An Anatomy of Chinese

An Anatomy of Chinese

Rhythm, Metaphor, Politics

PERRY LINK

HARVARD UNIVERSITY PRESS
Cambridge, Massachusetts, and London, England
2013

Copyright © 2013 by the President and Fellows of Harvard College
All rights reserved
Printed in the United States of America

Library of Congress Cataloging-in-Publication Data

Link, E. Perry (Eugene Perry), 1944–
   An anatomy of Chinese : rhythm, metaphor, politics / Perry Link.
      p.   cm.
   Includes bibliographical references and index.
   ISBN 978-0-674-06602-1 (alk. paper)
   1. Chinese language—Rhythm.   2. Chinese language—Metaphors.
3. Chinese language—Terms and phrases.   4. Chinese language—Semantics.
5. Chinese language—Political aspects.   I. Title.
   PL1279.L483   2013
   495.1'16—dc23   2012015096

To the sprightly spirit of Y. R. Chao — departed, and yet not — and to everyone else who loves the sounds and structures of spoken Chinese

Contents

Introduction   1

1 Rhythm   21
   The Prevalence of Rhythmic Patterns in Daily-Life Chinese   24
   Is Rhythm Unusually Common in Chinese?   37
   Speakers' Awareness of Rhythm   40
   Are There Fads in Rhythms?   44
   The Roots of Rhythms   49
   "External" Rhythms: Dominant and Recessive   54
   Recessive Rhythms of Favor   60
   How Recessive Rhythms Affect Structure   68
   How Universal Are the Preferred Rhythms of Chinese?   74
   Do Rhythms Have Meanings?   82
   What Other Formal Features Contribute to Meaning?   94
   Can the Users of Rhythm Be Unaware of Its Effects?   109

2 Metaphor   113
   How Do Metaphors Work in Ordinary Language?   115

Metaphor and Thought   128
Time   136
Color   147
Up and Down   155
North and South   162
Consciousness   169
The Self in Ancient Thought   171
Privilege in Dyads   174
Metaphors That Chinese and English (Pretty Much) Share   183
Metaphors in Chinese That Diverge from English in Significant Ways   198
Conceptual Differences That Are Rooted in Metaphor   209
Can Conceptual Metaphors Generate Philosophical Problems?   215
The Significance of Similarities and Differences among Conceptual Metaphors in Different Languages   231

3 Politics   234
A Bifurcation   235
Characteristics of the Official Language   243
The Language Game   278
How the Game Is Played: From the Side of the Rulers   295
How the Game Is Played: From the Side of the Ruled   321
Effects of the Language Game in the Mao and the Post-Mao Eras Compared   341

Epilogue   349

Acknowledgments   357
Index   359

Introduction

This book has grown from files that I have kept for more than three decades on items that have fascinated me about the Chinese language. When I dug into those files a few years ago I found that, in order to interpret their contents responsibly, I would need to read in a number of fields—prosody, cognitive science, philosophy of mind, comparative politics, even music theory—that were largely new to me. I asked colleagues for introductions to those fields and, with my store of Chinese examples serving as test cases, found the resulting exploration both pleasurable and rewarding.

Academic specialties in the early twenty-first century bristle with their own jargons, and nearly every area I turned to required an investment of time before I felt I was getting what was there to be got. Each investment, in the end, was worthwhile. Special jargon does serve a purpose when it allows expression of thought that could not have been put as precisely in ordinary language. But that said, I should say as well that I often found the jargon of subfields to be not entirely necessary: the same thought could often have been put, just as clearly or more so, in plainer language. Why we academics like jargon is an important question. It relates to why many humanities and social science disciplines are becoming more self-contained, growing as if in parallel universes; why students can be puzzled as they move from economics to anthropology to literature, even if their teachers claim to be sharing a subject ("China," for example); and why deans announce programs and deliver homilies to encourage "interdisciplinary" approaches. But an adequate analysis of the jargon problem is beyond my scope here. I mention it briefly only in order to suggest why I have tried to minimize it in this book. I admire the view of the eminent Chinese linguist Y. R. Chao, who wrote:

> [Usually] I shall prefer to use a familiar term, with a warning against making unwarranted inferences, in preference to using unfamiliar terms, which, though safe from being misunderstood, are often also safe from being understood.[1]

I will use technical terms only where I think plain language will not do. But my aim is clarity, not, alas, complete avoidance of tedium. Scholarship depends on attention to detail, and the demands of detail can make sentences and whole paragraphs sometimes seem dry, even if they are jargon free.

I want to start you where I started—noticing a few interesting little facts about the Chinese language that can lead, if one pursues them, into much larger areas.

In the fall of 1988, shortly after I arrived in Beijing for a year of work in the Beijing office of the Committee on Scholarly Communication with China (administered by the U.S. National Academy of Sciences), I noticed a sign that was intended for pedestrians crossing Haidian Road. In other countries such a sign might have said "Caution" or "Look both ways." But this one read: *Yi kan, er man, san tongguo* 一看，二慢，三通过 'First look, then go slowly, then cross'.[2] The phrase is not only rhythmic but exhibits the 1–2, 1–2, 1–2–3 pattern of syllables that is at least as old as mirror inscriptions of the Han period[3] and that has pervaded not only elite poetry but

---

1. Yuen Ren Chao, *A Grammar of Spoken Chinese* (Berkeley: University of California Press, 1968), p. 136.

2. The Chinese examples in this book are given in either traditional or simplified characters, 繁體字 or 简体字. Since examples are drawn from a range that extends from Zhuangzi to Hu Jintao, uniform restriction to either form might in some cases produce an unnatural feeling.

3. See Lin Suqing 林素清, "Liang-Han jingming suojian jiyu yanjiu" 兩漢鏡銘所見吉語研究 [Research into auspicious phrases seen in Han-period mirror inscriptions], in

folksongs, proverbs, and storytelling in many later eras. (In Chinese it is called *qiyan* 七言 'seven speakings', and I will ask the non-Chinese-speaking reader to adopt it as a technical term.) A banner stretched above the road's northbound lane, apparently intended for vehicles headed out of the city, read:

Gaogao xingxing chu cheng zou   高高兴兴出城走
An'an quanquan hui jia lai   安安全全回家来

Have a happy trip leaving the city, and be very safe in coming home.

Here was a couplet that exhibited not only the *qiyan* rhythm but grammatical parallelism and "semantic antitheticality" (i.e., paired opposites in meaning: *chu* 'exit' versus *hui* 'return' and *zou* 'leave' versus *lai* 'come') of a kind favored by classical poetry. The message seemed somehow more formal and exalted than if it had been put in ordinary language.

Formal? Exalted? I crossed the street and saw a public toilet. A sign warned: *Jinzhi suidi daxiaobian* 禁止随地大小便 'Don't just relieve yourself anywhere you like'. *Qiyan* again. The pattern seemed useful in a variety of contexts, exalted or not, but in any case seemed to bear a kind of authority. Its partner *wuyan* 五言, the equally classical 1–2, 1–2–3 syllabic pattern, was also widely in evidence. A television advertisement for cockroach killer promised: *Zhanglang siguangguang* 蟑螂死光光 'Cockroaches dead to the last one!' Somehow the poison seemed a bit more lethal in *wuyan*. A notice for a childbirth class promised *wutong fenmianfa* 无痛分娩法 'pain-free delivery'. Could *wuyan* mollify even labor pain? No, I thought. But it was apparent that someone, somewhere had felt that *wuyan* could add credibility to a claim about pain reduction.

These uses of classical rhythms were fairly obvious, I thought, and I guessed that both writers and readers of such phrases might have been

---

Handai wenxue yu sixiang xueshu yantaohui lunwenji 漢代文學與思想學術研討會論文集 [Collected papers of the Academic Conference on Han Literature and Thought], edited by Guoli Zhengzhi Daxue Zhongwen Xisuo, 161–188 (Taipei: Wenshizhe Chubanshe, 1991). Also "Liang-Han jingming chutan" 兩漢鏡銘初探 [Preliminary inquiry into Han-period mirror inscriptions], *Academia Sinica, Bulletin of the Institute of History and Philology*, 63, no. 2 (1993): 325–370.

aware of them. But sometimes I noticed *wuyan* and *qiyan* at work intuitively, as it were—buried inside phrases where they certainly made a difference but perhaps neither writer nor reader was consciously aware of them. Why, for example, do we find the opening line of Lu Xun's famous story "Kong Yiji" so lovely, so mellifluous? *Luzhen jiudian de geju, shi he biechu butong de* 魯鎮酒店的格局，是和別處不同的 'The layout of the taverns in Lu-town was different from those in other places'. The sentence is composed of two phrases of seven syllables each—not exactly parallel, to be sure, yet readable in something close to a 1–2, 1–2, 1–2–3 rhythm. Was Lu Xun conscious of the pattern when he wrote the line? Probably not, I guessed, although I think the line must have "felt right" to him even if he did not stop to examine the reasons. (Certainly I, as one reader of the line, sensed its rhythmical beauty before I ever thought of counting syllables.) Near the lugubrious end of Xu Zhenya's novel *Yulihun*, the narrator confesses *Yu yi shangxinren, xie ci duanchangshi* 余亦傷心人，寫此斷腸史 'I, too, am a grief-stricken person, writing this heart-breaking tale'.[4] The line is *wuyan*, and exhibits parallelism, but it is not presented in the text as poetry. For *Shangzhong hongling xia zhong ou* 上种红菱下种藕, the title of a novel by the celebrated contemporary novelist Wang Anyi, in English, we must settle for something unrhythmical like "planting red water nuts above and lotuses below," but the phrase's structure in Chinese includes *qiyan*, parallelism, and even a *ping-ze* 'level-oblique' tonal pattern.[5] Wang Anyi may (or may not?) have been consciously aware of these details when she created them. But how aware are her readers? Most, I would guess, feel that the result is pleasant but do not ask why, and are not consciously aware of the role that rhythm and parallelism are playing.

In musing over such questions, I found some of the most dramatic examples in the Mao Zedong era. During the Cultural Revolution, Mao exhorted the Chinese people to "smash the four olds": old customs, old culture, old habits, and old ideas. Certainly *wuyan* and *qiyan* should count as "old culture," yet Red Guards who gathered in Tiananmen Square at

---

4. Xu Zhenya 徐枕亞, *Yulihun* 玉梨魂 [Jade Pear Spirit] (Shanghai: Minquan chubanshe, 1914), p. 165.

5. On *ping-ze* and other technical matters, non-Sinologists may refer to James J. Y. Liu, *The Art of Chinese Poetry* (Chicago: University of Chicago Press, 1962), pp. 20–38.

the time chanted *Women yao jian Mao Zhuxi!* 我们要见毛主席 'We want to see Chairman Mao!' in a 1–2, 1–2, 1–2–3 pattern. Were they aware that they were using an example of the "four olds" in order to praise the leading opponent of the "four olds"? Was Mao himself aware? It seemed impossible. It seemed that no one noticed the irony, even as everyone was intuitively enjoying the lilt and rightness of the phrases. Then I began to notice that many phrases from the Cultural Revolution era used *qiyan*: *Fūnü neng ding banbiantian* 妇女能顶半边天 'Women can hold up half the sky';[6] *Linghun shenchu gan geming!* 灵魂深处干革命 'Make revolution in the depths of your soul!'; *Dahai hangxing kao duoshou* 大海航行靠舵手 'Sailing on the seas relies on the helmsman'. *Wuyan* seemed just as common. *Gongye xue Daqing, nongye xue Dazhai* 工业学大庆, 农业学大寨 'Industry should learn from [the] Daqing [oilfields], agriculture should learn from [the] Dazhai [commune]' was not only *wuyan* but parallel. It was interesting to me that these were all carefully crafted political slogans, things on which the creators must have spent considerable conscious effort. Have any cultural products—not only in Chinese history but in world history—ever been more closely scrutinized for political correctness than the model operas of the Cultural Revolution era? But one opera was titled *Hongse niangzi jun* 红色娘子军 (Red detachment of women) and another *Zhiqu weihushan* 智取威虎山 (Taking Tiger Mountain by strategy). Both are 1–2, 1–2–3 *wuyan*.

Whether or not they were used intentionally, the rhythms seemed to *add something* to the phrases they inhabited. What was it? Should we call it "meaning"? Can rhythms by themselves "mean"? *Women yao jian Mao Zhuxi!* somehow sounds more exalted, more righteous, than a plain *Women shi lai kan Zhuxi de* 我們是來看主席的 would sound. Similarly, *Yi kan, er man, san tongguo* 'First look, then go slowly, then cross' sounds more formal, more authoritative, than a casual *dajia xiaoxin guo jie, a!* 大家小心過街, 阿! 'Everybody be careful crossing the street, okay?' Certainly something is added by the rhythm, but one problem with calling this added thing "meaning" is that, as we have just seen, rhythms can be used without conscious awareness. Red Guards feel that they are praising, and Mao

6. I discuss the misleading translation of this statement as "women hold up half the sky" in Chapter 3.

Zedong feels praised, but neither side (most likely) is at all aware of thinking "We are using this rhythm for this purpose." Of words, we normally assume that they need to be used consciously in order to be "meant." Is this not true of rhythms? If we say that rhythms do not have "meanings," then what is the right word for what they add?

The way rhythms can "mean" seemed to me parallel to the sense in which certain grammatical constructions—all by themselves, independently of vocabulary—can, like rhythms, convey implications. In English, for example, "I threw her the ball" and "I threw the ball to her" both describe me as throwing a ball in her direction. But the former implies that she caught (or otherwise received) the ball, and the latter does not. The grammar seems primarily responsible for the implication of how successful the effort is. The same effect can be seen in "Jack sent Jill a package" and "Jack sent a package to Jill"; or "I taught Gladys Chinese" and "I taught Chinese to Gladys."[7]

I also began to wonder if rhythmical patterns were more common in ordinary Chinese than in ordinary English. Every human language uses stress, of course, and sometimes stress patterns take on aesthetic qualities when they "just feel right"—not merely because the accents are all on the right syllables, but because of something more than that. For example, most English speakers would probably say that "bright and shiny" sounds better than "shiny and bright," because TAH-ta-TAH-ta sounds better (has more natural balance than?) TAH-ta-ta-TAH.[8] The phenomenon is clear in things like slogans, chants, marches, and advertising jingles. Among the latter, we should note the pretechnological forebears known as hawkers' calls. China was once rich in hawkers' calls, and a few survive even in the West, for example in American ballparks, where a rhythmic pattern like "GET-cha HOT-dogs!" clearly assists in the hot dog vendor's delivery of a message. Here, I thought, the *rhythm itself* helps hearers to know instantly what the topic is. Rhythms in language must be universal and part of being human, yet I still felt that they seemed especially com-

---

7. I am indebted to Adele E. Goldberg for this insight. See her "Constructions: A New Theoretical Approach to Language," *Trends in Cognitive Sciences* 7, no. 5 (May 2003), 219–224.

8. I am indebted to James Richardson for this example (email message to author, September 18, 2002).

mon in Chinese. Beijingers could take *Yi kan, er man, san tong guo* in stride; what would New Yorkers think of being told in rhythm how to cross the street? What would they do if exhorted in parallelism to have a nice time in the country? How would they respond to a sign reminding them, in pentameter, where not to pee?

The public buses in Beijing, during that autumn of 1988 when I was working there, had ticket-sellers who would call out the names of bus stops in rhythmic patterns. One of these patterns was *Xia yi zhan*, X-X-X, *mei piao mai piao!* 下一站 X-X-X, 沒票買票 TAH-ta-TAH, TAH-ta-TAH, ta-TAH-ta-TAH! "Next stop is X-X-X, get a ticket if you don't have one!" Many of the bus stop names were three syllables (*zhongguancun* 中关村 'middle-gate village', *shuangyushu* 双榆树 'twin elms', *dongwuyuan* 动物园 'zoo', *baishiqiao* 白石桥 'white-stone bridge' etc.), which allowed the trisyllabic X-X-X almost always to fit. Where a stop had a longer name, like Nongye Kexueyuan 农业科学院 'Academy of Agricultural Sciences', it got a three-syllable abbreviation, Nongkeyuan, and the ticket-seller still could say *Xia yi zhan, Nongkeyuan, mei piao mai piao!* Conductors on New Jersey Transit trains between Princeton and New York City also sometimes enter a car and say, "Tic-KETS!" with a distinctive lilt. But if they went on for ten syllables, using the rhythm that their counterparts in Beijing do, it would not work. "Next stop IS, New BrunsWICK, show your TIX QUICK!" might frighten people off the train. In Beijing, even the three syllables of the stop names had a distinctive internal grammatical structure. Almost all were "two-syllable modifier plus one-syllable modified": *nongke + yuan; dongwu + yuan, tianan + men, wangfu + jing, baishi + qiao*, and so on. This structure clearly helped the rhythm. Or was the rhythm in charge of creating the structure? One should look into this, I thought.

Yet another aspect of that ticket-seller's call was interesting. She, like everyone who speaks Chinese, said *"xia" yi zhan* 'one stop "below"' for the "next" stop. Time was going "down." "Next week" is *xia ge xingqi* 下个星期, "next month" *xia ge yue* 下个月, and "next time" *xia ci* 下次. Similarly, "last month" is *shang ge yue* 上个月 'the month above', "last time" is *shang ci* 上次 'the time above', and so on. When you continue talking about something, you *shuo xia qu* 说下去 'go down with your talking'. Do we ever do this in English? I asked myself. We do say "down through the ages" and that inheritances get "passed down"—although for the latter case I wondered if "down" meant "later in time" or "lower in family status." In any case, even if we sometimes do use "down" for "future" in English, we don't use it as much as Chinese does. In English the time line seems horizontal. We say "front" for future: we look *forward* to things, to the glorious future that lies *before* us, and so on. But wait: Chinese does this, too. After Mao, Deng Xiaoping urged the Chinese people: *Xiang qian kan* 向前看 'Look forward'—clearly meaning "Look to the future." Was this usage a borrowing from Western language? No, because classical Chinese has *qian zhan* 前瞻 'forward outlook' for looking toward the future, and a term like *qiantian* 前天 'the day in front', meaning the day before yesterday, is not a borrowing from Western language.

But wait, again: *qiantian* refers to *the past?* Didn't *qian* 'front' refer to the future in *xiang qian kan* 'look forward'? How can you look forward to the day before yesterday? And why, in order to say "the day after tomorrow," does Chinese say *houtian* 後天 'the behind day'? The "behind day" is in the future? Is Chinese confused? "Future generations" are *houdai* 後代 'behind generations'. We all hope that future generations will have good "futures," or good *qiantu* 前途 'forward paths'. So we worry about *houdai de qiantu* 後代的前途, literally "the forward paths of the behind generation." Shouldn't we, perhaps, worry about our logic first?

English, it turns out, is no better. In English we look *forward* to the future, but our *fore*fathers reside in the past. They came *before* us, and therefore can be of no help with the problems that lie *before* us. Hmmm.

It suddenly seemed strange to me that human beings could talk with one another in either Chinese or English and remain clear about what was being said. Obviously they can, however. There must be rules that help people to keep things straight, even if they are not consciously aware of those rules.

I ran across *Metaphors We Live By* by George Lakoff and Mark Johnson, and it helped to clarify these problems, if not to solve them.[9] It was also my entrée into the field of cognitive linguistics, where the study of metaphor has grown considerably since Lakoff and Johnson published their

---

9. George Lakoff and Mark Johnson, *Metaphors We Live By* (Chicago: University of Chicago Press, 1980).

book in 1980. The book discusses the use of space as a metaphor for time (i.e., the question of which direction time "goes") and many other examples of daily-life metaphor that not only reflects the way we conceive the world but "structures" the way we are likely to continue conceiving it as new experience comes along. They point out, for example, that in English "consciousness is up, and unconsciousness is down."[10] Thus we *fall* asleep and wake *up*. We go *under* hypnosis or *sink* into a coma. The structuring power of this metaphor was evident when psychoanalysis came along and a *sub*conscious was metaphorically conceived as "below" the conscious level.

I read Lakoff and Johnson asking myself whether the "we" in their phrase "metaphors we live by" included Chinese speakers. Do different languages have different structuring metaphors that reflect, perhaps, partly different worldviews? It was interesting to me that a French translation of Lakoff and Johnson's book could use many, but not all, of the book's original examples. How different is Chinese? How important are the differences? In Chinese, for example, we do not use "up" and "down" for moving into and out of consciousness. When we do use spatial metaphors for this purpose, the movement is conceived as crossing a border within a single horizontal plane. Thus, in fainting we *yunguoqu* 暈過去 'faint and cross away', and in awakening we *xingguolai* 醒過來 'awake and cross toward here'. This is not terribly different from "pass out" and "come to" in English, but it was interesting to me that "up" and "down" were not involved in Chinese, except in modern terms, like *xiayishi* 下意識 'subconscious', that are clearly borrowings from Western languages. I thought of Zhuangzi's famous story of dreaming that he was a butterfly and then waking to wonder whether he was, indeed, a man who had dreamt of being a butterfly or was now a butterfly dreaming he was a man. Is the conundrum more puzzling when one thinks of Zhuangzi crossing over a line within a single plane than if one thinks of him rising and falling between levels? It felt so to me, but it was hard to say exactly why.

I became curious in the opposite direction as well: might certain Western philosophical conundrums appear differently if approached using Chinese metaphorical apparatus? For example, Lakoff and Johnson stress the importance of what they call "ontological metaphors" that turn complex

---

10. Ibid., p. 15.

processes into "entities," use nouns to label them, and thus make them easier to talk about. "Inflation," they say, is not originally an entity, but if we use an "ontological metaphor" to conceive it as such we can then "measure inflation," "combat inflation," and see inflation as an actor that "lowers our living standards," "takes a toll at the checkout counter," and so on. All of this seemed right to me, but then Lakoff and Johnson write: "ontological metaphors like this are necessary for even attempting to deal rationally with our experiences,"[11] and here I had my doubts. Students of Chinese philosophy have often noted that Chinese thinkers like to talk about "process" more than "thing," and, vaguely speaking, I had always felt that Chinese is by nature more verb-rich while English is more noun-rich. Thus in English we can find it natural, if not elegant, to utter a phrase like "the beginning of the development of the process of construction of bilateral relations" (in 1979 I had to translate this phrase in China for the vice-chancellor of an American university). The phrase strings together nouns that in a sense might be viewed as verbs ("begin," "develop," "proceed," "construct," "relate") in disguise. If we put the noun-rich phrase directly into Chinese and say *liangbian de guanxi de jianshe de guocheng de fazhan de kaishi* 兩邊的關係的建設的過程的發展的開始, we are grammatically correct but sound horrid, indeed so horrid that the meaning is not easy for a Chinese speaker to grasp. "Ontological metaphors," it seemed to me, just aren't as common or natural in Chinese as in English, and whenever they appear in abundance in Chinese, the Chinese takes on a flavor of "translatese."

But if that is so, then we need to doubt that ontological metaphors are all that "necessary" for "even attempting to deal rationally" with life, as Lakoff and Johnson write. How much a language uses them might vary quite a lot—with no difference in how "rationally" people can get through life. Indeed, to turn things around, it might be that Western languages talk about "entities" rather too much—perhaps thereby creating problems where there needn't have been problems, or at least not such tough ones. Western philosophers have long wrestled with what we mean by terms like "the good," "mind," "reality," and "existence." These are nouns, and we might ask how much of Western puzzlement over them has had to do

---

11. Ibid., p. 26.

with trying to figure out what "things" they are. In Chinese it is extremely awkward to translate "the good" as a noun; "reality" and "existence" as nouns are marginally more possible, but still are more easily discussed using verbs or other parts of speech. The Western "mind-body problem" somehow feels less problematic in Chinese; nouns like *xin* 心 and *shen* 身 are available, to be sure, but their use in grammatical context does not easily conjure the sort of radical mutual separateness of conceptual category that preoccupied René Descartes. I began to wonder if Chinese grammar might help with Western philosophical problems—not by "solving" them so much as suggesting ways they needn't be seen as problems in the first place.

Despite some very interesting contrasts, however, on the whole I found more similarities than differences in comparing the conceptual metaphors of Chinese and English. The puzzles about "before" and "after" as spatial metaphors for time led to very similar answers for the two languages. So did other examples, like being "red with anger" in English and *mian hong er chi* 面紅耳赤 in Chinese. Lakoff and Johnson suggest that the "experiential basis" of metaphor can often explain such similarity. Since it is true of human beings generally that intense anger causes blood to rush to the face, it is probably no accident that a red face should mean anger in several languages. Even something as basic as "high is more" (high level, high octane, etc.) can be seen as having the simple experiential basis that, originally, the more physical objects one puts in a place, the higher a pile becomes. Other theorists have gone further, claiming that it is not just common experience but the hardwiring of the human brain that leads to commonalities in perception. Kant claims this for concepts of space and time, and Chomsky for fundamental grammatical structures.

I was surprised to learn that contemporary neuroscience has found there are universal "best examples" of colors like "red" and "yellow." I had always assumed that the labeling of hues along the color spectrum was arbitrary in the sense that each language could do this as it pleased. In Chinese *huang* 黃, for example, is not coterminous with "yellow," because it spans from yellow all the way through tan to brown. The Huanghe 黃河 'Yellow River' is brown. But it turns out that this is only part of the truth. There are shades of certain colors like red, green, blue, and yellow that native speakers of different languages will tend to pick out as the best examples of the range within which they fall. These "focal colors" tend to be the same, it seems, because of the physiology of the human eye.[12] And so it happens that the two words *red* and *hong* 紅, for example—despite all of their different cultural and political connotations in English and Chinese—still lead native speakers of the two languages to identify the same "best example" on the color spectrum.

I began to wonder if there were parallel ways in which preference for certain *rhythms* might also be common to humanity at large. Is it only chance that rhythmic storytelling in China has often used 4:4 time, just as Western hymns and chants do? Might that be because all of us humans walk on two legs? Is it merely coincidence that the ten-syllable rhythm I heard on that Beijing bus (TAH-ta-TAH, TAH-ta-TAH, ta-TAH-ta-TAH) happens to be the same as the one I use when I say my ten-digit telephone number in the United States? This must, of course, be *partly* coincidence. Both ticket-sellers and telephone numbers can, and do, employ other rhythms. But is there, as it were, a certain repertoire of rhythms that the human brain prefers, and of which this is one? Here is another example: The Cultural Revolution song "The East Is Red" uses a rhythmic pattern of 1–2–3, 1–2–3, 1–2–3–4–5–6–7 (*Dongfang hong, taiyang sheng, Zhongguo chu le* [*ge*] *Mao Zedong* 东方红，太阳升，中国出了个毛泽东).[13] So does the Western nursery rhyme "This old man, he plays one, / he plays knick-knack on my thumb." So do Chinese riddles. So do a number of poems by the eighth-century Chinese poets Li Bai and Du Fu. It is hard to postulate "borrowing" over such a range of cases.

In thinking about whether rhythms might have "meanings" that users are not fully aware of, and also noticing how established metaphors seem to "structure thought," I wondered how such factors might relate to political uses of language. Some very astute observers of contemporary Chinese language use have raised the issue of how political usages—including, but not limited to, structural metaphors and rhythmic slogans—serve

---

12. Paul Kay and Chad McDaniel, "The Linguistic Significance of the Meanings of Basic Color Terms," *Language* 54, no. 3 (September 1978), 610–646.

13. There are syncopated beats in some of the lines, but this does not change the basic prosodic structure.

to shape thought in contemporary Chinese society. The Swedish scholar Michael Schoenhals, in writing about how to "do things with words in Chinese politics,"[14] unfolds many subtleties in the power engineering of political language in Communist, and especially Maoist, China. In a number of essays, the eminent literary critic Li Tuo has wondered whether Chinese writers, once acculturated to a "Mao literary form," can extricate themselves from its worldview—or even become aware that they in fact remain inside it. Li's observations in some ways recall eastern European writers like Miklos Haraszti and Czeslaw Milosz. In describing Hungarian writers in the 1950s as living inside a "velvet prison,"[15] Haraszti referred not only to the system of material rewards that lured and held them but also to the velvet unreality of official language that dulled their intellectual work. In *The Captive Mind,* Milosz went even further, explaining how language, gesture, and other aspects of personal presentation created a kind of public "role playing" that could become so thoroughgoing that eventually, "after long acquaintance with his role, a man grows into it so closely that he can no longer differentiate his true self from the self he simulates."[16]

What Milosz says of Communist Poland was, we know from literary accounts and memoirs, substantially the same in China during high Maoism. In the immediate post-Mao years, when I first lived in China, the all-consuming power of official language had receded somewhat, but there was still a clear—and very interesting—bifurcation between official and unofficial language. The official language was used in newspapers, on the radio, and at political meetings, and its distinctive features separated it clearly from everyday talk, which was used for buying fish, scolding children, gossiping about one's sister-in-law, and other such daily-life activities. Left alone, people preferred ordinary language, but in official contexts they needed to use officialese. All governments, of course—including premodern Chinese governments—have used officialese, but there are interesting

---

14. *Doing Things with Words in Chinese Politics: Five Studies* (Berkeley: Center for Chinese Studies, 1992).

15. *The Velvet Prison: Artists under State Socialism*, trans. Katalin and Stephen Landesman (New York: Basic Books, 1987).

16. *The Captive Mind* (New York: Knopf, 1953), p. 55.

differences of degree in how and how much it has been used. In Qing China, the *guanhua* 官話 'official talk' was left to officials. Ordinary people didn't need it for daily life. In Mao's China, politically correct verbal expression was not optional. Even for several years following Mao's death, political study meetings were mandatory, and one's "performance" had to be correct at them. Moreover, in order to get certain things that you needed in daily life—like bicycles, job assignments, or permission to marry—officialese had to be used correctly. The ordinary citizen had to abandon ordinary talk and play a kind of official "language game" in such contexts. For example, a professor I knew at Zhongshan University in Guangzhou, where I was doing research in 1980, wanted a bigger apartment for his family. The government had recently directed that universities treat professors better, in order to bring them back into the fold after their severe mistreatment during the Cultural Revolution. My friend knew about this policy. He went to his Party secretary, but did not ask "Can I have a bigger apartment?" He asked: "Do you think we can concretize Party Central's policy on intellectuals?"[17]

In graduate school I had learned much about different kinds of Chinese language: classical and vernacular, different forms of ancient language, and the many very different versions of modern oral Chinese, which are more nearly different languages than just "dialects," as they are sometimes called. But now I began to be interested in another axis on which the Chinese language divides into different versions—the official and the unofficial. I found some systematic differences. In vocabulary, for example, official Chinese used more borrowings from Western languages (primarily the neologisms introduced to China via Japan in the late-Qing years, with later additions from English, German, and Russian) than daily-life Chinese did. Terms like *xingshi* 形势 'situation' or *dongxiang* 动向 'trend' had an official flavor. They carried an aura of correctness but were usually abstract enough that one did not know exactly what they meant. This made them useful in obfuscating sensitive things. For example, to describe the persecution of people during the Cultural Revolution—

---

17. *Neng bu neng luoshi yixia zhongyang de zhishifenzi zhengce?* 能不能落实一下中央的知识分子政策?

INTRODUCTION   15

events for which ordinary language might use lively phrases like *hunfei posan* 魂飛魄散 'soul flies and spirit scatters—be scared out of one's wits' or *jiapo renwang* 家破人亡 'home wrecked and person perished'—the official language could retreat into a phrase like *caiqu cuoshi jinxing zhengdun* 採取措施進行整頓 'adopt measures to carry out reorganization'. *Cuoshi* and *zhengdun* are modern neologisms, and also what Lakoff and Johnson call "ontological metaphors," but the "entities" to which they are supposed to refer could hardly be more vague. I was reminded of George Orwell's famous essay "Politics and the English Language," in which he writes that political language "is designed to make lies sound truthful and murder respectable, and give an appearance of solidity to pure wind."[18]

Another interesting aspect of the official language was its implicit claim to moral weight. No matter how vague the cognitive meaning of *caiqu cuoshi jinxing zhengdun* might be, the implication was clear that it was a "correct" thing to do. Words that were not originally ethical terms could take on moral weight. For example, Mao Zedong liked the word *zui* 最 'most', and he liked to use it in series. In 1940 he called the great Chinese writer Lu Xun the "most brave, most correct, most firm, most loyal, and most ardent national hero."[19] In the high Maoism of the Cultural Revolution years, anything *zui* in the official language had to be good. Mao Zedong was *women xinzhong zui hong zui hong de hong taiyang* 我们心中最红最红的红太阳. An appearance of three *zui* in a row all but guaranteed that the adjective[20] that followed described a wonderful quality. Thus *zui, zui, zui hong* 最最最红 'most, most, most red' and *zui, zui, zui zhengque* 最最最正确 'most, most, most correct' both made sense, and indeed were common, in the official language; but to say *zui, zui, zui fandong* 最最最反动 'most, most, most reactionary'—although the phrase works fine grammatically and

---

18. "Politics and the English Language," in *A Collection of Essays* (Garden City, N.Y.: Doubleday Anchor, 1954), p. 177.

19. Widely quoted in later years, the phrase first appeared in January 1940 in "On New Democracy." See *Selected Works of Mao Tse-tung*, vol. 2 (Peking: Foreign Languages Press, 1967), p. 372.

20. Terms that I here call "adjectives" are different from adjectives in Western languages because they can follow subjects directly to form sentences, without any other verb. Some grammarians call them "stative verbs."

lexically—would have sounded wrong in the official language. There would have been something oddly contradictory about it, because *zui, zui, zui* primes the hearer for something good, and then *fandong* contradicts the priming. On the other hand, certain other phrases, although value-free in ordinary language, in the official language implied 'bad'. From the early 1950s (and perhaps earlier), the phrase *jishaoshu* 极少数 'tiny minority' in official language meant not just "small in number" but (morally or politically) "wrong" as well. When student demonstrators crowded Tiananmen Square in the spring of 1989 and Premier Li Peng charged that they were being manipulated by a "tiny minority" of troublemakers, he intensified both the cognitive and evaluative meanings by duplicating the phrase: a *jishaoshu de jishaoshu* 'tiny minority within a tiny minority' was causing all the trouble. The phrase could not have been used for something he favored. If he had wanted to say, for example, that Mao Zedong had been "a minority within a minority" of great world leaders, he would have had to say it some other way. To say *Mao Zedong shi jishaoshu de jishaoshu de weida lingxiu* 毛泽东是极少数地极少数的伟大领袖 would sound contradictory. In using this example in Chinese in lectures to Chinese audiences, I have found that it sometimes induces laughter.

Rhythms, too, I came to sense, had evaluative components in official language. To take another example from Cultural Revolution language, it was almost de rigueur in the late 1960s to refer to the Communist Party as *weida de guangrong de zhengque de gongchandang* 伟大的光荣的正确的共产党 'the great, glorious, correct Communist Party'. The three modifiers had to be in exactly that order for the result to sound right, and the rhythm was also fixed: ta-TAH-ta, ta-TAH-ta, ta-TAH-ta, TAH TAH TAH. The rhythm itself was so well associated with greatness, glory, and correctness that, I felt, even if one were to take the vocabulary out of it, a shadow of the meaning might still remain. I tested this notion by inserting opposed vocabulary to see what would happen. If we substitute Kuomintang for Communist Party, for example, and say not that it is great, glorious, and correct but shady, stingy, and disgusting, we can, in an identical rhythmic pattern, say *heian de xiaoqi de taoyan de guomindang* 黑暗的小氣的討厭的國民黨. This phrase, too, immediately elicits chuckles from people who know Cultural Revolution language. The message is contradictory: the denotative component of meaning says "bad" while the rhythm says "good." A similar test can show that even if we restrict ourselves to positive meanings, the rhythmic contribution to meaning emerges only in the official language, not the language of ordinary life. If we say (to be as positive as we can) "my beautiful, peaceful, comfortable home" and put the words into the same official-language rhythm, we could get something like *meili de anjing de shufu de wo jia* 美麗的安靜的舒服的我家. But this result is so awkward that, if heard in actual daily life, the hearer would wonder what is wrong with the speaker.

In any human language, of course, the patterns of set phrases (slogans, proverbs, idioms) are distinctive, and it is not hard to generate a sense of incongruity by inserting different vocabulary into them. In finding this phenomenon in official Chinese, we should not assume that it does not exist elsewhere. But there are differences of degree, and there are sometimes differences in form as well. It began to interest me that Chinese slogans, grammatically speaking, are usually presented as subjectless predicates: *dadao sirenbang* 打倒四人帮 'Down with the Gang of Four'; *quanxin quanyi gao sihua* 全心全意搞四化 'Give your full heart and mind to the Four Modernizations'.[21] In English, it is much more natural to use imperatives. And imperatives, grammatically speaking, are complete sentences. They don't take subjects; you cannot grammatically say "I down with the Gang of Four" or "You down with the Gang of Four." But Chinese slogans, as floating predicates, "invite" a subject and then leave the spot blank. Grammatically, one certainly *could* say *wo dadao sirenbang* 'I knock down the Gang of Four' or *ni dadao sirenbang* "you . . ." or *zanmen dajia yikuair dadao sirenbang* 咱们大家一块儿打倒四人帮 'all of us together . . .' Leaving the subject blank in Chinese slogans subtly gives a very different effect from the imperative form of English slogans. In English an implicit "I" is telling an implicit "you" to do something. Chinese has more the feel of "would that it be that [some result come about]." It is left unstated who does the action, or who tells whom to do it; the focus is on the end result.

From here, I began to notice other ways official Chinese had what might be called a "goal orientation." This was reflected not only in grammar (as in the slogan example) but in vocabulary as well. The "filler verb" *gao* 搞, for example, was in widespread use by the end of the Mao era, in

---

21. We can note in passing that these two slogans are *wuyan* and *qiyan*.

both official language and daily-life uses. (Mao Zedong favored the word, and it is used much less in Taiwan and overseas Chinese communities.) *Gao* is so flexible in its uses that one would need a fairly long list of English words to supply its counterparts: do, make, effect, perform, pursue, mess with, and so on. Fundamentally, it is just a device to transfer our attention to the goal expressed in its direct object. We have seen earlier the example *quanxin quanyi gao sihua*, which I translated (using an imperative, in English) as "Give your full heart and mind to the Four Modernizations." To reflect *gao*, I could have added a word like "pursue" before "the Four Modernizations," but it would not have mattered much. The point of *gao* is just to say "bring the goal about." How? *Gao* makes no comment. Just get it done. This characteristic of *gao* has made things convenient for policy-makers and bureaucrats. To issue a policy to *gao shehuizhuyi* 搞社会主义 'do socialism', *gao huanbao* 搞环保 'do environmental protection', or *gao shuangbai fangzhen* 搞双百方针 'go the double-hundred direction—give more latitude in literary expression' has allowed bureaucrats to tell what a certain result should be without having to take the responsibility (and therefore the political risk of a "mistake") for saying exactly how the result should be pursued. A Maoist slogan said *zhua geming, cu shengchan* 抓革命, 促生产 'grasp revolution, stimulate production'. Exactly what to "grasp" and exactly how one might "stimulate" were problems for the slogans' audience, not its issuers.

In sum, I came to feel that contemporary official Chinese did have a number of characteristics by which one could distinguish it from daily-life Chinese—not as different languages, of course, but as two distinct registers, or idiolects, of Chinese. The two idiolects were held together not only because they shared a common base but because there was frequent interchange, and sometimes borrowing, between the two. In unofficial contexts people talked, in ordinary language, about how they should play the chess game of the official language. Conversely, there could be talk, in the official language (at political meetings, for example), about how someone had spoken—or more likely, misspoken—in the unofficial language. There was also seepage of official vocabulary (as well as grammar, rhythms, and metaphors) into daily-life uses. *Gao*, for example, came to be used in a wide variety of daily-life contexts: looking for a spouse became *gao duixiang* 搞对象; cleaning the toilet *gao weisheng* 搞卫生; studying physics *gao wuli* 搞物理; hatching a plot *gao yinmou* 搞阴谋; cooking up a couple of dishes, *gao liang ge cai* 搞两个菜; and many more.

In the post-Mao years, some people began to worry, similarly to the way Li Tuo worried about writers, that the thinking of ordinary people had been shaped by unnoticed infusion of official language into daily-life language. Mao favored military metaphors, for example. Originally his movement annihilated the enemy (*xiaomie diren* 消灭敌人). But later the focus turned to annihilating errors (*xiaomie cuowu* 消灭错误), annihilating revisionism (*xiaomie xiuzhengzhuyi* 消灭修正主义), annihilating the rightist tendency to reverse correct verdicts (*xiaomie youqing fan'anfeng* 消灭右倾翻案风), and so on. Eventually, in daily life, people found themselves near the ends of meals urging one another to finish off the remaining food by suggesting "annihilation" of it. *Xiaomie shengcai* 消灭剩菜 entered the language as "finish off the leftovers." Chinese people in Taiwan and overseas do not use this metaphor and can find it startling when they first hear it. Mainland people who do use the metaphor, and who come to be aware of it, seem to feel a bit sheepish but not seriously upset. No one really approaches leftovers with violent intent, after all. But for some, the worry lingered. If we did not notice this militarism creeping into our thinking, how much else have we not been noticing? In the summer of 1989, when a group of Chinese dissidents, refugees from the June Fourth massacre in Beijing, met in Paris to draft a Declaration of the Chinese Democratic Front, they got into heated debates over language. Democratic *front*? Isn't "front" a military term? Mao used it, but should we? Everyone wanted to end the dictatorship of the Communist Party, but not everyone wanted to use terms like *tuifan* 推翻 'overthrow' or *dadao* 打倒 'knock down'. Two factions formed on the question, and each took itself to be the more radical. One side said, in effect, we do not compromise; we are willing to come right out and say "Down with the Communist Party." The other side said: you compromise by accepting the Communist Party's language; it is we who do not compromise; we say only "End one-party rule."

These Chinese were concerned, I realized, with the same kind of question that had intrigued me as I wondered about the "meanings" of rhythms and structural metaphors: how do these aspects of language that we use with ease every day, and that work very well for us in getting certain things communicated (even though we remain largely unaware of how they are doing so) relate to how we think? The chapters that follow explore three themes—rhythm, metaphor, and political rhetoric—in more detail.

1
Rhythm

The stress and intonation patterns in speech, which linguists call *prosody*, and which I am also calling, less formally, "rhythm," are universal in human languages, in fact essential to them. If you hear syllables pronounced in a manner that aims at uniformity in matters of stress, pause, and pitch, the utterances will seem to you to be coming perhaps from a computer, or an imaginary alien. In any case, they will seem "not human." Under a musicologist's rigorous definition of "rhythm," all phrases in spoken language necessarily have a rhythm, even if it is perfectly uniform or utterly random. The examples I discuss in this chapter might best be called "conventional rhythmic patterns"; in calling them "rhythms" I am simply using shorthand.

In English we speak of syllables within words "receiving accents"—and, for longer words, which syllables get primary and secondary accents. On a scale where 1 means most stress and 4 means least, in American English the word "constitution" is usually said 2–4–1–3. If the stress pattern of "constitution" strays very far from 2–4–1–3, native speakers of American

English will find that it "sounds funny." They will get this sense instantly, whether or not they have any conscious awareness of the pattern.

Stress patterns also play roles in phrases containing two words, three words, or more. For example, the name "Joey Davis," in American English, is usually said 2–4–1–3, using the same stress pattern as "constitution."[1] Again, a native speaker would find a radical diversion from this pattern to sound extremely odd. Said in a 4–2–3–1 pattern, the name "Joey Davis" might startle you, even cause you to keep your distance from Joey the person, and you might literally find it hard to pronounce the name in a pattern like 1–4–3–2. The ways some stress patterns naturally sound better than others can cause us, without being aware that we are doing so, to choose certain word orders over others. In English, for example, if we have a one-syllable word and a two-syllable word and want to connect them with "and," we find that it sounds better to put the one-syllable word first. "Salt and pepper" sounds better than "pepper and salt"; "bright and shiny" sounds better than "shiny and bright."[2] In general, TAH-ta-TAH-ta is more agreeable than TAH-ta-ta-TAH.

Syllabic "stress" can mean several things. It can mean that a syllable, compared to others near it, is (1) higher in pitch, (2) longer in duration, or (3) louder. Human languages, including the regional languages of China, differ in how "stress" is composed among these three elements. For Mandarin Chinese, Y. R. Chao has written that stress is "primarily an enlargement in pitch range and time duration and only secondarily in loudness."[3] In Cantonese, where "there is no neutral tone" (i.e., no syllable on which there is "completely weak" stress) as there is in Mandarin,[4] somewhat different rules apply. In mellifluous Cantonese, pitch plays a bigger role than it does in Mandarin, so even without neutral tones, there is plenty of room

---

1. Example is from Mark Liberman, "The Intonation System of English" (Ph.D. diss., Massachusettts Institute of Technology, 1975), quoted in Matthew Chen, "Metrical Structure: Evidence from Chinese Poetry," *Linguistic Inquiry* 10, no. 3 (1979), pp. 371–420, p. 413.

2. These examples are from James Richardson, professor of English, Princeton University. Email message to author, September 18, 2002.

3. Yuen Ren Chao, *A Grammar of Spoken Chinese* (Berkeley: University of California Press, 1968), p. 35.

4. Ibid., p. 38.

for "rhythm." In this book, my focus is on Mandarin, but only because I do not know other Chinese languages intimately enough to feel confident about examples.

I want to make clear, too, a general methodological point that will run through this chapter—and to a certain extent through the chapters that follow as well. It is this: I am not seeking rules that have no exceptions (although I welcome such rules if I find them); I am interested in patterns whether or not they have exceptions, and remain interested whether or not I can explain the exceptions. Take, for example, the pattern according to which "Joey Davis" is normally said with 2–4–1–3 stress. If someone mistook Joey Davis for his brother Louie, Joey might say, "No, I'm *Joey* Davis," and then he would probably use a stress pattern of 1–3–4–4. This pattern would be quite normal; both speaker and listener would find it so, and indeed would find it odd *not* to use such a pattern in such a case. Y. R. Chao offers the example *zhima da de shaobing* 芝麻大的燒餅, which, when said with slightly more stress on *da*, means "hot biscuits on which the sesame seeds are large" but with slightly more stress on *zhi* means "sesame-seed-sized [i.e., tiny] hot biscuits."[5] In simple cases such as these, we obviously are not dealing with an exception to a rule but with a more complex picture of how several rules apply. It is possible even to imagine a situation in which a native speaker of English, in saying "Joey Davis," might use the 4–2–3–1 stress pattern that I said is so unnatural-sounding as perhaps to frighten you away from Joey. Let's imagine that Joey, several hours ago, exited his house leaving the air conditioner on and all the windows open. His roommate, returning home, is disgusted to find that Joey has done this yet again, for the fourth time this week. The roommate hisses sarcastically, "Jo-EY Da-VIS!" in a 4–2–3–1 pattern. This pattern would be highly unusual, statistically speaking—but normal in context. My point is that this kind of "exception," or the much more common "exception" of 1–3–4–4 (for *Joey* Davis), does not undermine an interest in, or analysis of, the most common pattern of 2–4–1–3.

Could one, with care, delineate all the rules of stress in all imaginable contexts so that the rules applied with the same kind of exceptionlessness that we expect from mathematics? I think so. I doubt there is anything

5. Ibid.

ultimately mystical about stress patterns. But for my purposes in this book, the relevant question is "which level of analysis is most useful for showing what I want to show?" Do I want, primarily, to study forests or trees? For stress patterns, I do not find the leave-no-exceptions pursuit of apodictic certainty to be the most fruitful one for understanding the general cases, which in turn are often the best cases for illustrating how stress affects communication. So a few exceptions (or complexities, to put it more precisely) do not bother me. Of course, *too many* exceptions would indeed be a problem, because then a generalization itself comes into question. For my purposes here, a pattern that holds 80 or 90 percent of the time will be respectable; even if it holds only 60 percent of the time it might be worth noting. But the main point I want to leave with the reader is this: when I discuss a rhythmic "pattern," I am never claiming that examples that fall outside it are therefore "unsayable" or inauthentic.

The Prevalence of Rhythmic Patterns in Daily-Life Chinese

Rhythms in oratory and literature can be lengthy, complex, and variegated; they can be creative and therefore not at all "standard" in a sense in which one might say they are 80 percent or any other percent representative of anything else. In the next-to-last chapter of Lao She's novel *Camel Xiangzi*, for example, an elderly street vendor of fried cakes philosophizes at length, intermittently using creative rhythm that contributes a languid mood as well as a sense of depth to his soliloquy. He begins with some trochees: *Ni xiang duzi hunhao?* 你想獨自混好? TAH-ta TAH-ta, TAH-ta, then *Shei bushi name xiang de?* 誰不是那麼想的 TAH-ta-ta TAH-ta TAAA(elongated)-ta? Then, a moment later: *Yige ren neng you shenme beng? Kanjianguo mazha ba?* 一個人能有甚麼蹦? 看見過螞蚱吧?[6] TAH-ta-ta, TAH-ta, ta-ta-TAH. TAH-ta-ta TAH-ta-ta. The rhythm, although not a standard pattern, oozes from the language and enchants the reader. There are no formal signs to mark the rhythm, but readers who are native speakers of Chinese, asked to read the sentences aloud, consistently converge on

---

6. Lao She 老舍, *Luotuo Xiangzi* 駱駝祥子 (Hong Kong: Xuelin shudian, n.d.), pp. 284–285.

the same patterns.⁷ That the rhythms emerge from the syllabic patterns of the language, and not just from its meanings, is evident when one compares English translations of the same lines, in which the original rhythms are entirely lost: "So you think getting along on your own is best, do you? . . . Who doesn't think that way? . . . How far can one man hop? Have you ever seen a grasshopper?"⁸ The English has rhythms, to be sure, but they are different from the originals and deliver a somewhat different mood.

This kind of creative and complex rhythm is *not* the focus of this chapter. (It is a worthy topic, but one cannot do everything.) Here we will focus on shorter phrases that have relatively standard rhythmic patterns and are used in a wide variety of contexts within Chinese culture. The patterns are seldom creative, and are repetitive from case to case, but these facts do not prevent the patterns' details and uses from becoming extremely complex and interesting.

We can begin by sketching the wide variety of contexts in which rhythmic phrases appear. Five-character *wuyan* 五言 patterns and seven-character *qiyan* 七言 patterns have been extremely common in poetry and folksongs for a long time. This point hardly needs further comment, except perhaps to note that *wuyan* and *qiyan* patterns have persisted in twentieth- and twenty-first-century poetry much more than is commonly supposed. "Modernist" revolutions in the 1920s and 1980s brought free verse, French symbolism, and Western-flavored "misty" poetry to China, but these influences were always a matter of vanguard art and academic study. It remained true that when people wanted to express strong feelings about partings, deaths, or political events, they continued—overwhelmingly—to use *wuyan* and *qiyan* patterns. In 1976, after Zhou Enlai died, crowds of mourners gathered at Tiananmen Square seeking to reveal that, down deep, they preferred Zhou to the Maoists who had survived him. They brought thousands of poems to the square, nearly all of which were *wuyan* or *qiyan*.⁹ Fiction writers, as well, have borrowed *wuyan* and *qiyan*, especially when they have wanted to emphasize the depth, solemnity, or splendor of

---

7. I have run the experiment a few times. You can do it, too.

8. Lao She, *Rickshaw*, trans. Jean James (Honolulu: University of Hawaii Press, 1979), pp. 228–229. James's translation is excellent.

9. See Tong Huaizhou 童懷周, *Tiananmen Shiwenji* 天安門詩文集 (Collection of Tiananmen poetry) (Beijing: Beijing chubanshe, 1979), 2 vols.

26　　　　　　　　　　　　　　　　AN ANATOMY OF CHINESE

something. In writing of the Nanjing massacre of 1939, Wang Huo subtitled the three volumes of his *Zhanzheng he ren* 戰爭和人 (War and people) with *qiyan* phrases.[10] Some of the chapter titles use the pattern as well. As if to underscore the heartfelt sense that the pattern can convey, one chapter head begins with a sigh: *A! Xueyu xingfeng Nanjingcheng* 阿! 血雨腥風南京城 'Ah! Bloody rain and rancid wind course through Nanjing city'.

But *wuyan* and *qiyan* are not just for elite expression and solemn contexts. As any Chinese-reading visitor to tourist sites in China can observe, these patterns are favorites of graffiti artists as well. Phrases such as *daoci yiyou, hexu gui?* 到此一游何須歸 'visiting here, what need is there to leave?' are not hard to find. At the famous Mount Emei in Sichuan in the 1980s, an official display featured a *qiyan* poem by the celebrated poet and Communist elder Guo Moruo, who had extolled the beauty of the view. Scrawled on a post nearby was the sarcastic comment of someone who apparently thought the view had not been worth the hike. The graffiti artist took issue with Guo Moruo's aesthetic judgment but not with his choice of *qiyan* form:

Bushi Guo lao chui de xiong　　不是郭老吹得兇
Na ge jiuzi cai lai you?　　　　哪個舅子才來游

If our great Mr. Guo had not puffed this place up
What monkey's uncle would have wanted to come?[11]

Incidentally, in this book I often use what others sometimes call "free" translation, especially for items of popular culture and items for which rhythm and rhyme are important. In doing so, I do not see myself as sacrificing fidelity but, on the contrary, as trying to preserve fidelity to a va-

---

10. I.e., *Yue luo wu ti shuang man tian* 月落乌啼霜满天 [Moon falls, raven cries, frost fills the sky], *Shan zai xu wu piao miao jian* 山在虚无缥缈间 [Mountains dimly discernible in the mists], and *Feng ye di hua qiu se se* 枫叶荻花秋瑟瑟 [Maple leaves and reed flowers rustling in the fall]. Wang Huo 王火, *Zhanzheng he ren* 戰爭和人 [War and people], 3 vols. (Beijing: renmin wenxue chubanshe, 1993).

11. I am indebted for this item to a marginally educated woman from Sichuan who lives in New York but prefers to remain nameless. Even in 2007, she did not wish to be known as passing along a criticism of a Communist icon like Guo Moruo. She could not remember Guo's poem, only the satiric answer to it.

riety of things at once: meaning, rhythm, rhyme, register, and the holistic life of a phrase. I do not believe that a translation that kills a lively phrase and pickles its literal meaning has more "fidelity," overall, than one that keeps the life at the cost of some literal precision. This is why, for the couplet above, I allow myself the phrase "monkey's uncle" as an attempt to match the spirit of the line in popular American usage even though there is no monkey, but only a nondescript male relative, in the Sichuanese original. (I do not ask my reader to share my views on this point, but just to be aware of what they are.)

The "cultural T-shirts" (*wenhuashan* 文化衫) that began to appear in Chinese cities in the 1990s also make use of standard rhythms. In a piece of startling satire of plainclothes police, a T-shirt that appeared in 2006 read: *baoan xunluo zhiyuanzhe* 保安巡邏志願者 'volunteer security patrolman'.[12]

Some kinds of popular culture in China have shown a preference for four-syllable combinations. Menus, for example, easily show the cultural preference—not requirement, but preference—for four syllables in the naming of dishes: *gongbao jiding* 宮保雞丁 'kung-pao chicken', *mapo doufu* 麻婆豆腐 'pock-marked lady tofu', and so on. It doesn't matter much if the names are literal (*qingzheng liyu* 清蒸鯉魚 'steamed carp') or fanciful (*mayi shangshu* 螞蟻上樹 'ants climbing a tree—pork and vermicelli Sichuan style')—in any case four syllables are preferred. Their internal stress patterns can vary somewhat (to my ear *gongbao jiding* is close to 1–4–3–3 and *mayi shangshu* close to 1–4–2–1), but, grammatically and semantically, nearly every string splits into 2 + 2, not 1 + 3 or 3 + 1. The 2 + 2 pattern suggests and maintains a principle of balance.

Although poetry, fiction, graffiti, and menus are normally written forms, their rhythmic features suggest strong connections to spoken language. Rhythm in oral Chinese is even easier to find than in writing. Marches and chants, as in other languages, observe obvious rhythms. Chants that are used for popular purposes in Chinese sometimes take on the patterns of *wuyan* or *qiyan* and other patterns that are associated with poetry and song. I understand from an eyewitness (or should we say ear-witness?)[13]

---

12. Www.signese.com, July 9, 2006. Viewed June 21, 2012.

13. My source is Professor Hu Ch'ang-tu 胡昌度, Teachers College, Columbia University.

that in the 1940s, basketball cheerleaders at Nankai University in Tianjin chanted:

Yi, er, san; san, er, yi	一二三, 三二一,
Yi, er, san, si, wu, liu, qi	一二三四五六七
Jia-you, jia-you, duo yong li!	加油, 加油, 多用力!

One, two, three; three, two, one
One, two, three, four, five, six, seven
Step on it, step on it,[14] go all out!

The third line here is *qiyan*, and the first two are a pattern that I call 3-3-7 and will discuss in more detail below. The pattern 3-3-7 occurs in ancient poetry, and in modern times appears not only in basketball cheers but in many things, from the Cultural Revolution anthem "The East Is Red" to things like popular riddles that describe, in the following example, a peanut:[15]

Ma wuzi, hong zhangzi	麻屋子, 紅帳子
Li bian zhuzhe (ge) bai pangzi	裏邊住着个白胖子

A room of hemp, a curtain of red,
A little white fatty lies in bed.

It appears as well in nursery rhymes:

Ni pai yi, wo pai yi	你拍一, 我拍一
Yige xiaohair kai feiji	一個小孩儿開飛機

You pat one, I pat one
One little child flies the plane

Ni pai er, wo pai er	你拍二, 我拍二
Liang ge xiaohair diu shoujuanr	兩個小孩儿丟手絹(儿)

---

14. In midwestern American slang, "step on it" means "step on the accelerator," which approximates the Chinese *jiayou* 'add gas'.

15. In the second line, the *ge* shares a beat with the preceding *zhe*. This sharing does not change the overall rhythmic structure of the line. I have used "lies in bed" instead of "lives inside" in my translation for the sake of fidelity to the rhyme.

You pat two, I pat two
Two little children lose their hankies.
(and further verses)

The historical roots of these rhythmic patterns lie in popular sayings, songs, and proverbs as well as in elite poetry. It is not clear how much the seepage of such patterns was "top down," socially speaking, and how much was "bottom up." (Some have argued that popular sayings and folksongs might have become elite patterns when written down by literati scribes.) In any case, there is no doubt that *wuyan* and *qiyan* are found in many kinds of nonelite material. Common wisdom on how to predict the weather may have originated among farmers:

Ri mo yanzhi hong   日沒胭脂紅
Wu yu biyou feng   無雨必有風

When the sky is red at the end of the day
Wind if not rain will be on the way.

Popular sayings often include the "poetic" conventions of parallelism as well as those of rhythm:

Jian ren shuo ren hua   見人說人話
Jian gui shuo gui hua   見鬼說鬼話

Speaking human language to a person
And the devil's tongue to a devil

Qiyan is as easy to find as *wuyan* in sayings at the popular level. Examples are *Guilin shanshui jia tianxia* 桂林山水甲天下 'the scenery at Guilin beats any in the world' and *si zhu bupa kaishui tang* 死豬不怕開水燙 'dead pigs aren't afraid of boiling water' (a punishment, once it is applied, loses its deterrent effect).

Many contemporary examples can be found in the satiric "popular ditties" (*shunkouliu* 順口溜) that are passed around in Chinese society, orally and authorlessly, rather as jokes are passed around in Western societies. This example from the late 1990s protests the plight of elderly state-enterprise workers:

Qingchun xian gei dang　　青春獻給黨
Lao le mei ren yang　　　　老了沒人養
Shuo shi kao ersun　　　　說是靠兒孫
Ersun xia le gang　　　　　兒孫下了崗

I worked my whole life for the Party,
And had nothing at the time I retired;
Now they tell me to live off my kids,
But my kids one by one have been fired.

Qiyan examples of *shunkouliu* are even more numerous than *wuyan* examples. This one looks back on the course of the Communist revolution:

Xinxinkuku sishi nian　　　　辛辛苦苦四十年
Yi zhao hui dao jiefang qian　　一朝回到解放前
Jiran hui dao jiefang qian　　　既然回到解放前
Dang nian geming you wei shui?　當年革命又為誰？

For forty-some years, ever more perspiration
And we just circle back to before Liberation
And speaking again of that big revolution,
Who, after all, was it for?

With the rapid spread of handheld telephones in Chinese cities in the first decade of the twenty-first century, *shunkouliu*, which began as an oral medium, turned partly into the written medium of text messaging. The change did not affect the prevalence of rhythmic patterns.

Traditional popular arts such as storytelling, clapper-tales, drumsinging, and other forms known as *quyi* 曲藝 'song art' are waning in contemporary China, but the most adaptive among them, *xiangsheng* 相聲 'comedians' dialogues',[16] has remained popular in altered form. In *quyi*, including

---

16. The common mistranslation of *xiangsheng* as "crosstalk" appears to be based on a misreading of 相 in the fourth tone, where it means 'looks' or 'appearance', for the same character in the first tone, where it means 'mutual' or 'each other'. My rendition of "comedians' dialogues" avoids this pitfall, but has the flaw that while the great majority of *xiangsheng* pieces are performed by two people, some are done by one, three, four, or even more performers.

xiangsheng, rhythms of many kinds are consciously woven into the textures of language. An iconic *xiangsheng* piece called *Xiju yu fangyan* 戲劇與方言 (Drama and dialects),[17] made famous by Hou Baolin and Guo Qiru, opens with a 4:4 beat:

Zuo ge xiangshengr yanyuan,   做個相聲兒演員
Ke burongyi;   可不容易
qima de tiaojianr,   起碼的條件兒
dei hui shuo hua.   得會說話

Performing *xiangsheng* is no easy matter;
At the very least, you have to know how to talk.

It uses *qiyan* to say that their adorable popular dialect of Beijing is:

luoli luosuo yida dui   囉里囉唆一大堆

a big pile of loquaciousness

But returns to 4:4 in saying that "refined" Beijing dialect is

duan xiao jing han (er)   短小精悍 (而)
luojixing qiang   邏輯性強

terse, forceful, (and) powerful in logic

Elsewhere, 4:4 is prefaced by a heavy beat at the beginnings of two parallel lines:

Zher wumen yi xiang   這兒屋門一響
Nar fajue yi wen ...   那兒發覺一問

---

17. Hou Baolin 侯宝林 and Guo Qiru 郭启儒, "Xiju yu fangyan" 戏剧与方言, in Wang Wenzhang 王文章, ed., *Hou Baolin biaoyan xiangsheng jingpinxuan* 侯宝林表演相声精品选 (A selection of Hou Baolin's xiangsheng performance pieces) (Beijing: Wenhua yishu chubanshe, 2003), pp. 35–49.

Here, the door to the room makes a sound;
There, somebody notices and asks . . .

The couplet appears, periodically in the structure of the piece, five times.

The Maoist pressure to remake Chinese literature and art, and to get rid of "old" things, brought much change to *xiangsheng* but hardly got rid of its rhythms. Ma Ji's piece called *Baigujing xianxingji* 白骨精現形记 'White-boned demon revealed' complains that under the Gang of Four, whatever you did could be called wrong, even to the extent that (in *wuyan*):

Shang ye shang buqu　上也上不去
Xia ye xia bulai　下也下不來
Huo ye huo buliao　活也活不了
Si ye si bucheng　死也死不成

Go up?—You can't go up
Down?—You can't go down
Live, you can't live
Die, you can't die!

This piece is said to have been created underground during the final years of Mao Zedong's rule and then, after his death, appropriated for official use when the new leadership found it useful in discrediting the "all-evil [Maoist] Gang of Four." Whether or not these claims are true for this particular piece and this particular rhythm, it is easily demonstrable, in general, that Chinese governments have adopted popular rhythms in their "propaganda work." The phenomenon was especially obvious during the Mao era, but it did not begin then. The Nationalists used rhythmic slogans in the 1930s and 1940s, and continued to use them in Taiwan after 1949. A public billboard in Taipei in the 1960s read, in *wuyan*:[18]

renren zuo hao ren　人人做好人
riri zuo hao shi　日日做好事

18. I am indebted to Andrew Plaks, professor emeritus of East Asian Studies, Princeton University, for this example, October 4, 2006.

Everyone be a good person.
Every day do good deeds.

Mao Zedong is said to have favored rhythmic phrases in his personal speech. Whether or not this is so, it is certainly true that he used them in political slogans at many points in his life. On August 5, 1966, Mao issued a "big-character poster" that was later viewed as a turning point in bringing on the violent phase of the Great Proletarian Cultural Revolution. The poster's title was a *wuyan* phrase followed by a *qiyan* phrase: *paoda silingbu: wode yige dazibao* 炮打司令部: 我的一个大字报 'smash the headquarters: a big-character poster of mine'. Then, in calling on young people to support him with their own big-character posters, Mao chose *qiyan* again: *daming, dafang, dazibao!* 大鳴大放大字報 'big outcry, big release, big-character posters'. I have cited other examples of *wuyan* and *qiyan* in Maoist language in the Introduction, so will not list more here, but I will speculate that Mao's preference for these patterns may help to account for why they became so prevalent in political struggle throughout Chinese society during the late Mao years. To cite just one of a great number of examples, in the 1957 Anti-Rightist Movement, He Chi, a gifted writer of *xiangsheng* pieces, was attacked for "hating socialism" and "organizing an anti-Party clique." During a "struggle session" organized by local officials to humiliate him, he heard:[19]

Dadao He Chi dayoupai　　打倒何遲大右派
Mandi dagun shua wulai　　滿地打滾耍無賴

Knock down the big rightist He Chi
Writhing around on the ground in his lies

To what extent have Chinese officials been conscious of the ways they use rhythms? This is hard to say, and almost certainly varies from case to case. When officials during the Cultural Revolution used old rhythms in order to attack "old culture" (which certainly would include old rhythms),

---

19. He Chi, *He Chi zizhuan* (Autobiography of He Chi) (Beijing: Zhongguo minjian wenyi chubanshe, 1989), pp. 287–88.

they likely were not very conscious of the self-contradictory nature of their activity. (In the political context of the time, it would have been frightening to arrive at such consciousness.) Yet they must have been aware of the rhythms at *some* level, because the rhythms in their phrases must have been part of what made them feel that the phrases were fitting.

There is good evidence that at least some people in the government have been highly conscious of rhythm and have fashioned it consciously in propaganda work. A man named Peng Ruigao, of the Shanghai Municipal Propaganda Bureau, told *New York Times* reporter Craig Smith in 2001 that "slogans require the writing techniques and rhythms of classical poetry to make them palatable to the people."[20] Putting rhythms into slogans was part of Peng's job. Signs of conscious word craft are apparent, as well, at the very highest levels of Chinese government, for example in the "Eight Honors and Eight Shames" (Barong Bachi 八荣八耻) of the Hu Jintao regime. These eight couplets, memorized by schoolchildren across China, asked people to regard "loving the country (or state)" as an honor and "hurting the country (or state)" as a shame; to regard "resolute struggle" as an honor and "wallowing in luxury" as a shame; and so on. Each line is seven syllables long (although the rhythmic pattern is not the same as in *qiyan*), and the evidence of conscious craft is overwhelming. The first syllable of each line is *yi* 以, and the sixth is *wei* 为 'take [something] as [something else]'; the seventh syllable in each line is either *rong* 荣 'honor' or *chi* 耻 'shame' in alternating lines; and the four syllables from number two to number five are all balanced 2 + 2 phrases, the first five of which are a two-syllable transitive verb followed by a two-syllable object, and the last eleven of which are parallel two-syllable verbs. There can be no doubt that the ideological content of the Eight Honors and Eight Shames was carefully debated at high levels; there also can be little doubt that their form was consciously crafted as well.

Government slogans on other topics often made use of *wuyan* and *qiyan* patterns as well. Rhyme and parallelism could be involved, as the following examples from the years 2006 and 2007 make clear.[21] Central Chinese Television (CCTV) sometimes exhorted youth to idealism with the *wuyan*

---

20. Craig S. Smith, "Shanghai Journal; Political Power Grows from the Point of His Pen," *New York Times*, June 14, 2001.

21. I am grateful to Mao Sheng for most of these examples.

phrase *rexin xian shehui, zhenqing ai renjian* 热心献社会, 真情爱人间 'dedicate yourself to society with ardor, love humanity sincerely'. Warnings to drive safely, written on public walls and blackboards in several towns and county seats around the country, read *shouwo fangxiangpan, shike xiang anquan* 手握方向盤, 时刻想安全 'grip the steering wheel, always think of safety' and *siji yibei jiu, qinren liang hang lei* 司机一杯酒, 親人两行淚 'one cup of wine for the driver, two streams of tears for the family'. Walls and blackboards also carried calls to protect the environment. In *wuyan*, there was *diqiu shi wo jia, lühua kao dajia* 地球是我家, 绿化靠大家 'the globe is our home, greenification depends on everyone', and in *qiyan*, there was *yihua yicao jie shengming, yizhi yiye zong guanqing* 一花一草皆生命, 一枝一叶葉总关情 'every flower and blade of grass is life, care for every branch and leaf'. Family planning examples included the *wuyan* example *jiating zinü duo, xiaokang hui huapo* 家庭子女多, 小康会滑坡 'with many children in a family, middle-class lifestyle declines' and *zinü zhiliang gao, shenghuo shuiping gao, xingfu zhishu gao* 子女质量高, 生活水平高, 幸福指数高 'quality of children high, standard of living high, happiness index high'. In *qiyan* there was *chusheng quexian ganyu hao, bang ni sheng ge hao baobao* 出生缺陷干预好, 帮你生个好宝宝 'it's best to intervene on birth defects; it'll help you produce a good little treasure' and *sheng nan sheng nü yiyang hao, nüer yeshi chuanhouren* 生男生女一样好, 女儿也是传后人 'having boys or girls is equally good; girls keep the family line going, too'.[22]

It should be no surprise that commercial advertisements have also employed *wuyan* and *qiyan* rhythms. In 2008 Nescafé coffee was advertised under the slogan *weidao haojile* 味道好极了 'the taste is excellent'. In English this might seem dull, perhaps even self-defeating as an advertisement, but in Chinese, thanks in part to its *wuyan* structure, the phrase is far more effective.[23] A newspaper advertisement for a restaurant in Shaoxing, Zhejiang Province, called Donghu Leyuan (East Lake Paradise) advertised in 2006: *jiewen jiujia hechu hao, donghu leyuan jiujia you!* 借問酒家何處好, 東湖樂園酒家優 'May I ask where the good restaurants are? The

---

22. From "Jihua shengyu xin biaoyu chutai neiqing" 计划生育新标语出台内情 (The inside story on the promulgation of the new birth-control slogans), *Nanfang zhoumo* 南方周末 (Southern Weekend), August 23, 2007.

23. I am indebted to David Moser for this example. Email message to author, April 13, 2008.

East Lake Paradise restaurant is fine!'[24] Even McDonald's was using *qiyan* on CCTV: *shike changxiang maidanglao* 时刻畅想麦当劳 'always keep McDonald's on your mind'. *Qiyan* could help sell tonics: *xueqi chongzu cai jiankang, buxue renzhun jiuzhitang* 血气充足才健康, 补血认准九芝堂 'health requires that the blood-spirit be ample, and to bolster the blood you need Jiuzhitang'; also *jinnian guojie bu shou li, shou li zhi shou naobaijin* 今年过节不收礼, 收礼只收脑白金 'don't take gifts at New Year's this year unless the gift is Naobaijin'. If health fails, at least one can look good with cosmetics, now offered in *wuyan: xiangyao pifuhao, zaowan yao dabao* 想要皮肤好, 早晚要大宝 'if you want good skin, sooner or later you'll need Great Treasure Cream'. You're obese? A guaranteed diet is offered in *wuyan: jianfei bu fantan, fantan bu shoufei* 减肥不反弹, 反弹不收费 'cut the fat and keep it off, if the fat comes back there'll be no charge'. An advertisement for sanitary pads on CCTV used the phrase *nüren yue zuo yue kuaile* 女人越做越快乐, making use not only of *qiyan* rhythm but a pun on *yue*, which could be either 越 'more' or 月 'month', so that users could be either "happy every month" or "more and more happy," depending on how one took the phrase. A poster advertising English lessons makes its appeal in a very Chinese rhythm: *Yingyu xuexi xintupo* 英语学习新突破 'A new breakthrough in the study of English'.[25] Even the sale of gasoline warrants rhythm: *jiayou zhong shi hua, fangxin pao tianxia* 加油中石化, 放心跑天下 'fill up with China Petrol and go wherever in the world you want'.[26] An email provider, in touting the freedom of expression that its services made possible, came up with the *qiyan* phrase *wode dipan wo zuo zhu* 我的地盘我做主 'I am master in my own domain'.

From an historical point of view, the widespread use of rhythm in commercial advertising might be entirely expected, since its roots can be found in the hawkers' calls that lasted into the early twentieth century and that almost invariably used distinctive rhythms. Hawkers' calls included an immense variety, perhaps because each hawker wanted to sound distinctive. Refuse collectors who called out a phrase like *shou polanr de!* 收破烂儿的 'taking in junk!' might truncate the *po* to make the effect *shou*

---

24. *Zhejiang ribao* 浙江日报 (Zhejiang Daily), March 12, 2006.
25. Available at www.signese.com, July 13, 2006. Viewed June 21, 2102.
26. All of the examples in this paragraph, unless otherwise noted, are from CCTV in 2006 or 2007.

p'lanr de ta-ta-TAH-ta. It is extremely rare in Mandarin Chinese for the first syllable of a compound to be unstressed (pronounced in "neutral tone"), but that is what a refuse collector could do with *polan*, in order to help everybody know exactly who was heading down the street.

In all such examples, it seems to me, the rhythm adds something to the message. It makes the message seem not just more pleasant and memorable but also somehow more natural, more right, more authoritative, more exalted—or something like that. I will discuss the possible meanings of rhythm below, as well as questions of which rhythms seem particularly "Chinese," and why. But first I want to address a prior question Chinese linguists sometimes raise: "Why are rhythms so common in everyday Chinese?" Is there something unusual about the nature of the language?

Is Rhythm Unusually Common in Chinese?

Rhythmic patterns in Chinese are sometimes determined by grammar. Consider, for example, verb-object constructions of two syllables plus two syllables (which I abbreviate as "2 + 2"). Phrases like *yuedu baozhi* 阅读报纸 'read newspapers' can regularly be shortened to 1 + 2 *du baozhi* or to 1 + 1 *du bao* but not, normally, to 2 + 1 *yuedu bao*. But 2 + 2 phrases in which the first two syllables *modify* the second two normally follow a different rule: *shoubiao gongchang* 手表工厂 'wristwatch factory' can shorten to 2 + 1 *shoubiao chang* or to 1 + 1 *biao chang*, but not to 1 + 2 *biao gongchang*. In all of the above cases, moreover, the syllables come in neat packs of 2, 3, or 4. The counterpart phrases in English include four and five syllables and cannot be manipulated in regular patterns of the kinds Chinese allows. Noting such examples, Lu Bingfu and Duanmu San conclude that "we are not aware of any other language in which syntax and word length show such a striking relation."[27] This has to do, they show, with the distinctive rhythmic flexibility of Chinese.

In Chinese, morphemes, or minimal grammatical units, are almost always monosyllables. They combine easily with one another to produce standard word lengths, and often produce balance as well. For example,

---

27. Bingfu Lu and San Duanmu, "Rhythm and Syntax in Chinese: A Case Study," *Journal of the Chinese Language Teachers Association* 37, no. 2 (May 2002), p. 134.

daxiang 大象 'big-elephant' is "elephant" and *yachi* 牙齿 'tooth-tooth' is "tooth." "Ivory" borrows one morpheme from each to make *xiangya*, in two syllables, while "ivory chopsticks" can be *xiangya kuaizi* 象牙筷子 or *xiangyakuai*, three syllables or four, as one prefers.[28] This kind of recombinatory power is easy to find in other languages, but Lu and Duanmu are probably right that the neatness of syllabic structure is distinctive to Chinese. Compare, for example, "electrocardiogram" and *xindiantu* 心电图 'heart-electric-chart'. Although *electro* and *dian*, *cardio* and *xin*, and *gram* and *tu* each can combine with other morphemes to make other words, in Chinese, *but not English*, the morphemes that move around are reliably one syllable (not two, three, or more). This makes creation of rhythm much easier. A Chinese poet (or other phrase-maker) can quite easily produce lines of five syllables each; a French or English poet, attempting comparable craft, might produce five *beats* per line, but to try to line up rows of exactly five *syllables* apiece turns phrase-making into an arcane exercise in which technical demands eclipse other aspects of art or meaning. Written form only reinforces the difference, because, in Chinese, five syllables are reliably five Chinese characters, which standardly yield lines of exactly the same length, since each character is conceptually square.[29] A French or English poet who tried to produce lines of exactly equal length would feel almost impossibly constricted, and achievement of the goal, if someone could do it, would likely appear to the reader as an oddity, a technical tour de force whose form, not content, would dominate attention.[30]

---

28. I am indebted to David Moser for this example. Email message to author, May 8, 2004.

29. Even a character that is not square, like 一 'one', is usually "conceptually square" because it occupies the center of an imaginary square space on a printed page. See Martin J. Heijdra, "Typology and the East Asian Book: The Evolution of the Grid," in Perry Link, ed., *The Scholar's Mind: Essays in Honor of Frederick W. Mote* (Hong Kong: Chinese University Press, 2009), pp. 120–125.

30. In an effort to illustrate this problem, David Bellos, professor of comparative literature at Princeton University, has translated the *shunkouliu* above ("For forty-some years, ever more perspiration/And we just circle back to before Liberation," etc.) in four lines of exactly twenty-one bits apiece: "Blood sweat and tears/Over forty long years/Now it's utterly over/Who stole the clover?" See David Bellos, *Is That a Fish in Your Ear? Translation and the Meaning of Everything* (London: Particular Books, 2011), p. 135.

In Chinese, with its monosyllabic morphemes, lines of equal length are much easier to produce. The phrase-maker has much more flexibility to arrange content within a set form. A phrase can fall into a formal pattern without seeming in any way odd, and there is no sense that the formal requirements of a phrase are attracting too much attention to themselves. Indeed there is something of the opposite sense: that the form of the phrase actually adds to its depth or credibility. Something that in English might seem "too cute" can seem perfectly natural in Chinese. And because this sort of naturalness has been around for a long time, Chinese culture tends to value it. Consider the following mundane example. A sign in the men's toilet at CCTV in the early 2000s reminded users to flush the toilet even if they were in a hurry. It read *congcong er lai, chongchong er qu* 匆匆而来, 冲冲而去.[31] The phrase has rhythm, rhyme, grammatical parallelism, and antithetical semantic parallelism (*lai* 'come' versus *qu* 'go'). In Chinese it feels natural, even cheerful. But what happens if one tries to put it into English? The meaning is "flush the toilet even though you're busy," but how would one imitate the form? "Come in a flash, go with a flush" captures the four-syllable structure, some of the parallelism, and some of the rhyme. The lines are of equal length, but maybe a bit too long. "Enter rushing, exit flushing" is terser, and also has the right number of syllables and equal line length, and some rhyme. But note: we are now playing a game in English, and in that game any effort seems awkward if it is bad and too cute if it is good.

Chinese people have noticed the remarkable flexibility of their language and sometimes make up games and puzzles that depend on the monosyllabicity of morphemes. The recombinatory cleverness that results goes well beyond anything one could even contemplate in a Western language. On the lid of a teapot, for example, the characters *keyi qingxin ye* 可以清心也 can be inscribed in a circle so that, wherever one chooses to begin, one can read around the circle and the result makes sense:[32]

---

31. I am indebted to David Moser for the example and for the "come in a flash, go with a flush" translation cited below. Email message to author, May 8, 2004.

32. I am indebted to Hu Ping for this example. Email message to author, June 9, 2007.

可以清心也	You can clear the mind
以清心也可	You can also take it as mind-clearing
清心也可以	Clearing the mind is also possible
心也可以清	The mind, too, can be cleared
也可以清心	You can clear the mind, too

But if morphemes are almost always monosyllabic in Chinese, it is quite another matter, and grossly incorrect, to say that words are. The often-heard statement that Chinese is a "monosyllabic language" makes sense only if one is speaking of morphemes. The word *word* is not always easy to apply to Chinese,[33] but whatever the definition, there are a great number of unproblematic examples of polysyllabic *words*. Many of these, too, have reliable stress patterns. In modern Mandarin *doufu* 豆腐 is 'bean curd'. In writing the two characters, a person might conceive 豆 and 腐 as "monosyllables." But for most people most of the time (including buyers, sellers, and eaters of bean curd who may have been illiterate), *doufu* was a two-syllable word. Moreover it had a clear internal stress pattern: always *DOUfu*, never *douFU*. Examples of other two-syllable words or phrases are innumerable. Rhythmic patterns become more complex, as we shall see, when three or more syllables are involved.

Speakers' Awareness of Rhythm

If someone were to go to the market and ask for *douFU*, he or she would probably get the stuff, but everyone within earshot would know "something's wrong." The ability to recognize that "something's wrong" in cases like this extends well beyond the small group of people who can explain—in terms of syllables, stresses, and so on—*why* it is wrong. This simple example shows that there are two levels in what we can mean by "awareness" of stresses or rhythms. When a person hears or uses a stress pattern that follows convention, it "sounds right" or "feels good." When used incorrectly, it sounds wrong. Should we say that the user is *conscious* of this connection between rhythm and rightness? The question is subtle.

---

33. See Y. R. Chao, *Grammar of Spoken Chinese*, p. 136.

We cannot say that users are not consciously aware, because the sense of rightness (or of wrongness, for mistakes) is indubitably a conscious feeling. But it is also true that the great majority of users of stress patterns do not make conscious decisions when selecting patterns and cannot explain what they have done once the sounds have been pronounced.

The "tones" of Chinese are a good example of this phenomenon. If, following Y. R. Chao, we regard voice pitch as part of what we mean by "stress," then we can take Chinese tones as miniexamples of stress patterns. A native speaker of Chinese—including any dialect—will immediately feel that something's wrong when a tone is wrong. This feeling will be just as clear as it is for an English speaker who hears "gat" when he or she can infer that "get" is what the speaker meant to say. But here's the point: native speakers of Chinese, unless they are specially trained, usually cannot identify which tone was said and which was meant. Many will have learned labels for the tones in school (first tone, second tone, etc.) but still will not be able to say "that was second tone, it should have been fourth," or even "your voice pitch was rising and it should have been falling." At that level, they normally are not *conscious* of pitch. But the same people will be immediately aware of any mistake, and can very easily *pronounce* what the proper sound should have been.

This two-levelledness in the awareness of pitch and stress can create ironies. I noted in the Introduction how Red Guards, in the late 1960s, assembled in Tiananmen Square chanting an "old" *qiyan* rhythm *(women yao jian Mao zhuxi)* in praise of the man who was urging them to reject everything old. I doubt that the Red Guards were aware of this contradiction.

What about Mao himself? At which level, if any, might he have been aware of such things? There is ample evidence that Mao was willing, in general, to exempt himself from rules that he applied to others. In 1963, for example, he published a volume of his classical poetry, in *qiyan* and other forms, *Mao Zhuxi shici sanshiqi shou* 毛主席詩詞三十七首 (Thirty-seven poems by Chairman Mao). By 1974 the little book had been reprinted fourteen times.[34] For nearly everyone else in China during those

---

34. Mao Zedong, *Mao Zhuxi shici sanshiqi shou* 毛主席詩詞三十七首 [Thirty-seven poems by Chairman Mao] (Beijing: Wenwu chubanshe, 1974).

Cultural Revolution years, any public show of favor toward classical poetry might be dangerous, possibly even lethal. Mao's book not only contained classical poetry; it imitated traditional, a.k.a. "feudal," style in many other ways: it used traditional characters, arranged them vertically in unpunctuated lines, opened from the right-hand side, and was composed of pages bound with string between covers of blue paper. In many ways it was made to resemble books of the Ming-Qing era. Its design features were unavailable to any other mainland Chinese who produced books during the late-Mao era, a time when many traditional-style books, including genuine Ming-Qing volumes, were being burned. Can we imagine that the whole production of Mao's poetry book happened without the conscious awareness of its makers of what they were doing? Hardly. Can we suppose that Mao himself did not consciously approve? Again no. This is almost impossible to imagine. It is much easier to imagine that the principle "Mao is an exception to Maoist guidelines" was in use.

Yet, despite the obvious exceptionalism, I would guess that Mao seldom, if ever, was consciously aware of Red Guard use of *qiyan* rhythm to praise him. It seems more plausible that he just felt—rather as the user of correct tones in ordinary Chinese *just feels*—that the phrases sounded right. This hypothesis gains strength when we consider the many examples of his use of such rhythms in watchwords that he intended for others. I noted several of these in the Introduction (*Funü neng ding banbiantian* 妇女能顶半边天 'Women can hold up half the sky'; *Linghun shenchu gan geming!* 灵魂深处干革命 'Make revolution in the depths of your soul'; *Nongye xue Dazhai* 农业学大寨 'Agriculture should learn from Dazhai'; etc.). When Mao wanted to warn that there are a lot of good-for-nothings hidden in the shallow waters at the august Peking University, his phrase *Beida shui qian wangba duo* 北大水浅王八多 'The water is shallow and the turtles are many at Peking University' no doubt just felt better to him because of its *qiyan* rhythm.

Qiyan and *wuyan* rhythms are in fact easier—not, as one might expect, harder—to find in the public political language of high Maoism. These rhythmic habits not only appeared in national campaign slogans and the names of the model operas but seeped into daily-life political struggle as well. At the two sides of a makeshift stage used for "struggling class enemies" in Harbin, two vertical banners bore the *wuyan* matching couplet *buwang jiejiku, laoji xueleichou* 不忘阶级苦, 牢记血泪仇 'don't forget class bitterness; remember forever blood-and-tears enmity'.[35] In Sichuan an art student remembers a chant, in *qiyan*, of *yao zuo, yao zuo, hai yao zuo* 要左, 要左, 还要左 'left, left, ever more left'.[36] These are but random examples in an ocean of others.

The irony of articulate intent versus inadvertent use of rhythm is sharpest for the Mao years but hardly limited to them. Fifty years earlier Hu Shi, in his famous 1917 essay "My Humble Opinion on the Reform of Literature" called on Chinese writers to "pay no attention to parallelism" (*bujiang duizhang* 不講對仗).[37] But Hu himself, in promoting the scientific method,[38] called for these actions:

Dadan de jiashe	大膽地假設	Hypothesize boldly.
Xiaoxin de qiuzheng	小心地求證	Seek evidence carefully.

Hu's phrases are not only *wuyan* but elegantly parallel ("big gall this, little heart that"). We can imagine that Hu might explain this gap between his theory and his practice by holding that his rule about parallelism applies to literary essays, whereas aphorisms of the kind I have quoted here serve a different purpose. Still, it is interesting that Hu seems to have felt, at least for aphorisms, that *wuyan* rhythm and parallelism *add something*, or somehow make things better. When his friend and fellow reformer Chen Duxiu followed Hu's "Humble Opinion" with a more hard-hitting essay titled "On Literary Revolution," Chen called for "knocking down" all kinds of "ornate," "rotten," "extravagant" old forms and styles and creating "colloquial social literature."[39] Chen's essay itself, though, was written

---

35. Exhibition of the photography of Li Zhensheng 李振盛, California Museum of Photography, University of California, Riverside, April 28–July 7, 2007.

36. From the memory of Tang Shaoyun 唐绍云, professor of art, Xiamen University.

37. Hu Shi 胡適, "Wenxue gailiang chuyi" 文學改良芻議, *Xinqingnian* 新青年 [New youth], no. 1 (January 1, 1917).

38. Hu Shi 胡適, "Qingdai xuezhe de zhixue fangfa" 清代學者的治學方法 (1921) in *Hu Shi wencun* 胡適文存 (Collected works of Hu Shi), collection 1, volume 2 (Hefei: Anhui jiaoyu chubanshe, 2003) (1921).

39. Chen Duxiu 陳獨秀, "Wenxue geming lun," *Xinqingnian* 新青年 [New youth], no. 2 (February 1, 1917).

in a classical style that can only be called fairly ornate and a bit extravagant. Here, too, an ironic gap opens between "what I say should be done" and "what I am doing." Two levels of awareness—focused consciousness and inadvertent habit—are in play.

Are There Fads in Rhythms?

Fads in language use can originate in a number of ways, some of them purposeful, but they seem often to spread at the same less-than-conscious level that explains much use of rhythm in language. People sense that it feels good to use a certain word or phrase without specifically noting that they are following a trend in doing so. In the modern West teenagers are held to be major purveyors of language fads, but in fact the adult worlds of business, government, and academe are also full of examples. In the late twentieth century words like "interface" and "module" were stylish in American bureaucratic language. In the twenty-first, "robust," "compelling," and "multiple" have received faddish attention. There are plenty of other examples.

It seems that not only words but rhythms can be involved in faddishness. This notion first occurred to me for the case of contemporary Chinese when I noticed how many slogans of the Great Leap Forward years (1958–60) seemed to be four-syllable phrases:

Duo kuai hao sheng!	多快好省	More, faster, better, thriftier
Chao Ying gan Mei!	超英赶美	Surpass England and catch up with America.
Li gan jian ying	立竿见影	Erect a pole and see a shadow—get instant results.
Tu fei shui zhong	土肥水种	Earth, fertilizer, water, seeds
Mi bao guan gong!	密保管工	Dense protect manage labor. [Mao's formula for miraculous crops]

And so on. To test my hypothesis rigorously one would need to count the occurrences of different kinds of rhythms from a variety of randomly selected texts (and where possible, recordings) from different time periods. I have not done this kind of rigorous study, but have examined, in the spirit of a pilot study in that direction, headlines and slogans in the *People's Daily* for the month of October in 1951, 1958, and 1966, respectively.[40] I chose these three years in order to highlight the slogans of three prominent campaigns (i.e., those called Suppression of Counterrevolutionaries, The Great Leap Forward, and The Great Proletarian Cultural Revolution). In using the *People's Daily* as my source I was aware of the bias toward official and political language as opposed to daily-life usage, but still, the easy comparability of three months of the *People's Daily* made systematicity possible, so the effort seemed worthwhile.

I found standard patterns of four, five, and seven syllables in all three periods. In October 1951 an unusually large number of paired slogans appeared that used an eight-syllable line followed by a seven-syllable line. For example:

Gonggu renmin minzhu zhuanzheng 鞏固人民民主專政
Jianjue zhenya fan'geming 堅決鎮壓反革命

Consolidate the people's democratic dictatorship.
Resolutely suppress counterrevolutionaries.[41]

Kuoda chengxiang wuzhi jiaoliu 擴大城鄉物質交流
Fazhan gongnongye shengchan 發展工農業生產

Expand material exchange between city and countryside.
Develop industrial and agricultural production.[42]

Patterns of nine syllables also seemed unusually common in 1951:

Dazhang qigu zhenya fan'geming 大張旗鼓鎮壓反革命

Roll out the banners and drums in suppressing counterrevolutionaries.[43]

40. I am grateful to Mao Sheng for assistance in this work.
41. *Renmin ribao* 人民日報 [People's daily], October 3, 1951, p. 3.
42. Ibid., October 20, 1951, p. 2.
43. Ibid., October 3, 1951, p. 3.

Zhongguo renmin datuanjie wansui   中國人民大團結萬歲

Long live the great unity of the Chinese people.[44]

In 1958, by contrast, four-syllable lines seemed unusually common, and they were often paired with a second line that might have four, five, or seven syllables. An example of a four-four pair is:

Loushang louxia, diandeng dianhua   楼上楼下电灯电话

Electric lights and telephones upstairs and down.

A four-five pair:

Qingzhu woguo nongye dafengshou   庆祝我国农业大丰收

Congratulate our country's big agricultural harvest.[45]

And a four-seven pair:

Quanmin dongyuan   全民动员
Baozheng gangtie fan yi fan   保证钢铁翻一番

Mobilize all the people to guarantee a redoubling of steel.[46]

In the fall of 1966 rhythms of all kinds were more common in the pages of the *People's Daily* than they had been in either 1951 or 1958. The Cultural Revolution rhythms seemed, too, to carry a more palpable "beat" than others. For example:

Weida de daoshi, weida de lingxiu,   伟大的导师, 伟大的领袖
Weida de tongshuai, weida de duoshou,   伟大的统帅, 伟大的舵手
Mao Zhuxi wansui!   毛主席万岁!

---

44. Ibid., October 5, 1951, p. 3.
45. Ibid., October 1, 1958, p. 4.
46. Ibid., October 1, 1958, p. 9.

Long live the great teacher, great leader, great commander, great helmsman Chairman Mao![47]

In this example the first four phrases are not only five syllables in length but invite a heavy lilt: ta-TAH-ta-ta-TAH, ta-TAH-ta-ta-TAH. . . . The crucial contribution of the little particle *de* 的, which precedes the modified nouns, is worth noting. It not only prevents a reading of the five-syllable lines in the customary pattern of 2 + 3, with a pause after the second syllable (as would certainly happen if, for example, the line were *weida zongsiling* 伟大总司令 'great commander-in-chief'). It also, because it is repeated in parallel, magnifies the lilt. English, which has no corresponding marker, does not have the same lilt-inducing tool available to it. "Great teacher, great leader, great commander, great helmsman" can be said with rhythmic parallelism, to be sure—but not with the swing that comes naturally to *weida de daoshi, weida de lingxiu, weida de tongshuai, weida de duoshou*. Or consider the example I noted in the Introduction of the Cultural Revolution phrase *weida de guangrong de zhengque de gongchandang* 伟大的光荣的正确的共产党 'great, glorious, correct Communist Party'. Compared to the ta-TAH-ta, ta-TAH-ta, ta-TAH-ta rhythm of the Chinese, the English phrase "great, glorious, correct" sounds flat.[48]

In 1958 a casual comment from Mao Zedong seems to have led to a rhythmic pattern that took at least two different shapes during China's late Mao years. In early August 1958, when Mao was on an inspection tour of prototypes of the communes (*dashe* 大社) that he was planning, a local official in Shandong reportedly asked him what these new organizations should be called, to which he reportedly answered: *haishi jiao "renmin gongshe" hao* 还是叫"人民公社"好 'It's probably best to call them "People's Communes"'.[49] Mao's grammar in this sentence was fine, but when his sentence was shortened, as it was in *People's Daily* headlines and in many other places, to *renmin gongshe hao!* 人民公社好!, the result was a saying that observes *wuyan* rhythm but is not, when lifted from context, a grammatically natural phrase. (Without *hen* 很 or *ting* 挺 or some other adverb

---

47. Ibid., September 27, 1966, p. 4.
48. I am indebted to David Moser for this insight on *de*. Email message to author, April 13, 2008.
49. Renminwang 人民网 [People.com], http://cpc.people.com.cn/GB/64162/64170/4467343.html. Viewed June 23, 2012.

of degree preceding *hao*, the sentence technically means "the People's Communes are better [than some alternative].") But the phrase *renmin gongshe hao* was repeated so often that it not only came to seem natural but also established the pattern *A–B–C . . . hao*, which spread, especially during the Cultural Revolution, to refer to a variety of politically correct things: *shehuizhuyi hao* 社会主义好 'socialism is good'; *dazibao hao* 大字报好 'big-character posters are good'; *wenhua dageming hao* 文化大革命好 'the Great Cultural Revolution is good'; *geming weiyuanhui hao* 革命委员会好 'the revolutionary committees are good'; *fuke nao geming hao* 复课闹革命好 'it is good to return to class to make revolution';[50] *haishi laoshi dian hao* 还是老实点好 'it's better to be a bit more sincere after all'.[51] The pattern survived even as late as 2005 and 2006 in the family-planning slogans *jihua shengyu hao* 计划生育好 'the planning of births is good' and *zhisheng yige hao* 只生一个好 'producing only one is good'.[52]

It seems that Mao added a permutation to the pattern with another inadvertent comment in the summer of 1966, when he said that the rebellious spirit of the Red Guards was *hao de hen* 好得很 'really good'. The August 23, 1966, issue of the *People's Daily* published a front-page editorial under the headline *hao de hen*, and in the ensuing days this headline appeared three times: *hongweibing de wuchanjieji geming zaofan jingshen hao de hen!* 红卫兵的无产阶级革命造反精神好得很 'The proletarian revolutionary rebellious spirit of the Red Guards is really good!'[53] Then many other things became *hao de hen* as well. On September 6, 11, and 24, it was reported that foreign friends from Albania, Japan, Congo, Chile, Cuba, and elsewhere were sending in messages that *Zhongguo wuchanjieji wenhua dageming hao de hen* 中国无产阶级文化大革命好得很 'China's Proletarian Cultural Revolution is really good'.[54] Eventually other phrases that used a

50. *Dongfang hong* 东方红 [The east is red], November 3, 1967, p. 2.

51. *Hongqi zhanbao* 红旗战报 [Red flag warfare] (Xinjiang), January 20, 1968, p. 1. For many of the examples in this paragraph I am indebted to Mao Sheng, "Geming weiyuanhui hao" (The revolutionary committees are good), unpublished manuscript, March 2007.

52. Mao Sheng, "Geming weiyuanhui hao."

53. *Renmin ribao* 人民日报 [People's daily], August 24, 1966, p. 3; August 26, 1966, p. 2; August 27, 1966, p. 3.

54. Ibid., September 6, 1966, p. 5; September 11, 1966, p. 4; September 24, 1966, p. 4.

rhythmic pattern of TAH-ta-TAH (resembling *hao de hen*) seem also to have become stylish. In the August 24 *People's Daily*, right below a headline that ended in *hao de hen!*, another ended in *gan de hao!*: *shoudu guangda gongnongbing relie huanhu "hongweibing" gan de hao!* 首都广大工农兵热烈欢呼 '红卫兵' 干得好 'Broad ranks of workers, peasants and soldiers in the capital cheer the "Red Guards" for doing well'.[55]

There is room for further research in this area, but in any case the hypothesis that rhythms have gone through passing fads in contemporary Chinese, in political language and elsewhere, seems plausible in a number of ways.

The Roots of Rhythms

Rhythms in language can result from set forms, as in songs or chants, or from less consciously observed rules that involve grammar, meaning, emphasis, or simply convention. In Mandarin Chinese it is easy, for example, to notice conventional stress patterns in which the second syllable of a two-syllable compound or phrase is an unstressed "neutral" tone: *er.duo* 耳朵 'ear', *qing .ni* 请你 'invite you' and so on. (Here and below I follow Y. R. Chao in using a dot to precede a syllable that is pronounced in the unstressed "neutral" tone.) It is also easy to note how an unstressed syllable can take on stress when a speaker's meaning calls for it: *wo qing **ta**, bu qing **ni*** 我请她, 不请你 'I invited *her*, not *you*'.

Other things being equal (and I will consider some of those "other things" below), Mandarin Chinese has a clear preference for maintaining syllabic balance. One syllable plus one syllable naturally form a balance, and so do two plus two. When three syllables are involved, it sometimes (not always) happens that the three are reduced to two so that balance can be maintained. For example, "school" is *xuexiao* 学校 in two syllables. To say "middle school" (which is high school, in American usage) the modifier *zhong* 中 needs to come first, but this would make a three-syllable *zhongxuexiao*, which feels awkward. So Chinese drops the *-xiao*, and the word for high school becomes *zhongxue*, where the *xue* stands in for all of *xuexiao*.

---

55. Ibid., August 24, 1966, p. 3.

Then, among *zhongxue*, one can subdivide to either *chu* 初 'beginning' or *gao* 高 'high' levels (i.e., junior or senior high), but again *chuzhongxue* and *gaozhongxue* are both three syllables, so again are shortened. *Chuzhong* becomes the word for "junior high school" and *gaozhong* the word for "senior high school." But the original word *xuexiao*, which now is dropped completely, is clearly understood. Similarly, for "hold a meeting" Chinese uses either *kai hui* 开会 in two syllables or *juxing huiyi* 举行会议 in four, split 2 + 2. A three-syllable *kai huiyi* feels a bit awkward, and *juxing hui* sounds pretty awful. In four-syllable phrases, the overwhelming tendency is to break the syllables 2 + 2, and this preference for 2 + 2 holds across different kinds of grammatical structure.[56] For example *yuyan yanjiu* 语言研究 'the study of language' is 2 + 2, and so is *yanjiu yuyan* 研究语言 'study language'. (There are rare cases in which four-syllable phrases can be broken 1 + 1 + 1 + 1, or 3 + 1, or 1 + 3, or even 1 + 2 + 1, and we will visit some of these odd cases later; their oddness only serves to underscore the preference for balance when a balanced alternative is available.)

Stress patterns become more complicated—and interesting—in cases where three syllables more or less *have to* be involved. In three-syllable strings, it is rare that each syllable is equally weighted, although examples like Alabo 阿拉伯 'Arabia' and *jiguanqiang* 机关枪 'machine gun' come close. Nearly always, the three syllables cluster as either 2 + 1 *pingguo da* 苹果大 'the apple is big' or 1 + 2 *da pingguo* 大苹果 'big apple'. The break in such phrases often is not a pause so much as a minor slowing down leading to slightly more stress on the syllable that follows. A "pause" exists only by comparison to transitions that pause less. For example, to say that there is a break between *guo* and *da* in *pingguo da* means only that there is less of a break (or none at all) between *ping* and *guo*. This kind of a subtle stress pattern, because it depends on comparison, cannot obtain when only two syllables are involved. *Er.duo* 'ear' has an obvious stress pattern, but it is not the same as—indeed is usually more prominent than—stress patterns of the kind I am analyzing here, the kind that result from three- or four-syllable clustering.

---

56. See Feng Shengli, "Prosodic Structure and Its Implications in Teaching Chinese as a Second Language," unpublished, April 2003, pp. 12–13.

In three-syllable phrases, grammar and meaning usually determine whether the clustering is 2 + 1 or 1 + 2. Examples where the break comes between subject and predicate are trivially easy to cite: *women yao* 我们要 'we want' is 2 + 1, and *ta buxin* 她不信 'she doesn't believe' is 1 + 2. The breaks in modifier-plus-noun phrases are often determined by the grammar and meaning of the component words. A *fujingli* 副经理 'deputy manager' is always a *fu* + *jingli*, never a *fujing* + *li*, and *doufutang* 豆腐汤 'bean-curd soup' has to be *doufu* + *tang*, never *dou* + *futang*.

Other questions of where breaks occur are more subtle. An interesting subfield in Chinese prosody, recently pioneered by Duanmu San, Feng Shengli, and others, has studied what happens in stress patterns when phrases are shortened. The results vary with grammatical structure. In phrases where a verb is followed by a second verb, called a "complement" (the relation of verb and complement in Chinese is similar to *scared stiff* or *tickled pink* in English), shortenings from 2 + 2 syllables to either 1 + 1 or 1 + 2 are both all right, but 2 + 1 normally is not. For example, *baifang zhengqi* 摆放整齐 'arrange into neat order' can shorten to either *fang qi* or *fang zhengqi*, but not *baifang qi*.[57] Similarly *jiangjie qingchu* 讲解清楚 'explain clearly' can become either *jiang qing* or *jiang qingchu*, but not *jiangjie qing*.[58] In short, rhythmic factors not only induce certain patterns but can rule out patterns as well.

Verb-object constructions normally observe the same rule, for example, *yuedu baozhi* 阅读报纸 'read a newspaper' can be either *du bao* or *du baozhi* but not *yuedu bao*; similarly, *zhongzhi shumu* 种植树木 'plant trees' can be *zhong shu* or *zhong shumu* but not *zhongzhi shu*.[59] Exceptions like *taoyan gou* 讨厌狗 'find dogs disgusting' can be explained by the fact that *gou* 'dog' does not have an easy two-syllable alternative. The rule is, as it were, "soft," in the sense that it describes a definite preference but allows exceptions for good reason. Feng Shengli points out another interesting exception: 2 + 1 for verb-objects is all right when the verb includes a neutral

---

57. The example is from Feng Shengli, "Facts of Prosodic Syntax in Chinese," unpublished paper, p. 34.
58. The example is from Lu and Duanmu, "Rhythm and Syntax in Chinese," p. 126.
59. Examples from ibid., p. 123.

tone, as in *xi.huan qian* 喜欢钱 'likes money' or *xia.hu ren* 吓唬人 'frighten people'.[60]

In cases where both modifier and modified are two syllables, a difference emerges depending on whether the modifier is a noun or an adjective. When a noun modifies a noun, the preference in shortening four syllables to three is 2 + 1, not 1 + 2. Thus *meitan shangdian* 煤炭商店 'coal store' shortens to *meidian* or to *meitan dian*, but not to *mei shangdian*.[61] On the other hand, when the two-syllable modifier is an adjective, 1 + 2 is preferred: *nüxing gongren* 女性工人 'female worker' shortens to *nügong* or to *nü gongren* but not to *nüxing gong*.[62] In addition to this puzzling difference, another difference between adjective modifiers and noun modifiers is that only adjective modifiers can take the particle *de*. One can say *nüxing de gongren* for "female worker," but not *shoubiao de gongchang*. (If we did say the latter, its meaning would switch, and be odd. It would mean something like "a factory belonging to wristwatches.")

Most of these patterns can be explained by what Duanmu San and others call a "nonhead stress rule." (The "head" of a phrase is the top of the tree-structure in a phrase diagram.) In a verb-object or verb-complement structure, the verb is the head; in a modification structure, the modified noun is the head (unless the modifier is an adjective, in which case the implied particle *de* is the head). In all cases, the component of a phrase that is *not* the head receives stress. Duanmu discusses apparent exceptions to the nonhead stress rule and on the whole defends the rule well.[63]

The rule applies to phrases longer than the four-syllable strings we have been considering. In verb-object constructions, where the nonhead object needs more stress, a two-syllable verb cannot go with a one-syllable object: hence *du bao* 'read the newspaper' is all right, but *yuedu bao* sounds wrong. Similarly, a three-syllable verb sounds wrong with a two-syllable object. We can say *fuze bingfang* 负责病房 'take responsibility for the

---

60. Feng Shengli, "Facts of Prosodic Syntax in Chinese," p. 5.
61. Lu and Duanmu, "Rhythm and Syntax in Chinese," p. 123.
62. Ibid., p. 128.
63. Ibid., pp. 126–133. See also San Duanmu, "Stress and the Development of Disyllabic Words in Chinese," *Diachronica* 16 (1999), pp. 15–16, and *The Phonology of Standard Chinese* (Oxford: Oxford University Press, 2000), ch. 6.

[hospital] ward' but not *fuzeren bingfang* 负责任病房 (of the same meaning). Feng Shengli points out that here it is the nonhead stress problem, not the 3 + 2 clustering of syllables, that rules out *fuzeren bingfang*. *Dui bingfang fuze* 对病房负责 'be responsible for the ward' is also three syllables plus two, and is quite fine, because now *dui bingfang* is the nonhead.[64]

While the nonhead stress rule and related grammar rules can, as we have just seen, be "strong" enough to rule out certain phrases (i.e., make them what grammarians call "unsayable" in normal usage), it is also true that they are sometimes *insufficient* to determine how a string of syllables should be said, or set to rhythm, or understood. In such cases *meaning* also plays a role. This point is clear if we look at strings of nouns in which the possibilities of modification are ambiguous. Feng Shengli uses the example *pi* 皮 'leather,' *xie* 鞋 'shoes,' and *chang* 厂 'factory' to illustrate. Each of these syllables by itself is a noun, and the three start, as it were, on equal footing. If we string them together as *pixiechang*, it is possible (if we imagine a certain context) to understand the phrase as three nouns meaning "leather, shoes, and factories" (1 + 1 + 1). A person could say, for example: *pi xie chang, women Lanzhou dou you* 皮鞋厂我们兰州都有 'leather, shoes, and factories—we've got them all in Lanzhou'. But when we consider the more likely case in which the nouns can modify one another, the question of clustering arises. In writing, *pixiechang* could be seen as either 2 + 1 *pixie chang* 'leather-shoe factory' or 1 + 2 *pi xiechang* 'shoe factory made of leather' (or, more intriguing, 'naughty shoe-factory'). In deciding between these two (and the 1 + 1 + 1 alternative), meaning makes the difference in our choice, and the "right answer" is fairly obvious. There is no *grammatical* reason to prefer *pixie chang* over *pi xiechang*, but we realize that (in the normal world, anyway) a leather-shoe factory is a more plausible thing than a shoe-factory made of leather. This recognition guides our interpretation of the grammar and also tells us where the pause and stress should go if we read the phrase aloud.

In a startling footnote, Duanmu San points out that meaning is sometimes strong enough not only to decide among grammatical possibilities within a string of syllables but also, like grammar rules themselves, to

---

64. Feng Shengli, "Facts of Prosodic Syntax in Chinese," pp. 36–37.

render certain things "unsayable."⁶⁵ In certain pairs of statements of the forms 'X is P' and 'X is not-P', only one of the two can normally be said. (The point here is not the logical point that 'X is P' and 'X is not-P' cannot simultaneously be *true;* the point is that only one of the two forms is normally "sayable," regardless of whether it is true.) A two-syllable adjective with a positive meaning like *qingchu* 清楚 'clear' or *anquan* 安全 'safe' can be preceeded by *hen bu* 很不 'very not': *hen buqingchu* 'very unclear', *hen buanquan* 'very unsafe', and so on. But two-syllable adjectives of *negative* meaning, like *mohu* 模糊 'muddled' or *weixian* 危险 'dangerous' do not similarly follow *hen bu.* No one (except in odd contexts) says *hen bu weixian* 'very not-dangerous'. To compound this peculiarity, the point *exactly reverses* when one makes the minor change of talking about one-syllable adjectives instead of two-syllable adjectives. Now adjectives with negative meanings take *hen bu* (*hen bushao* 很不少 'quite a few'; *hen buruo* 很不弱 'very not weak—pretty strong'), but adjectives of positive meaning do not. Normally no one says *hen buqiang* 很不强 'very not-strong'. The mystery gets even deeper if one reverses *hen bu* to *buhen.* Now only adjectives with positive meanings—regardless of whether they are one syllable or two—can be accommodated. One can say *buhen qingchu* 'not very clear' or *buhen da* 'not very big', but not *buhen mohu* 'not very muddled' or *buhen shao* 'not very few'. Duanmu presents these data but cannot explain them, and neither can I. My purpose here is simply to illustrate further the point that sometimes the meanings of phrases—not just their grammar—go into determining whether native speakers find them "sayable."

"External" Rhythms: Dominant and Recessive

We have seen how grammar can affect the rhythms of phrases and how, when phrases in written form are ambiguous, meaning can make the difference in determining grammatical relations and associated rhythms. But there are also rhythms in language that originate outside of grammar

---

65. Lu and Duanmu, "Rhythm and Syntax in Chinese," p. 133, n. 7. The authors credit Lü Shuxiang, "Hen bu . . ." [Very not . . .], *Zhongguo Yuwen* [Chinese language] 5 (1965), for the original insights on *hen bu.*

or meaning. I will use the term "external rhythm" to refer to these. These are cultural artifacts that are used and understood independently of—and sometimes despite—what grammar requires.

Some cases of external rhythm are hard to miss. In any human culture, poetry, songwriting, and things like chants and marches include meter that has patterns that are external to the requirements of grammar. I will call these kinds of external rhythms "dominant." By "dominant" I mean that the people who put them to use—and very often the people who receive them as well—are consciously aware of what is going on. When a poet or songwriter composes a line in a dominant pattern, the rhythm is "there first," as it were, and the poet or songwriter's task is to select and arrange words to fit it. The pattern is "strong" enough that it can be acceptable even for a poet or songwriter to overrule normal grammar in order to accommodate a rhythm.

Normally, for example, the English phrase "the button he pressed" would be understood as a noun phrase meaning "the button that he pressed." In a limerick, though, it can mean "he pressed the button." This inversion of verb and object is justified—and does not confuse a cooperative reader—because the demands of the dominant rhythm (and in the following case, rhyme, too) need to be met:

Endeavored a boy of No. Dak.
To picture a bear with a Kodak.
The button he pressed,
And the bear did the rest—
The boy stopped running in So. Dak.[66]

The first line above, like the third, reverses the normal subject-predicate order, but in neither case do we mind. In a limerick, even such fixed aspects of language as spelling and pronunciation can bow to rhythm and rhyme: No. Dak. and So. Dak. are made to rhyme with Kodak. Limericks are, to be sure, extreme cases. They are an especially mischievous form to which we give especially broad license. But for that very reason they are

---

66. Cyril Bibby, *The Art of the Limerick* (Hamden, Conn.: Archon Books, 1978), p. 193. I have taken the liberty of substituting "boy" for "lady" in Bibby's version.

good examples of what I want to call "external" rhythm of the "dominant" kind. The rhythm in a limerick is unapologetic about its formal demands, makes both writer and reader quite aware of what these demands are, and can, if necessary, push around other facets of language.

But there is another kind of cultural rhythm, which is still "external" in the sense that it is not required by grammar, but is not as explicit or nearly as pushy as the dominant kind. I will call this kind "recessive." In the Introduction, I cited the example of the *qiyan* pattern that underlies the first line of Lu Xun's story "Kong Yiji": *Luzhen jiudian de geju, shi he biechu butong de* 魯鎮酒店的格局, 是和別處不同的 'the layout of the wineshops in Lu-town was different from those in other places'. Few ordinary readers will be consciously aware that *qiyan* rhythm undergirds this line, but few, too, will not sense the grace it adds. Ian McEwan has noted a similar way iambic pentameter underlies John Updike's line "the rooms are quadrants of one rustling heart," which, McEwan writes, produces a "sweetly pitched" description of a house in which lovers are obliged, by the presence of others in a house, to enjoy each other quietly.[67]

Some recessive rhythms are standard parts of a language, even when they are not consciously noticed. An example from contemporary American English is the pattern (which employs pitch as well as rhythm) that goes "low-low-low-HIGH, low-low-low-HIGH, low-low-low-HIGH . . ." (The number of "low" syllables can vary.) For example, if I had a bad day at the mall I might say, "First it *rained*, then I couldn't find *parking*, then I lost my *credit card* . . ." and so on. This pattern usually tells the listener three things: (1) I am giving you a list of related items; (2) This list has no certain end; and (often, but not always) (3) I feel exasperation about the items on the list.

Unlike their "dominant" cousins, "recessive" rhythms defer to other facets of language. They have ways that they work within the rules of grammar but still make important contributions to the way phrases "feel" in the minds of speakers and hearers. Speakers and hearers, while remaining largely if not entirely aware of the rhythms, use them as they use most grammar and pronunciation rules—automatically, as it were. They do not

---

67. Ian McEwan, "On John Updike," *New York Review of Books* 56, no. 4 (March 12, 2009), p. 6.

give them the conscious notice that they normally give to word selection (at least for the crucial words in an utterance) or, when they are present, to "dominant" rhythms, either. But recessive rhythms, even though used in this less than fully conscious way, are still *cultural* in the sense that they are the artifacts of certain cultures and not necessarily of others.

In distinguishing "dominant" and "recessive" rhythms, I am not claiming that every example of a rhythm has to be one or the other kind. Limericks, to be sure, are sufficiently distinctive that we might say they are always dominant. (Can we imagine a person producing a limerick, or passing one along, inadvertently?) There are also complex poetic forms, such as the *qinyuanchun* 沁園春 'spring in Qin's garden' form, which is so dominant that even Mao Zedong obeyed it and so ornate that anyone who seeks to use it needs to be quite aware of exactly what he or she is doing. But the great majority of rhythms that I discuss in this book, including *wuyan*, *qiyan*, and other examples in both Chinese and English, are not essentially either dominant or recessive but can be, and very often are, either one. Rigorously speaking, what I am distinguishing here are not two sets of examples of rhythms but two ways rhythms can function.

Enough prologue. What are the "external rhythms" of Chinese? Can we uncover them? The "dominant" ones have been well catalogued by scholars of Chinese poetry. This is a vast and rich field, in which there is always more to learn, but the importance of rhythms in it hardly needs to be "uncovered." The "recessive" patterns, though, are another matter. They have not been studied, and it is tricky to figure out how to uncover them. The problem is not just that people are unaware of them and therefore not able to identify them. The problem is also that the rhythms, being "recessive," defer to other aspects of language structure. They are camouflaged, as were, within syntax. Consider again the example (from the Introduction) of the Red Guards in Tiananmen Square chanting *women yao jian Mao zhuxi!* 'we want to see Chairman Mao' in a *qiyan* pattern of 2–2–3 syllabic structure. Can we say, from this evidence, that 2–2–3 is an "external" pattern of the "recessive" kind? No, we cannot, because grammar easily explains the 2–2–3 pattern as well. The first two syllables of *women yao jian Mao zhuxi* are its subject, the next two are its verb, and the last three its object. The 2–2–3 pattern comes right out of the grammar, and there is no need to postulate an "external" rhythm. To be sure, we might speculate that the Red Guards hit on this particular combination of subject, verb, and object because they started, somewhere in their quasi-consciousness, with a sense that *qiyan* rhythm "sounds good." That would be plausible, but hard to prove.

Other examples I have discussed are equally frustrating from this point of view. In *yi kan, er man, san tongguo* 'first look, then go slowly, then cross', *qiyan* rhythm coincides with grammar in a similar way. So does *wuyan* rhythm in *zhanglang, si guangguang!* 'cockroaches—dead to the last one!' An interesting question thus emerges. Are there *intrinsic* preferences for certain kinds of recessive rhythms in Chinese, where by "intrinsic" I mean preferences that exist independently of the pushes and pulls of grammar? If so, is there any way we can identify these preferred rhythms? If we want to say that recessive rhythms are cultural items in their own right, that speakers and writers are expressing preferences when they decide to use them or not, and that the rhythms contribute some kind of sense or feeling to a phrase (all of which are claims that I want to make in this chapter), then we will need, somehow, to separate rhythms from grammar, to see what rhythmic preferences might obtain when grammar does not dominate. But how?

In his article "On the 'Natural Foot' in Chinese,"[68] Feng Shengli has come up with an ingenious method for doing just what we need—isolating recessive rhythms. (Feng's term "natural foot" is synonymous with what I am calling "recessive rhythm.") Feng reasons that if we can find strings of syllables that are *exactly parallel* grammatically, then grammar will not be the explanation for any rhythms that might appear within them. If rhythms do appear, and if they fall into consistent patterns (that is, are not just random from case to case), then the patterns must be intrinsic preferences of Chinese culture.

Feng does his experiment using two kinds of parallel syllables. One kind are the syllables that are used for sound only in the transliteration of foreign words. For example, just as "Joey Davis" has an internal stress pattern in English, so does "Mayakovsky" in Russian. But when

---

68. "Lun Hanyu de 'ziran yinbu'" 论汉语的 "自然音步" [On the 'Natural Foot' in Chinese], *Zhongguo yuwen* 中国语文, no. 1 (January 10, 1998).

"Mayakovsky" is transliterated into Chinese *Ma-ya-ke-fu-si-ji* 瑪雅可夫斯基, the lilts of Russian are lost. The syllables undergo a radical homogenization, reducing to something like tat-tat-tat-tat-tat-tat and, as it were, "starting over" rhythmically. If any patterns in the new string happen to emerge, they will come from *Chinese* cultural preferences, not Russian. And no grammar, either Chinese or Russian, will get in the way.

Feng's second method of testing uses items in series. In referring generically to kitchen utensils, for example, the Chinese language sometimes uses the set phrase *guo wanr piao penr* 鍋碗瓢盆 'woks, bowls, ladles, and pots'. For kitchen staples, there is *chai mi you yan jiang cu cha* 柴米油鹽醬醋茶 'kindling, rice, oil, salt, soy sauce, vinegar, and tea'. I will call such examples "item lists." The items that they contain are often nouns, but do not have to be. Dissolute behavior can be summarized in the verbs *chi he piao du* 吃喝嫖赌 'eat, drink, brothel, gamble', and the basic colors are *hong huang lan bai hei* 红黄蓝白黑 'red, yellow, blue, white, black'. The only requirement of item lists is that the items be parallel.

Item lists usually involve things with much more cultural content than we encounter in transliterations like *Ma-ya-ke-fu-si-ji*. The choice of which kinds of items to put into such lists is a cultural choice, and the order in which they appear is also fixed by cultural convention. (If, for example, you accused someone of *he du piao chi* instead of *chi he piao du*, people might worry about you as much as the accused.)[69] But even if item lists do open the door to small cultural influences, Feng Shengli is right to include item-list examples in his experiment because the cultural elements are not *grammatical*. There is no grammatical reason to insert either stresses or pauses inside a string like *hong huang lan bai hei*. Feng is right that if a pattern does appear, then a "recessive" rhythm must be at work.

Let us see what happens when we do Feng Shengli's experiment on syllable strings of various lengths, using both transliterations and item lists.

---

69. I say transliterations "usually" have less cultural content because, as marketers of Western products in China have discovered, a transliteration can be made to suggest a meaning as well. *Baishi kele* 百事可乐 transliterates "Pepsi-Cola" but also means, to the Chinese ear, "everything's felicitous."

Recessive Rhythms of Favor

Two-syllable strings often give equal stress to each syllable: plunk, plunk. Examples are Aiji 埃及 'Egypt', a transliteration, and *yinyang* 阴阳 'yin and yang', an item list. Since clustering is impossible with only two syllables, variation in the length of pauses cannot be a factor. Many two-syllable words that use "neutral tones" in modern Mandarin put a stress on the first syllable: *di.di* 弟弟 'younger brother', *ma.fan* 麻烦 'trouble(some)', and so on.[70] But these imbalances do not happen (or anyway are extremely rare) in transliterations or item lists. *Dong.xi* 东西 '(concrete) thing' stresses the first syllable, but the same characters *dongxi* meaning 'east and west' are an item list and give equal stress to each. I believe it is possible—barely—to hold that two-syllable transliterations that end with a syllable pronounced in a fourth tone, such as *ka-te* 卡特 'Carter', tend to stress the fourth-tone syllable a bit more than its predecessor. Fourth tones, because they fall sharply and relatively far, can naturally seem more emphatic. But this effect, to the extent that it exists, probably owes something to the fact that the fourth-tone syllable is the second of the two in *ka-te*. In a word like Beining 贝宁 'Benin', the effect disappears.

With transliterations or item lists that contain three syllables, a "plunk, plunk, plunk" pattern of equal stresses without clustering (i.e., 1 + 1 + 1) is often a norm. Luoshanji 洛杉矶 'Los Angeles' is said this way, as is the item list *tian di ren* 天地人 'heaven, earth, human being (the cosmos, in sum)'. It would be awkward to insert major pauses or stresses into such phrases. Feng Shengli notes, however, that sometimes, in some transliterations, a subtle 2 + 1 clustering does emerge. Xiyatu 西雅图 'Seattle', Jia'nada 加拿大 'Canada', and Moxige 墨西哥 'Mexico' can all be said 1 + 1 + 1, especially if said slowly. But when spoken quickly and fluently, a subtle tendency toward 2 + 1 is detectable. The very slight clustering creates not

---

70. Duanmu San notes that disyllabic words, whether including neutral tones or not, became the norm in Chinese during the twentieth century. An extensive study by the Chinese Language Reform Committee in 1959 showed that 69.8 percent of the three thousand most commonly used words were two syllables. "Stress and the Development of Disyllabic Words in Chinese," pp. 4–5.

even a pause, but only a brief slowing-down that results in slightly more emphasis on the syllable that follows. I will make a slash (/) stand for this brief slowing-down. If we listen carefully, with Feng Shengli, we can hear that Xiyatu is Xiya/tu; Jia'nada is Jia'na/da; and Moxige is Moxi/ge. The subtle difference emerges more clearly if we compare 2 + 1 to 1 + 2. Try (if you speak Chinese) saying Xi/yatu or Jia/nada. These just don't work as well as Xiya/tu or Jia'na/da. The same seems to hold for item lists. Pronounced slowly, *shulihua* 数理化 'math, physics, and chemistry' and *fulushou* 福禄寿 'wealth, position, and longevity' are both 1 + 1 + 1. But said fluently, *shuli/hua* sounds better than *shu/lihua* and *fulu/shou* better than *fu/lushou*. I believe that even in such tiny differences as these we can begin to feel the "meaning" of Chinese rhythms. I think a Chinese speaker would feel a bit more comfortable with a promise of *fulu/shou* than of *fu/lushou*. And I would guess that if you interviewed would-be Chinese tourists about tour packages to Seattle, they might be slightly more attracted to Xiya/tu than to Xi/yatu.

Recessive rhythms begin to emerge more clearly when we look at syllable-strings longer than three. In four-syllable examples, a preference for 2 + 2 is quite clear. Feng Shengli notes that Sri Lanka is normally said as Sili/Lanka 斯里兰卡, Pakistan is Baji/sitan 巴基斯坦, and Tanzania is Tansang/niya 坦桑尼亚, all with a slight slowing-down between the second and third syllables; similarly for item lists, Chinese speakers tend to say *dongxi/nanbei* 东西南北 'east, west, south, north', *chaimi/youyan* 柴米油盐 'firewood, rice, oil, salt', and *jiajian/chengchu* 加减乘除 'addition, subtraction, multiplication, division'.[71] The preference for 2 + 2 is confirmed in cases where a matching line is also 2 + 2. *Chi he piao du* 'eat, drink, brothel, gamble', for example, is commonly followed by *wu e bu zuo* 无恶不作 'no evil not done'. In *wu e bu zuo* grammar intervenes to reinforce the 2 + 2 pattern, but this intervention only confirms that 2 + 2 is the right way to say the first line.

Rhythmic preferences become considerably more obvious in cases of five-character and seven-character strings. This is not surprising, in view of the prevalence of *wuyan* and *qiyan* patterns in Chinese culture that I have noted in a variety of examples. Five-syllable transliterations tend to

---

71. Feng Shengli, "Natural Foot," p. 42.

split 2 + 3 in standard *wuyan* form. Aerbaniya 阿尔巴尼亚 'Albania' tends to be Aer/baniya, and Bolshevik is Buer/shiweike 布尔什维克. In item lists, the five elements tend to be pronounced as *jin mu/shui huo tu* 金木水火土 'metal, wood, water, fire, earth', and the five metals as *jin yin/tong tie xi* 金银铜铁锡 'gold, silver, copper, iron, tin'.[72] In seven-syllable examples, Buyinuosiailisi 布宜诺斯艾利斯 'Buenos Aires' tends to be Buyi/nuosi/ailisi, and the list of every item one standardly needs in the kitchen, *chaimiyouyanjiangcucha* 柴米油盐酱醋茶 'kindling, rice, oil, salt, soy sauce, vinegar, and tea', tends to be *chaimi/youyan/jiangcucha.*

The breaks in all these phrases—which are 2/3 for *wuyan* and 2/2/3 for *qiyan*—are the same as in classical Chinese poetry (in the study of which they are referred to as "caesuras"). In many cases a minicaesura among the final three syllables in a *qiyan* line, that is, 2/1, is also detectable. (The last three syllables of Buyinuosiailisi, for example, are subtly closer to *aili/si* than to *ai/lisi*.)

The breaks that emerge in transliterations and item lists are normally much briefer than those involved in the oral reading of poetry. When classical poems are read aloud, the pauses can be emphasized—drawn out and savored—to marvelous effect. To do the same with Albania, or salt and soy, would be comical.

Sometimes, too, classical poets alter the standard pattern of caesuras for deliberate artistic effect. Matthew Chen cites two seven-character lines by Ouyang Xiu (d. 1072 CE) in which a "mismatch" between syntax and 2 + 2 + 3 rhythm creates "metrical tension" that seems clearly to be part of the poet's art:[73]

jing ai zhu shi lai ye si	靜愛竹時來野寺
Du xun chun ou guo xi qiao	獨尋春偶過溪橋

A quiet lover of bamboo, I come often to the rustic temple
Alone in search of spring, I happen across the bridge over the brook

---

72. Ibid., p. 41.
73. Matthew Y. Chen, "Metrical Structure: Evidence from Chinese Poetry," *Linguistic Inquiry* 10, no. 3 (1979), pp. 406, 412.

Here the grammar clearly asks for a 3 + 2 + 2 rhythm, generating "mismatch" with the standard 2 + 2 + 3 pattern. The poet is playing with us. "Handle the mismatch," he seems to be saying, "and feel its exquisiteness." The 3 + 2 + 2 mismatch appears in more popular forms as well, for example in the title of a story by Feng Menglong (1574–1646): "Maiyoulang duzhan huakui" 賣油郎獨占花魁 (The oil vendor wins the courtesan). But 3 + 2 + 2 does not, as far as I can tell, appear in transliterations or item lists, where the standard patterns of 2 + 3 for *wuyan* and 2 + 2 + 3 for *qiyan* are, even if articulated faintly, overwhelmingly preferred.

But just now, in considering five-syllable and seven-syllable strings together, I skipped over the case of six-syllable strings. What about them? And what about strings of eight, nine, or more syllables? Are cultural preferences in rhythm still involved? Six-syllable rhythmic patterns do exist in Chinese. Classical *pianwen* 駢文, with roots as old as the Han period, observes a pattern of four plus six syllables. *Pianwen* was a refined art, and its rhythms were normally "dominant" in the sense in which I am using the term. They were consciously employed, but also restricted, it seems, to a cultural elite; there is no evidence that they ever had the kind of general use that *wuyan* and *qiyan* have today.

Whether indirectly related to *pianwen* or not, modern phrases of six syllables can be found, although they are not nearly as common as *wuyan* and *qiyan*. A prominent Cultural Revolution slogan was *zhua geming, cu shengchan* 抓革命, 促生产 'grasp revolution, promote production'.[74] A 2004 advertisement on CCTV said *pifu hao, yong dabao* 皮服好, 用大宝 'for good skin, use Great Treasure Cream'. In these cases, the six syllables are balanced 3 + 3, but there are also cases of 2 + 2 + 2. Lesson 15 of a textbook aimed at spreading literacy among farmers, published in Sichuan in 1979, opens with *zhengyue lichun yushui, eryue jingzhe chunfen* 正月立春雨水, 二月惊蛰春分 'in the first month spring arrives and the rains come, in the second month the insects awaken and spring begins' and continues with twelve lines of six characters apiece, all in a 2 + 2 + 2 pattern.[75] (This

---

74. *Renmin ribao* 人民日报 [People's daily], September 7, 1966, p. 1.
75. Mianyang diqu wenjiaoju 绵阳地区文教局, *Nongmin shizi keben* 农民识字课本 (A textbook for teaching literacy to farmers) (n.p., 1979), p. 22.

clearly is a case of "dominant" pattern use.) A 2007 family-planning slogan also used a 2 + 2 + 2 arrangement: *kongzhi renkou shuliang, guan'ai diqiu muqin* 控制人口数量，关爱地球母亲 'control population numbers, care for Mother Earth'.[76]

But why are six syllables in a rhythmic string far less common than five or seven? There seems to be a cultural preference for five or seven that steers usage in those directions. For example, the lesson text in the farmers' textbook that I just cited, near the bottom of the page, abandons its six-syllable pattern and uses seven-syllable lines. When this happens a tone shift seems to occur; the seven-syllable lines are weightier; they sum up the truth of the lesson. The six-syllable lines bring us through all the farming routines of the twelve months of the year, and these lines somehow almost suggest incompleteness: with each there is a next step to come. But with the seven-syllable lines at the end, the tone suggests summary and wisdom:

Meiyue liang jie bubiangeng　　每月两节不变更
Zuiduo xiangcha yi liang tian　　最多相差一两天
Buwu nongshi yao zhuajin　　不误农时要抓紧
Kexue zhongtian duo gaochan　　科学种田夺高产

Two periods in each month without exception
Never differing by more than one or two days
We must watch closely to miss no farming times
And reap high production through scientific planting.

If there is indeed a cultural preference for five syllables or seven, as opposed to six, we should expect it to show up on the neutral turf of transliterations and item lists. Does it? Is there a tendency (where a choice is possible) to choose five or seven syllables in a transliteration, instead of six? Or to make item lists five or seven items long, rather than six (or, perhaps, eight)?

Yes, there does seem to be such a tendency, and we can test the case by adding or subtracting syllables and observing what happens.

For item lists, we should begin by noting that some lists are not arbitrarily expandable or contractible. "North, south, east, west," for example,

---

76. From "Jihua shengyu xin biaoyu chutai neiqing."

is 2 + 2 in Chinese, and either *dongnan/xibei* or *dongxi/nanbei*, but we cannot make the number of directions three or five just by wanting to. (We could include the intermediate directions *dongnan* 东南 'southeast', *xibei* 西北 'northwest', etc., but then our list would automatically jump to eight, making it impossible to test for the appeal of five or seven.) Luckily, for our purposes, most item lists in Chinese are arbitrary. They could, in theory, easily be more or fewer in number, so a fact that they tend to settle at five or seven (or whatever number) can be considered a cultural preference.

We saw such preferences in the examples *jin yin / tong tie xi* 'gold, silver, copper, iron, tin' for metals and *chai mi / you yan / jiang cu cha* 'kindling, rice, oil, salt, soy sauce, vinegar, and tea' for kitchen supplies. Now let's do a thought experiment. What if someone said, of the metals list, "We should add aluminum. In the modern world we no longer have tin cans—they're mostly iron or aluminum. If tin deserves to be on the list, aluminum certainly does, too." So we add *lü* 铝, and what happens? It doesn't sound very good. *Jin yin tong tie xi lü* seems awkward, and it doesn't help much to break it up as *jin yin / tong tie / xi lü* or as *jin yin tong / tie xi lü*. But if we could come up with one more metal, to make seven, then we would be in good shape again. Let's add zinc *xin* 锌. *Jin yin / tong tie / xi lü xin* now feels much better. The seven-syllable phrase is not standard in the language, and my point is not that it is or that it should be. My point is that if Chinese *were* to go beyond five items on the metals list, it is likely that seven *would* be the pattern—whether or not aluminum and zinc were the two metals that were added.

A thought experiment on the kitchen staples yields a similar result. Among *chai mi you yan jiang cu cha* 'kindling, rice, oil, salt, soy sauce, vinegar, and tea,' we might ask "Why is kindling there?" People don't ingest kindling, as they do the other items, so maybe it should not be on the list. But does *mi you yan jiang cu cha*—six syllables—sound as good? Hardly. So let's put the kindling back. But then what about garlic *suan* 蒜? What is Chinese food without garlic? It would seem as important as the others, so what happens if we add it and go to eight items? *Chai mi you yan jiang cu cha suan* is not too bad, actually. Eight syllables, if not as elegant as seven, seems better than six. (Some scholars have held that the seven syllables of *qiyan* are actually eight with a musical rest at the end; this seems right, and makes it easier to understand why the expansion from seven syllables to eight seems natural.) But what if we add ginger *jiang* 姜, to make nine? *Chai mi you yan jiang cu cha suan jiang* is cumbersome, and not very good. Nine syllables or more may begin to be too long to feel like a single phrase, and it may be that limits of this sort inhere in the human brain.[77]

In addition to thought experiments, there are real-world examples to suggest a tendency to prefer item lists of five or seven rather than other nearby numbers. In the early stages of the Cultural Revolution, for example, Mao Zedong named "five black categories" of people: landlords, rich peasants, counterrevolutionaries, bad elements, and rightists. Each was summarized in a one-syllable abbreviation: *di fu fan huai you* 地富反坏右. One might say, of course, that "five" was not Mao's preference; maybe it just naturally happened that there were five kinds of bad people in China, just as there are naturally four directions. But later, as further problems popped up for Mao, other categories bad people had to be labeled. There were capitalist-roaders, rightist-tendency elements, reactionary scholarly authorities, and others. At different times and places, the five black categories expanded to higher numbers. But they didn't seem to stop at either six or eight. Eventually two versions, the "five" and the "seven" black categories, became standard.[78]

Syllable strings of nine or more, if they do have set rhythms, are likely to be built from shorter phrases. Take, for example, the pattern that I called "3–3–7" earlier, a pattern that feels natural in a variety of contexts, from cheerleading to singing a national anthem. The "3–3" part of it, by itself, can feel awkward. We have noted that an expansion of the five metals to six does not sound very good: *jin yin tong tie xi lü* 金银铜铁锡铝 is awkward, whether read as 2 + 2 + 2 or as 3 + 3. The metals sound better in either five or seven syllables. But watch: six metals sound just fine if you follow them with a list of seven more to make 3–3–7: *jin yin tong, tie xi lü,*

---

77. The psychologist George Miller, in his seminal article "The Magical Number Seven, Plus or Minus Two," *Psychological Review* 63 (1956), pp. 81–97, summarizes studies that show that the human ear and brain normally can handle discriminations of pitch and of loudness up to a limit of seven or so, after which confusions happen more easily than before.

78. See Guo Jian, Yongyi Song, and Yuan Zhou, *Historical Dictionary of the Chinese Cultural Revolution* (Lanham, Md.: Scarecrow Press, 2006), pp. 13–14.

qian bo you gang lei nie wu 金银铜, 铁锡铝, 铅铂铀钢镭镍钨 'gold, silver, bronze; iron, tin, aluminum; lead, platinum, uranium, steel, radium, nickel, tungsten'. The whole phrase sounds so nice that a person might want to go out and buy all thirteen metals.

In any case, I think we can conclude that cultural preferences in rhythm are strong enough to help shape the length and internal structure of item lists. There are plenty of examples. It thus becomes interesting to note that, by comparison, rhythms seem to have less power in shaping transliterations. As noted above, Feng Shengli seems right to observe a subtle preference for Xiya/tu over Xi/yatu when saying 'Seattle'; but in lengthier transliterations the cultural shaping seems to lose power. For example, Chinese uses six syllables to transliterate Uzbekistan as Wucibiekesitan 乌慈别克斯坦, which is normally said as 2 + 2 + 2. The Uzbek language uses four syllables for this word, and English also uses four. Why does Chinese use six? Apparently, this is an effort to account for all of the Uzbek consonants. The desirability of covering all the consonants seems to outweigh the question of syllables, even when an awkward "six" is the result. There are other cases where "six" might be avoided but is not. For example, Czechoslovakia was called Jiekesiluofake 捷克斯洛伐克—six syllables, and again 2 + 2 + 2. English adds a "ia" to the end of the country's name, and there is no reason Chinese could not have done so as well. If it had, then we would have the seven-syllable Jiekesiluofakeya 捷克斯洛伐克雅—easily, and pleasantly, pronounced as 2 + 2 + 3. Yet this did not happen. It felt all right to keep the syllables at six.

Why might this be? Why should item lists tend to observe the *wuyan* and *qiyan* preferences more than transliterations do? I wonder if the difference has to do with the cultural familiarity of item lists as opposed to the alien flavor of transliterations. Names like Czechoslovakia are, after all, the creations of foreigners. Chinese speakers may feel, whether consciously or not, that if such names don't sound quite mellifluous in Chinese, well, there is something appropriate about that. We Chinese should respect the clunkiness of the Czech language; it's not our business to be making adjustments for others. But when we refer to oil, soy, and tea, we are on home turf, as it were; here our intuitive sense of the "right feel" is indeed our own business, and we deal with it.

How Recessive Rhythms Affect Structure

I have noted how the rhythms of phrases can make them seem more graceful or authoritative and will address these "meanings" of rhythms in a separate section below. Here I want to address the question of how rhythms can make a difference in the structure of phrases. The point is obvious for "dominant" rhythms (as in the limerick about No. Dak). But for recessive rhythms, I have said earlier that they "defer to other aspects of language" and "have ways that they work within the rules of grammar." Still, recessive rhythm in Chinese does affect structure in several ways.

It can, first of all, cause the addition or subtraction of syllables from a phrase. We have seen how *zhong xuexiao* automatically shortens to *zhongxue* 'high school' and *chu zhongxue* to *chuzhong* 'junior high'. This dropping of syllables suits a rhythmic preference for two-syllable balance. On the other hand, Duanmu San has shown how syllables can be *added* to produce balance.[79] When nonheads are stressed, they must have at least as many syllables as the head. *Zhong suan* 种蒜 'plant garlic' is all right, but *zhongzhi suan* 种植蒜 is not. If *zhongzhi* becomes two syllables, then *suan* has to become *dasuan* 大蒜. The *da* 'big' is there for rhythmic balance only and is semantically empty (i.e., the garlic does not have to be big). In modification phrases, where the nonhead comes first, the pattern reverses. *Mei dian* 煤店 'coal store' cannot be *mei shangdian* 煤商店. If you want to use the two-syllable *shangdian*, then you have to say *meitan* 煤炭 for 'coal', even though *tan* (literally 'charcoal') does not do anything to change the meaning of *mei* 'coal'. Duanmu notes that "the extra syllable in the disyllabic form is semantically redundant or vacuous."[80]

In some compounds of modern Chinese, a redundant second syllable is added even when "nonhead stress rules" do not require it. For example, in

---

79. San Duanmu, "Stress and the Development of Disyllabic Words in Chinese," pp. 9–10, 24–25. See also Lü Shuxiang, "Xiandai Hanyu dan shuang yinjie wenti chu tan" 现代汉语单双音节问题初探 [A preliminary study of the problem of mono- and bisyllabic expressions in modern Chinese], *Zhongguo Yuwen* [Chinese language] 1 (1963), pp. 11–23; Duanmu, *Phonology of Standard Chinese*, pp. 140–142; and Feng Shengli, "Facts of Prosodic Syntax in Chinese," unpublished paper, pp. 3–7.

80. San Duanmu, "Stress and Development of Disyllabic Words in Chinese," p. 3.

classical Chinese both *yi* 衣 'upper clothing' and *shang* 裳 'lower clothing' could be used independently, but in modern Chinese *shang* cannot stand alone. It is useful only as a second syllable to tack onto an *yi* in order to make *yishang* 'clothes'.[81] Similarly, *hu* 虎 'tiger' is conventionally prefixed with *lao* 老 'old' to make *laohu* 'tiger', even though *lao* has nothing to do with the age of the tiger. A baby tiger is a *xiao laohu* 小老虎 (literally "young old tiger" but actually just "young tiger").

The addition of redundant or vacuous syllables to accommodate culturally favored rhythms such as *wuyan* and *qiyan* seems also to happen. We saw the example *rexin xian shehui, zhenqing ai renjian* 'dedicate yourself to society with ardor, sincerely love humanity'. The final *renjian* 'humanity' could as easily have been the single syllable *ren* if terseness had been the main concern. But obviously *wuyan* rhythm was more important. In *zhanglang, si guangguang!* 'cockroaches—dead to the last one!', why is the second *guang* there? Isn't *si guang* 'dead with none remaining' dead enough? Why make it *si guangguang?* Might the second *guang* be there to underscore the thoroughness of the annihilation? Perhaps. Is it there to make the rhyme with *zhanglang* better (completing a pleasant AABAA) pattern?[82] Perhaps. But it can also be viewed as a redundant fifth syllable put there in order to complete a *wuyan* pattern.

In some cases it seems that more than one syllable is added in order to complete a rhythmic pattern. In 1972, when U.S. journalists were allowed into China with the Nixon entourage, one Western reporter is said to have asked a group of Chinese on a Beijing street where the mysterious Lin Biao had gone, to which a young boy reportedly called out: *Gerpi zhaoliang dahaitang!* 嗝屁着凉大海堂 'Croaked with a belch and a fart', that is, died. *Gerpi zhaoliang* is standard slang roughly equivalent to "croak" or "kick the bucket" in American English. One interpretation of *zhaoliang*, literally "catch cold," is that it evolved from *chaoliang* (朝梁 'face the rafters'), describing the attitude of a corpse lying supine. I cannot vouch for this view. What I want to point out here are the last three syllables, *dahaitang*, literally "great sea hall." They seem to make no semantic contribution to

---

81. Ibid., p. 30.
82. I am indebted to James R. Pusey for this insight. Correspondence with author.

the phrase at all. Why are they there? Somehow they contribute panache to the phrase, and at least some of that panache, I believe, derives from the completeness of the *qiyan* rhythm.

Another way rhythm can impinge on structure involves no change in words or word order. The role of rhythm can be simply to induce the listener or reader to interpret a string of syllables in one way instead of another. Consider, for example, the five syllables *ni qu wo ye qu* 你去我也去, literally "you go I also go." In one rhythm this means "You are going and so am I." In another it means "If you go, I'll go, too." Implied conditionals that have no markers except stress pattern and context are much more common in Chinese than in English. Here is another example, picked from a myriad of other options. *Zhu tao le zenme ban?* 猪逃了怎么办？ can mean either "the pig has escaped; what should we do?" or "what should we do if the pig escapes?"

First-year students of Chinese know that *lian* 连 and *dou* 都 combine to express the notion of "even": *wo lian bao dou bukan* 我连报都不看 'I don't even read newspapers'; *ta lian yidian dou buxiang chi* 她连一点都不想吃 'She doesn't want to eat even a bit [of it]'. It is common, and widely observed, that *lian* can drop out of such phrases: *ta yidian dou buxiang chi* works just as well as the sentence just cited. Less widely noticed is the fact that *lian* and *dou* can sometimes *both* be omitted, while the notion of "even" continues to be implied: *yi dian guanxi meiyou* means the same as *lian yidian guanxi dou meiyou* 连一点关系都没有 'it doesn't matter in the slightest'. The writer Wang Shuo has a novel entitled *yidian zhengjing meiyou* 一点正经没有 (Utterly lacking in decency)[83]—which means, clearly, *lian yidian zhengjing dou meiyou*, although a cool writer like Wang Shuo would never do anything so uncool as to spell things out for dullards.

So how does a reader or listener know when to infer *lian . . . dou* if neither is actually used? Context clearly helps, but another reason, I believe, is that a stress pattern distinctive to *lian . . . dou* usage can help. A phrase like *yi dian guanxi meiyou* has a distinctive lilt. A phrase like *yi wen bu zhi* 一文不值 'not worth a penny—worthless', condensed from *lian yi wen dou buzhi*, is readily understood because it is a cliché, although theoretically

---

83. Wang Shuo 王朔, *Yidian zhengjing meiyou* 一点正经没有 (Beijing: Zhongguo dianying chubanshe, 2004).

one could understand it as a subject plus transitive verb (awaiting an implied object): "a penny is not worth [something else]."

An imaginary example might show the point most clearly. For a sentence like *ta yidian mingqi meiyou le* 他一点名气没有了, speakers of Chinese will naturally supply the *lian . . . dou* idea, apply its associated rhythm, and understand it to mean "he completely lost his fame." But without the *lian . . . dou* idea, we can take the same eight syllables in another way. Imagine a classroom teacher who is angry because he thinks some of his students have been cutting class. The students say they are innocent and challenge him to call the roll. When he calls roll and finds that, yes, everyone indeed is present, his anger completely subsides, that is, *ta yi dianming, qi mei you le* 'as soon as he calls roll, anger is no longer there'. This second interpretation is actually more parsimonious than the first, because it requires no importation of understood items. It also has a very different rhythm from the first. In spoken language, there would be no ambiguity at all, because rhythm alone—without even the help of context—would decide the matter.

In rare cases, three or even four different interpretations of a phrase can result from rhythmic variation. In a short novel by Gao Yubao entitled *Gao Yubao*, which was famous in China in the late 1950s, a man shouts for others to get out of bed and go to work because dawn has arrived.[84] He presses his point by saying *ji dou jiao le* 鸡都叫了! 'it's cock-crowing time already!' and everyone knows what he means. The same four syllables could, though, be read in different rhythms to mean, variously: (1) All the chickens have crowed; (2) Even the chickens have crowed; (3) The chicken even squawked (because, for example, something hurt it).

At their most "pushy," recessive rhythms sometimes override considerations of grammar or meaning. In this they resemble what I have called dominant rhythms, although the crucial difference that remains between recessive and dominant rhythms is that speakers and listeners are usually aware of dominant rhythms, while recessive rhythms almost always work their effects unnoticed. A simple example is how the preference in a four-syllable string for 2 + 2 balance can intrude in a phrase. A *gongsi jingli* 公司经理 'company manager' is 2 + 2, both grammatically and rhythmically.

---

84. Gao Yubao, *Gao Yubao* (Beijing: Zhongguo qingnian chubanshe, 1955) p. 110.

A *fu zongjingli* 副总经理 'deputy to the general manager' is 1 + 3 grammatically (or, at a finer level, 1 + [1 + 2]). We might expect the phrase to be pronounced 1 + 3, but normally it is not. What people actually say for *fu zongjingli* is *fuzong/jingli*, not *fu/zongjingli*.[85] It just feels better. By stretching logic, one might conceive the phrase as 2 + 2, that is, *fuzong* 'deputy general' + *jingli* 'manager'. But even the wildest logic cannot explain a case that Y. R. Chao gives to show how the 2 + 2 rhythmic preference can superimpose itself on other structures. Chao's example is *wufeibingniu* 無肺病牛, which reasonably clusters as either *wu feibingniu* 'there are no cattle with pneumonia' or *wufeibing niu* 'cattle that are free of pneumonia'. To Chao's astute ear, however, people still tend to say 2 + 2, *wufei bingniu*, as if they mean "sick cattle without lungs."[86]

In some cases a recessive rhythm can become assertive enough that it alters the number or order of syllables in a phrase. Examples can be found among phrases of a type sometimes used in Chinese that we might call "false verb-object compounds." These phrases are distinctive and delightful even though they seem to have no formal name. I mean ones like *majie* 骂街 'scold the street', that is, shout abuse in public, or *yangbing* 养病 'nourish illness', that is, nourish oneself back from illness. In such phrases the noun in the object position does not name the *receiver* of the action but something else. I suspect that these interesting phrases come about in part because of the allure of 1 + 1 or 2 + 2 rhythm. *Majie* must have evolved from something more unwieldy, like *zai jieshang ma* 在街上骂—but 1 + 1 was neater and caught on. In *yangbing*, what one nourishes is not the illness but more nearly the opposite, yet a phrase like *yang kangbing yinsu* 养抗病因素 'nourish factors that resist illness' is awkward and hard to put into pleasant rhythm. *Chang dagu* 唱大鼓, literally "sing the big drum," omits the important word *shu* 书 'stories' (*dashu* 大书 'big stories'—meaning stories about major figures in history—are what actually are getting sung) and does not make clear that *da* here does not modify *gu* (the drum in fact

---

85. Feng Shengli, "Natural Foot," p. 46.
86. "Zhongwenli yinjie gen ticai de guanxi" 中文里音节跟体裁的关系 [How syllables affect meaning in Chinese], in *Lishi yuyan yanjiusuo jikan* 历史语言研究所集刊 [Journal of the research institute for historical language] (Taipei: Taiwan zhongyang yanjiuyuan, 1968), vol. 40, part 1.

is small). Instead, all of the complexities behind the phrase bow to a 1 + 2 rhythm that conforms with the nonhead stress rule. Modern terms follow rhythmic conventions in similar ways. *Dasao weisheng* 打扫卫生 'sweep sanitation—clean up' would need many more syllables to spell out properly what is involved. But the verb-object compound, with 2 + 2 balance, feels good.

Wuyan and *qiyan* patterns, used "recessively," can influence syllable arrangement as well. Duanmu San offers the example *xiangxin mixin, xiangxin gui* 相信迷信相信鬼 'believing in superstition and believing in ghosts' and notes that the phrase does not work nearly as well the other way around: *xiangxin gui, xiangxin mixin* is awkward, and a preference for the 2 + 2 + 3 rhythmic pattern is what makes the difference.[87] In this case it is easy to switch *mixin* and *gui*, so there is no cost, as it were, for accommodating the rhythm. But in other cases such costs do exist, and this fact shows how subtle the power of a recessive rhythm can be. For example, the political slogan *reai renmin reai dang* 热爱人民热爱党 obeys the 2 + 2 + 3 structure of *qiyan* and sounds good for that reason. Normally, however, there is a strong preference in the official language of Communist China to put *dang* before *renmin* (as in, e.g., *Shaanbei dang yu renmin datuanjie* 陕北黨與人民大團結 'the great unity of the Party and the people in Shaanbei'). In placing *renmin* before *dang*, the phrase *reai renmin reai dang* has flouted a political rule. The advantage of preserving 2 + 2 + 3 rhythm has outweighed the importance of putting the Party before the people. (*Qiyan*, one might say, has been able to achieve what Chinese democrats have not.)

Recessive *qiyan* can alter even the grammar of a phrase. When Chinese Premier Zhou Enlai died in January 1976, headlines in many Chinese newspapers read *renmin zongli renmin ai* 人民总理人民爱. The straightforward way to say "the people loved the people's premier" would, of course, be the other way around, *renmin ai renmin de zongli*, but the latter just doesn't sound as good. For headline writers, the importance of recruiting a 2 + 2 + 3 lilt seems to have outweighed the importance of standard subject-verb-object word order. Even Chinese-language teachers have been known to compromise grammar for the sake of rhythm. In the 1990s an American

---

87. Lu and Duanmu, "Rhythm and Syntax in Chinese," p. 127.

university announced a study program in China under the slogan *xuexi Hanyu zai Beijing* 学习汉语在北京 'study Chinese in Beijing'. Textbooks in the program taught the standard pattern "*zai* [place word] + verb + object"—for example, *zai guanzili chifan* 在馆子里吃饭 'eat in a restaurant'. And to follow this pattern students should have said *zai Beijing xue Hanyu*. Why the shift to *xuexi Hanyu zai Beijing?* To reach out to English-speaking students by imitating English word order? Perhaps. More likely, the genie of *qiyan* rhythm was again at work.

How Universal Are the Preferred Rhythms of Chinese?

If all human languages have rhythms, and if the rhythms of languages fall into more or less standard patterns, then it becomes interesting to ask how much those patterns tend to be the distinctive products of a given culture and how much they might derive from human experience that is common to many or all cultures. There are prima facie reasons to take both sides of this question.

To argue the side of cultural uniqueness, one could note that the patterns I am calling *wuyan* and *qiyan* arose in China and spread elsewhere in East Asia; or that the limerick arose in Britain and likewise spread elsewhere. (By the way, it spread even to China. The Chinese poet Xu Zhimo [1897–1931] borrowed the limerick form for his poem "Ouran" 偶然 [By chance].)[88] The very idea of "borrowing" such forms shows that we regard them as distinctive cultural inventions. On the other hand, to argue for universality, one could easily note that a tendency toward "plunk-plunk, plunk-plunk", or "4:4 time," in things like chants and marches, seems universal. Occasionally, much odder similarities pop up as well. Is it just chance, for example, that the ten-syllable lilt of ticket-sellers on Beijing buses (*xia yi zhan, nongkeyuan, mei piao mai-piao!* 'next stop is Academy of Agricultural Sciences, get a ticket if you don't have one!') is the same as the ten-syllable lilt in U.S. telephone numbers? Here there is no question of cultural borrowing, so we might ask if there is something about the

---

88. See Julia Lin, *Modern Chinese Poetry: An Introduction* (Seattle: University of Washington Press, 1972), pp. 103–104.

human brain that just "likes" this particular rhythm. Or are such resemblances mere coincidence?

If there are commonalities in human preference for rhythms, where do they come from? Historians of music have wondered whether 4:4 time derives somehow from the physiology of the human body, such as the beat of the heart or the two-legged walk. If so, there would be a good basis for explaining commonality across human experience. It seems dubious that the heartbeat could directly induce a penchant for 4:4 rhythm, since the heart does not beat a regular two beats. But perhaps it creates a tendency toward universal preference for some other rhythm. The two-legged walk theory, on the other hand, may indeed provide a plausible explanation for a preference for 4:4 among humans (and might raise, incidentally, the unfathomable question of whether horses or insects would find 4:4 time congenial).

Whatever the explanation, the following regularity concerning four-beat rhythm does seem to hold, at least for Chinese and European cultures: the more popular a form, the more likely it is to use four-beat rhythm. Chaucer, Shakespeare, and other elite English poets often used five-beat meter, while ditties, hymns, and other popular forms in English commonly use four beats. In China, seven-syllable *qiyan* lines tend be read 1–2, 1–2, 1–2–3 as elite poetry but turn into 4:4 time when popularized. For example, lines of Shandong "fast tales" (rhythmical storytelling accompanied by the percussion of wooden or metal clappers) appear on paper as *qiyan*:[89]

Kan zhe / guniangr / danr zhen da!   看這姑娘膽真大
Pao lai / huche / ba wo ma!   跑來胡扯把我罵

Look at the gall of this girl! Running up to berate me with her nonsense!

In performance, though, accompanied by the domineering beat of a clapper, *qiyan* gives way to a swinging four-beat line:

---

89. I am indebted to Wu Xiaoling for this and the following example.

KAN zhe GUniangr DANr zhen DA!
PAO lai HU che(zhe) BA wo MA!
(*Zhe* 着 here is a syncopated beat added in performance.)

Similarly in Henan ballad-singing (*zhuizi* 坠子):

Gonggong / mingzi / Yan Bairui　　公公名字嚴百瑞
Nüxu / ming jiao / Yan Jing'an　　女婿名叫嚴景安

The father-in-law's name was Yan Bairui; the son-in-law's name was Yan Jing'an

Turns into:

GONGgong MINGzi YAN BaiRUI
NÜxu MING jiao YAN Jing'AN

Similarly, the example of Red Guards at Tiananmen chanting *women yao jian Mao zhuxi* 'we want to see Chairman Mao' is formally *qiyan*, but when the chanting became feverish it resolved into four-beat mode: *WOmen YAO jian MAO zhuXI*. A satire of official language that circulated by text messaging in 2006 began:

Huiyi meiyou bu longzhong de, bimu meiyou bushengli de;
Jiang hua meiyou bu zhongyao de, guzhang meiyou bu relie de;
Jueyi meiyou bu tongguo de, renxin meiyou bu guwu de . . .

会议没有不隆重的, 闭幕没有不胜利的;
讲话没有不重要的, 鼓掌没有不热烈的;
决议没有不通过的, 人心没有不鼓舞的 . . .

No meeting is un-magnificent, no closing ceremony un-victorious;
No address is un-major, no applause un-thunderous;
No resolution is un-passed, no heart is un-moved . . .

The piece has a clear four-beat rhythm and goes on—mesmerizingly—for sixty lines.

In his essay "The Neural Lyre," Frederick Turner speculates on whether commonalties in poetic meter across cultures might have to do not just with legs or heartbeats but with the structure of the human brain.[90] Turner finds that the poetic line, worldwide, varies from seven to seventeen syllables in length (four to twenty at the extremes) and takes between 2.5 and 3.5 seconds to pronounce (2 to 4 seconds at the extremes). He finds that even a mime, performing wordlessly, tends to use a three-second "phrase."[91] He then makes the bold claim that "the similarities between metered verse in different cultures are real and . . . indicate a shared biological underpinning."[92] Turner is a professor of English, so we might want, ideally, to find confirming evidence in the fields of psychology and neuroscience. In his classic 1957 article "The Magical Number Seven, Plus or Minus Two," psychologist George Miller showed that the human ear and brain normally can handle discriminations of pitch and of loudness up to a limit of seven or so, after which confusions happen more easily than before.[93] Miller finds, in addition, that short-term memory seems to break down after roughly seven items, although he argues that the underlying processes of perception and memory, and thus the reasons for the "roughly seven" limit in the two cases, are fundamentally different. It is hard to say whether or not the brain's natural limits, as Miller views them, are causally related to the consistency of poetic line length that Turner observes. But Turner and others feel that they could be.

The plausibility of claims that the human brain might have inborn affinities for rhythm has been strengthened by studies of infants. In their very first months of life, before they can have learned very much of arbitrary cultural patterns, infants have been shown to recognize rhythmical features in human speech. Peter W. Jusczyk, in summarizing the results of studies on infants and speech rhythms, goes beyond saying that infants can "recognize" prosodic differences to say they are "well attuned to"

90. Frederick Turner, "The Neural Lyre," in *Natural Classicism* (New York: Paragon House, 1985), pp. 61–108.
91. Ibid., pp. 74–75.
92. Ibid., p. 80.
93. *Psychological Review* (1956), 63, pp. 81–97.

them from birth.[94] Here Jusczyk's word "attuned" reflects his claim that there are natural tendencies in the brain at birth, and the studies he cites seem to support this claim.

Exactly how much is inborn and how much learned in the formation of rhythmic preferences is a complex and difficult question that is beyond our scope here. I do wish, however, to consider one rhythmic pattern that has appeared in such different times and places that it makes the question of what gives rise to such patterns especially interesting. This is the syllabic pattern 1–2–3, 1–2–3, 1–2–3–4–5–6–7, for which I have used the abbreviation of "3–3–7." It appears in *shunkouliu* like the following example, from early 2007, that satirizes the way local officials in China pass false reports upward in a bureaucracy and only pay lip service to instructions that come back down:[95]

Cun pian xiang, xiang pian xian, yizhi pian dao guowuyuan;
Guowuyuan, xia wenjian, yiceng yiceng wang xia nian;
Nian wan wenjian jin fandian, wenjian genben bu duixian.

村骗乡, 乡骗县, 一直骗到国务院
国务院, 下文件, 一层一层往下念
念完文件进饭店, 文件根本不兑现

The village fools the township, the township fools the county, and the fooling goes on up, right to the State Council;
The State Council, then, sends its orders back down, where, level by level, they are dutifully read;
When the readings are over there's a banquet for all, while the orders are just set aside.

In this example, two 3–3–7 lines are followed by two *qiyan* lines. This combination of 3–3–7 and *qiyan*, which is common, invites the suggestion

---

94. Peter W. Jusczyk, *The Discovery of Spoken Language* (Cambridge, Mass.: MIT Press, 1997) p. 54.
95. "Rang Wen Jiabao nankan de shunkouliu" 让温家宝难堪的顺口溜 (Shunkouliu to make Wen Jiabao uneasy) *Pingguo ribao* [Apple Daily] (Hong Kong), March 12, 2007.

that 3–3–7 at a deeper level is a version of 4–4–8, with a "rest" after each 3 and after the 7. Whether or not this is so, 3–3–7 remains distinctive not only because of the distinctive lilt with which it is pronounced but because the whole thing, the two 3's *and* the 7, need to be present in order for the pattern to feel satisfying. (We saw this fact in sensing how an item list of six metals can sound a bit awkward while a list of thirteen can sound fine.)

The pattern 3–3–7 followed by a *qiyan* line occurs regularly in the children's nursery rhyme *ni pai yi, wo pai yi, yige xiaohair kai feiji; ni pai er, wo pai er, liang ge xiaohair diu shoujuanr*, and so on. Remarkably, this pattern is the very same that is found in an English counterpart: *This old man, he plays one, he plays knick-knack on my thumb . . . this old man, he plays two, he plays knick-knack on my shoe*, and so on.[96] The striking similarity seems enough to suggest that China might have borrowed the rhythm from the modern West, just as it borrowed the rhythm of "Frère Jacques" to make the rhyme "San zhi Laohu" 三隻老虎 (Three tigers) or "Happy Birthday to You" to make "Zhu ni shengri kuailuo" 祝你生日快樂. The presence of *feiji* 飛機 'airplane' in the Chinese rhyme shows it to be of twentieth-century vintage, which seems to add plausibility to the hypothesis that some kind of borrowing happened.

But 3–3–7 is too deep and pervasive in Chinese culture to be explained by modern borrowing alone. As noted above, it appears in things as varied as popular riddles, cheerleaders' chants, and the Cultural Revolution anthem "The East Is Red."[97] It seems to have roots in rural culture as well as urban. On a public wall in a mountain village in Sichuan in 2007 someone had scrawled this protest against forcible family planning:[98]

Yitai sheng, ertai za　　　一胎生, 二胎扎
Santai, sitai—gua! gua! gua!　　三胎四胎—刮! 刮! 刮!

Fetus one leads to birth, fetus two to tying tubes
With fetus three and fetus four—scrape! scrape! scrape!

96. A "dotted" variation occurs in another English nursery rhyme, "A-tisket, a-tasket, a green and yellow basket . . ."
97. See the Introduction and earlier in this chapter.
98. I am grateful to Mao Sheng for this example.

Examples of 3–3–7 also popped up during the Great Leap Forward of the late 1950s, when Chinese farmers were encouraged to "produce more" of virtually everything, including poems. Here are two:[99]

Dazibao! Dazibao!   大字报! 大字报!
You xiang xingxing you xiang pao!   又像星星又像炮!

Big-character posters! Big-character posters!
They are like stars and also like cannon!

Jinhuang di, jinhuang shan,   金黄地, 金黄山
Jinguang shanshan ran hong tian   金光闪闪染红天

Golden earth, golden mountains,
Golden light glimmers through the red sky.

At the height of the Cultural Revolution, Red Guards swore fealty to Mao Zedong with this chant:

Tou he duan, xue ke liu   头可断, 血可流
Geming jingshen bu ke diu!   革命精神不可丢!

Cut off my head, and let my blood flow,
But my revolutionary spirit will not go!

Evidence that 3–3–7 has premodern roots in Chinese popular culture comes from *Pekinese Rhymes*, a little book published in 1896 by Guido Vitale, an Italian diplomat.[100] Its 274 pages contain children's rhymes and other popular verse that, Vitale writes, were "composed by illiterate people who have no knowledge of the written language." Vitale's examples show no sign of borrowing from the West, and not even much preference for standard *wuyan* and *qiyan* patterns. There are many three-syllable lines,

---

99. Quoted in Xiao Yuying 蕭育瀛, "Ping 1958 nian xin min'ge yundong" 評一九五八年新民歌運動 [Evaluating the new folksongs of 1958], unpublished conference paper, 1979.

100. *Chinese Folklore: Pekinese Rhymes* (Peking: Pei-t'ang Press, 1896; reprint, Hong Kong: Vetch and Lee, 1972).

and the mix of line lengths and irregular patterns does seem to suggest the kind of unschooled earthiness that Vitale claims. It is interesting, therefore, that even in this context 3–3–7 pops up fairly often.[101]

The possibility that 3–3–7 in China is the result of modern borrowing is definitively ruled out by the simple observation that many examples appear as early as the Northern Dynasties (fifth and sixth centuries). A folksong from that era (generally recognized as being borrowed from a northern, non-Sinitic language) goes:[102]

Tian cangcang, ye mangmang　　天蒼蒼, 野茫茫
Feng chui cao di xian niu yang　　風吹草低見牛羊

Deep blue sky, boundless prairie
The wind blows, the grass bows, sheep and cattle appear

Examples of classic poetry from the Tang period and later use 3–3–7 as well.[103] Li Bai (701–762) uses it in his poem "Jiang jin jiu" 將進酒:

Wu hua ma, qian jin qiu　　五花馬, 千金裘
Hu er jiang chu huan mei jiu　　呼兒將出換美酒

Magnificent steed, resplendent fur
I call a boy to bring some good wine

As does Du Fu (712–770) in "Bing ju xing" 兵車行:

Ju linlin, ma xiaoxiao　　車轔轔, 馬蕭蕭
Xingren gongjian ge zai yao　　行人弓箭各在腰

Chariots rumbling, horses neighing
Soldiers marching, bows readied at the waist

---

101. Ibid., pp. 31, 95, 150, 154–155, 159, and elsewhere.
102. Cited in Ogawa Tamaki 小川環樹, "Chokuroku no uta" 敕勒の歌 "Song of Chile River," in *Chosakushū* 著作集 [Collected works] (Tokyo: Chikuma Shōbō), 1997), vol. 1, pp. 323–337; p. 324.
103. I am grateful to Wang Wei for pointing out the following two examples, and many others.

Where, then, did 3–3–7 originate? The eminent Japanese Sinologist Ogawa Tamaki has suggested that it might have spread to China in pre-Tang times from origins in Central Asia or the Near East.[104] If this is right, then we still might count our observed similarities as a kind of "borrowing." We might even ask—although I have no evidence for the hypothesis—whether 3–3–7 in the ancient Near East might explain 3–3–7 in the English nursery rhyme "This Old Man." England was not the only European place to come up with 3–3–7 subsequent to the era Ogawa has studied. A 3–3–7 chant that was used in Soviet-dominated Poland (about the Union of Polish Youth, Zwiazek Mlodziezy Polskiej, or ZMP) went this way: *My ZMP, my ZMP; reakcji nie boimy sie* 'We ZMP, we ZMP, we fear no reactionary'.[105]

It is possible, of course—perhaps even likely—that 3–3–7 has had origins in different places independently. Especially when we remember that, as noted, the addition of "rests" easily turns 3–3–7 into 4–4–8, it may be that human bipeds in several places discovered the pattern without needing to borrow anything. In any case, the short answer to the question "Are rhythms culturally determined or common to human beings everywhere?" seems inevitably to be "Both."

Do Rhythms Have Meanings?

The question of whether rhythms can have meanings raises a prior question, itself extremely large and complex, of what we mean by "meaning." An adequate review of this larger question in either Eastern or Western philosophical tradition is well beyond our scope here. But since we need at least an implicit answer to it for the case of the "meanings" of rhythms, I would like to address the topic here briefly. I will begin by asking what the *uses* (or functions) of linguistic rhythms are. This question is easier to get a handle on than "meaning"; once we identify some functions, it might then be easier to estimate whether they involve "meaning"—and if so, of

---

104. Ogawa Tamaki 小川環樹, "Chokuroku no uta" 敕勒の歌.
105. Anna Wierzbicka, "Antitotalitarian Language in Poland: Some Mechanisms of Linguistic Self-Defense," *Language in Society* 19 (1990), p. 12.

what kind and how much. (The approach seems not bad, since many modern philosophers, following Ludwig Wittgenstein, J. L. Austin, and others, see "meaning" as pretty much amounting to "use" in any case.)

One function of rhythm in human language—so broad that it almost need not be mentioned—is to signal that "this is human language." The variations of pitch, timing, and loudness that constitute "rhythm" are not things that mechanical voice simulators can easily imitate. Despite advances in early twenty-first-century technology, simulated human voices on telephone recordings remain easy to distinguish from human voices.

A more obvious use of stress patterns is in making distinctions. I have noted how "Joey Davis" might change in stress pattern from 2–4–1–3 to 1–3–4–4 if Joey's purpose becomes one of distinguishing himself from his brother Louie. (Already, here, we see the beginning of what J. L. Austin would call "meaning," because the "speech acts" of (1) introducing oneself and (2) distinguishing oneself from another are different acts with different "meanings.") Y. R. Chao notes that the riddle "Why do birds fly south?—Because it's too far to walk" would lose its point if stress were applied to *fly*.[106] Native speakers of English (or of Chinese, if the riddle is translated) are easily and automatically aware of the difference the stress makes. Chao also notes the difference between *wo de mingzi shi Yuehan* 我的名字是約翰 'my name is John' (i.e., not Bill or Pete) and *Yuehan shi wo de mingzi* 'John is my name' (i.e., not title or nickname). Here, Chao says, stress is "a marker of the logical predicate," which most native speakers handle with no problem even though they do not notice that they are handling anything.[107] Sometimes, as I have noted, stress can help to determine which of more than one grammatical structure should apply to a string of syllables. *Ni bu shuo, meiyou ren shuo* 你不说没有人说 can be, with different stress, either "you didn't say it; nobody said it" or "if you don't say it no one will."

A considerable range of the conscious use of rhythm in human life has to do with helping people to coordinate their activity. A single person can sing, dance, march, chant, or haul loads, but when two, a dozen, or a hundred want to do these things in unison, rhythm becomes an invaluable

---

106. Chao, *Grammar of Spoken Chinese*, pp. 79–80.
107. Ibid., p. 79.

tool. Things would go haywire rather quickly without it, and excellence or efficiency can depend on how tightly a rhythm is applied. A crew team could not go as fast if a coxswain did not use rhythm. The laborers who chant pile-driving songs outside the hotel window at the beginning of act 2 of Cao Yu's play *Sunrise* are doing it, at least in part, in order to apply more thud to the earth per unit of expended energy.[108]

Rhythms are also useful in aiding memory. Most people remember rhythmic phrases much more easily than nonrhythmic ones. To confirm this simple fact, try saying your own telephone number to yourself. If you are an American, your phone number is ten digits long, and you probably use the standard 1–2–3, 1–2–3, 1–2–3–4 pattern to say it. Now trying saying the same number in some other pattern, like 1–2, 1–2–3–4, 1–2–3, 1. Just from memory, you probably will not be able to do this. In order to use this other rhythm, you will probably have to write the digits down and then read them off. This shows that you remember your telephone number only in a certain rhythm. Similarly, you probably know your nine-digit Social Security number in a 3–2–4 rhythmic pattern, but could not easily say it in a different pattern. Telephone and ID numbers in other countries observe other patterns; but the fact that people use patterns to memorize numbers appears to be the same everywhere.

Rhythm is an aid not only to personal memory but to community and cultural memory. Because rhythms make memorization easier, they are useful in any verbal art that is passed around orally—songs, nursery rhymes, *shunkouliu*, and other such things. The rhythmic lines in these oral compositions are able to remain consistent over wide spans of time and place without necessarily being written down. (Examples do admit variation, of course, but the degree to which they remain consistent is remarkable.) This ability to achieve consistency without recourse to writing has an additional use in repressive societies: without paper trails, it is much harder for authorities to find and punish authors. On the Underground Railway, the clandestine network that helped fugitive slaves escape the American South, people passed messages by song. In China today, rhythmic *shunkouliu* and text messages thrive in part because authors cannot be traced.

108. Cao Yu 曹禺, "Richu" 日出 [Sunrise] (Singapore: Youth Book, 1966), p. 85.

But to say that rhythms are useful in remembering phrases that have meanings is not the same as saying that the rhythms themselves—on their own—"mean" something. Do they? Consider a hawker who uses a distinctive rhythm to call out something like *shaubing youtiao!* 烧饼油条 'sesame cakes and deep-fried dough-sticks!' In such a case, it is not just the four syllables he chooses but the distinctive voice, including the lilt, that does the work of communication for everyone within earshot. The purpose of the hawker's cry is less to inform people of a denotative meaning ("I sell sesame cakes and dough-sticks") than to remind them of a daily routine ("Here I am again!" or "Now's your chance to buy again!"). Would this level of hawker's meaning get through if he used a very different lilt? Probably not—at least not until his customers got used to the new lilt and associated it with him. In this sense the lilt seems to have its own "meaning."

It would be, though, a meaning that applies only in particular circumstances. The hawker's call signals "it's me again!" only for that hawker or for others in a group of hawkers who have decided to employ the same oral tag. It is a somewhat different question to ask whether a rhythm can "mean something" regardless of who (within a much larger culture) uses it. Are there such examples? To address this question requires, whether we like it or not, that we have a definition of what we mean by "mean," so let me offer this one: for my purposes in this book, a rhythm has "meaning" if and only if native speakers of a language that customarily uses the rhythm take from a phrase that employs it a different understanding or feeling, however slight, from what they would have taken from the same phrase pronounced without the rhythm. Further, in order to qualify as "meaning" in this sense, the production of an "understanding or feeling" must be reliable, that is, it cannot be idiosyncratic (e.g., as a particular hawker's call) but has to be similar among the majority of speakers within a culture or subculture. Theoreticians of poetic meter seem generally to agree that meter itself does have "meaning" of this kind, although it is not easy to specify what it is.[109]

---

109. Frederick Turner, for example, writes that meter "has significance," although its "'message' . . . is rather mysterious." "Neural Lyre," spp. 81–82.

I have noted the pattern in American English that uses "low-low-low-HIGH, low-low-low-HIGH, low-low-low-HIGH . . ." to express (1) I am giving you a list; (2) the list is indefinitely long; and, often, (3) it involves some exasperation. Perhaps we can test whether the rhythm itself "means" these things by trying it out, for example, on items that do not make sense as a list. If I use the low-low-low-HIGH pattern to say "The cat is on the mat, two plus two is four, the cow jumped over the moon," it takes considerable imagination to conjure a situation in which the rhythm would "make sense." A similar problem would arise if my list were finite and listeners knew it. If I said, for example, that I have three children, and (in the low-low-low-HIGH pattern), "one is named Jane, one is named Joe, and one is named Jill," people would find me odd—and, if they thought about it, a bit self-contradictory. The "meaning" of my rhythmic pattern would be suggesting indefinitely many children, even though I had said up front that there were exactly three.

Rhythms that suggest humor, like that of the limerick, are perhaps an even better example. The words in limericks are often witty, but I want to set that point aside. The point I wish to make is that the *rhythm itself* suggests whimsy. We can test for meaning in the "rhythm itself" by combining the limerick form with somber content and seeing whether a sense of incongruity emerges. For example, Macbeth's soliloquy ("Is this a dagger which I see before me, the handle toward my hand? . . .") in limerick form might be:

> That dagger just hung in the air
> Where it gave to Macbeth a great scare:
> "What specter can such be?
> Come, let me clutch thee,
> To hang there like that isn't fair!"

Incongruous? Quite. The whimsicality and the seriousness do not match. The key question is where the whimsicality comes from. Certainly not from the words, so it must come from the rhythm. But if that is so, then the rhythm "means something" in the sense I have defined above. It brings "funny," or at least "lighthearted," into the mix. Whether this funniness is set by culture or, perhaps, is rooted in human nature is an interesting but largely unfathomable question. Could there be a culture in which the limerick rhythm suggested seriousness? Or is the bouncy lilt something that would naturally tend to strike the human mind—any mind, anywhere—as whimsical?[110] I lean toward the latter view but wonder if I am culture-bound.

The question can be pondered for Chinese as well, where certain rhythmic patterns, like the limerick, suggest "this is a bit funny"—although do not do it quite so brazenly as the limerick does. The rhythmic patterns in *luan qi ba zao* 乱七八糟 'chaotically messy' and *hu li hutu* 糊里糊涂 'muddle-befuddled' are examples.[111] A normal stress pattern for four-syllable strings, apparent in transliterations like Gelunbiya 哥伦比亚 'Columbia' or item lists like *dong nan xi bei* 东南西北 'east, south, west, north', is 1–3–2–4. *Luan qi ba zao* and *hu li hutu*, however, are closer to 3–1–2–4. *Luoli luosuo* 啰里啰唆 'long-winded', which also is whimsical, is close to 3–1–3–3, which also differs from the normal 1–3–2–4. In these phrases, the lilt itself seems to suggest that something is out of control in a mildly comical way. If you refer to Columbia or the four directions with this kind of comical lilt, they seem to lose some of their dignity.

There are other stress patterns in Chinese that seem to suggest "meaning" in the broad sense I am using. In addressing or referring to people, for example, a 2 + 2 syllabic balance seems to imply affectionate respect. If I address my distinguished colleague Yu Ying-shih as *Yu xiansheng* 余先生, I sound a bit formal. If I address him as *Yingshi xiansheng* 英時先生, I sound just as respectful but closer and more affectionate. In part, of course, this is because I am using his given name instead of his family name. But the effect also has to do with the pleasant four-syllable rhythmic balance of 2 + 2, *Yingshi xiansheng*. The enhanced pleasantness of 2 + 2 (compared to 1 + 2) can be seen in the fact that when a person has a one-syllable given name then *both* surname and given name are used in order to join with the two syllables of *xiansheng* to make a pleasant 2 + 2 balance.

---

110. Xu Zhimo's use of the limerick form in poems like "Ouran" (see note 88 above) is not a good test of the question. While "Ouran" imitates the limerick in line length and rhyme scheme, it does not capture the limerick lilt. And if it did, it would likely produce the same "incongruity" effect that my imaginary example of Macbeth in limerick produces, because Xu puts serious romance into his poem.

111. I owe this insight to Feng Shengli, email message to author, October 17, 2002.

With a name like Li Rui, for example, one would say *Li Rui xiansheng* 李锐先生, not *Rui xiansheng*. The convention extends even to such unusual contexts as the top of the Communist Party of China. In *Zhongguo liusi zhenxiang* 中國六四真相 (The true story of June Fourth),[112] when the Communist elders and Politburo members address or refer to one another informally as "Comrade So-and-so," they invariably do it in balanced four-syllable phrases: *Xiaoping tongzhi* 小平同志, *Ziyang tongzhi* 紫阳同志, *Yibo tongzhi* 一波同志, and so on. But when the given name is only one syllable, as in Li Peng or Qiao Shi, no one says *Peng tongzhi* or *Shi tongzhi*. To do so would sound funny, even a bit disrespectful. The comrades preferred *Li Peng tongzhi* 李鹏同志 or *Qiao Shi tongzhi* 乔石同志. In other words, if one is to preserve the sense of affectionate respect, the principle of rhythmic balance turns out to be more important than the question of whether one includes the family name.

The pursuit of 2 + 2 balance in name-plus-title can run into problems when names are unusual. Duanmu San, the name of the talented linguist whom I have quoted several times, is an example. One-syllable given names, like San, are fairly common, although not nearly as common as two-syllable given names; two-syllable surnames, like Duanmu, are not very common; and the combination of a two-syllable family name and a one-syllable given name is highly uncommon. What happens if we want to address Duanmu San with affectionate respect, as we could by saying *Yingshi xiansheng*? *San xiansheng* would be three syllables and hence call for a fourth; a fourth would normally be borrowed by adding a one-syllable family name. But if we add the two-syllable Duanmu, we now have five syllables—*Duanmu San xiansheng*. We have "jumped over" the rhythmic 2 + 2 and have something that sounds too formal to convey affection. This is just his bad luck. Duanmu San deserves both respect and affection, but there is no way we can use this particular rhythmic mechanism to express them. A similar problem, which Duanmu himself points out,[113] occurs

---

112. Zhang Liang, *Zhongguo liusi zhenxiang* 中國六四真相 (The true story of China's June Fourth) (New York: Mingjing chubanshe 明鏡出版社, 2001), abridged and edited by Andrew Nathan and Perry Link as *The Tiananmen Papers: The Chinese Leadership's Decision to Use Force against Their Own People* (New York: Public Affairs Press, 2001).

113. San Duanmu, "Development of Disyllabic Words in Chinese," pp. 29–30.

when the familiar (and often affectionate) prefixes *lao* 老 'old' and *xiao* 小 'young' are used before surnames: *lao Zhang* 老張 'old Zhang', *xiao Li* 小李 'young Li', and so on are perfectly natural as long as two-syllable balance applies. People surnamed Ouyang 歐陽, Duanmu 端木, or Situ 司徒 by (rhythmic) custom are denied the privilege of having the friendly *lao* or *xiao* prefixed to their names.

The question of meaning for longer and more complex rhythms—such as *wuyan*, *qiyan*, or 3-3-7—is harder to pin down. Regardless of whether the rhythms are dominant or recessive, what they "mean" can be as vague as a fog. But that hardly means they are evanescent or unimportant. They sometimes make a considerable difference, even if the difference is impossible to specify. In this sense, they resemble the meaning of music. In what follows I am going to use words like *authority*, *naturalness*, *exaltation*, *memorability*, and *finality* to discuss them. None of these words is ideal; yet none is useless, either, and that is the interesting point.

What is the difference between a line in *qiyan* like *yi kan, er man, san tong guo* ('first look, then go slowly, then cross'—cited in the Introduction) and an equivalent in plain language like *dajia xiaoxin guo jie* 大家小心过街 'everybody be careful crossing the street'? The *qiyan* line is smoother and more aesthetically pleasing, to be sure; but there is something more. With *qiyan* the message seems, somehow, to come from a more formal or authoritative source. This is true even if the source of the *qiyan* message (the author of the road-crossing sign) is not physically present, as the crossing guard is. The crossing guard also possesses a definite authority, but this derives from his or her social role, and perhaps from a uniform, not from the rhythm of the phrase *yi kan, er man, san tong guo*. Frederick Turner, in writing about what meter "means" in world traditions generally, says it gives "a sense of power combined with effortlessness."[114]

In the early 1950s, Chinese demonstrators who marched in support of China in the Korean War could enhance their tone of authority by setting aside random shouts in favor of the *qiyan* slogan *kang Mei yuan Chao gan dao di!* 抗美援朝幹到底 'resist America and aid Korea to the end!' In this case the slogan chanters were in plain view, on the streets; but *qiyan* can convey a sense of authority even when the "speaking authority" is

---

114. Turner, "Neural Lyre," pp. 92–93.

elusive or abstract, indeed as abstract as something like "nature itself" or "just the way things are." Who, for example, is the implied authority for *Guilin shanshui jia tianxia* 'the scenery at Guilin beats any in the world'? Here, I would argue, the *qiyan* pattern still conjures a sense of authority—more authority than would be present if the same idea were put in ordinary language—but what authority is it, other than "the natural order of things"? Turner refers to "a pleasing sense of 'fit' and inevitability," which seems to impart "mysterious wisdom."[115] Similarly, Edward Slingerland, in studying the *Book of Odes*, finds that morally powerful words and actions are those that show "effortless accordance with what is 'proper' or what 'fits.'"[116]

In a modern context, this sense that words are "fitting" often amounts to a claim that "what is expressed here is *true*." This apparent claim of truth can be laid bare if we consider rhythmic phrases that imply such a claim but, if properly analyzed, are not so obviously true. Take, for example, the *qiyan* proverb that warns that Sichuan is a rebellious place: *tianxia wei luan, Shu xian luan* 天下未亂蜀先亂 'While all under heaven is still quiet, Sichuan leads the way to chaos'. Spoken in plain language, the claim would surely raise eyebrows. How does one know such a thing? Has anyone actually counted the rebellions that started in Sichuan, and then compared that number to the numbers of rebellions that arose in other provinces? Probably not. But when *qiyan* takes charge, it is as if we agree to suspend our critical faculties. Something that sounds "proper" does not get proper scrutiny. *Wuyan* has a similar power. To say that little girls change in many ways as they grow up, the Chinese proverb says *nü da shibabian* 女大十八變 'a growing girl changes eighteen times'. Eighteen? Not more, not less? And little boys are different? None of these questions occur—although they certainly would if someone were to make such an arbitrary claim in ordinary language.

In his brilliant article "Symbols, Song, Dance, and Features of Articulation," Maurice Bloch has argued that formalized language—in religious ritual, political discourse, song, and elsewhere—includes set features (one

---

115. Ibid., p. 77, 73.
116. Edward Slingerland, *Effortless Action: Wu-wei as Conceptual Metaphor and Spiritual Ideal in Early China* (Oxford: Oxford University Press, 2003), p. 40.

of which is rhythm) that make the claims of what is articulated seem more authoritative.[117] "The notion of true or false or better or worse," Bloch writes, "has been eliminated by the way the proposition has been put."[118] It is ironic that this sense of authority accompanies—indeed depends on—what Bloch calls the "impoverishment" of language. Impoverishment is his name for the fact that formal language cuts off alternate possibilities of expression; it is in that very cutting off that its own authority arises. The stricter the formal features are, the stronger the authority sounds. At the extreme, as Bloch rightly observes, "you cannot argue with a song."[119]

Should we go so far as to say that rhythm, in a certain sense, tells lies? Frederick Turner almost says so. He observes that metrical poetry, by "presenting an experience [that] gives a false impression of reality and separates one from the harsh world" raises the question of whether "poetry deceives."[120] The examples I have cited in which *wuyan* and *qiyan* have been used in advertisements of things like cosmetics, tonics, and gasoline do suggest a deliberate manipulation in which the "meanings" of rhythms can add up to something close to lying. But "deception" in a broader sense (and Turner is clear on this) is not necessarily dishonorable. It includes inadvertent deception and several kinds of self-deception in which the deceived are happy to participate. After all, "separation from the harsh world" can lead to transcendence, sublimity, and religious experience—not just squalid ignorance. Scholars in several fields have pointed out that poetry, ritual, chants, song, and other forms in which rhythm is involved can impart a sense of rising above the world, approaching the sacred, and even entering a trance-like state.[121] Such "rising above" does not need sophisticated art. It requires only that someone, in fact, be moved. The quip that "all bad poetry springs from genuine feeling," widely attributed to Oscar Wilde, makes a fair point.

---

117. Maurice Bloch, "Symbols, Song, Dance and Features of Articulation *or* Is Religion an Extreme Form of Traditional Authority?," *Archives Européennes de Sociologie* 15, no. 1 (1974), pp. 55–81.
118. Ibid., p. 66.
119. Ibid., p. 71.
120. Turner, "Neural Lyre," p. 99.
121. A classic statement of this effect is in Bloch, "Symbols, Song, Dance, and Features of Articulation."

When a rhythm helps to produce a sense of "rising above," what exactly is it that rises? The speaker? The hearer? The object referred to? In the case of songs and rituals, we would probably think first of the hearer as the one who is elevated. The singer of a song or the producer of a ritual might also rise, but not necessarily, because one can imagine a priest who is simply going through some motions, and a song, if it is recorded, can move people long after the singer has departed. Sometimes the thing that is elevated is the object referred to—or, more precisely, the status of that object in the estimation of the speaker or hearer. This apparently is the point of using *wuyan* rhythm to sell China Petrol: *jiayou zhong shi hua, fangxin pao tianxia* 'fill up with China Petrol and go wherever in the world you want' (cited above). The hearer (i.e., the potential buyer of China Petrol) might or might not feel personally elevated at the thought of buying a spiffy brand of gasoline, but the main point, surely, is to exalt the petrol itself. In some cases the hearer (or other receiver) of the message becomes quite irrelevant, and only speaker and object are importantly elevated. When Red Guards chanted *women yao jian Mao zhuxi* 'we want to see Chairman Mao' at Tiananmen, they were certainly exalting Mao, and their own spirits just as certainly were being made high. Were there third parties, listening and thereby also elevated? Perhaps, but they would have been incidental, and the chanting would have gone on whether or not they were there.

Rhythm can also contribute to making a line memorable. It can, as we have seen, help us to remember things like telephone numbers and Social Security numbers, but that is different from what I mean here by memorability. By "memorable" here I mean *worthy* of being remembered—because of the special wisdom or the historical importance of the phrase, but also for its aesthetic value of harboring a rhythm. For example, Mao Zedong's phrase *Zhongguo renmin zhanqilai le* 中國人民站起來了 'the Chinese people have stood up' is 2–2–3 *qiyan* plus a particle. Franklin Roosevelt's famous line "the only thing we have to fear is fear itself" has twelve syllables that divide pleasantly into clusters of 4 + 4 + 4. It is easy to find many other examples in poetry. In order to understand the aesthetic value of this kind of rhythm, it is no longer necessary to be concerned with the difference between speaker and hearer (unless, perhaps, we want to distinguish between "me now" and "my memory of then"). The "meaning" of rhythm—be it exaltation, authority, the invocation of naturalness, or whatever—can now be something that happens entirely within a single mind.

Both the mnemonic value of rhythm and its aesthetic value contribute, I believe, to the telling fact that we often can remember the rhythm of a phrase while forgetting some of its words. This is what might lead us to sing, in English, "I come from Alabama with a banjo something, something" when we cannot remember "on my knee" or, in Chinese, to say *yue luo, shenme, shenme, shuang man tian* 月落甚麼甚麼霜滿天 'the moon falls, whatever, whatever, frost fills the sky' when we forget *wu ti* 烏啼 'raven cries' in the middle.[122]

Along with authority and memorability, it seems to me that sometimes rhythm can convey a sense of finality or completeness—although this aspect of the "meaning" of rhythm is one I feel least confident about. Let's consider one more time *Guilin shanshui jia tianxia*. Doesn't the phrase convey the sense of 'the scenery at Guilin beats any in the world (and that's the last word)'? And isn't the 2–2–3 rhythm part of what gives it that sense of "the last word"? Or take *renren zuo hao ren, riri zuo haoshi*. To me it feels like 'everyone be a good person, every day do good deeds (and that will leave the world in fine shape)'. Or consider again the Great Leap slogan *loushang louxia diandeng dianhua* 'electric lights and telephones upstairs and down (and with that you're all set)'. This kind of "finality" or "completeness" message might be especially clear, I feel, with 3–3–7. I will leave the reader to experiment with various examples of 3–3–7, but of the ones I have cited, the cheerleaders' chant seems to be an especially good example of letting a rhythm make a completeness-claim:

Yi, er, san; san, er, yi　　一二三, 三二一,
Yi, er, san, si, wu, liu, qi　一二三四五六七

Here nothing but numbers is involved, so the test of whether rhythm can suggest "completeness" is especially pure. If the sense is there, it has to be the rhythm, not the numbers, that delivers the result. There is no reason

---

122. From the famous (eighth-century) poem "Fengqiao yebo" 楓橋夜泊 [Night mooring at maple bridge], by Zhang Ji 張繼.

in arithmetic for *qi* 'seven' to feel "final," but here *qi* comes down with a thud that seems to say "I am the last item you would ever want to ask about." It is 3–3–7 that makes this happen.

What Other Formal Features Contribute to Meaning?

If rhythm alone can create differences in meaning (where "meaning," remember, is taken in the broad sense I am using of making at least some kind of difference in a received message), are there other formal features of language—having to do, for example, with things like pitch or parallelism—that can do this as well? There are. It is beyond our scope to examine each in detail, but they are worth noting as we pass by, because the ways they operate in the mind—gently effective although largely unnoticed—are similar to the ways rhythm operates.

Tones. Here I do not mean literary tone. I mean the categories of pitch variation in which syllables of Chinese are pronounced and of which Mandarin Chinese is conventionally said to have four. Tones are "phonemic" in the sense that they change the reference of a syllable in the same way vowels and consonants do—the same way, for example, that *b* and *g* make the difference between *bet* and *get*. Like *b* and *g*, tones do not "mean" anything on their own.

But I want to suggest that sometimes, subtly, they might. In choosing names for their children, Chinese parents sometimes worry over whether the sound of the name itself is "smooth" (especially for a girl) or "strong" (especially for a boy), and part of the feeling of smoothness or strength derives from patterns of tones.

Sometimes (by no means always, but sometimes) the "fourth tone" in Mandarin, in which the voice falls rapidly, suggests authority or finality. This effect is roughly similar to the "finality" effect of certain rhythms. Consider again the example *renren zuo hao ren, riri zuo haoshi* 'everyone be a good person, every day do good deeds'. I claim above that the phrase ends with a sense of finality because of its rhythm. But does the effect perhaps also derive from the fact that *shi* 事 'things, deeds' is fourth-tone? Let's try, for example, reversing the two lines to get *riri zuo haoshi, renren zuo hao ren*. This does not sound quite as good—or at least, not as "final." The two basic ideas "everybody be good" and "do a good deed daily" can be put in either order with not much difference, and the rhythm is the same in either case, but the feeling of finality or authority is stronger when the whole thing ends with the fourth-tone *shi* than when it ends with the second-tone *ren* (in which the voice pitch rises).

Do other aphorisms or slogans sound more authoritative if they end with fourth-tone syllables? A 2007 sex education slogan was *waichu wugong yao fang ai, qianwan bie hai xiayidai* 外出务工要防艾，千万别害下一代 'when you leave home to do work, watch out for AIDS; you absolutely must not harm the next generation'.[123] Here we have both *qiyan* as well as rhyme among *ai*, *hai*, and *dai*, and all of this may contribute to a sense of rightness or authority. But I suspect that the fact that *dai* is fourth-tone also contributes. There seems to be an implied exclamation point at the end, and it seems to come in part from the falling tone on *dai*. Would it be there if a similar slogan referred, say, to "watching out for bugs" (*fang chong* 防虫) and ended with "young children" (*ertong* 儿童)? Could a second-tone ending conjure the same sense of authority and finality? On the whole not, I think.[124]

Consider a phrase that uses all fourth tones, like *zhengque duidai di'erci shijie dazhan* 正确对待第二次世界大战 'regard World War II correctly'. This phrase (partly because it is a string of fourth tones?) carries an assertive and authoritative air, and might even seem a bit pompous. But is that because of the content or because of the tones? What about other phrases

---

123. From "Jihua shengyu xin biaoyu chutai neiqing."

124. If fourth tones at the ends of phrases do indeed have an effect of lending authority, one might expect that, on average, aphorisms would tend to end in fourth tones just in order to borrow that authority. But this seems not to be the case. A survey of all the *wuyan* and *qiyan* examples in the first fifty pages of a standard modern dictionary of Chinese idioms, Tang Shu 唐枢, ed., *Chengyu shuyu cihai* 成语熟语辞海 [Dictionary of idioms and familiar expressions] (Taipei: Taiwan wunan tushu chuban gongsi 台灣五南圖書出版公司, 2000), shows that 27 percent of the *wuyan* examples (among a total of 237) and 19 percent of the *qiyan* examples (among 488) end with fourth-tone syllables. This puts final fourth tones in the range of normal distribution, or even a bit below it. So if we wish to test whether fourth tones do contribute to "meaning" (broadly conceived), we appear to be left with the subjective task of judging whether phrases that do happen to use fourth tones tend to "feel different."

that use only fourth tones but whose meanings are less austere, for example, *Zhao taitai zhan zai podeng shang kan dianshi* 赵太太站在破凳上看电视 'Ms. Zhao is standing on a broken stool watching television' or *daxiang shou pohai hou daochu luan fang pi* 大象受迫害后到处乱放屁 'after their mistreatment the elephants wandered around farting'? Here we may laugh. But do we laugh only because the examples are inherently droll, or partly because—and this is the key question—the hacking assertiveness of the fourth tones somehow does not match the playful content of the phrases? Do the tones keep frowning, as it were, saying "listen to me," while the content is saying "relax, this is fun!"—and does this incongruity contribute to the humor? We might test the case by considering an example that uses second tones only: *youyu shichang huilai wanr piqiu* 鱿鱼时常回来玩儿皮球 'the squid often return to play with leather balls'. Here the content again is playful, so we can ask whether the same mismatch between tones and message appears. Do second tones fit playful messages better than fourth tones, while fourth tones are a better fit with austere messages? Such tendencies, if they do exist, are subtle and unusual. But even if they explain only why something like *renren zuo hao ren, riri zuo hao shi* sounds slightly better than *riri zuo hao shi, renren zuo hao ren*, they are still worth consideration.

Vowels and consonants. If tones, whose normal role is phonemic (not semantic), can nevertheless suggest subtle differences of meaning, we should ask whether other phonemes—vowels and consonants—can do so as well. In English, for example, is it merely chance that so many verbs ending in *-ash* have to do with violent motion: crash, clash, mash, bash, trash, slash, splash, dash, lash, and so on? Does *-ash* itself "mean something"? Does *-umble* have to do with incompetence: mumble, fumble, bumble, jumble, tumble? In onomatopoeia, we expect sounds in language to imitate sounds in nature, but the question here is different: whether clusters of sound can move from word to word carrying a bit of "meaning baggage" with them. In Mandarin Chinese, the *mo* sound seems to conjure a family of meanings. First-tone *mo* 摸 is for rubbing something gently, like tousling a child's head, or feeling something lightly, like passing a finger over the blade of a knife to see if it is sharp. *Mo* 摩 in second tone is to rub harder or to scrape, as in scraping the skin off your knee. *Mo* 磨, also in second tone, is rubbing hard enough to polish a marble floor, or to grind, as a knife blade against a sharpening stone (before you gently *mo* 摸 to check on your results). Metaphorically speaking, you can *mo shijian* 磨时间 'grind time', meaning "while it away," or *moren* 磨人 'rub somebody', rather as we "rub someone the wrong way" in English. Third-tone *mo* 抹 is rubbing gentler again, and is used for applying cosmetics to the face or spreading butter across a slice of bread. So does the vowel-consonant cluster have a substratal "meaning" here? I am not sure that -*ng* at the ends of Mandarin syllables ever "means something," but it is an interesting fact that *wuyan* and *qiyan* proverbs and aphorisms end with -*ng* syllables at a rate significantly higher than normal.[125]

A small subfield of cognitive science has studied this question and seems to have found that human beings do indeed tend naturally to associate certain kinds of (nononomatopoetic) sounds with certain kinds of meanings. A famous early study by Wolfgang Köhler found that people, when presented with a softly roundish shape and a sharply angular one, and then are given the nonsense words *maluma* and *takete* to apply to them, prefer to call the round thing "maluma" and the pointy thing "takete."[126] Another study got the same result using *bouba* and *kiki*.[127] (You can guess which sound matched which feeling.) Moreover, such results seem to hold across language and cultures; similar results were found among children in England and Tanzania.[128] Why might this be? Some have hypothesized that the tendency to associate roundness with sounds like *maluma* and *bouba* comes from the fact that a human being needs to round

---

125. In the first fifty pages of Tang Shu, *Chengyu shuyu cihai*, 41 percent of both *wuyan* and *qiyan* examples end with -*ng* syllables. This compares with 20 percent in a randomly selected page from the writing of the eminent contemporary literary critic Liu Zaifu and 29 percent from a randomly selected page from the fiction of the famous contemporary novelist Jin Yong, *Liu Zaifu sanwenshi heji* 刘再复散文诗集 [Collected prose poems of Liu Zaifu] (Beijing: Huaxia chubanshe, 1988), p. 134, and Jin Yong 金庸, *She diao yingxiong zhuan* 射鵰英雄傳 [Chronicle of the eagle-shooting heroes], ch. 4 (Hong Kong: Yuluo chubanshe, n.d.), 1:67.

126. Wolfgang Köhler, *Gestalt Psychology* (New York: Liveright, 1929).

127. V. S. Ramachandran and E. M. Hubbard, "Synaesthesia: A Window into Perception, Thought, and Language," *Journal of Consciousness Studies* 8, no. 12 (2001), pp. 3–34.

128. R. Davis, "The Fitness of Names to Drawings: A Cross-Cultural Study in Tanganyika," *British Journal of Psychology* 52 (1961), pp. 259–268.

the lips in order to make the sounds. To say *takete* or *kiki*, the lips are more angular. Others hypothesize that the universal tendencies are rooted somewhere deeper in the human brain.[129] There seems to be no consensus on this question, but the field does agree that at a primitive level, sounds themselves do sometimes suggest meanings.

Wondering whether Mandarin Chinese sounds might be guides, however subtly or marginally, to their meanings, I devised an experiment in 1996. Setting aside cases that are arguably onomatopoeia (like *pa!* 啪 for a slapping sound or *wang* 汪 for the bark of a dog), I wanted to see whether sounds might suggest meanings in a broader sense. I made a list of twenty paired opposites in Chinese: *qianhou* 前后 'front and back', *daxiao* 大小 'large and small', *kuaiman* 快慢 'fast and slow', and seventeen others. I brought the list to classes of seventh-graders at the John Witherspoon Middle School in Princeton, New Jersey. I offered a lesson in beginning Chinese, so the students and their teacher might feel all right about me. Then I handed out lists in English of the twenty pairs of opposites and read the sounds of the paired opposites in Chinese, asking the students to guess which Chinese sound "sounded like" which meaning. For example, the students looked at the words "front" and "back" while I read the sounds *qian* and *hou*; then they used their pencils to mark on their sheets whether "the first sound" meant "front" and "the second sound" meant "back," or vice versa. I flipped a coin twenty times, in advance, to determine the order in which I would read the paired words in Chinese, so that customary patterns in the orders of such things (which tend to be the same in the two languages, e.g., we conventionally say *front* before *back* in English and *qian* before *hou* in Chinese) theoretically would be neutral. I also requested that any student who knew any Chinese at all not participate in the fun. By chance, there were exactly one hundred students participating. The table on the next page gives the results.

An average number of right guesses only slightly higher than 50 percent is not a very strong basis for claiming that sounds themselves have

---

129. Ramachandran and Hubbard, "Synaesthesia"; Daphne Maurer, Thanujeni Pathman, and Catherine J. Mondloch, "The Shape of Boubas: Sound-Shape Correspondences in Toddlers and Adults," *Developmental Science* 9, no. 3 (2006), pp. 316–322.

Results of my 1996 experiment

	Correct guesses	Incorrect guesses	No guesses (left blank)
Qianhou 'front and back'	61	36	3
Daxiao 'big and little'	49	49	2
Kuaiman 'fast and slow'	33	67	0
Gaoai 'tall and short'	50	49	1
Haohuai 'good and bad'	58	41	1
Shangxia 'up and down'	54	46	0
Duoshao 'many and few'	37	62	1
Qingzhong 'light and heavy'	90	10	0
Ruanying 'soft and hard'	44	56	0
Yuanjin 'far and near'	64	36	0
Maimai 'buy and sell'	52	48	0
Baoe 'full and hungry'	24	76	0
Baohou 'thin and thick'	70	30	0
Xinjiu 'new and old'	50	50	0
Fangyuan 'square and round'	60	40	0
Meichou 'beautiful and ugly'	77	23	0
Zaowan 'early and late'	46	53	1
Shenqian 'deep and shallow'	14	86	0
Gaodi 'high and low'	43	57	0
Qingchu/hunzhuo 'clear and muddy'	86	14	0
Average	53.1%	46.4%	0.5%

meanings. I do find some of the particular results interesting, however. The pair that was guessed most accurately was *qingzhong* 'light and heavy', and a correct-guess rate as high as nine out of ten strongly suggests that there might be a reason. Does the *i* sound in *qing* 轻 sound "light"? Or perhaps the palatal initial *q-* contributes to this feeling? Might it be that the fourth (falling) tone on *zhong* 重 contributes to a "heavy" feeling? On similar grounds, it seems natural that the students guessed well (86 percent) on *qingchu* 清楚 for 'clear', leaving *hunzhuo* for 'muddy'. Some of the examples on which the guesses were worst seem to raise the question whether, despite being wrong, the guesses may have made some sense. A student commented to me afterward, for example, that he thought *e* 饿 'hungry', with its falling tone, sounded like being overstuffed and about to vomit—rather the opposite of hungry. And *shen* 深 'deep' and *qian* 浅 'shallow' might have misled students because of the tones. *Shen* has a first (high) tone and *qian* a third (low) tone—the opposite of what one would expect for 'deep' and 'shallow'.

Another sense in which sound itself can have meaning seems to be especially important in Chinese. This effect happens when one meaning carries a second meaning with it—only because of a sound. Any human language has homonyms, and sometimes homonyms create "double meanings." Puns are a common example, and Chinese has plenty of puns. But I am not speaking here of puns. In a pun, the whole point is that a single sound has two different meanings that *cannot* carry over from one to the other. What makes a pun funny is precisely the "fraudulent claim," as it were, that one thing can be another. For example, when the famous Chinese *xiangsheng* performer Hou Baolin says that he is a *zuojia* 作家 'author' because all day he *zuo jia* 坐家 'sits at home', no one thinks that sitting at home really does make him an author. The sound *zuojia* does not have this power. But in another function of "double meaning" that is very common in Chinese culture, sound itself *is* assumed to carry meaning along with it. No sense of fraud is involved, and nothing is funny. Quite the contrary, the topic is often serious. At New Year's, for example, Cantonese eat *facai* 髮菜 'hair vegetable', a stringy black vegetable that looks a bit like hair but—importantly, at New Year's—is a near homonym of *facai* 發財 'get rich' (*fat choi* in Cantonese). It is also good to eat *yu* 鱼 'fish' at New Year's, because *yu* 餘, also second tone, is 'bounty'. When my Princeton colleague James Wei, a dean of engineering and a brilliant man, went to grade school in Shanghai in the 1930s, his mother put onion (*cong* 葱), garlic (*suan* 蒜), and chicken hearts (*ji xin* 雞心) in his lunch box. This was to be sure that he would be smart (*congming* 聰明), be good at mathematics (*suanshu* 算術), and have a good memory (*jixing* 記性). Terese Bartholomew has published a 350-page book on more than three hundred examples of this kind of meaning-transfers, which she calls "hidden meanings," that regularly appear in Chinese art and are meant to help people achieve happy marriage, wealth, longevity, official career, and passing of exams.[130] The care with which Chinese parents traditionally choose their children's names sometimes also includes this kind of calculation. The

---

130. Terese Tse Bartholomew, *Hidden Meanings in Chinese Art* (San Francisco: Asian Art Museum, 2006).

Anhui novelist Chen Dengke 陈登科, for example, has a fine name that suggests "Chen who rises in the examination system." A family named Wei 魏, however, would likely avoid such a choice, lest the name suggest "has not passed the exams" 未登科. The exiled Chinese political philosopher Hu Ping 胡平 has a son named Hu Pan 胡畔; when a daughter was born, he and his spouse were considering Hu Sha 胡莎 for her name but later thought better of it. If the two children were attracted to legal careers, they would be at a big disadvantage: one *hupan* 胡判 'crazily sentencing' and the other *husha* 胡杀 'crazily killing'.[131] Similarly, in moving to an English-speaking country, a Chinese family might, if they could manage it, avoid a dentist named Dr. Paine or a surgeon named Dr. Slaughter.

Pitch. We have already seen examples where voice pitch (which combines with loudness and duration to constitute what I have defined as "stress") is useful in making distinctions of meaning. When we emphasize that *Joe*y Davis is not *Lou*ie Davis, pitch is part of what makes the difference. When we distinguish between birds *flying* south and birds flying *south*, pitch again pitches in. In English, pitch differences can convey skepticism or surprise. In "Where did you go?" the voice normally falls at the end; but in "You went *where?*" it rises. In "Would you like coffee or tea?" if the *cof-* in "coffee" is spoken in a relatively high pitch and *tea* in a relatively low one, the meaning is *ni yao kafei haishi cha?* 你要咖啡还是茶? 'which would you like—coffee or tea?'. But if the last four syllables are said with relatively high and rising pitch, the meaning is *ni yao buyao kafei huozhe cha?* 你要不要咖啡或者茶? 'would you like either coffee or tea [yes or no]?' In the fall of 2009, after two sets of tennis doubles, one of my fellow players asked the rest of us if we would like to play a third set. Two people answered "I'm good" but meant exactly opposite things by it. One used a pitch contour that resembled the Mandarin Chinese first tone (high level) followed by a second (rising) tone; this meant "yes, bring it on." The other used two falling pitches, like the fourth tone in Chinese; this meant "no, I've had it." No one was puzzled by the two answers. Both were perfectly clear in meaning. In fact, no one (except me, later) seemed to notice that the same two syllables had been used and that it was pitch alone that had made the difference.

131. Hu Ping, email message to author, November 23, 2007.

Pitch in Chinese (in addition to its normal role in tones) does many similar things, and we cannot address all of them here. But, for example, the particle *lou* that gets added to the ends of Cantonese utterances to mean something like "of course!" or even "only an idiot would need to be told this!" is consistently said in a high pitch. In Mandarin, skeptical questions employ a higher-than-normal pitch, as they do in English. This holds even when a "falling tone" (fourth tone) appears in a question that wants a higher-than-normal pitch. For example *shi ma?* 是吗? 'is that right?' is said in higher-than-normal pitch but still allows, within the elevated pitch range, for a falling pitch on the fourth-tone syllable *shi*. In skeptical questions of greater length, like *nandao ta shuo de dui ma?* 难道他说得对吗? 'Could it be that what he said was right?' a higher pitch runs through several syllables at the end of the phrase, but again allows room for fourth-tone syllables (*dui*, in this case) to fall in pitch appropriately. Y. R. Chao has used the image of ripples riding on waves to describe this phenomenon; Chao observes that what the voice actually does is an "algebraic sum" of the two effects.[132]

George Lakoff and Mark Johnson, in their brilliant little book *Metaphors We Live By*, assert that "tone languages generally do not use intonation to mark questions at all."[133] The error is glaring, yet the notion that seems to have led to it—that languages very different from English might follow different customs in intonation—is important. In English the voice rises at the end when we say "you mean this one?" or simply "this one?" But by custom in northern Mandarin Chinese, the voice drops in saying the corresponding phrase *zhei g'a?* 这个啊?[134] For another example, in English the voice drops on the last syllable of the phrase "what do *you* think?" It would be very easy to use the same pattern in Mandarin, where a ready match is available in the combination of first tone followed by neutral tone in a phrase like *women ting le* 我们听了 'we listened'. But, despite its easy availability, Mandarin does *not* use this ready-made pattern in phrases that correspond to "what do *you* think?" In *ni shuo ne?* 你说呢? 'what do *you* say?' the final *ne* does not drop but stays high, about where *shuo* is.

132. Chao, *Grammar of Spoken Chinese*, p. 39.
133. George Lakoff and Mark Johnson, *Metaphors We Live By* (Chicago: University of Chicago Press, 1980), p. 138.
134. Yuen Ren Chao, *Mandarin Primer* (Cambridge, Mass.: Harvard University Press, 1948), lesson 2, n. 3, pp. 129–130.

A feature that is sometimes related to pitch in Chinese intonation is elongation of syllables. If a nervous mother in China asks a teenage daughter if she has ever driven long distance before, the daughter might answer *k-a-a-a-i-i-i-i guo!* 開──過! 'y-e-e-s-s-s-s-s, I have', where the drawing-out of *kai* emphasizes the point in a way designed both to reassure the mother and to suggest that she needn't have asked.[135]

The full picture of intonation in Chinese is a large and complex topic. The purpose here is only to illustrate it briefly and to note its relation to the question of rhythm.

Parallelism. Just as rhythm can produce senses of naturalness, authority, or "fit," it seems clear that parallelism can do the same. Indeed parallelism and rhythm—as classical Chinese poetry richly shows—often work together. As with rhythm, the success of parallelism in producing meaning in Chinese seems attributable, in part, to the flexibility of the single-syllable morphemes that compose Chinese.

Consider again the four-syllable Great Leap Forward slogan *li gan jian ying* 'erect a pole and see a shadow—get instant results'. Even in such a simple example, the grammatical parallelism of verb-object followed by another verb-object seems (at least to me) to suggest a sense of "rightness." I have also noted the Great Leap slogan *loushang louxia, diandeng dianhua* 'electric lights and telephones upstairs and down'. Here the double parallelism of *lou-A lou-B, dian-X dian-Y* is, to my ear, even more effective in suggesting "fittingness." The terseness of the phrases enhances the power of their parallelism, and the result is nifty penetration. What could possibly be better, as it were, than *loushang louxia diandeng dianhua*?

The power of parallelism to create a sense of fit appears in sharper relief in examples where the words themselves are relatively empty. Take, for example, the Cultural Revolution slogan *zhua geming, cu shengchan* 抓革命, 促生產 'seize revolution, stimulate production'. What exactly did it mean, in daily life, to *zhua* revolution? Everyone at the time knew that this was a good thing to do, but what exactly did it mean? (Work harder? Obey your leader? Pick on your politically tainted neighbor?) "Promote production," although somewhat clearer, is still fairly general and abstract, as an

---

135. The example is borrowed from Ta-tuan Ch'en et al., *Chinese Primer* (Princeton, N.J.: Princeton University Press, 2007), vol. 1, p. 85, and vol. 2, p. 183.

instruction. But note: when the two phrases are put side by side, somehow the grammatical parallelism (verb-object) and rhythmic parallelism (1–2, 1–2) generates a tight sense of fit. The phrase, if not its meaning, is lean and neat. And it exudes "rightness."

In poetry and many kinds of popular phrases, the effects of parallelism are enhanced when parallel syllables are semantically antithetical. A traditional *shunkouliu* says:

Hai ren zhi xin bu ke you　害人之心不可有
Fang ren zhi xin bu ke wu　防人之心不可無

The will to harm others you must not have
The will to resist others you must not lack

Here we have both *qiyan* and an unusually close parallelism: five middle syllables are identical, while the framing syllables at either end are grammatically parallel and semantically antithetical. In elite poetry, such features might seem only the technical features of a genre—or even, if they are overdone, ostentatious wordplay. In popular culture, though, I believe the effect has been somewhat different. I believe it creates an aura of dignity and credibility about what is expressed. The message becomes right, natural, fitting, wise.

This tradition has been strong enough to persist through China's Communist revolution and into the market economy of today. In the early years of the revolution, a slogan aimed at preserving forests was *fandui langfei mucai, fandui lanfa linmu* 反對浪費木材, 反對濫伐林木! 'oppose the waste of lumber; oppose rampant cutting of forests', in which the grammatical parallelism is reinforced by the repetition of *fandui* as well as by the quasi rhyme of *langfei* and *lanfa*.[136] A campaign against corruption and waste used a slogan that comprised three "verb plus object" phrases in parallel: *qingli zichan, heding zijin, fandui langfei!* 清理資產, 核定資金, 反對浪費 'clean up property, check on ownings, oppose waste!'[137] By 1966, Mao Zedong had decided that "old culture" should be thrown out, but he still

---

136. *Renmin ribao* 人民日報 [People's daily], October 23, 1951, p. 2. The unusual six-syllable rhythm is worth noting here.

137. Ibid., October 28, 1951, p. 2.

used parallelism. A photograph in the *People's Daily* in fall, 1966 shows Mao waving in front of a large billboard that reads:

Dapo yiqie boxuejieji de jiu sixiang, jiu wenhua, jiu fengsu, jiu xiguan!
Dali wuchanjieji de xin sixiang, xin wenhua, xin fengsu, xin xiguan!

大破一切剥削阶级的旧思想, 旧文化, 旧风俗, 旧习惯!
大立无产阶级的新思想, 新文化, 新风俗, 新习惯!

Demolish the old thinking, old culture, old customs, and old habits of all the exploiting classes!
Establish the new thinking, new culture, new customs, and new habits of the proletariat![138]

The two phrases are semantically antithetical in five places and, except for *yiqie* 'all', are exactly parallel as well. The power of the lines clearly derives in part from the parallelism, and it seems likely that Mao and his followers appreciated the power without noticing its old-culture roots. Essentially the same power of parallelism extends into the commercial culture of the post-Mao era, for example in an advertisement for White Beauty Soap (*baili xiangzao* 白丽香皂) that appeared on Shanghai television in 2000: *shi toufa gengen rouruan, ling pifu cuncun nenhua* 使头发根根柔软, 令皮肤寸寸嫩滑 'makes each one of your hairs soft, makes every inch of your skin smooth'. The seven-syllable rhythm here is an unconventional "dotted" 4:4 pattern, but the parallelism is impeccable from start to finish. Similarly, a warning to motorists not to drink and drive that was posted on public blackboards in Beijing and elsewhere in 2007 read *hejinqu ji di meijiu, liuchulai wushu xuelei* 喝进去几滴美酒, 流出来无数血泪 'imbibe a few drops of fine wine, shed countless more in blood and tears'. My English translation does not fully capture either the rhythm or the parallelism of the original, whose impact is to convey a sense something like: "this can't be wrong."

Although the "meaning" that rhythm, parallelism, and semantic antitheticality can conspire to produce has especially strong cultural roots in Chinese popular culture, there is obviously something universal about it as well. It also appears, if perhaps not as frequently, in English-speaking

---

138. Ibid., October 21, 1966, p. 4.

cultures, for example in the famous lines in John F. Kennedy's 1961 inaugural address "United there is little we cannot do, divided there is little we can do" (in which the combination of rhythm, parallelism, and antitheticality could not be more "Chinese") or his statement that if a free society "cannot help the many who are poor, it cannot save the few who are rich." Why are such phrases effective? Do the rhetorical features themselves not make the messages seem more right, natural, and fitting than they otherwise would? Whether in Chinese or English, rhyme, rhythm, parallelism, and antitheticality, separately or in concert, can convey the sense that "this is the real truth" or "this resonates with nature." An adequate account of these rhetorical devices, in the history of either Chinese or Indo-European languages, is beyond our scope here.

Chiasmus. A distinctive version of parallelism, sometimes called "chiasmus,"[139] combines rhythmic and grammatical parallelism with semantic inversion. "Eat to live, don't live to eat" is an example, and it is easy to find others, in both Chinese and English, from the twentieth and twenty-first centuries. Kennedy's "ask not what your country can do for you; ask what you can do for your country" in his inaugural address is a famous example, as is Mao Zedong's Cultural Revolution slogan

Jiefangjun xue quanguo renmin 解放军学全国人民
Quanguo renmin xue jiefangjun 全国人民学解放军

The Liberation Army should learn from all the people of the nation
All the people of the nation should learn from the Liberation Army.

Intellectuals have used chiasmus as well. In his 1918 essay "On Establishing a New Literature," Hu Shi distilled his main message into the phrase *guoyu de wenxue, wenxue de guoyu* 國語的文學, 文學的國語 'literature in the national language and a national language's literature'.[140] More recent

---

139. See Mardy Grothe, *Never Let a Fool Kiss You or a Kiss Fool You* (New York: Viking Books, 1999). Grothe also has a website, www.drmardy.com, accessed June 23, 2012.
140. Hu Shi 胡適, "Jianshe xin wenxue lun" 建設新文學論 [On building a new literature], quoted in "Jianshe de geming wenxue lun (I)" 建設的革命文學論 (I) [On a con-

scholars have given their essays titles like "Shehui de xianshi he xianshi de shehui" 社会的现实和现实的社会 (Social reality and present-day society), "Cong wenxue de chengshou dao chengshou de wenxue" 从文学的成熟到成熟的文学 (From the maturation of literature to literature that is mature), and "Beiai de zhishifenzi he zhishifenzi de beiai" 悲哀的知识分子和知识分子的悲哀 (Sorrowful intellectuals and the sorrow of intellectuals).[141] A freshman seminar at Princeton University in 1999 was named "Deforming Codes, Decoding Forms"; around the same time, a bon mot from Toni Morrison appeared on the wall of the Princeton student center: "The Place of the Idea, the Idea of the Place."

The "value added" of chiasmus is a bit mysterious. What is it, and what does it come from? We might test the question by separating the two halves of certain examples, thereby destroying whatever additional effect is caused by the pairing of lines. Each phrase in "ask not what your country can do for you" and "ask what you can do for your country" can make sense independently, although the parts somehow seem less than the whole. Something extra seems to emerge when the two parts are joined. Another example where each of the two halves makes a good point independently is the popular Chinese saying about Communist Party meetings *xiao huiyi zuo da jueding, da huiyi zuo xiao jueding* 小会议做大决定, 大会议做小决定 'small meetings make big decisions and big meetings make small ones', that is, important choices are made by a few people in small rooms, and routine approvals are given in huge conference halls. Each half of this chiasmus has something important to say, and the fact that the two comprise the chiasmus form is a kind of bonus. On the other hand, sometimes the two halves of chiasmus seem redundant (what does "the sorrow of intellectuals" add to the idea of "sorrowful intellectuals"?). Nonetheless—and this is the crucial point—juxtaposing the two seems to make a claim that "something extra," even something a bit mysterious or

---

structive revolutionary literature], www.mianfeilunwen.com/Wenxue/Hanyuyan/31407.html, accessed June 23, 2012.

141. The first two of these titles are from a conference on 新时期的中国文学 (Chinese literature in the new era) at Zhongshan University, Guangzhou, 1979. The third is from the conference "The Course of Contemporary Chinese Intellectuals: An International Symposium Commemorating the Fiftieth Anniversary of the Anti-Rightist Movement Campaign," University of California, Irvine, July 29–30, 2007.

profound, is going on. In some cases, the extra element is so important that if one takes the chiasmatic juxtaposition away, the two parts do not stand up at all on their own. By itself, for example, either "The Place of the Idea" or "the Idea of the Place" would look odd on the wall of a campus center. Only when the two are side by side does it suddenly become all right to put them there; and the result, somehow, even seems to lay claim to a special wisdom. In complex instances of chiasmus, concrete meaning might not be as important as the aesthetic satisfaction one feels just from seeing all the parts coordinate like clockwork. In analyzing the late-Qing novel *Niehaihua*, for example, David Wang writes that it "literally politicizes the sport of desire as much as it eroticizes the game of power."[142] The reader does not need to dig for the ultimate meaning of the phrase in order to enjoy its craft.

The "extra something" that chiasmus lays claim to is hard to pin down. It seems to me akin to the claims of *wuyan* and *qiyan* rhythms: that there is something right, fitting, or authoritative about the message that the phrase bears. But in chiasmus, the claim may be even a bit stronger, reaching toward the realm of "deep" or "mystical." This relatively strong claim in chiasmus is most visible when it is overdone, by which I mean when the rightness or profundity of the message does not measure up to what the chiasmus form seems to be claiming. For example, if a professor is proud of his verbal integrity and says "I said what I meant and I meant what I said," we accept it as a successful emphatic statement; but if he is proud of his dress and says, in parallel chiasmatic form, "I wear suits when I lecture and I lecture when I wear suits," we would have to say that chiasmus had seduced him into saying something whose detailed implications he had not considered. This is an imaginary example, but many actual examples raise the same question in varying degrees. In 2002, for example, U.S. congressman John Dingell summed up the behavior of Enron executives as "either criminally stupid or stupidly criminal."[143] Exactly what the difference is between "criminally stupid" and "stupidly criminal" was not clear, and how one might determine which of the two was actually the case—as the statement suggests one could do—was also murky. But I would guess that these questions did not even occur either to Dingell or

---

142. David Wang, *Fin-de-Siècle Splendor: Repressed Modernities in Late-Qing Fiction, 1849–1911* (Stanford: Stanford University Press, 1997), p. 106.

143. *ABC News with Peter Jennings*, January 24, 2002.

to many of his listeners, for whom the charm of chiasmus was likely enough to make the statement seem not just acceptable but memorably wise. Similarly, a campaign slogan for healthful sex practices in China in 2007 was *chenggongde nanren yao jiankang, jiankang de nanren geng chenggong* 成功的男人要健康，健康的男人更成功 'successful males want health, and healthy males are more successful'.[144] Here it is not clear what *chenggong* 'success' means because "success at what?" is not specified; the only real meaning of the phrase is a vague positive valuation: whatever it is, *chenggong* is "what you'd want to be." But if that is the case, then it becomes banal to say that *chenggong* males would want to be healthy, and to turn the phrase around to say that healthy males are more *chenggong* is equally vacuous. Yet despite all these weaknesses, the charm of chiasmus was enough to lead Chinese slogan writers to feel that the words might have persuasive power, and they probably were right in that judgment.

Can the Users of Rhythm Be Unaware of Its Effects?

At several points in this chapter I have noted that the meanings of rhythms (and some related devices) are sometimes not fully noticed by those who use them. I have employed a broad definition of "meaning" by which merely "a different understanding or feeling, however slight," can count as meaning even if users are not aware of just what is causing the small difference. In one sense, though, to speak in this way is odd. Normally, we assume that meaning implies *intent*. When we "mean" something, how can we be unaware of it? How can we say that rhythms "mean" things when people are not meaning them to do so?

But perhaps this is not so strange after all. Compare for a moment "meaning" as it applies to words. Normally, when A says or writes a word, like "book," and B receives and interprets the word, we assume the following conditions:

1. that a meaning has passed between A and B, and
2. that both A and B might be—and often are—conscious of the word's role in conveying the meaning.

144. From "Jihua shengyu xin biaoyu chutai neiqing."

Neither condition ensures that A and B understand each other perfectly, of course. A might consciously intend one thing (e.g. in saying "cook the books!"), and B might consciously infer something else (by placing the books into a steamer). But even in *mis*communication such as this, A and B are both conscious of a meaning for the word "book." It is true that in fluent speech we may not consciously notice every word as it flies by, and also true that in some cases meaningful words emerge from our subconscious minds (in Freudian slips, for example, or, more radically, in talking in one's sleep). But still, for most words most of the time, we are aware of our word choices, and sometimes even think long and hard in choosing words. For words, conditions 1 and 2 both apply.

For such things as rhythm and parallelism, though, condition 1 holds while condition 2 almost never does. A poet or trained linguist—or a reader of this book—might notice the rhythm in a phrase and be able to interpret its contribution to "meaning," but ordinary native speakers of a language do not do such things. They do use rhythms, and using them does make differences to them and to the people with whom they communicate. But they do not notice. Chinese schoolchildren learn characters, memorize sentences, and are explicitly told that these are vessels of meaning. They are not given tables of rhythms to memorize.

Can we say simply that rhythmic meaning is subconscious and let it go at that? Cognitive scientists are apparently comfortable with the assumption that, at a minimum, "unconscious thought is 95 percent of all thought."[145] If that is so, why can't rhythm just be unconscious meaning? The main problem with such a stance is that the mind *is* to some degree conscious of the various effects that rhythm produces—authority, rightness, whimsy (for a limerick), and so on. Even if people are not aware of the causes of these effects, they are certainly aware of the effects. So it appears that we must say that while some aspects of what rhythms are doing impinge on consciousness, others do not.

This situation of "partly conscious and partly not"—aware of effects but not what causes them—seems in some ways parallel to the ways grammar rules operate in the mind. Few speakers of Chinese, for example, are aware of the very powerful rule in Chinese that modifiers—whether of

---

145. George Lakoff and Mark Johnson, *Philosophy in the Flesh: The Embodied Mind and Its Challenge to Western Thought* (New York: Basic Books, 1999), p. 13.

nouns or verbs, and regardless of length—precede what they modify. Yet the same adept speakers have no trouble obeying the rule or feeling consciously that something's wrong when the rule is violated. Moreover, the force of the rule is strong enough that it can bend apparent exceptions to its will. For example, the fluffy dried meat known as *rou song* 肉松 might appear to be a noun (*rou* 'flesh') followed by an adjective (*song* 'loose'), but in the Chinese mind the modification relation still works in the standard way: *rou song* is "fluff" of the "meat" variety; it is "meat fluff." Similarly, *putao gan* 葡萄乾 'raisin', composed of *putao* 'grape' and *gan* 'dry', is not a grammatical reversal of "dry grape" into "grape dry". Like *rou song*, it too, conceptually, is a modifier preceding a noun. A raisin is a "grape-derived dry-thing." The strong grammar rule, applied to the mind subconsciously, helps to turn this trick.

Another revealing example of subconscious obedience of rules is the common pattern in Chinese of four-syllable phrases in which two of the syllables are numbers: *yi qing er chu* 一清二楚 'crystal clear'; *bu san bu si* 不三不四 'shady (character)' *dian san dao si* 颠三倒四 'confused, incoherent'; *shuo san dao si* 说三道四 'speak irresponsibly'; *wu yan liu se* 五颜六色 'varied in color'; *luan qi ba zao* 亂七八糟 'utterly messy'; and others. There are some exceptions, but such phrases tend to observe these two rules:

1. the two numbers are adjacent integers (n and n + 1), and
2. of the two integers, the odd one comes first.

The second rule holds even when the odd number is the larger of the two, as in *san yan liang yu* 三言兩語 'in two or three words' or when the integers are not adjacent, as in *jiu niu er hu zhi li* 九牛二虎之力 'the strength of nine bulls and two tigers—tremendous effort'. It is not hard to find exceptions to either rule. For example *wu hua ba men* 五花八門 'multifarious' violates rule 1, and *si qin san hao* 四勤三好 'four diligents and three do-wells', a slogan that was used to fight SARS in 2003, violates rule 2.[146] Big numbers

---

146. The "four diligents" were diligently wash hands, diligently wash face, diligently drink water, and diligently ventilate; the "three do-wells" were wear face masks well, regulate moods well, and exercise the body well. I am grateful to David Moser, who observed signs bearing the slogan in Beijing; email message to author, May 8, 2004.

also ignore the rule, as in *qian fang bai ji* 千方百計 'by every possible means'.[147]

But the two rules usually do hold, and moreover seem to influence choices when Chinese speakers invent new phrases. For example, when Communist Party leaders decided in 1981 to promote improvement in public behavior, they came up with the formula *wujiang simei* 五讲四美 'five pay-attentions and four beautifuls'. The pay-attentions were attention to civility, politeness, hygiene, order, and morality. The four beautifuls were beautiful spirit, beautiful language, beautiful conduct, and a beautiful environment. The meanings seemed good, the composite phrase sounded good, and the phrase spread easily through the nationwide bureaucracies and publicity system. It obeyed the two rules, and that obedience probably had to do with why it "sounded right" to everyone. But how many people were consciously aware of the two rules? Were the creators themselves aware? Likely not, I would guess. *Wujiang simei* just sounded better than *simei wujiang*.

What happens here is similar to what happens with unnoticed rhythms because, in both cases, grammatical arrangements happen and results sound good even if people are not aware of the reasons why. The pattern 2–2–3 just sounds better than 3–2–2, hence people say *renmin zongli renmin ai*, not (as grammar would have it) *renmin ai renmin de zongli* ('the people love the people's premier'). It is worth noting that shortly after *wujiang simei* was promulgated, Party leaders felt that "three loves" (love of the Communist Party, love of the motherland, and love of socialism) should be added. So how did they add it? They did not say *san'ai* 三爱 'three loves' but *san reai* 三热爱 'three ardent loves'. It is, of course, natural that they would want love of the Party to be "ardent," but it is more likely that *re* was added for rhythm, in order to make the whole phrase a nice-sounding *qiyan* pattern: *wujiang simei san reai* sounds better than *wujiang simei san'ai*. And you don't even have to think about it.

---

147. I do not consider examples like *qian pian yi lü* 千篇一律 'stereotyped' or *bai fa bai zhong* 百發百中 'unfailing accuracy' to be exceptions, because of their different underlying grammar.

2
Metaphor

In 1935 a young American named Graham Peck, fresh from Yale and seeking adventure, set out for China, where he traveled widely, often by bicycle, making sketches, taking notes, and picking up some Chinese. In 1940 he went to China again, this time for a longer stay during which he took a post with the U.S. Office of War Information. Eventually, he became frustrated with a gap he perceived between official U.S. hopes for China and the abysmal conditions he found on the ground. After the war he put his perceptions into a book that was excellent in many ways but bore the unfortunate title *Two Kinds of Time*.[1]

Peck explained his title this way: "By one Chinese view of time, the future is behind you, above you, where you cannot see it. The past is before you, below you, where you can examine it. Man's position in time is

---

1. Graham Peck, *Two Kinds of Time*, rev. ed. (Boston: Houghton Mifflin, 1967) (originally published 1950). Information in this paragraph is drawn in part from the introduction to the revised edition by John K. Fairbank.

that of a person sitting beside a river, facing always downstream as he watches the water flow past."[2] Peck goes on to tell about Chinese gardens in which a gentleman meditating next to an artificial stream sits in that same downstream-facing position while servants, standing behind him, fill cups with wine and float them down to him. The gentleman drinks when the cups arrive, but never knows just when they will. Peck's point is that Chinese culture looks at what has passed, not at what is coming. This, for him, is "one kind of time." The other kind is found in "America and other Western countries," where

> man faces in the other direction, with his back to the past, which is sinking away behind him, and his face turned upward toward the future, which is floating down upon him. Nor can this man be static: by our ambitious Western convention, he is supposed to be rising into the future under his own power, perhaps by his own direction. He is more like a man in a plane than a sitter by a river.[3]

Apparently aware that his analysis might leave the Chinese side looking inferior, Peck points out the weakness of the forward-gazing airplane rider: because he does not look back at the past, he flies blind into the future.

Peck's characterizations of Chinese and "Western" concepts of time are oversimplified and, even in the simple terms in which he presents them, garbled. For neither Chinese nor English is his account complete, and the claim that the two languages and cultures conceive radically different "kinds of time," as we shall see below, is false. Still, his speculation on the ways time is conceived in terms of space is—as Mark Twain said of Richard Wagner's music—not as bad as it sounds. Peck's rudimentary speculations were headed in an important direction. He anticipated by forty years a subfield of cognitive science that has shown clearly both that (1) his notion that conceptual systems are built on the metaphor that "time is space" is correct and well worth studying, and (2) his particular conclusions about Chinese and English are off the mark.

Late twentieth- and early twenty-first-century studies have found that the "time is space" metaphor is apparently universal in human languages.

2. Peck, *Two Kinds of Time*, rev. ed., p. 7.
3. Ibid., p. 8.

In a 1994 book, Hoyt Alverson examines conceptions of time in English, Chinese, Hindi, and Sesotho and finds similarities that are strong enough to lead him to hypothesize that "the experience of time is based on a universal template of human experience."[4] An anthropologist, Alverson is committed to reasoning from empirical data, and he reflects this commitment in his book's title, *Semantics and Experience*. One might wonder how a strictly empirical approach can get Alverson from four particular languages to universal claims for all languages. His use of the word "template," although vague, suggests that he feels his study of four languages reveals something that might be necessary for, or built into, human perception generally. If this is his claim, it is not a strictly empirical approach, yet this kind of claim does have a fine pedigree. Immanuel Kant listed time and space as "synthetic a priori categories of the pure understanding," that is, necessary conditions in the human mind for any possible experience. And if Noam Chomsky is right that fundamental grammatical concepts are built into the human mind, it is at least plausible that conceptions of time and space—or here, more precisely, time *as* space—might be so as well.

In this chapter I will be working from examples in Chinese and English, noting both similarities and differences, and to this extent will be working empirically. There are demonstrable and interesting differences among conceptual metaphors in Chinese and English. There are also striking similarities. Where I find similarities, I will not be assuming that the overlap is mere chance. I will at least open the door to the kind of universal theorizing Kant and Chomsky have done and even an anthropologist like Alverson apparently allows.

How Do Metaphors Work in Ordinary Language?

The study of creative metaphor in the literary arts is a wonderful and endless field that no writer can encompass, and I will not try to. In this chapter I will look at the more restricted field of metaphor that pervades

---

4. Hoyt Alverson, *Semantics and Experience: Universal Metaphors of Time in English, Mandarin, Hindi, and Sesotho* (Baltimore: Johns Hopkins University Press, 1994), p. xii.

daily-life expression. Cognitive scientists sometimes call this "conceptual metaphor" or "structural metaphor." When a person is angry, we might say in English she is "all steamed up" or "hot under the collar"; similarly, in Chinese she *huor le* 火儿了, literally "is on fire," or *shengqi* 生气, literally "emits vapor." Speakers of Chinese or English understand the underlying metaphor, which in this case is similar in the two languages, that "anger is heat" or "anger is gas under pressure." Lakoff and Johnson, who pioneered this kind of inquiry in 1980 in *Metaphors We Live By*, explain the general human need for conceptual metaphor this way:

> Because so many of the concepts that are important to us are either abstract or not clearly delineated in our experience (the emotions, ideas, time, etc.), we need to get a grasp on them by means of other concepts that we understand in clearer terms (spatial orientations, objects, etc.).[5]

Lakoff and Johnson claim not only that "many" of our concepts are metaphorical but that "*most* of our normal conceptual scheme" is "metaphorically structured; that is, most concepts are partially understood in terms of other concepts."[6] This "structuring" involves a capture, in only one or a few abstract words, of highly complex processes whose literal and detailed exposition would require many, many more words. An example is monetary "inflation," which is not only a one-word summary of a complex phenomenon but something that, in our ordinary language, we speak of as a "thing," sometimes even a living thing. We say things like "inflation is killing us," "inflation shows up at the checkout counter," and so on. Lakoff and Johnson call the turning of something like inflation into a "thing" an "ontological metaphor."[7] They cite examples to show that even respectable natural scientists commonly use this kind of metaphor to make concepts easier to pass back and forth. They cite a 1997 issue of *Science* that contains these sentences, asking us to take note of the italicized words:

---

5. George Lakoff and Mark Johnson, *Metaphors We Live By* (Chicago: University of Chicago Press, 1980), p. 115.
6. Ibid., p. 56, emphasis added.
7. Ibid., p. 25–32.

Most of the neurons in that very early processing stage merely *report* what is happening on the retina. *To do its job*, however, this cortex *must cooperate with* connected sensory regions that hold and use the information for briefer periods of time.[8]

Could the scientists have described their findings without metaphorically imputing intentions to neurons? Yes, probably. But it would have taken much longer and been much more tedious. On the other hand, nothing seems to be lost by the shorthand of metaphor, so long as both reader and writer understand it correctly. Lakoff and Johnson argue that ordinary language has become so immersed in conceptual metaphor that it would be very hard to do without it even if we were to try. They write: "If we consciously make the enormous effort to separate out metaphorical from non-metaphorical thought, we probably can do some very minimal and unsophisticated nonmetaphorical reasoning. But almost no one ever does this."[9] The philosopher John Searle goes further, claiming that sometimes *only* metaphor can say exactly what a speaker wishes to say. "It is often the case," Searle writes, "that we use metaphor precisely because there is no literal expression that expresses exactly what we mean."[10]

How does daily-life metaphor work? Why can we say something like "the ship plows the sea"—something that, if taken literally, is patently false—yet have listeners not only understand us but think, "right, I see what you mean"? A brief detour into the field of metaphor theory in cognitive science will be useful here.

Although scholars vary in their terminology, the field consistently distinguishes (1) the thing described from (2) the nonliteral way it is described. "Sam is a pig," for example, singles out Sam and then tells us nonliterally, via "pig," something about him—that he is filthy, gluttonous, sloppy, or the like. In the professional literature, "Sam" in such a sentence is sometimes called the "defined concept" and piglike behavior the "defining concept"; alternatively, "Sam" is sometimes called a "topic" and piglike

---

8. Lakoff and Johnson, *Philosophy in the Flesh*, p. 217.
9. Ibid., p. 59.
10. John R. Searle, "Metaphor," in Andrew Ortony, ed., *Metaphor and Thought*, 2nd ed. (Cambridge: Cambridge University Press, 1993), p. 111.

behavior a "vehicle." The topic is sometimes said to fall within a "target domain" while piglike behavior is in a "source domain." (It is interesting that these bits of jargon—"target," "vehicle," and "domain"—are themselves metaphors, which the theorists themselves build easily and understand without much problem.) The field also uses the term "mapping" as if it were a metaphor—for example, "mapping" a source domain onto a target domain—but this usage often is not clear or rigorous.[11]

Metaphor theorists generally agree on the logical processes that a hearer or reader uses in order to interpret conceptual metaphor.[12] These processes happen quickly and often without being noticed by the interpreting mind, so what follows is meant not as a description of conscious experience but as an answer to the question I just posed: how does conceptual metaphor work? Step 1 is to recognize the literal meaning of a proposition and see if that makes sense. If I say "Sam is a bowler," you do not need—unless I offer you some kind of signal—to start asking yourself "what does he mean by *bowler?*" But if I say "Sam is a pig" (when Sam is, in fact, a human being), then my very statement gives you a signal to start casting about for metaphorical understandings. This "casting about" is step 2. Steps 1 and 2 need not come in order; research has found that people seem to process literal and available nonliteral interpretations simultaneously.

Step 3 is to choose among the likely possibilities that turn up after the casting about is done. These possibilities depend on custom and culture. In modern English, ". . . is a pig" conventionally offers such options as: messy, gluttonous, filthy, selfish. And how does the hearer choose among them? The choice depends on context, where "context" includes surmise

11. The function of a map is not analogical in the way that "Sam is a pig" is; literally, a map stands in relation to the ground it maps by (1) miniaturizing it, (2) marking certain features (roads, towns, whatever) that it wishes to highlight by using amplification, coloring, etc., and (3) eliminating all other features of the ground. This is hardly what is going on between "target" and "source," or "topic" and "vehicle," when metaphors are used. In mathematics there is a more rigorous definition of "mapping"—by which the elements in one set are assigned to elements in another—but this is not what metaphor theory is doing, either.

12. My description here is drawn primarily from Sam Glucksberg, *Understanding Figurative Language: From Metaphors to Idioms* (Oxford: Oxford University Press, 2001), pp. 8–11, and from Searle, "Metaphor," pp. 102–108.

about what is in the speaker's mind. If Sam never washes or makes his bed, and the speaker is his roommate, then "Sam is a pig" will likely be understood as "Sam is messy" or "Sam is filthy" (or both). If Sam ate the whole pumpkin pie and the speaker is someone else at the table who did not get any, then "Sam is a pig" will likely mean "Sam is a glutton" or "Sam is selfish." If the common cultural possibilities run out, then the hearer has to look further into the context and/or do further speculation about the speaker's mind. If Sam is, for example, neat, clean, anorexic, and self-effacing, and if someone nevertheless says, "Sam is a pig," it might be because Sam cheers for the Arkansas Razorbacks. It could also be because he is a Chinese born in 1971 or 1983. The hearer needs to cast around.

Obviously, too, the hearer must have a cooperative attitude toward the speaker's utterance. After hearing that "Sam is a pig" one could, if one chose to be difficult, logically infer any of literally hundreds of statements about Sam, including "Sam is a vertebrate," "Sam has bristles," and many other propositions that would not be, in most contexts, what the speaker had in mind. But people seldom do this—and when they do, they generally know they are mischievously "breaking the rules." The philosopher Paul Grice has noted the operation of a "cooperative principle" by which participants in conversation expect that each will make a "conversational contribution such as is required, at the stage at which it occurs, by the accepted purpose or direction of the talk exchange."[13] Grice's famous principle applies to the interpretation of metaphor. When Shakespeare says "Juliet is like the sun," no one is confused. We know that he means "Juliet is bright and warm," not "Juliet is for the most part gaseous" or "Juliet will incinerate you if you get too close"—even though the latter two are well-known facts about the sun.[14] Lakoff and Johnson, in noting this feature of metaphor, point out that the "defining concept" in metaphor always contains more stuff than is carried over to the "defined concept." The conceptual metaphor "ideas are food," for example, leads English speakers to speak of "raw facts" or "half-baked notions"—but, Lakoff and Johnson observe, this conventional metaphor does not normally

---

13. H. P. Grice, "Logic and Conversation," in Peter Cole and Jerry L. Morgan, eds., *Syntax and Semantics*, vol. 3, *Speech Acts* (New York: Academic Press, 1975), pp. 45.

14. See Searle, "Metaphor," p. 96.

lead to many other possibilities, such as "sautéed, broiled, or poached ideas."[15]

It is important to note that the implicit claims of metaphor do not have to be *true* for metaphor to work properly. "Richard is a gorilla" can mean—and be correctly understood to mean—that Richard is fierce and nasty, even if it is false that gorillas are fierce and nasty. If the speaker's meaning is that Richard is fierce and nasty, then, in order for the metaphor to work properly, it need only be true that both speaker and hearer are familiar with a cultural convention that views gorillas as fierce and nasty; the literal proposition does not have to be true, and it does not even have to be the case that speaker and hearer believe it to be true.[16] Consider the two statements "my daughter is an angel" and "my daughter is no angel." For any human being with a daughter, the first of these statements is literally false and the second is literally true. Moreover, in literal terms the two statements are contradictory, that is, in no possible world could both be true at the same time. But as metaphor, both statements *can* be true of the daughter (at different times), and both can be easily and correctly understood, provided that speaker and hearer are on the same wavelength ("cooperating," as Grice would say) about what "angel" and "no angel" entail.

The fact that a person needs context in order to interpret a metaphor has led some to suppose that this is what distinguishes metaphor (and other figurative speech) from literal expression. But the matter is not that simple. Searle has rightly observed that the interpretation of some kinds of literal expression also requires context.[17] "Mary is tall," for example, cannot be interpreted without reference—whether explicit or implicit—to the group of people with whom the speaker is comparing Mary. Is she a fourth-grader? A volleyball team member? "Tall" would refer to different heights in these two cases. Rigorously speaking, "Mary is tall" means "Mary is taller than most of the people within the reference group I have in mind." Searle is also very good at showing how metaphorical expression is only one example of nonliteral expression that obeys the same general set of rules that metaphor interpretation obeys. Irony, for example,

15. Lakoff and Johnson, *Metaphors We Live By*, p. 109.
16. Ibid., Searle, "Metaphor," pp. 92–93.
17. Ibid., pp. 85–86.

also asks the hearer to begin by ruling out the literal interpretation of an utterance; it then asks the hearer to accept an opposite meaning.[18] Here intonation can be a cue, as when you say "*Won*derful!" after I have knocked over and shattered your Ming vase. But often it is context alone that leads the hearer to interpret an ironic utterance correctly. Sometimes "speech acts" as well follow the same general rules. When I say "Can you pass the salt?" my hearer normally rules out the possibility that I mean to ask a question about your ability to pass salt. He or she instead just passes the salt—and in that, of course, reflects a correct understanding of the utterance.

The standard use of questions like "Can you pass the salt?" to mean "Please pass the salt" or "How are you?" to mean "Hello" has a counterpart in the often-noted phenomenon of the "dead metaphor." Most metaphor theorists allow that daily-life metaphors can and do die. After death they often remain useful, however, in much the same way literal words or phrases are useful. For example, if I say "Interstate 95 goes to Boston," the metaphor that suggests that the road itself "goes somewhere" is utterly dead. It is hardly different from the literal statement that "Interstate 95 is a road." The metaphor's deadness is so well established that any effort to bring it to life would seem perverse. If you say "Interstate 95 goes to Boston," and I say, "Nonsense, Interstate 95 just lies there on the ground," we both know that I am breaking rules that are so well established that we normally do not even notice them. Owen Barfield has pointed out that etymology, if pressed far enough, shows that nearly every word has roots that refer either to "a solid, sensible object, or some animal (probably human) activity," and that everything else, in a sense, is dead metaphor; for example *elasticity* has roots in 'draw' and *abstract* in 'drag'.[19]

Dead metaphors, we can assume, usually or always began as live ones. Lakoff and Johnson have written that conceptual metaphors often had "physical" or "experiential" bases in their beginnings. For example the ideas of "up" and "more"—as pure concepts—have no essential connection. Yet we commonly use the conceptual metaphors "more is up" and "less is down" to say things like "murders are up," "foreclosures are down," and so on.

---

18. Ibid., pp. 109.

19. Owen Barfield, *Poetic Diction: A Study in Meaning* (Middletown, Conn.: Wesleyan University Press, 1973), p. 64.

Lakoff and Johnson hypothesize that the "physical basis" for this usage is the simple fact that when you get more of something, and put it in the same place, a pile forms. Pile tops go up, so "more" becomes "up."[20] This theory gets support from the fact that many languages use the metaphor. In China, as elsewhere, things like pile tops and fluid levels go up when more of something is in one place, or in one container; accordingly, Chinese says things like *jiaqian gao* 价钱高 'the price is high' and *shuiping di* 水平低 'the level is low'. Such usages have been influenced by modern Western languages and so might not seem good evidence for the universality of the "physical basis" for "more is up." Other examples, though, make the point without ambiguity. In English we say "red in the face" to mean angry or agitated, and in Chinese say *mianhong erchi* 面红耳赤 'face red ears red' in quite the same way. Here there is no sign of borrowing; there is, though, a plausible common "physical basis" in the fact that for human beings in any language or culture, blood tends to rush to the face when one is angry or agitated.

An important characteristic of conceptual metaphor is that it is not just used in one or two phrases but can underlie a variety of related expressions. Lakoff and Johnson cite the example "love is a journey," which can underlie a variety of expressions: our relationship "is at a crossroads," "has hit a dead-end," "is spinning its wheels," or "has entered the fast lane" or "we are going in different directions," and so on.[21] Lakoff and Johnson might better have called this metaphor "a romantic relationship is a journey," not "love is a journey," since there are many kinds of love for which "journey" is harder to apply. ("I love chocolate ice cream," "God so loved the world . . ." etc.) But the point itself—that metaphorical expressions tend to come in families—is important. Not only do the various expressions associated with a conceptual metaphor tend to cohere; sometimes conceptual metaphors become strong enough that they can shape the way people absorb new experience as it arises. I have noted Lakoff and Johnson's identification of the English conceptual metaphor "consciousness is up and unconsciousness is down" according to which we *fall* asleep and

---

20. Lakoff and Johnson, *Metaphors We Live By*, p. 16.
21. Lakoff and Johnson, *Philosophy in the Flesh*, p. 123.

wake *up*, *sink* into a coma, and so on.[22] When such metaphors become established in a culture, they tend to shape understanding of new experience. When Freud began to speak of the less-than-conscious mind, for example, it was natural to speak of a "sub"-conscious." This kind of fact is what leads Lakoff and Johnson to claim that conceptual metaphors are "metaphors we live by." They also claim that strong, broad metaphors have a power to govern smaller clusters of others. For example, the broad metaphor "life is a journey" (e.g., "she got a head start in life," "he's never let anyone get in his way") can be seen as subsuming, and perhaps giving rise to, conceptual metaphors of smaller domain such as "love is a journey" ("We're in the fast lane," etc.) and "a career is a journey" ("He's on the fast track," etc.).[23]

Lakoff and Johnson have been criticized for claiming too much structuring power for conceptual metaphors. While it may be true that we often *conceive* things in terms of metaphor, can we go further, as Lakoff and Johnson do, to claim that "it structures the *actions* we perform"?[24] When I embark on a romantic relationship, do I actually behave differently because I am thinking in terms of "love is a journey"? A key question here has been whether established metaphors are "automatically accessed" or not. If, for example, an English speaker thinks of a romantic relationship, does "love is a journey" *always* kick in, or is it optional? Psychologists Sam Glucksberg and Matthew McGlone devised an experiment in which American college students were asked what "our love is a voyage to the bottom of the sea" or "our love is a bumpy roller-coaster ride" might mean. Here the verbal cues clearly set the stage for conceptions of the "love is a journey" sort. If conceptual metaphor is accessed automatically, one would expect the student responses to mention discovery, roads over rolling hills, "uncharted waters," "where we are headed," and other phrases consistent with "love is a journey." And a few of Glucksberg and McGlone's

---

22. Lakoff and Johnson, *Metaphors We Live By*, p. 15. Noted in the Introduction.

23. George Lakoff, "What Is a Conceptual System?," in Willis F. Overton and David S. Palermo, eds., *The Nature and Ontogensis of Meaning* (Hillsdale, N.J.: Erlbaum, 1994), p. 62.

24. Lakoff and Johnson, *Metaphors We Live By*, p. 4. Boaz Keysar, Yeshayahu Shen, Sam Glucksberg, and William S. Horton explicitly argue against this claim by Lakoff and Johnson in "Conventional Language: How Metaphorical Is It?," *Journal of Memory and Language* 43 (2000), p. 578.

responses were indeed of this type. But, significantly, most were not. Most students thought the given phrases meant "we don't talk enough," "we're drowning in each other's problems," "our love is exciting but not very stable," and other such things.[25] Experiments like this show that conceptual metaphors do have influences on the way we conceive things, but that they are not obligatory. They are more like arrows in a quiver—to be drawn on when useful, otherwise not.

Work by Boaz Keysar and others has found the interesting result that *very* conventional metaphors—or "dead" metaphors—have fewer connections to underlying concepts than fresh metaphors do. In the metaphor "happy is up, sad is down," for example, we have English examples like "she's feeling low," "I'm depressed," and so on. Similarly, in Chinese we have *gaoxing* 高兴 'high mood—happy' and *diluo* 低落 'low fall—downcast'. Keysar and his colleagues argue that a conventional phrase like "I'm depressed" normally is understood lexically, hardly different from how "I'm a professor" is understood. The hearer does not need to draw on the underlying concept of "sad is down" in order to understand. Similarly, a hearer would probably not need "happy is up" in order to understand "I'm on cloud nine" or "she's higher than a kite," because these familiar clichés are hardly different from ordinary words. But it is precisely when *new* expressions come along, Keysar argues, that conceptual metaphors are useful and perhaps even necessary if correct understanding is to result. In a case like "I'm feeling lower than a piece of gum stuck on the bottom of your boots," a hearer will likely need to draw on "sad is down" in order to make sense of the phrase.[26] Here again we see conceptual metaphors waiting in abeyance, as it were—ready to help when needed, but not demanding to be used.

What happens when two or more metaphors are used together? In literary matters "mixed metaphor" is supposed to be a mistake, largely for aesthetic reasons, but what happens when daily-life conceptual metaphors come together? Do they collide? Muddle the underlying concept? Or does it not matter?

---

25. Sam Glucksberg and Matthew S. McGlone, "When Love Is Not a Journey: What Metaphors Mean," *Journal of Pragmatics* 31, no. 12 (1999), p. 1547.

26. Keysar et al., "Conventional Language," p. 579.

Experiments in the psychology of metaphor have shown that hearers tend to prefer consistent metaphors. For example, to describe someone speaking and acting in anger, people prefer "she fumed and exploded" to "she fumed and growled." Even when different subjects are involved—thus allowing a bit more "space" in which to accommodate different metaphors, people still prefer "she fumed; he exploded" to "she fumed; he growled." But preferences aside, the same experiments show that the mixing of conceptual metaphors normally does not inhibit understanding or even slow down reading speed.[27] This result is further evidence that dead or frozen metaphor is processed in the mind more or less as ordinary words are. "Conceptual clash" appears not to be a problem.

These experiments were done in English. Does the point hold for Chinese as well? Although no experiments are available, I believe the point does hold. It is easy to find examples of clashing dead metaphors in Chinese, and such clash does not seem to cause any confusion among users. Ning Yu, an analyst of conceptual metaphor, cites the example *gaiguo shenghuo shuiping bi mouxie fada guojia luohou wushinian* 该国生活水平比某些发达国家落后五十年 'the living standard in this country is fifty years behind certain developed countries'.[28] Here are clashing metaphors: the development "water level" (*shuiping*) of a country "falls behind" (*luohou*) those of other countries. "Water level" implies vertical movement, because water levels go only up or down, not left or right; but "fall behind" normally implies horizontal movement left or right. (It is true that *luo*, literally "fall," can be conceived vertically, but when it fuses with *hou*, literally "behind," *luohou* is pretty clearly horizontal.) Do these clashing metaphors cause puzzlement that slows people down? I doubt it. It is more likely that the metaphors are simply accepted as lexical items.

The point also seems plain when one considers the ease with which Chinese speakers use different metaphors for a "next" or "last" time period. The day after tomorrow is *houtian* 後天 (literally "the behind day"), where the metaphor *hou* 'behind' implies a horizontal time line. Similarly

---

27. Glucksberg and McGlone, "When Love Is Not a Journey: What Metaphors Mean," pp. 1553–1554.

28. Ning Yu, *The Contemporary Theory of Metaphor: A Perspective from Chinese* (Amsterdam: Benjamins, 1998), p. 120.

qiantian 前天 'the day before yesterday', *qiannian* 前年 'the year before last' *hounian* 後年 'the year after next', and metaphors such as *guo qu le* 過去了 'has passed (away)' all imply a horizontal time line. On the other hand, for weeks and months, the implicit time line is vertical: *xia xingqi* 下星期 (literally 'the week below'), *shang ge yue* 上個月 ('the month above'), and so on. Do users of Chinese get confused or slowed down by having to "change conceptual schemes" every time they shift from days to weeks, or from months to years? The answer is so obviously no that an experiment almost seems a waste of time. In a sentence like *ta bushi shang ge yue lai de, shi qiannian lai de* 她不是上個月來的, 是前年來的 'she came the year before last, not last month', the metaphor shift will not even be noticed, let alone be troublesome. A statement like *shangge libai yijing guoqu le* 上個禮拜已經過去了 'last week has already passed' might seem irritating, but only because it is a worthless tautology, not because of the metaphor clash between *shang* (implying a vertical time) and *guo qu* (implying a horizontal one).

Edward Slingerland, who has used contemporary metaphor theory to study ancient Chinese thought, has concluded that "literal consistency is not something that we require of our metaphors."[29] Here Slingerland's "we" includes people living in pre-Qin China as well as today. He notes, for example, that in ancient Chinese—just as in modern English—the self can be metaphorically divided into two: a self that acts and a self that is acted on. In modern English we can say "I dragged myself out of bed" or "he lost control of himself," and Slingerland notes examples from *Zhuangzi*, including *zi shi* 自失 'lose oneself' and in particular the statement of Zi Qi of Southwall that *wu sang wo* 吾喪我, literally "I lose me," that seem to illustrate a similar metaphorical split between "subject" (the actor) and "self" (the acted-on).[30] Verbs in pre-Qin texts that metaphorically describe self-cultivation in terms of "following" nature (either one's own nature or a transcendent nature)—for example *cong* 從, *yin* 因, *yi* 依, and *shun* 順—all can be seen as implicitly assuming this distinction between subject and self. But another family of metaphors that conceive the self, which Slingerland calls the "at ease" group (*an* 安, *shu* 舒, *jing* 靜, *xi* 息, *xiu* 休, *you* 游, and others) implicitly assume a unitary self that admits

---

29. Edward Slingerland, *Effortless Action: Wu-wei as Conceptual Metaphor and Spirit Ideal in Early China* (Oxford: Oxford University Press, 2003), p. 36.

30. Ibid., p. 31.

no split between actor and acted-on.[31] How can we reconcile the two sets of metaphors? Slingerland argues that we do not have to, and indeed that it would be a mistake to demand that we try. It is a mistake because underlying human nature (in ancient China no less than today) is complex enough to be difficult to capture from a single point of view. Differing metaphors illuminate different facets of it, but none is or can be comprehensive, hence there is no requirement that every useful metaphor should fit with every other.

We are left with a theory of conceptual metaphor in which metaphorical expressions are useful to our thinking and communicating but only as assistants, as it were, in getting at one or another aspect of complex topics. There is no contradiction between using metaphors that clash and holding that a full view of complex issues can be coherent and internally consistent. As long as metaphors get their particular jobs done, it is not terribly important whether they fit together, clash, or are mutually irrelevant. None by itself can or should be viewed as reflecting a unified worldview.

Sometimes one conceptual metaphor piggybacks on a second and, as it were, invades its territory. But here, too, pragmatism seems to trump purity: if the result works, no one minds. Consider the sportscaster who comments before a basketball game that "Georgia Tech will have to keep the game in the sixties; anything north of that and they're in big trouble."[32] He means that the Georgia Tech players are specialists in defense and will need to keep the score low in order to exploit their comparative advantage. He combines the well-established conceptual metaphor "more is up" with the modern cartographical convention "up is north" to yield the piggybacked metaphor "more is north." Another sportscaster—this one commenting on the U.S. Open tennis tournament in September 2005—observed that "men north of thirty," who were beyond their prime, would have a tougher time competing. Hearers of such phrases are not startled into asking themselves "Hey, how do I put this conceptual clash into a coherent worldview?" The metaphor serves its purpose, and that is enough.

---

31. Ibid., pp. 29–30.
32. Christopher Russo on *Mike and the Mad Dog*, WFAN radio, April 5, 2004, 7:32 P.M.

But if conceptual metaphor behaves this way, if it can do flips and twists in the service of underlying ideas, are the cognitive scientists who claim that "conceptual metaphor" sometimes shapes our thinking therefore wrong? Not necessarily. It can remain true in some cases that our habits in metaphor guide the ways we think. At a minimum, we can make the empirical observation that metaphorical expressions in human languages do tend to occur in internally consistent families such as (for modern English) "consciousness is up, unconsciousness is down," "more is up, less is down," "a romantic relationship is a journey," and others. Given that these family resemblances among metaphors do exist, it is reasonable to infer that the resemblances are not accidental but must have some cause. But then we should ask: which way does the causality go? Is there something about the commonality of human experience—or perhaps the structure of the human mind—that causes metaphors to bunch in consistent families? Or do the bunchings themselves take over the ways we think and give rise to their own consistency? (Or both?) There have been scientific experiments in this area; there are also some unsettled controversies. We turn to some of them next.

Metaphor and Thought

Lakoff and Johnson hold a strong position on the relation between metaphor and thought. The back cover of the paperback edition of *Metaphors We Live By* claims that "reality itself is defined by metaphor, and as metaphors vary from culture to culture, so do the realities they define." The authors' claim for metaphor can be viewed as a particular instance of what Benjamin Whorf claimed in 1939 for language in general—to paraphrase the famous "Sapir-Whorf hypothesis," that the language a person speaks affects the way he or she thinks. Whorf has drawn much criticism from later cognitive scientists, in part because his reasoning can seem circular. As satirized by Steven Pinker, for example, Whorf claims that "[Eskimos] speak differently so they must think differently. How do we know that they think differently? Just listen to the way they speak!"[33] Pinker holds—

---

33. Steven Pinker, *The Language Instinct* (New York: Morrow, 1994), p. 61.

and others, including Noam Chomsky and Jerry Fodor, hold similar positions—that at least some human thinking, including the fundaments of grammar, is built into the human mind, therefore universal, and therefore not subject to cultural variance.[34]

There are two different kinds of arguments in the field for why "concepts," including metaphorical concepts, sometimes appear to be universal. The Pinker-Chomsky-Fodor kind of argument about the structure of the mind is one; Lakoff, Johnson, and others espouse a different sort of argument, which is that the physical experience of human beings—which after all shares a great deal in common, no matter where or in what culture one lives—naturally induces the same kinds of metaphors in any language. Studies have shown, for example, that heart rate and body temperature both tend to rise when people feel anger, or even when they are asked only to imagine anger or to simulate it in their bodily movements.[35] If this is true, then it is not surprising that "hot with anger" occurs in English and *huor le* 火儿了 'on fire—angry' is used in Chinese. Environmental commonalities can have the same effect. "More is up" is a natural inference to draw in any context where physical objects and gravitational force are both present.

It is unfortunate that Lakoff and Johnson often use the word *embody* to refer to the relation they find between physical experience and conceptual metaphor, because this use of the word clashes with the normal sense of it. When Lakoff and Johnson write that "the mind is inherently embodied"[36] they mean that it is "shaped by the body's experience." But in common use (as well as in dictionaries), *embody* means "put into a body" or "give a material or concrete character or form to."[37] Lakoff and Johnson's

---

34. Noam Chomsky, *Reflections on Language* (New York: Pantheon, 1975); Jerry Fodor, *The Language of Thought* (Cambridge, Mass.: Harvard University Press, 1975).

35. Paul Ekman, Robert W. Levenson, and Wallace V. Friesen, "Autonomic Nervous System Activity Distinguishes among Emotions," *Science* 221, no. 4616 (September 16, 1983), pp. 1208–1210.

36. Lakoff and Johnson, *Philosophy in the Flesh*, p. 5.

37. Definitions from *The Shorter Oxford Dictionary on Historical Principles* (Oxford: Clarendon Press, 1933), 1:598. The phrase "the embodied mind," in terms of these dictionary definitions, would have to mean something physical, like "the brain," or at least something metaphorically substantive, like Immanuel Kant's *Critique of Pure Reason*. But a reader who conscientiously follows Lakoff and Johnson's usages in this direction will find that the pursuit is futile.

idiosyncratic usage thus might cause confusion where there needn't have been any, but this should not obscure the value of their basic claim, which is that one important reason why human beings sometimes think and speak similarly is that they all have bodies.

Lakoff and Johnson's kind of reason for conceptual commonality differs from that of Pinker, Chomsky, and others, in that it is based in experience. This means that at least in theory, concepts that are held in common might vary from context to context. Gravity varies from place to place only by minuscule amounts, and bodily responses to anger might be the same everywhere; but in other aspects of living, cultural as well as physical, there can be significant differences, and metaphors might therefore be different. When Lakoff and Johnson postulate that both metaphors and thought patterns vary from culture to culture, they implicitly raise the "Whorf" question: Do different languages induce different ways of thinking?

Psychological experiments in the early twenty-first century have lent new credibility to at least some parts of the Whorf hypothesis. Lera Boroditsky, who sets aside the "strong Whorfian view" that "thought [is] entirely determined by language," nevertheless defends a weaker version according to which "frequently invoked mappings may become habits of thought."[38] For example, Boroditsky notes—correctly—that Chinese uses a "future is down" metaphor more often than English does; she then tests in several ways the hypotheses that Chinese speakers tend to think vertically about time more easily than English speakers do and that English speakers tend to think horizontally about time more easily than Chinese speakers do. She does this by presenting vertical and horizontal cues (a fish apparently in motion is a horizontal cue, for example) and then tests to see how quickly native speakers of the two languages can confirm that March precedes April (where "precedes" moves either horizontally or vertically, depending on language habits). As hypothesized, Chinese speak-

---

38. Lera Boroditsky, "Does Language Shape Thought? Mandarin and English Speakers' Conceptions of Time," *Cognitive Psychology* 43 (2001), pp. 2 and 7. Lakoff, the senior figure in the group that holds this view, sometimes carries it so far that he undermines his credibility. See Lakoff, "Staying the Course Right over a Cliff," op-ed, *New York Times*, October 27, 2006, p. A19.

ers in her experiments performed better after seeing a vertical display, and English speakers did better after seeing a horizontal display. The results suggest that in matters of time, Chinese speakers were "ready to think" vertically more easily than English speakers, who were more "ready to think" horizontally.[39] In a related experiment, Boroditsky found that English speakers did better with vertical thinking about time after practicing imaginary English examples of it—such as "Nixon was president *above* Clinton."[40] She concludes that "language is a powerful tool in shaping thought about abstract domains."[41]

Boroditsky has been challenged by Jenn-yeu Chen, who did not get the same results from the same experiments. Chen also correctly points out that the differences between Chinese and English in the use of "horizontal" versus "vertical" time lines are only a matter of degree and that, in fact, horizontally conceived usages in Chinese outnumber vertically conceived usages by about five to three.[42] Chen's challenge to Boroditsky casts considerable doubt on the claim that Chinese speakers really do have a penchant for vertical conception of time. But Chen does not undermine, indeed seems to accept, the larger claim that languages tend to "shape thought about abstract domains."

One important objection to the work of both Boroditsky and Chen could be the one I attributed above to Pinker: that the reasoning seems circular—one claims that language shapes thought, but the evidence for the shaped thought is the very language that does the shaping.[43] In an apparent effort to skirt this objection, Boroditsky and nine colleagues devised some clever ways to test how people think of time in terms of

---

39. The Chinese speakers had to overcome a flaw in Boroditsky's experiment design. Her vertically arrayed fish are moving up, but Chinese time—when it does move vertically—moves down. Hence for Chinese speakers in the experiment, the preference for verticality in general had to be stronger than the preference for direction within the verticality.

40. Boroditsky, pp. 17–18.

41. Ibid., p. 1.

42. Jenn-yeu Chen, "Do Chinese and English Speakers Think about Time Differently? Failure of Replicating Boroditsky (2001)," *Cognition* 104 (2007), pp. 429–430.

43. Boroditsky's data are "response times," which themselves are not verbal, but they are triggered by verbal cues.

space *without* using language—by using only spatial images on a computer monitor.[44]

These experiments by Boroditsky and her colleagues study speakers of English, Indonesian, Greek, and Spanish. The researchers begin by showing that all four languages use both *length* and *volume* as spatial metaphors for time, for example, in English, a "I waited a *long* time" or "the meeting took *much* time." They then show that in daily-life language, English and Indonesian tend to use the length metaphor much more often than the volume metaphor, while Greek and Spanish use the volume metaphor much more often than the length metaphor. They then pose the question whether these different habits in language use might induce different habits of thought, including thought that is *not* expressed in language. They showed subjects a line that grows in length across a computer monitor; then they showed more such lines that grow at different speeds and extend to different lengths. Subjects used the click of a mouse (not language) to indicate which lines were longer in length and which took longer in time to complete. No one had much trouble identifying which lines were longer in length. But for the metaphorical question of which lines took "longer" in time, the physical length of lines was shown to interfere with people's judgment. People thought that a longer line "took longer" in time to complete than a shorter line, even if the time duration of the two lines was the same; similarly, they thought that physically shorter lines lasted less time than lengthier ones even when this was not the case. They continued to make these mistakes even after being apprised of the trickiness of the stimuli. So here was evidence that a mental habit that apparently originated in metaphor was indeed affecting the way people think, even before anything was expressed in language.

Speakers of all four of the languages involved seemed to be influenced by the metaphorical habits of their own languages. When presented with

---

44. Daniel Casasanto, Lera Boroditsky, Webb Phillips, Jesse Greene, Shima Goswami, Simon Bocanegra-Thiel, Ilia Santiago-Diaz, Olga Fotokopoulu, Ria Pita, and David Gil, "How Deep Are Effects of Language on Thought? Time Estimation in Speakers of English, Indonesian, Greek, and Spanish," *Proceedings of the 26th Annual Conference of the Cognitive Science Society* (Hillsdale, N.J.: Erlbaum, 2004), pp. 575–580.

lines across a screen, speakers of English and Indonesian, in which "time is length" metaphors are common, had much more trouble than did speakers of Greek and Spanish, where "time is length" is less common. The mental habit of "time is length" was evidently more deeply ingrained for English and Indonesian speakers. But Boroditsky and her colleagues did another experiment where, instead of presenting growing lines to represent "more time," they presented containers being filled; these "filled up" to different degrees and at different speeds in a manner that was parallel to the "growing lines" of the first experiment. Now the results reversed: Greek and Spanish speakers experienced more "interference" from irrelevant cues than did English or Indonesian speakers. For Greek and Spanish speakers, the mental habit of "time is volume" appeared to be more deeply ingrained.

Although this work by Boroditsky and her colleagues is impressive evidence for one side in the debate over Whorf, in one respect it also tends to confirm the other side, even though they do not say so. By showing that native speakers of four languages have conceptual habits that correspond to the "time is space" metaphors that are characteristic of their languages, the work of Boroditsky and her colleagues tends to confirm Whorf. But by showing, for all four languages, that spatial metaphors interfere with judgments about time *but not vice versa*, the work tends to confirm the views of Chomsky, Pinker, and others who claim that there are conceptual structures in the mind that no language or culture can affect. Boroditsky and her colleagues observe that although their subjects were sometimes confused when physically longer and shorter lines took an equally "long" time, "line duration did not affect subjects' distance estimates."[45] The length of a line was easy to conceive regardless of how much time elapsed in completing it, but the reverse was not the case: the time a line took to grow was not easy to conceive as length varied. The authors call this an "asymmetric relation between space and time," and it deserves more careful thought. What exactly is this asymmetry? Might it be something that is "given" in the human mind? Lakoff and Johnson, Boroditsky, and many others have observed that in general, human languages conceive

---

45. Ibid., p. 577.

time using spatial metaphors.[46] Why don't we conceive space using temporal metaphors? Can such a thing even be done? Will the structure of the mind allow it? I doubt it. Here the "innate-structure" notions of Pinker, Chomsky, Kant, and others seem vindicated.

One kind of example of "space in terms of time" is easy to observe: we all say things like "the library is just five minutes from here" or "Philadelphia is an hour away." But these are only ways of *measuring* distance in terms of the assumed average speed of certain vehicles, in these two cases, our legs or our automobiles. Measuring can be done a number of other ways, for example in money. Farmers in rural Guangdong use money to measure distance. *Hin-gong yat ho mm (Xian'gang yi-hao wu)* 蚬岗一毫五 'Xian'gang is fifteen cents (in bus fare) from here'; *Fat-san gaw-yee (Foshan ge er)* 佛山个二 'Foshan is 1.20 yuan away'. But these ways of measuring—by vehicle speed, vehicle fare, or whatever—are matters quite different from the question of *conceiving* space as time. In order to do that conceiving, we would have to be able to make sense of phrases that somehow do the inverse of what phrases like "a long time" do. Can we? Let's try by substituting "space" for "time" in that phrase, and then try to substitute a modifier that corresponds to "long" but refers to time. It is hard to think of such a modifier, and it is worth reflecting on why this is so hard. Will "ancient" or "eternal" work, perhaps? Can we conceive an "ancient space" or "eternal space" in a way that delivers the notion of "a very large space" just as easily as "a long time" delivers the notion of a very large time? We normally do not do such things, and it is far from clear that we *can* do them. What, to ask a parallel question, would be the time-for-space analogue of "a short time"? Can we conceive "a brief space"? To the extent that our minds do make sense of phrases such as "an ancient space" or "a brief space," I still do not feel that we are conceiving space in terms of time, but are probably doing smaller, more poetic things. "An ancient space" feels as if it might mean something like "a musty crypt with Dead Sea scrolls stacked in a corner." And "eternal space" still summons the idea

---

46. Lakoff and Johnson, *Philosophy in the Flesh*, p. 139; Boroditsky, "Does Language Shape Thought," p. 4; Ning Yu, *Contemporary Theory of Metaphor*, p. 84. Ning Yu suggests that the commonality may have an experiential basis simply because objects in space can be pointed to, whereas objects in time cannot be.

of a long-lasting space, not necessarily an endlessly expansive one. It is true that in real life we do use phrases like "a two-hour space," but note that here we are not conceiving space in terms of time but reverting—once again—to the "time is space" metaphor to which our minds are well accustomed. "A two-hour space" likely refers to a block of *time* on a chart. In short, it may be no accident that human languages the world over conceive time in terms of space but not space in terms of time. There is something about the structure of the human mind that makes this so.

But if that is so, then both sides in the Whorfian debate have part of the truth. Does one language lead its speakers to think differently from the ways speakers of other languages think? Yes, for some concepts. But does the structure of the human mind condition and limit the ways any person thinks, regardless of language or culture? Also yes. It is not contradictory to hold both positions.

In the remainder of this chapter, I will not be concerned with trying to winnow evidence in search of the borderlines between the two basic positions on Whorf but will look primarily at the side on which Whorf is right, that is, I will be interested in showing how two different languages, Chinese and English, correspond to different ways of conceiving things. The exercise is especially useful for languages that differ considerably, as do Chinese and English. To compare neighboring languages, like French and English, is not as mind-stretching. I have noted in the Introduction that when Lakoff and Johnson's *Metaphors We Live By* was translated into French, most of their examples went into French easily. For example, when the authors point out the metaphor "causation is emergence" and give examples like "He shot the mayor *out of* desperation" and "He dropped *from* exhaustion," these became French easily as "De désespoir, il a tué le maire" and "It est tombé d'épuisement."[47] But, for complex reasons—some of which I will address below—the "causation is emergence" metaphor is not available in Chinese. The translator's task would be much more difficult in producing a Chinese version of Lakoff and Johnson's book. The work would involve not only a wider search for examples but, more often

---

47. George Lakoff and Mark Johnson, *Les métaphores dans la vie quotidienne* (Paris: Editions de Minuit, 1986), trans. Michel de Fornel Jean-Jacques Lecercle, ch. 14, "La causalité: En partie émergente et en partie métaphorique."

than for French, some fundamental rethinking of the theory that generates them. The Chinese language sometimes structures things very differently, and the differences are interesting. On the other hand, similarities can be interesting as well. In a world where cultural differences are sometimes assumed to be great or even daunting, it can be refreshing to note cases where human beings *do* think alike, even when, using the same basic cranial equipment, they do not need to.

Time

Although it is universal, or at least nearly so, that human languages use space as a metaphor for time, this metaphor can work in a variety of ways, even within a single language. Events in time can be ordered either horizontally or vertically (conceivably, of course, they could be ordered on other axes), can "move" either toward or away from "us" at the conceptual center. They can unfold either "in front of" you (where your face defines your front) or behind you. It is noteworthy that in Chinese and English (and in many other languages) events in time are arranged in one-dimensional space. The human mind easily conceives three dimensions of space—and, as we have seen, sometimes uses two dimensions, or three, in describing amounts of time. But we seem uniformly to adopt only one—a "line"—when dealing with the order of events in time. We do not use a sheet or a block for this purpose—and it is not clear that we could do so even if we wanted. The "time lines" humans invent are not strictly one-dimensional, rigorously speaking. They are conceptually "fat" enough to carry an event with them, as when we say "Christmas is coming," and also are fat enough to accommodate simultaneity, as when we say *fu wu shuang zhi* 福無雙至 'blessings don't arrive in pairs'. Still, they remain basically lines.

By the early twenty-first century, scholars had pretty well figured out the time lines of Chinese and English. Both languages use two different kinds of horizontal time line plus a vertical time line, and in both languages these three time lines can work together as "mixed metaphors" without confusing people. Moreover, the three time lines are conceptually very similar in the two languages. It is true that modern Chinese has been influenced by Western languages, but the fundamental congruity between Chinese and English time lines is something that well predates that influence. Graham Peck's romantic notion that "two kinds of time" undergird radically different worldviews has been thoroughly "deconstructed."

The only significant difference between time lines in Chinese and English lies not in their conceptualization but in the relative frequency of their use. Vertical metaphors of "past is up, future is down" are common in Chinese: *shang ge yue* 上個月 'last month', *shuo xia qu* 說下去 'keep on talking', *cong tou lai* 從頭來 'start from the head [i.e., beginning]', and so on. Jenn-yeu Chen, using searches of Yahoo and Google Chinese news as data for a study published in 2007, found that 36 percent of the time metaphors in these sources were vertical.[48] Chen did not gather parallel data for English, but no English speaker will doubt that "past is up, future is down" metaphors are used much less than 36 percent of the time in English. Indeed, they are rare enough that one needs to reflect in order to realize that they exist at all. We refer in English to "high antiquity" and to "descendants" from earlier generations, and we call clothes given to younger siblings "hand-me-downs." But there are not many such examples. Amanda Scott counted eleven instances of *shang* 'up' or *xia* 'down' as temporal metaphors within a twenty-five-page 1987 Chinese drama script; she could find no instances of "past is up, future is down" within a ninety-five-page 1972 English drama script.[49]

To say that Chinese and English are alike in their metaphorical conceptions of time is not to say that the patterns are easy to see. On the contrary, they present some difficult puzzles. But it is significant that the puzzles themselves are very similar in the two languages. In the Introduction I noted the oddity of a phrase like *houdai de qiantu* 後代的前途, which could be translated as "the future path of future generations" even though the first "future" in this phrase reflects the word *hou* 'behind' and the second reflects *qian* 'in front of'. The oddity that attends such a phrase is not just its contradictory metaphors but the fact that the phrase is quite

---

48. Jenn-yeu Chen, "Do Chinese and English Speakers Think about Time Differently?," pp. 429–430.

49. Amanda Scott, "The Vertical Dimension and Time in Mandarin," *Australian Journal of Linguistics* 9 (1989), p. 308.

clear and unremarkable to people who use it. It does not give its users any sense of contradiction or confusion.

All by itself, the single syllable *qian* 'in front of' can illustrate the problem of a radical ambiguity that somehow leads to no confusion in understanding: *qiancheng* 前程 is "the road ahead," and *qianchen* 前塵 is "the dust of the past." Moreover, *chen* and *cheng* are both second-tone, so only that little *-g* makes all the difference, orally, between past and future.[50] Ning Yu, whose book *The Contemporary Theory of Metaphor: A Perspective from Chinese* provides the most systematic account we have of time metaphors in modern Chinese, notes a similar puzzle: *guoqu de shiwu nian li* 过去的十五年里 'in the past fifteen years' and *shiwu nian lai* 十五年来 'for the past fifteen years' both refer to the same fifteen-year time span, that is, the span that began fifteen years ago and ends now, even though one expression says the years are "gone" (*qu*) and the other suggests that we have (or someone has) been "coming" (*lai*) through them.[51]

In Ning Yu's analysis, the horizontal conception of time in Chinese has two fundamentally different modes, which he calls case 1 and case 2. (The vertical conception of time movement is a third and separate matter.) In horizontal case 1, events in time form a linear sequence that moves out of the future and toward "us" (speaker, listener, etc.) and then passes us as it heads into the past. Yu uses a sketch of a passing railroad train to illustrate case 1.[52] This conception of time in Chinese well preceded the advent of railroads, so the illustration is anachronistic; but conceptually it is very apt. Case 1 can explain the phrase *guoqu de shiwu nian li*, because the fifteen years in question are the ones that have just gone by us and are now heading into the past. The general term *guoqu* 'in the past', without any time period attached, is also governed by case 1. Terms meaning "the future," like *weilai* 未来 (literally "the not-yet-come") or *jianglai* 将来 (literally "the will come") obey case 1 as well, because *weilai* or *jianglai* are, as it were, the cars near the end of the train that are still on their way toward us. Case 1 can also explain why *houtian* 后天, literally "the behind day,"

---

50. More amazingly still, people who live along the Yangzi River, from Jiangsu to Sichuan, speak dialects that drop even the *-g*, or sometimes add it when it should not be there. Yet life goes on.

51. Ning Yu, *Contemporary Theory of Metaphor*, p. 106.

52. Ibid., p. 107.

means "the day after tomorrow"; this is because *mingtian* 明天 'tomorrow' has not yet arrived, and *houtian* is that day waiting "behind" *mingtian*, one day further from us in the line of arriving days. Similarly, *qiantian* 前天 'the day before yesterday' is that day out there "in front of" yesterday in the train of events that is headed into the past. The general terms *yiqian* 以前 'in the past' and *yihou* 以后 'in the future' are also governed by case 1.

When we recall things in Chinese, we can *zhuixiang* 追想 or *zhuinian* 追念, literally "chase after" thoughts or ideas. In reminiscing, we *zhuiyi* 追忆 'pursue memories'. Ning Yu points out that this mental "pursuit" of things that have passed us by is also based on a case 1 understanding of time.[53] We look into the past and "catch up" with events that have already gone past us. The same concept explains why *zuxian* 祖先, literally 'clan firsts', means "ancestors," and *qianbei* 前辈 'the in-front generation' means the elder generation. These are the people who were out in front on the train of events.

This case 1 conception of time is used in English as well, where we speak of "forebears" using the same metaphor as *zuxian* in Chinese, and say "Christmas is coming" with the same metaphor of "the future is coming" that *weilai* uses. Chinese and English also share the notion that arriving events can have impacts on people. In English we say "Christmas brought great joy" (or maybe "brought a lot of family squabbles") just as in Chinese we can say *chuntian dai gei le renmen wuxian meihao de xiwang* 春天带给了人们无限美好的希望 'spring has brought people unboundedly beautiful hopes' (the example is from Ning Yu).[54] With this kind of example in mind, Ning Yu claims that there is a "time is a changer" metaphor, but this is a mistake that confuses *time* with *events in time*.[55] After all, it is spring, not time, that causes the hopes; and certain *events* at Christmas, not

---

53. Ibid., p. 102.
54. Ibid., p. 114.
55. Ibid., p. 117. Yu appears to have misunderstood George Lakoff and Mark Johnson, who observe in their *More Than Cool Reason: A Field Guide to Poetic Metaphor* (Chicago: University of Chicago Press, 1989, p. 40) that "because changes occur as time passes, it is possible to personify time itself as being the agent of change." We say, for example, that "the passage of time brought wrinkles to the old man's face" as a shortcut for saying that events that occurred during the time that passed are what brought the wrinkles.

time itself, cause the joys or the headaches. Yu is similarly imprecise when he labels his case 1 "time as a moving object."[56] The things that move in case 1 are events in time, not time itself. But this minor imprecision does not affect the basic soundness of Yu's analysis of case 1.

Case 2 describes time in a fundamentally different way. Here we are looking toward the future, as in *qiancheng* 前程 'road ahead', *qiantu* 前途 'path ahead', *qianjing* 前景 'scene ahead', or, in more classical style, *zhanwang* 瞻望 'looking forward'. Past events lie behind our backs, out of view unless we turn around, which we do when we *huigu* 回顾 'turn around and look' or *huishou* 回首 'turn [our] heads'. In case 2, we can be stationary, but need not be. We can *zou xiang xin shiji* 走向新世纪 'march toward the new century' and if we really get excited can do something like *ben xiang canlan de mingtian* 奔向灿烂的明天 'gallop toward a brilliant tomorrow'.[57] Similarly, when we turn around to look at the past (*huigu* or *huishou*), we might not just look but actually "go backward," *wang hui zou* 往回走, into the past.

One key difference between cases 1 and 2 is that in case 1 it does not matter which way we are facing but in case 2 it does. *Qian* and *hou* in case 1 are defined by the order of the train of events that is passing by us, not by which direction we are looking. We could be mere points, without eyes or noses at all, and words like *qiantian* 'the day before yesterday' and *houtian* 'the day after tomorrow' would still make perfect sense. But in case 2 it is crucial which way we are facing, that is, where our eyes and nose are pointing. If we were mere points, a phrase like *qianjing* 'scene ahead' or *xiang qian kan* 向前看 'look forward' would be uninterpretable, and turning around to *huigu*, look at the past, would be equally so.

There are difficult examples of case 2, in both Chinese and English, where we speak as if time or something that measures time were moving with us in the same direction, sometimes as a competitor. We can say in English that we are "in a race with time" or that we need to "beat the clock," or in Chinese that *shijian budeng ren* 时间不等人 'time does not wait for people' or *women bixu genshang shidai de bufa* 我们必须跟上时代的

---

56. Ning Yu, *Contemporary Theory of Metaphor*, p. 105.
57. Example from ibid., p. 119.

步伐 'we must catch up with the pace of the times'.[58] It can seem in such phrases that "time itself" is moving and therefore that there must be some kind of variant of case 2. But I think not. In such phrases the word "time," I believe, is always some kind of metonym (abbreviation) for other more understandable and temporally bounded things. In *shijian budeng ren*, for example, *shijian* could mean a deadline to accomplish some task, or the aging process that affects everyone all of the time, or something like that. Similarly, *shidai de bufa* does not imply that "time itself" is pacing forward (what *could* such a phrase mean?) but that some process within time—the spread of the Internet, the advance of human freedom, or whatever—is going forward and needs to be kept up with. Ever since social Darwinism entered Chinese thinking in the late Qing years, and especially after Marxism came in a few years later, the notion that history "moves forward" has tended to imply change for the better, or "advance." If someone "cannot keep up with the times" (*genbushang shidai* 跟不上时代), it is clearly the times—not the things that lag behind them—that are to be preferred. *Women yao shizhong zou zai shidai de qianmian* 我们要始终走在时代的前面 'we want always to walk at the forefront of the times' suggests a quest to be the best, not merely the newest.[59]

The case 1 and case 2 analyses of horizontal time lines in Chinese are clear and consistent. The reasons why puzzles can arise have to do, usually, with "interference" between the cases. If, following case 2, we look forward (*xiang qian kan*) toward the future, it can somehow feel awkward, or downright wrong, that one of the future days we are looking at is, according to case 1, *houtian* or the "behind day." But the two concepts themselves are clear; only their combination is awkward. And it is worth stressing again that ordinary people in ordinary life are not bothered by such puzzles; only people who try to think systematically about language are. Graham Peck was a very intelligent man, and it is understandable that his thinking about time got tangled. Even Ning Yu, inventor of the terms "case 1" and "case 2" that I have been using here, occasionally shows slippage between his concepts of the two cases. For example, he summarizes

---

58. These examples are from ibid., pp. 125 and 127.
59. Examples from ibid., p. 128.

case 1 by writing that "times are moving objects, with their fronts toward the face of the Observer."[60] Here we must understand "times" to mean not "time itself" (which would make the statement uninterpretable) but "events in time," whether large or small—such as Christmas, next Saturday, the Tang dynasty, or whatever. Yu's "slippage" occurs because, as we have seen, case 1 usages are indifferent to the direction the observer faces; it is case 2 that wants the observer facing this way or that. But here, in speaking of case 1, Yu asks that the fronts of events be "toward the face of the Observer." In another sign of slippage, Yu speaks of events themselves as having fronts or backs: "their fronts" point toward the observer, he writes. But what can that mean? When a human head has a "front," or a store has a "front," it is because of distinctive features on one side of the thing. What could it mean for Christmas or the Tang dynasty to have a "front"? For Christmas it might mean the first few hours of the day, and for the Tang it could mean the first few years or decades of the dynasty. But if that is all "front" means, then it is tautological to say "the front comes first." Moreover, as soon as the "front" passes the observer and goes into the past, it no longer points toward the observer. Ning Yu's sentence should have said something like this: "events in time are objects that move from the future toward the observer, reach the observer, and then move away from the observer into the past." At least part of the inaccuracy in Yu's original sentence seems attributable to interference from case 2.

If case 1 and case 2 are kept analytically clear and are applied to the "puzzles" that I originally noted in this discussion, the mysteries about them pretty much dissolve. In *houdai de qiantu* 'the future path of future generations', the *hou* in *houdai* is a case 1 metaphor, and the *qian* in *qiantu* a case 2 metaphor. Only linguists, not ordinary people, worry about the effects of putting them into a single phrase. Similarly, *qianchen* 'the dust of the past' is a case 1 example, and *qiancheng* 'the road ahead' a case 2 example. *Guoqu de shiwu nian li* 'in the past fifteen years' is a case 1 example and *shiwu nian lai* 'for fifteen years' a case 2 example. A cliché like *huishou qianchen* 回首前尘, literally "turn the head to look back at earlier dust," switches from case 2 to case 1 exactly in its middle. *Gu qian bugu hou* 顾前不顾后 is an intriguing case. Because *qian* and *hou* are standard opposites,

---

60. Ibid., p. 117.

it seems easy to analyze the phrase as "looking one way but not the other," but this interpretation does not square with its standard meaning (confirmed by dictionaries) of "forging ahead without considering the consequences."[61] In *gu qian bugu hou* we look toward the future, but those "consequences" (*houguo*, here abbreviated to *hou*) are also out there in the future. No "looking in different directions" happens. Like *huishou qianchen*, the phrase "switches modes" in midstream. *Gu qian* is case 2, looking forward; *bugu hou* is case 1, failing to look at the *houguo* that are coming down the pike. This kind of combining of case 1 and case 2 time metaphors is common in English and other languages as well.[62]

We might ask in passing whether horizontal time lines in Chinese conceive the past on the left and the future on the right or the other way around. There is nothing intrinsic to terms like *qian* and *hou* that would tilt the balance either way on this question. In theory a horizontal line could go either way, or indeed on any axis within a horizontal plane. The drawings in Ning Yu's book, as well as the time lines in standard Chinese language textbooks, put the past on the left and the future on the right.[63] This direction accords with left-to-right writing across the page in European languages. It seems, too, to accord with a larger left-to-right bias in modern English-speaking cultures, or at least American culture. Of the thirty-two teams of the National Football League, twenty have logos with a left-to-right orientation (i.e., with the panther, the raven, or whatever

---

61. From Beijing waiguoyudaxue yingyuxi cidianzu, *A Chinese-English Dictionary* (Beijing: Foreign Language Teaching and Research Press, 1995), p. 350. I have substituted "forge ahead" for "drive ahead" in the dictionary's rendition.

62. Lakoff calls the phenomenon "simultaneous mappings." George Lakoff, "The Contemporary Theory of Metaphor," in Ortony, *Metaphor and Thought*, pp. 218–219. Although correctly noting the existence of the phenomenon, Lakoff writes about it incorrectly. He uses the example of "within the coming weeks" and claims that "*within* makes use of the metaphor of time as a stationary landscape which has extension and bounded regions, whereas *coming* makes use of a metaphor of times as moving objects." (p. 219). But "within" does not imply "stationary," as Ning Yu's "case 1" (for which there are many examples in English as well as Chinese) clearly shows. The moving "train of events" does have extension and can indeed be bounded, but it is not stationary.

63. Ning Yu, *Contemporary Theory of Metaphor*, pp. 99, 105, 106; Ta-tuan Ch'en et al., *Chinese Primer: Notes and Exercises* (Princeton, N.J.: Princeton University Press, 1989), pp. 64, 74.

looking rightward) while none have right-to-left orientations. (Twelve have neutral orientations.) On U.S. paper currency, the $10 bill shows Alexander Hamilton looking leftward, but the gentlemen on the $1, $2, $5, $20, $50, and $100 bills all look to the right.[64] Even professional linguists who work on Chinese, in which the traditional order of writing was from top to bottom and in columns right to left, adopt the left-to-right metaphor of European languages when they write, for example, that "disyllabic feet are built from left to right."[65] Do speakers of Arabic or Hebrew, where writing goes right to left, conceive time lines in that direction? In what direction did Chinese conceive time lines before the arrival of European-language influences? This is hard to say. My point is only that the left-to-right convention that predominates today is arbitrary, and could well be otherwise.

Next to Ning Yu's cases 1 and 2 we should postulate, as a case 3, the vertical metaphor "past is up, future is down." Jenn-yeu Chen has shown that this occurs about 36 percent of the time in Chinese, but it is important to note that it does not happen any time you want it to. It requires certain grammatical contexts, like [verb] *xiaqu* 下去 'continue [verb]ing' or certain lexical contexts, like *xingqi* 星期 'week' or *yue* 月 'month' but not *tian* 天 'day' or *nian* 年 'year'. (There are dialects in which *shang* 'up' can work with *tian* 'day', but these patterns are still set, and not up to the speaker's preference.) There is a word *xiachang* 下场 'down-field', meaning "situation one ends up in," but no *xiajing* 下景 'down-scene', even though this metaphor would make just as much sense for the same idea. Vertical metaphors also cannot work with certain other common metaphors, like *daolu* 道路 or *lucheng* 路程, that mean "road." Perhaps because vertical roads are awkward to picture in the mind, *daolu* and *lucheng* keep to horizontal metaphors like *qian*, *hou*, and *guo* 过 'cross'.

---

64. I do not wish to overstate this point. Among major league baseball teams, for example, twenty-three have orientationally neutral logos, five look left, and only two look to the right. Of the common U.S. coins, only the penny looks squarely to the right; the half-dollar, quarter, and dime all look to the right, and until recently the nickel did as well. On 2006 nickels, like 2007 dollar coins, the gaze is slightly to the right.

65. Bingfu Lu and San Duanmu quoting Feng Shengli, "On the 'Natural Foot' in Chinese," in Bingfu Lu and San Duanmu, "Rhythm and Syntax in Chinese: A Case Study," *Journal of the Chinese Language Teachers Association* 37, no. 2 (May 2002), p. 127.

I have noted that English also uses "past is up, future is down" metaphors (as when we say "down through the ages" or speak of a person's "descendants") but uses them less often than Chinese. Television hosts sometimes refer to "the top of the show" to mean its beginning. Hence it is a puzzle that in English we also say "*up*coming events" or "let's move the meeting *up* a week," because these usages seem to suggest a "past is down, future is up" metaphor that goes oppositely from the normal direction. Lakoff and Johnson try—not quite successfully, in my view—to explain this usage by observing that, as physical objects come nearer to us, their images appear larger and the tops of the images are therefore farther "up."[66] To me it makes more sense to abandon the notion that *up* has to have a literal basis in such phrases and just let it be (metaphorically) horizontal. *Up* plainly does have such horizontal uses, even when used strictly spatially, as in "up to the water's edge." Since water necessarily must be *below* the ground at the water's edge, "up to the water's edge" cannot be a vertical conception and therefore must be horizontal. But if "up" can be horizontal, then upcoming events might simply be events that, in accordance with Ning Yu's case 1, are headed toward us horizontally. Events "down the road" might similarly exist within a horizontal conception.

A number of cognitive scientists have speculated on what the "physical basis" for vertical time metaphors might be, but their results have in general been unsatisfying. Ning Yu has argued that "later is down" can be derived from the horizontal "case 1," in which later things are "behind" in the train of events, because, Yu reasons, when one stands up from a lying position, one's head, which was in the front-of-the-train or "earlier" position, is now up, which therefore becomes the "earlier" position in vertical terms; meanwhile one's feet, which began in the back-of-the-train position or "later" position horizontally, are now down, in the "later" position when measured vertically.[67] But Yu gives no reason why one metaphorically "lies" with one's head or feet either this way or that. He also gives no reason why we should employ horizontal case 1 instead of horizontal case 2 to interpret the vertical metaphor, and horizontal case 2 would seem to lead to an opposite conclusion. Hence his effort is valiant but

---

66. Lakoff and Johnson, *Metaphors We Live By*, p. 16.
67. Ning Yu, *Contemporary Theory of Metaphor*, pp. 111–112.

unpersuasive. Amanda Scott has suggested that vertical time might derive from the rise and fall of the sun in the sky. Here, to be sure, we are speaking of a natural vertical movement (only an *apparent* one, of course—as we know from Copernicus) that corresponds to earlier and later times.[68] The problem with Scott's explanation is that the sun moves both up and down in equal measure, and Scott has no explanation for why such movement could be the basis for a metaphor that, in both Chinese and English, moves only down.

A letter to the editor of the *Wall Street Journal*, commenting on an op-ed essay by Lera Boroditsky, claims that gravity is the basis: "if you drop something, the past is where it was (above) and the future is where it will be eventually (below)."[69] Other speculations about the origins of vertical time metaphors for Chinese in particular look not to "physical bases" but to human creations like the writing system. The plausibility here comes not just from the fact that the *next* character one writes is indeed *below* the current one (if one's paper is vertical) or that to continue writing is to *xie xiaqu* 写下去 'write down' in a literal sense. It comes as well from a general drift in temporal thinking that the writing system both reinforces and obeys. But this "general drift" is also what makes the theory questionable as a causal theory. Which way does the causality go? Did a predilection in thought lead to the writing custom, or did the direction of writing create the habit of thought? (Once the pattern was established, causality no doubt continued for centuries to go both ways.) Scott speculates that other metaphorical uses of *shang* 'up' to mean "high (in status), excellent" and *xia* 'down' to mean "low, inferior" might seep into the connotations of the two words when they mean "past" and "future."[70] But this seems far-fetched. It is true that the ancient past in China has been regarded as glorious, but to hold that in modern Chinese *shang* for the past and *xia* for the future reliably connote "better" and "worse" would mean, for example, that future weeks and months (where *xia* is used) are consistently drearier in the Chinese mind than future days and years (where horizontal metaphors are used), and there is no evidence for such a difference.

68. Scott, "Vertical Dimension and Time in Mandarin," p. 307.
69. Letter from Sean Cox, July 31, 2010.
70. Ibid., pp. 312–313.

In sum we can say that there are four kinds of metaphorical expression that use space to conceive events in time in Chinese: two kinds of horizontal time lines (Ning Yu's cases 1 and 2), a vertical time line, and, as a fourth category, a variety of mixtures among the first three. English usage draws on the same four categories, although in somewhat different proportions. After finishing his systematic study of time metaphor in Chinese and comparing his findings to Lakoff's for English, Ning Yu feels that he has found "strong evidence in favor of certain universals in the human cognition of time."[71] This claim, which echoes Alverson's hypothesis of "a universal template" in the human experience of time, is persuasive. Are there "universal templates" in human experience of other things, such as color?

Color

It is easy to note that in any language colors are used metaphorically, as in English when we have the blues, are green with envy, are yellow-bellied cowards, get red-faced (or even livid, i.e., white) with anger, compile blacklists, and so on. Is all of this cultural invention, or are there universals to be found? The question depends on a prior question: to what extent are the definitions of colors the same across languages? That is, before we study how the metaphorical uses of *hong* 红 and *red* compare, it seems important to know how much we are comparing the same things: how well do *hong* and *red* (and *rouge* in French, *akai* in Japanese, and so on) pick out the same spans on the natural color spectrum?

This question is not the same as the philosopher's metaphysical question of whether one person's qualia (phenomena of subjective experience) are the same as another's. Your experience when you see red and mine when I see red might be different, even radically different, even while our talk using the word "red" proceeds without a hitch. But this philosophical question is untestable and beyond our scope. Here, by "see red" I mean only "have qualia that allow one to use the word 'red' in a way that accords with how other people use it (whatever their qualia may be)" or,

---

71. Ning Yu, *Contemporary Theory of Metaphor*, p. 113.

alternatively, "perceive with eye and brain light waves that fall within a certain span."

A cursory comparison of how the Chinese and English languages label colors lends considerable support to a view that has been called "linguistic relativity" in color definition. (The view derives from Sapir and Whorf and was dominant around the middle of the twentieth century.) In Chinese, for example, the term *huang* 黄 does not correspond well to any English word. Dictionaries cite "yellow," but *huang* covers much more of the spectrum than yellow does. It begins with yellow, spans all of tan, and goes pretty far into brown. As noted in the Introduction, China's Huanghe 黄河, Yellow River, is brown, not yellow. A *huang gou* 黄狗 in Chinese is a brown dog, or at the lightest a tan one, hardly a yellow one. I teach classes wearing *huang pixie* 黄皮鞋, 'brown leather shoes' and might think twice about going to class if they actually were yellow. When Western languages arrived in China with their major distinction between "brown" and "yellow," modern Chinese responded by using other brown-like words—such as *hese* 褐色 'earth-tone brown' and *zongse* 棕色 'palm-fiber brown'—to serve as counterparts of "brown." But in daily-life Chinese usage, *hese* and *zongse* have never really competed with *huang*, and, when they do get used, they refer to much narrower bands on the color spectrum than *huang*. A similar problem attends *qing* 青, which can be green as in *qingjiao* 青椒 'green pepper', blue as in *qingtian* 青天 'blue sky', or even black as in *qingbu* 青布 'black cloth'. Examples such as these would seem to lead to the conclusion that divisions within the color spectrum are arbitrary. Indeed, we might feel that they *must* be arbitrary. The spectrum is, after all, a continuum; no natural line separates blue from green, orange from red, and so on, so any language *of course* must be arbitrary in saying where one color ends and the other begins. Or so it would seem.

In their 1969 book *Basic Color Terms*, Brent Berlin and Paul Kay presented research results showing that we should not make this assumption.[72] Berlin, Kay, and their students found that some factors that go into the naming of colors are constant across languages. They presented speakers of twenty different languages with varying shades of red, blue, green,

---

72. Brent Berlin and Paul Kay, *Basic Color Terms: Their Universality and Evolution* (Berkeley: University of California Press, 1969).

and so on, and then asked them to identify which was the most standard or representative example within each family of shades. They found considerable agreement on which were the "best red," "best blue," and so on. This agreement held not only among speakers of the same language but also—and here is the key point—across speakers of *different* languages. The favored examples of *red, rouge, hong, akai,* and so on tended to be the same shade regardless of language. Berlin and Kay gave the name "focal colors" to these favored shades: focal *red,* focal *blue,* and so on. They found that agreement was clearest for what they identified as the "basic colors" black, white, red, green, yellow, blue, and brown. After comparing data in secondary material for seventy-eight languages in addition to the twenty they had studied directly, Berlin and Kay concluded that "the foci of basic color terms are similar in all languages."[73] The *fringes* of a color's definition—where red blends into orange, and so on—varied considerably among languages, but the "focal" cases did not.

Berlin and Kay make some further claims that seem doubtful, in part because their own color terms, which are based in English, lead them to pose questions that preclude certain answers that other languages might produce. For example, they argue that there is a natural order in which labels for the basic colors enter human languages. They find, arguing from empirical survey, that all languages have black and white, and that, when a third basic color enters a language, it invariably is red. For languages that go to four basic colors, the next to be added is either green or yellow, and when there are five, *both* yellow and green are on the list. For six-color languages, blue is added; for seven, brown; and after that purple, pink, orange, and grey all arrive, although these four observe no particular order.[74] Berlin's and Kay's extensive data do seem to confirm this pattern, but one needs to wonder how much English-language categories shaped the very data they were working with. When they say that green is the fourth or fifth color to arrive in languages, a Chinese speaker might ask "do you mean here *qing* 青 or *lü* 綠?" (It is not clear whether there are "focal" shades of both these Chinese notions of "green.") Or one might ask "In what order does *huang* arrive?" Would it be in fourth or fifth place

73. Ibid., p. 10.
74. Ibid., pp. 2–3.

(where "yellow" is) or seventh (where "brown" is)? These objections do not seriously impair Berlin's and Kay's argument for the existence of "focal colors"; but they do question some of their related claims.

If "focal colors" exist, it is natural to ask *why* they exist. Studies in the late 1960s of the neurophysiology of the eye of the macaque, a primate whose visual system is close to that of humans, showed that four "response cells" in the eye of the macaque had to do with the perception of red, green, yellow, and blue, while two others had to do with brightness, which helps to explain the perception of black and white.[75] Later cognitive scientists, including Paul Kay and George Lakoff, have claimed that neurophysiology can explain the phenomenon of the focal colors.[76] Lakoff holds that in addition to neurophysiology, there is a "something else" (his term) that might account for "different values in different cultures." But he does not explain clearly what that "something else" might be. (We are told only that it "consists of a complex cognitive mechanism incorporating some of the characteristics of fuzzy set theory union and intersection" and that it "has a small number of parameters" that make the difference.)[77] In any case, at bottom, the Kay-Lakoff argument depends on the assumption that a relatively simple physiological source (a certain neuron for "red," for example) can explain a natural preference for a certain hue. Combinations of firings for red and yellow produce orange, for blue and red produce purple, and so on, while subtler shades presumably involve more complex firings.

Kay and Lakoff's theory raises thorny issues in what Western philosophers have called the "mind-body problem." How do neural firings in the (physical) brain relate to perceptions—such as colors—in the mind? Kay and Lakoff do not address this question but do make an assumption about its answer when they assume that relatively simple neural firings correspond to perceptions of "focal" colors. That may be so; but it is also

---

75. R. L. DeValois, I. Abramov, and G. H. Jacobs, "Analysis of Response Patterns of LGN Cells," *Journal of the Optical Society of America* 56 (1966), pp. 966–977; R. L DeValois and G. H. Jacobs, "Primate Color Vision," *Science* 162 (1968), pp. 533–540.

76. Paul Kay and Chad McDaniel, "The Linguistic Significance of the Meanings of Basic Color Terms," *Language* 54, no. 3 (1978), pp. 610–646; Lakoff, *Women, Fire, and Dangerous Things*, pp. 26–30.

77. Lakoff, *Women, Fire, and Dangerous Things*, p. 30.

possible that it is not so. Might it not also be that the firings that produce what a human being chooses to call "best red" are complex? Kay and Lakoff seem to have an assumption that a comparatively simple or basic neural experience will lead a person to feel "right" or "primary" (or something like that) about the corresponding subjective impression. But is this necessarily so?

Consider, by analogy, the taste sensation. If we gave bits of chocolate of slightly different flavors to people (professors of Chinese literature do not have research budgets for this kind of experiment, so this is a thought-experiment only) and found that the subjects generally agreed that sample 7 was the "most chocolate-y" of the lot, would we want to assume that "most chocolate-y" corresponds to relatively simple physical stimuli? Or to stimuli created by chocolate of the simplest chemical composition? I think we would not want to make such assumptions. The addition of sweetness from an admixture of sugar, for example, might well enhance a sense of chocolate-ness. And what about wine? Would "focal chardonnay" be the one that corresponds to simpler physical stimuli than those of other chardonnays? If so, any connoisseur could tell us that focal chardonnay is not the best chardonnay. I don't mean to satirize Kay and Lakoff here; they may still be right. But their argument does contain a hole. A correspondence between simpler neural activity and more "focal" subjective experience needs to be demonstrated, not just assumed.

But even if the connections to neural bases are not well understood, the empirical finding of focal colors is an important result. It can give us confidence, as we begin to compare metaphorical uses of color-terms across languages, that we are dealing with the "same thing"—or more precisely, in the jargon of the field, the same "vehicle" or "defining concept." Thanks to the discovery of focal colors, we can be fairly certain that *hong* and *red*, *hei* 黑 and *black*, and *bai* 白 and *white* are very close to the same for native speakers of Chinese and English. *Hui* 灰 'grey' and *zi* 紫 'purple' also probably correspond well. Special problems involving colors like *qing* and *huang* will require that we be careful before using English to interpret Chinese metaphors that use such colors.

Now let us turn from colors themselves to the question of their metaphorical uses. One of the bases for commonality in color metaphors across languages is (as noted earlier) what metaphor theorists call the "physical" or "experiential" bases of metaphor. I have noted the example in which blood rushing to the face during anger apparently has led to metaphors like "red in the face" or "seeing red" in English and *qi hong le lian* 气红了脸 'angered [oneself] red-faced' or *mian hong er chi* 面红耳赤 'face and ears red' in Chinese. Note also that blood gathering in the facial capillaries can have causes other than anger and that, correspondingly, this particular "physical basis" can undergird metaphors for conditions other than anger: embarrassment, for example, as when we say *lian hong* 脸红 in Chinese or "red-faced" in English. Robust health or cold air can also bring blood into the facial capillaries, which leads us to say *manmian hongguang* 满面红光 'bright red fills face' in Chinese or "rosy cheeks" in English.[78] In extreme frustration, so much blood might rush to the head that we say, in English, one is "blue in the face"; intense anger might also bring blueness or, as both Chinese and English suggest, drain the blood from the face, so that one is "livid" in English or, in Chinese, *qi de lian hong yi zhen bai yi zhen* 气得脸红一阵白一阵 'so angry that the face alternated between red and white'.

The commonality by which "green" tends to mean "young" seems to have an obvious physical basis in the vivid greenness of young plants. In English we say a neophyte is "green," and in Chinese *qingnian* 青年 'green years' refers to young people. The physical basis connecting "green" with "young" is perhaps most apparent in *qingchun* 青春 'green spring—youth', where the young sprouts of spring embody both greenness and newness. In Su Xiaokang and Wang Luxiang's famous 1988 television series *Heshang* (River elegy), *huang* 'brown' served as an extended metaphor for "conservative, hidebound, or inward-looking." Even this had an indirect physical basis. *Huang* is the color of the earth in the inland region of north China; that is where, for Su and Wang, the earthbound, uncosmopolitan side of Chinese culture was rooted; it is also where the Communist Party had its base in Yan'an in the 1940s; a continuing "feudal" mentality was still alive in the 1980s, according to the television series, and it could be symbolized as *huang* or "earth-colored" culture.

78. For this and a number of other promptings about the metaphorical meanings of colors, I owe a debt to Ye Minlei.

But if these color metaphors can be traced to physical bases, there are a large number, probably a majority, that cannot be. These other metaphors apparently have arisen from more accidental causes and are better viewed as cultural creations in which the connection of ideas to specific colors is arbitrary. Why, for example, are we "green with envy" in English but have *hongyanbing* 红眼病 'red eye disease—envy' in Chinese? Why are pornographic films "blue movies" in English but *huangse dianying* 黄色电影 'yellow movies' in Chinese? Why is "blue" in English "sad, depressed," whereas *qing* 'blue or green' in Chinese can be upbeat, as in *mingchui qingshi* 名垂青史 'name suspended through (blue or green) history—go down in history'. Is it not just arbitrary that "red" in English signifies danger (red flag, red alert, etc.) and *lü mao* 绿帽 'green hat' in Chinese is what a cuckold wears? To account for all such ad hoc color metaphors would be to write a short encyclopedia.

A single color can have very different connotations even within the same language. In Chinese, *bai* 'white' is a good thing in *jiebai* 洁白 'clean, pure' or *qingbai* 清白 'stainless, immaculate', but stands for evil in the *bailian* 白脸 'white face' of popular opera. Red is especially rich and versatile. In addition to "angry," "embarrassed," "healthful," and "envious," noted above, *hong* can mean "hot, popular" as in *hong mingxing* 红明星 'popular star'; "favored," as when person A is a *hongren* 红人 in the view of person B; "lucky," as when somebody *zou hong* 走红 'gets lucky' or has *hongyun* 红运 'good luck'; "beautiful," as in *hongfen jiaren* 红粉佳人 'red-powder beauty' or *hongyan yilao* 红颜易老 'red face ages easily—beauty does not last'; "loyal" as in *chidan zhong xin* 赤胆忠心 'red gall loyal heart—utter devotion'; and even "ordinary, pedestrian" as in *kanpo hong chen* 看破红尘 'see through the red dust [of the ordinary world]'.

Modern borrowings from Western languages have added even more meanings of red to Chinese. "Red ink" meaning debt has come into modern Chinese as *chizi* 赤字 'red characters'. Red to mean "Communist" has given new meaning to *hongqi* 红旗 'red flag', *hongjun* 红军 'red army', and many other terms. Some of the traditional positive connotations of *hong*—such as "favored" and "loyal"—have seeped into the new usage of *hong* as "Communist." The *hong wu lei* 红五类 'five red categories' (workers, poor peasants, revolutionary officials, revolutionary soldiers, and revolutionary martyrs) were the bedrock Communist people during the Cultural

Revolution, but also the "favored" and "loyal" ones—making them safe on both grounds from persecution.

Other obvious modern borrowings of color metaphors include "black" to mean "secret" or "nefarious," in terms such as *hei shehui* 黑社会 'black society—underworld', *hei mingdan* 黑名单 'blacklist', *heishi* 黑市 'black-market', and others. After a borrowed metaphor takes root, it can take on a power to structure new concepts (can be a "metaphor people live by," as Lakoff and Johnson would say) and produce terms in the borrowing language that did not exist in the lending language. For example, Chinese farmers who live in cities without legal urban residence permits are said to have *heihu* 黑户 'black residence' in the cities. *Huang* meaning "pornographic" arose in the twentieth century in China after evolving from the English term "yellow journalism," whose roots were in New York of the 1890s. In the United States, though, the term has meant scandal-mongering and sensationalism, not specifically pornography, as it does in Chinese.

One possibility in explaining similarity in metaphors across languages is, of course, simply coincidence. This happens, after all, even with ordinary terms, such as *low* meaning "mean or base" in English and *lou* 陋 meaning "mean or base" in Chinese. In both languages, "colorful" can mean "rich, interesting." We can have a "colorful life" in English and a *duoziduocai de shenghuo* 多姿多彩的生活 'multiappearance multicolor life' in Chinese. Is this coincidence, or might there be a subtle "experiential basis" at work—in that different colors might imply variety, therefore interest, maybe even travel?

Although color metaphors can seem highly contingent, they also can have considerable power. In October 1988, at a high-level conference on Sino-American scholarly exchange, the distinguished American historian Frederic Wakeman, of the University of California at Berkeley, borrowed Su Xiaokang's term "yellow" to describe the inward-looking side of Chinese civilization and contrasted it with the "blue" side (also Su Xiaokang's term) that looked across the ocean (hence "blue") at the international world. Wakeman observed that scholarly exchange might play a role in China's transition toward a blue civilization out of a yellow one. Yan Dongsheng, chief of the Chemistry Division of the Chinese Academy of Sciences, heard the term "yellow civilization" as "pornographic civilization" and rose to denounce Wakeman in terms so impassioned that no one at the meeting (including me) could recover in time to explain that a color metaphor had been misunderstood. Explanations had to wait until the next day.

Up and Down

We have seen how *shang* 'up' and *xia* 'down' are useful in the vertical conception of time in Chinese. But *shang* and *xia* have a wide variety of other uses as conceptual metaphors, as do *up* and *down* in English. The two languages sometimes resemble each other in these matters, but sometimes they do not—and sometimes they present puzzles. Why, in English, after chopping a tree down, do we chop the wood *up?* Why, in Chinese, do we memorize something down (*beixialai* 背下来) but remember it up (*jiqilai* 记起来)?

The conceptual metaphor "more is up, less is down" is well established in both languages. This fact is not surprising, because, as noted, the "physical basis" of the metaphor is universal: for speakers of any language, "more" of something tends to create a pile, and a pile top tends to go up. During the twentieth century—in Chinese, English, and many languages—abstract uses of the metaphor, in phrases like *tonghuo pengzhang shangqu le* 通货膨胀上去了 'inflation has gone up', became increasingly common. Uses of terms like *gao* 高 'high' and *di* 低 'low' to fit the metaphor also seem to have increased: *xinshui hen gao* 薪水很高 'salary high' means more money, *wendu jiang le* 温度降了 'temperature fell' means less heat, and so on. Such usages are now so common in both Chinese and English that we usually forget that they are metaphors. But they are: originally, after all, "up" and "more" are unrelated concepts.

From *up* meaning "more in quantity" it is but a small shift—which Chinese, English, and many languages have made—to the meaning "more in quality." In Chinese, both ancient and modern, a *shangce* 上策 is a good plan, a *xiace* 下策 an inferior one. Mao Zedong urged students to *haohao xuexi tiantian xiangshang* 好好学习天天向上 'study hard and go up [i.e., get better] every day'.

Such examples usually refer to technical quality, but examples of moral quality are even more numerous. *Up* connotes virtue; *down*, baseness. We can say in English that someone is "upright" or "high-minded," and in

Chinese *gaoshang* 高尚 'high-esteemed—noble' or *gaoming* 高明 'high-bright—enlightened'. In English we "stand up for principle," and in Chinese *tingshen er chu* 挺身而出 'straighten the body and go out—step boldly forward'. These images vary, but all reflect a connection between "up" and "morally right." Similarly, a moral scoundrel in English can be "low-down" and others might need to "stoop" to his level. In Chinese such behavior is *beixia* 卑下 'base, low', and perhaps *xialiu* 下流 'mean, obscene'. There do exist exceptions to the pattern, however, and these seem perhaps more common in Chinese than in English. Ning Yu cites examples where Chinese uses the metaphors basically the other way around: *wenzhong* 稳重 'stable and heavy' and *chenwen* 沉稳 'weighty and stable' both mean "solid and reliable" in a positive sense, whereas *qingfu* 轻浮 'light and floating' and *piaofu* 漂浮 'drifting and floating' mean "frivolous, flighty" in a negative sense.[79] Similarly, in English "flighty" combines *up* with a negative connotation.

Another use of "up" or "high"—in Chinese, English, and many languages—is to indicate more status or power within an administrative structure. In English an official can be "high-ranking" and on completion of a term of service might "step down." In premodern Chinese, *da* 大 'big' and *xiao* 小 'little' were used in this regard: a high official was a *daguan* 大官 'big official'. But in recent times, the term *gaoji guanyuan* 高级官员 'high-ranking official' has become more common.

Desmond Tutu and others who ran the Truth and Reconciliation Commission (TRC) in South Africa after 1994 consciously sought to counter the "up is good" and "up is powerful" metaphors that were implicit in both English and South African languages by having everyone at hearings sit on the same level. "We had to avoid any impression that [the witnesses]

---

79. Ning Yu, *Contemporary Theory of Metaphor*, p. 65. The terms *gexia* 阁下, literally 'below the pavilion' and *zuxia* 足下, literally 'beneath the feet,' both of which are ways to say "you" in premodern polite language, also might appear to be exceptions, because normally Chinese honorifics *elevate* the person to whom they refer. But these are not exceptions. The sense of *gexia* (or *zuxia*) is 'you, the one beneath whose pavilion (or feet) I (stand to) address'. The dictionary *Cihai* explains that, because it might seem too audacious to address an august personage directly, *gexia* is used to make the approach indirect by addressing the servants and retainers who are arrayed below. Cihai bianji weiyuan hui, *Cihai* (Sea of words) (Shanghai: Cishu chubanshe, 1979), p. 2016.

were in the dock," Tutu has written, "so they sat on the same level as the TRC panel hearing their testimony."[80]

In a metaphor that combines the concepts "up is more power" with "up is to go on stage—that is, be more visible and responsible," Chinese says *shangtai* 上台 'move up onstage' when an official assumes office and *xiatai* 下台 'move down offstage' for leaving office. "Up" is sometimes used in Chinese not only for a person who is administratively higher but for a geographical place that is. In Wu dialect, for example, *shangqu* 上去 'go up' is used to mean "go to the city" while *xiaqu* 下去 'go down' means "go to the countryside."[81] It is probably more than just administration that explains the "up"-ness of an urban area, because the city has more of other things as well: markets, entertainment, population, and general bustle. But sometimes the political implications are clear. When a political leader makes an inspection tour of the countryside, it is *xiaxiang kaocha* 下乡考察 'go down to the countryside to inspect'. When youth in the Mao era left the cities to "learn from the peasantry," one might have expected the prestige of the peasantry—a "revolutionary class" in Maoist ideology and the putative "teachers" in this project—to put them higher than the youngsters coming from the cities. But this did not happen, at least not at the level of the conceptual metaphors in daily life. The phrases *xiaxiang* 下乡 'go down to the countryside' and *xiafang* 下放 'transfer down' remained standard. Whether people noticed the implication or not, the metaphorical lowness of the countryside outweighed the political ideal that the peasants should be teachers.[82]

Lakoff and Johnson (and many others) have noted "happy is up, sad is down" as another example of a standard metaphorical meaning of "up" in English. We say in English that our spirits "rise" or that they get a "boost";

---

80. Desmond M. Tutu, *No Future without Forgiveness* (New York: Doubleday, 1999), p. 110.

81. I am grateful to Ye Minlei for this example. Email message to author, March 7, 2008.

82. The full four-syllable phrase *shangshan xiaxiang* 上山下乡 only reinforces the metaphoric significance of *xia*, because *shang* here is literal. Going up a mountain is a matter of altitude; going "down" to the countryside is seldom a matter of altitude. (On average, cities are at lower altitudes than farms.) So *xia* in the phrase needs to have a metaphorical understanding.

but our spirits can "sink," after which we feel "down," "low, or "depressed."[83] We can be "on cloud nine"; we also can be "down in the dumps." Some theorists have speculated on what possible "physical basis" there might be for the notion that "happy is up." Lakoff and Johnson, and Ning Yu, think that such expressions "arise from the fact that as humans we have upright bodies."[84] Perhaps so, but the assertion needs further explanation. Is the point that when our bodies are not upright we are often not fully alert, as when we are ill or asleep? Can we say in general that we are happier standing up than lying down? Zoltán Kövecses has a different theory. He suggests that "up" reminds us of birds—which are above us, and seem free, and thus seem happy.[85] But Kövecses's explanation seems to risk circularity. Do birds, who seem happy, cause us to associate *up* with *happy*? Or do we, perhaps, attribute happiness to birds *because* they are "up there"? This is hard to say.

Whatever the physical basis for the "happy is up, sad is down" metaphor might be, it is a simple matter to show that it occurs in Chinese as well as in English. In Chinese we have *gaoxing* 高兴 'high spirit—happy' or *xingfen* 兴奋 'spirit-lift—(pleasantly) excited' on the one hand and *diluo* 低落 'low fall—downcast' or *chenmen* 沉闷 'sink stifled—in low spirits' on the other.[86] On the whole, though, *up* and *down* as metaphors for happy and unhappy may be less common in Chinese than in English. David Moser has correctly observed that Chinese tends to use container metaphors such as *open* or *unfettered* for happy and *boxed in*, *cornered*, or *faced with barriers* for unhappy.[87] Thus *kaixin* 开心 'open heart' is "happy" and *xi chu wang wai* 喜出望外 'joy overflows outwards' is something like "exuberant," and *nanguo* 难过 'hard to cross over (something)' means "sad." *Kai* also has associations of "free, happy" when used as a verbal complement in phrases such as *jiekai* 解开 'untie open—solve (a puzzle or mystery)', or *xiangkai* 想开 'think open—rise above (something)'—a phrase that can

---

83. Lakoff and Johnson, *Metaphors We Live By*, p. 15.

84. Ning Yu, *Contemporary Theory of Metaphor*, p. 61; Lakoff and Johnson, *Metaphors We Live By*, p. 15

85. Zoltán Kövecses, "Happiness: A Definitional Effort," in *Metaphor and Symbolic Activity*, 6:29–46.

86. Ning Yu, *Contemporary Theory of Metaphor*, p. 63.

87. Letter to the author, October 25, 1993.

be used in advising a person how to get over a personal loss. *Shunxin* 顺心 'accord with heart' indicates a happy contentment, and when things go wrong a feeling of *bushun* 不顺 'nonaccord' arrives. The word *men* 闷 captures the metaphor well all by itself (even the character—a heart enclosed by a door—suggests the metaphor). Spoken in first tone, *men* refers to stuffy air, muffled sound, keeping quiet (i.e., not talking), or shutting oneself indoors; it is also what you do to tea leaves when you trap them under a tight lid and steep them in hot water. In the fourth tone, *men* means bored, depressed, or sealed off. These uses of "open" and "closed" in Chinese as metaphors for "happy" and "unhappy" exist alongside "up" and "down" for the same ideas. As with different directions for time lines, the mix causes few, if any, problems in getting through daily life.

There is another set of *up* and *down* metaphors that seem conceptually at odds in both Chinese and English. Sometimes *up* suggests "unknown" or "unsettled" and *down* almost the opposite. We say "that's still *up in the air*" and then, when the matter is decided, that "it's settled."[88] On the other hand, we sometimes use *up* to suggest "finished" or "all set," as when we "chop up," "wrap up," or "dress up." The meaning of *up* is elusive here, but it does seem to suggest that something did in fact get chopped or wrapped or dressed. The effect seems to survive even when the result is not a pleasant one. If we "mess up" or "screw up," *up* still seems to spotlight the end result—rubbing it in, as it were.[89] The fixity of *up* and indeterminacy of *down* are also illustrated in what Lakoff and Johnson call the "control is up" metaphor, for which they cite "I'm on top of the situation" as an example.[90] Here the notion is that things down below, far from "settled," are in some kind of confusion that calls for control.

Although parallels with Chinese are not perfect, they are sufficiently similar to be intriguing. In English when we memorize something we

---

88. These examples are from Lakoff and Johnson, *Metaphors We Live By*, pp. 120, 137.

89. I am claiming here only that "finished" is a common meaning of *up* after a verb, not that it is the only one. A phrase like "put up with idiocy" would likely need a different explanation.

90. Lakoff and Johnson, *Philosophy in the Flesh*, p. 53. The authors hypothesize that the "experiential basis" for this metaphor is that "it is easier to control another person or exert force on an object from above, where you have gravity working with you."

might say we have it "down pat," while in Chinese we say it has been *bei xialai le* 背下来了 'memorized down'. Chinese also uses *luoshi* 落实, literally "descend to facts," when something theoretical, like a government policy, is put into practice. Of a group of noisy children Chinese can say they *anjing xialai* 安静下来 'quiet down', just as English says "quiet down." Something can be "up for grabs" in English, and in Chinese can "hang" (*xuan* 悬) awaiting decision, as in *zhe shir buneng lao xuanzhe* 这事儿不能老悬着 'this matter can't keep on hanging there'.[91] These several examples, in both languages, illustrate the conceptual metaphors "*up* is unknown, or in flux," and "*down* is known or settled."

What about the opposite case, where *up* suggests "all set" or "in control" and *down* suggests "indeterminate" or "in flux"? Chinese seldom uses *shang* 上 the way English uses "up" in a phrase like "chop up." (*Ganshang* 赶上 'catch up' is an unusual exception.) But Chinese has other phrases that fit the metaphor fairly well. We just saw that *luoshi* can mean "descend to facts"; but Chinese also says *luokong* 落空 'descend to emptiness' when an idea or plan falls through or comes to naught. A term like *zhenya* 镇压 'repress' (*zhen* and *ya* both mean "press down") also accords with the metaphor in that it suggests that control is on top and chaos, which needs control, reigns below. *Qiyi* 起义, literally "rise righteousness," a common term for rebellion, might seem from the point of view of the rebels to mean "headed upward, toward the sky." But from the viewpoint of the ruling dynasty, the rebellious activity is taking place "down below," and *qi* thus means "moving upward toward us," which creates the need to *zhenya* or "press down."[92] Other examples in which "here, the present level" seems standard and clear while "the level below" seems murky or questionable are phrases like *shuo bu shanglai* 说不上來 'can't come up with [a word, explanation, etc.]' or *xiang bu qilai* 想不起來 'can't recall', in which *shang* and *qi* tell us that the movement is upward or rising and *lai* tells us that it is

---

91. The example is from Beijing waiguoyudaxue yingyuxi cidianzu *A Chinese-English Dictionary*, p. 1151.

92. It is worth noting that another conceptual metaphor in Chinese, which might be called "control is clenching," uses the verbal complement *zhu* 住 'hold in place', and has examples like *na zhu* 拿住 'hold fast (with hand)', *yao zhu* 咬住 'clench (with teeth)', or *kongzhi zhu* 控制住 'bring under control'. In Chinese, this metaphor of "control is clenching" is far more common than "control is up."

toward the speaker. This combination of notions—"up" and "toward the speaker"—implies that the loose accumulation of words or memories one is trying to draw on lies somewhere beneath one. In *xia hai* 下海 'jump into the sea', which by extension, in the late twentieth century, came to mean "leave the state employment system and jump into the free-market economy," the notion of *down* applies in the literal sense that the sea is downhill from the land. But it also applies in the sense that the free-market economy, down "below," is murky and beyond easy control.

Still other uses of *shang* that suggest determinacy (or in this case, formality) and of *xia* that suggest the opposite (flexibility or informality) are their uses as transitive verbs. *Shang ban* 上班, literally "go up to the group," means "go to work" or "be on duty"—that is, be constricted to a certain role—while *xia ban* 'go off duty' releases one to go do anything else. *Shang ke* 上課 'go to class, hold class' and *xia ke* 'get out of class' have similar implications, as do *shang* (or *xia*) *tai* 上(下)台 'go onstage (or offstage, literally or figuratively)'. Literal meanings of *shang* and *xia* tend to trump figurative ones; a miner who joins his group to head down into the mines, for example, is more likely to *xia kuang* 下礦 'go down into the mine' than to *shang ban* 'go to work'. But underlying conceptual metaphors survive such temporary trumpings.

Can we make sense of the fact that major conceptual metaphors using *up* and *down* seem to contradict each other? Why is "fixity" sometimes down and other times up? To revisit an earlier example, why do we memorize something down (*beixialai* 背下来) but remember it up (*jiqilai* 记起来)? It might seem, for an example like this, that we can unify the concepts by saying that we store something *down* in the bank of memory (*beixialai*) until we need to draw on it, when we recall it back *up* (*jiqilai*). But the little word *lai* 'come', which appears in both phrases, is a major problem for this interpretation. *Lai* means "move toward the speaker." Therefore, *beixialai*, literally "memorize down toward us," suggests that the galaxy of unmemorized language is hanging over our heads before we begin to memorize. Then, as we memorize, the memorized phrases come "down" to our level. The puzzle is that *jiqilai* also uses *lai*, so here again the motion is conceived as moving toward the speaker. But if the phrases that are being recalled *rise* toward the speaker, as *qi* suggests, then they had to have started out beneath the speaker. This contradicts the implicit claim of *beixialai*, which tells us that memorized phrases come down from above.

One might try to rescue the *jiqilai* example by arguing that *lai* does not *have to* imply "toward the speaker" when used with *qi*. In other colloquial uses in standard Chinese, it sometimes does not. For example if you are lying in bed next to your partner on Saturday morning, arguing about who is going to get up to feed the dog, you say *ni qilai, wo buxiang qilai* 你起來, 我不想起來 'you get up, I don't feel like it'. You use *lai*, not *qu*, even though the motion of "getting up" is clearly "away from the speaker." This "illogicality" is conventional in modern Mandarin, where *qiqu* 起去 'rise go [away from the speaker]' is extremely rare (although it is more common in other regional Chinese languages). But even if *jiqilai* might be unified with *beixialai*, the many other examples of clash between "fixity is up" and "fixity is down" would still remain. There is no possible way, I believe, to unify *luoshi* 'descend to facts' and *luokong* 'descend to emptiness'. We just need to accept that both conceptual metaphors are available and that speakers and listeners draw on them as needed, and without confusion. This kind of drawing on what you need in order to make your point applies to proverbs in a language as well as metaphors. In English we say both "look before you leap" and "he who hesitates is lost"; the two are exactly contradictory, yet each is regarded as wise. Contradiction of this kind is not a barrier to efficient communication.

North and South

Yet another intriguing metaphorical use of *up* and *down* involves the four directions. Human cultures everywhere, from ancient times, seem to have accepted the "fourness" of the basic directions. This may be, as some have speculated, because of the arc of the sun across the sky. In any case, the fourness is a human convention, not a fact of nature.

Literally speaking, of course, none of north, south, east, or west is *up*. In the real world, each of these directions is perpendicular to up.[93] When we

---

93. Or very nearly so—a caveat we need to add because of the slight curvature of the earth.

take north to be up, as nearly all modern maps do, we are observing a metaphorical convention—and, strictly speaking, one that applies only when a map is vertical, as when it is on a wall. When a map lies horizontal on a table, two metaphors need to piggyback: "north is up" combines with "up is the direction away from the viewer" to yield "north is the direction away from the viewer."

On a stone-engraved map of Mesopotamia that dates from around 2300 BCE, in the dynasty of Akkad, the mapmaker engraved "east" at the top edge of the map. (We know which edge was the "top" because of the orientation of script and symbols on the map.) "West" was engraved at the bottom, and "north" at the left.[94] Since the map in this case is a block of stone, it is probably anachronistic to imagine that users placed it vertically or thought of it in vertical terms. We need to remember that "top" is a modern metaphor for "the side away from the viewer," just as "bottom" is "the side toward the viewer."

The earliest maps we have from China are a group of seven dating from around 300 BCE that were unearthed from a tomb in Tianshui 天水 city in Gansu Province in 1986.[95] Drawn in black ink on wood, these maps primarily show rivers and their tributaries, although mountains, roads, and timber sites are shown as well. It is impossible to say that any particular sides of these maps were considered the correct sides from which to view them. With few exceptions, the characters that label the streams and rivers follow, from top to bottom, the direction of the water flow. (The direction of flow can be inferred from the tributary structure.) As rivers do not all flow in the same direction, the characters on the maps do not either and are thus of no use in defining which side should be "up" for any of the maps. One map, which scholars have agreed to call "number 2," has

---

94. Alan R. Millard, "Cartography in the Ancient Near East," in J. B. Harley and David Woodward, eds., *The History of Cartography* (Chicago: The University of Chicago Press, 1992) vol. 1, bk. 1, pp. 113. Millard does not state how he knows which side of the stone-engraved map (pictured on p. 114) is up, but the orientations of the script and map conventions (overlapping semicircles for ranges of hills) seem to make this clear. I am grateful to Wang Haicheng for assistance with this and other ancient maps.

95. See Cao Wanru 曹婉如, "Youguan Tianshui fangmatan Qinmu chutu ditu de jige wenti" 有关天水放马滩秦墓出土地图的几个问题, *Wenwu* (Beijing) 403 (December 1989), pp. 78–85; also Mei-ling Hsu, "The Qin Maps: A Clue to Later Chinese Cartographic Development" *Imago Mundi* 45 (1993), pp. 90–100.

the odd feature of including the character *shang* 上 at one of its edges, and some have argued that this character indicates "top of map." But there are two major problems with such a claim.

One problem is that "top" is a metaphor that makes sense only when the habit of displaying maps vertically has been established. Was there such a habit in 300 BCE? On a more sophisticated map from about 130 years later, the more understandable labels *dong* 東 'east' and *nan* 南 'south' are written at two of the map's edges. There is no sign of *shang* 'up', even though this later map, which is painted on silk, not wood, would have been more amenable to vertical display.

The other major problem in interpreting *shang* 上 on map number 2 as indicating "top of map" is that the character points inward, toward the center of the map. If one turns the map (or oneself) so that the *shang* is at the map's "top" (away from viewer), the character is upside-down. Why would a mapmaker do that? Mei-ling Hsu sensibly recommends that we turn the map back around so that *shang* is right-side up, but this puts the *shang*, necessarily, at the "bottom" of the map. Hsu then makes the somewhat far-fetched claim that the character *still* indicates "top of map" because, while resting at the bottom, it "points to the top."[96] Hsu further assumes that the *shang* character is pointing "north," as a compass needle does, even though 300 BCE was several centuries before the appearance of the compass in China and even though, when the compass did appear, it was considered by convention to be "pointing south" (*zhi nan* 指南), not north.

My own guess is that *shang* is on the map for some reason other than to tell us which side of the map is "up." I further suspect that the mapmaker(s) may have felt no need for an "up." The ground was lying there, and so was their sketch; who needs an "up"? In any case, if we cannot know which way, if any, was considered up, there is no way to determine which of the four directions up might have been.

The "more sophisticated" map I just referred to is one of three dating from the second century BCE that were excavated from a Han tomb in Changsha, Hunan Province, in the early 1970s.[97] One of these three is a

---

96. Mei-ling Hsu, "Qin Maps," p. 92.

97. See Mei-ling Hsu, "The Han Maps and Early Chinese Cartography," *Annals of the Association of American Geographers* 68, no. 1 (March 1978), pp. 45–60, and Kuei-

city map that was found in such bad condition that scholars have not been able to make much of it. The other two were in good condition and were restored well enough that useful copies of them could be made.[98] They are drawn on silk and include both symbols and written characters that indicate features both natural (streams and mountains) and human-made (roads and settlements). One is called a *zhujuntu* 駐軍圖 'military map' and the other a *dixingtu* 地形圖 'topographic map'.

Again, it is not easy to determine which side, if any, the mapmaker(s) regarded as "up," but for these two maps there is more to work with than there was with the Qin maps. On the military map, an especially large *dong* 東 'east' is written at one edge and another large *nan* 南 'south' at another. (The other two edges indicate nothing about direction.) *Dong* and *nan* are written with the "tops" of the characters pointing off the edge of the map, the opposite of the way the *shang* is written on Qin map number two. Therefore, viewing *dong* and *nan* in their "upright" positions, it becomes very plausible that either east or south is the "top" (or, without the vertical metaphor, the "away from viewer side") of the map. The question then becomes whether there is a way to decide between east and south. On the map itself, there are about seventy-five written labels for various things, and if the characters for these labels all observed a certain orientation, that would be strong evidence for which way is "up." But the labels are written in various directions, including diagonally. (We can infer "diagonal" if we take *dong* and *nan* as defining vertical and horizontal). My best count of these labels finds twenty-seven pointing south, twenty-two east, twenty-two west, and thirteen north. (I say "best count" because one needs to be a bit arbitrary in deciding which way a slanted column *basically* is pointing). This distribution is good evidence that south was preferred to north as the "up" direction, but only slim evidence for saying that south was preferred to east (which is the question we were trying to decide).

To further complicate the matter, the labels that point in a given direction (east, south, whatever) are not clustered in one part of the map; they

---

sheng Chang, "The Han Maps: New Light on Cartography in Classical China," *Imago Mundi* 31 (1979), pp. 9–17.

98. Mawangdui Hanmu boshu zhengli xiaozu, *Guditu* (Beijing: Wenwu chubanshe, 1977).

are scattered everywhere on it, mixed among one another. This fact suggests that the mapmakers did not expect viewers to turn the map (or move themselves around it) in order to study one part of it from one side, then another part from another, and so on. It seems, rather, that they expected all of the map to be useful when viewed from any side, even though viewers looking southward (in the terms of the map) had an advantage over northward-lookers in that they needed to read fewer characters upside down. Whether this small bias in favor of south was conscious design, unconscious cultural habit, or just accident is an interesting question but impossible to answer.

However, the maker(s) of the other Han map, the "topographical" one, *did* orient the characters in their labels in a consistent direction, thus making it clear which side they expected people to view it from—or, in our modern metaphorical terms, which side was "up." Unfortunately, they did not write *dong*, *nan*, or anything else on the map to indicate which direction that was. This problem is easy to solve, however, because the congruity of the ancient map with modern maps of the same area is very good. The ancient map shows a body of water at its "top" (inferable from the orientation of the characters on it), and modern maps make it clear that that water is the Xi Jiang 西江 estuary that leads to the South China Sea off the coast of Guangdong Province. Hence, for this map, we may be certain that "south is up." Whereas the military map "faces south" only ambiguously and very slightly, on the topographical map the privileging of south is clear.

In later times, as is well known, Chinese culture has favored south in a variety of ways. Residences, including those of emperors, faced south. The compass has been called a *zhinanzhen* 指南針 'south-pointing needle', as Chinese culture has preferred to see that needle (which after all "points" both north and south) as pointing south. A reference as early as the first century CE mentions a *sinan* 司南 'take charge of south', which apparently was a spoon-like object that a lodestone could pull as a way to indicate south.[99] A *zhinanche* 指南車 'south-pointing chariot', said to be invented

---

99. See Li Shu-hua, "Origine de la Boussole II: Aimant et Boussole," *Isis* 45, no. 2 (July 1954), pp. 175–196.

by the legendary Yellow Emperor, bore a wooden rider whose hands were supposed to point south regardless of which way the chariot turned.

Can there be any reason for favoring either north or south—any "physical basis," as contemporary metaphor theorists might say? The Han-era dictionary *Shuowen jiezi* 說文解字 defines *yin* 陰 'dark, female, negative' as *an ye shui zhi nan shan zhi bei ye* 暗也水之南山之北也 'dark; south of water, north of mountains'.[100] Later texts echo this formula, and in modern Chinese the saying *shannan shuibei wei yang, shanbei shuinan wei yin* 山南水北為陽, 山北水南為陰 'south of mountains and north of water is yang, north of mountains and south of water is yin' continues it.[101] It makes sense that the south sides of mountains should be yang (bright, sunny, and warm) and the north sides yin (dark, shaded, and cool) because of the angle from which the sun shines on the earth in the Northern Hemisphere. But why would it be the opposite for water? Why, for water, is north especially yang and south especially yin? This is not a minuscule academic question. It has been important enough to affect the names of some very large cities—Luoyang 洛陽 is on the north side of the Luo River, for example, and Jiangyin 江陰 is on the south side of the Yangtze (Changjiang). A clue to this puzzle appears in Cheng Dachang's Song-period (960–1279 CE) *Yu Gong shanchuan dili tu* 禹貢山川地理圖 (Geography of the mountains and rivers in Yu Gong): *gu yi shannan wei yang shuibei wei yang yi shouyang zhi fang ming zhi ye* 古義山南為陽水北為陽以受陽之方命之也 'the ancient notion that both south-of-the-mountain and north-of-the-water are yang comes from their both being places that receive sunlight'.[102] Here I have translated the second *yang* in the quotation as "sunlight" in order to emphasize what clearly appears to be the key natural fact that underlies the

---

100. *Shuowen dazidian* 說文大字典 (Shuowen jiezi 說文解字) (Taipei: Xuehai chubanshe 學海出版社, 1982), 7:91.

101. I am indebted to Ye Minlei for reporting how she was asked to memorize this line in elementary school in the 1990s. Email messages to the author, March 5 and 7, 2008.

102. Cheng Dachang 程大昌 (1123–1195), *Yu gong shanchuan dilitu* 禹貢山川地理圖 [Geography of the mountains and rivers in Yu Gong] (Shanghai: Shangwu yinshuguan, 1936), vol. 1 卷上, p. 50. Also in *Yingyin wenyuange sikuquanshu: jingbu* 影印文淵閣四庫全書•經部 [Jing section of the photocopied Wenyuange Complete Library in Four Divisions] (Taipei: Taiwan Commercial Press, 1983), 56: 129.

usage: river banks on north sides of rivers get more direct sunlight than do banks on south sides. (The opposite would be true in the Southern Hemisphere.) The puzzle (if there still is one) is why early European mapmakers, who were located in the Northern Hemisphere, as the Chinese were, chose to privilege the colder and darker north direction.

Several hundred years after the invention of the compass in China, "pointing south" came to mean not just showing direction but showing *correct* direction. In the poetry of Zhang Heng 張衡 (78–139 CE), Li Shangyin 李商隱 (813–58 CE), and elsewhere, *zhinan* shifts from physical matters to the ethical domain and comes to mean "pointing the way to appropriate behavior."[103] Eventually, the guidance that *zhinan* offered came to refer to a wide spectrum of life. In 1936 when the Zhonghua Book Company published a comprehensive guide to Shanghai, a city that people from elsewhere in China could find mind-boggling, editors called it *Da Shanghai Zhinan* 大上海指南 'Guide to great Shanghai'—or, more literally, "pointing south in big Shanghai."

Given this cultural favoring of south, it is interesting, and somewhat puzzling, that maps in China's Northern Song period (960–1127 CE) began to use a convention of "north is up." Several stone-carved maps of the whole of China, one from 1121 CE and others from 1136 CE and later, clearly show the Yellow River, the Yangzi River, the Shandong peninsula, and other well-known features of China's topography. Two of these, the *jiuyu shouling tu* 九域守令圖 'map of nine governing districts' and the *hua yi tu* 華夷圖 'map of the Chinese and barbarians', inscribe *bei* 北 at their "top" (away from viewer) edges, *nan* 南 at the bottom edges, *xi* 西 at the left, and *dong* 東 at the right. Both maps, moreover, contain hundreds of characters all of whose "top" sides consistently point north.[104] In sum the "north is up" orientation is strong and unambiguous. Because the elapsed time between these maps and their Han predecessors is nearly thirteen

---

103. Zhang Heng, "Dongjing fu" 東京賦, contains the line *xing jianzhinan yu wu zi* 幸見指南于吾子 'fortunate in receiving guidance from you', and Li Shangyin, "Xianji xianxianggong qi" 獻集賢相公啟, includes the line *wei baidai zhi zhinan, jiuzhou zhi muduo* 為百代之指南, 九州之木鐸 'as the [moral] compass for a hundred generations, and [moral] teacher for China'. Cihai bianji weiyuan hui, *Cihai*, p. 1586.

104. See Cao Wanru 曹婉如 et al., eds., *Zhongguo gudai dituji* 中国古代地图集 (Beijing: Wenwu chubanshe, 1990), vol. 1 (zhanguo-yuan), plates 62, 63, and 65.

centuries, we cannot speak of a "sudden" change, but it is a 180-degree change and raises the interesting question of what brought it about. Was there some influence from the Indo-European world, either over the Silk Route or over the oceans? The question is made no easier by the paucity of maps from the intervening years. One does exist, though not from the heart of China. A circular "world map" drawn in Kashgar (in contemporary Xinjiang) probably between 1072 and 1076 CE by a Turkic scholar named Mahmūd al-Kāshgarī shows Arabic script that implies an orientation in which east is the "up" (away from viewer) direction, west is down, north is left, and south is right.[105] What to make of this is hard to say.

Consciousness

Scholars who have studied metaphor in European languages have observed that "up" and "down" relate to consciousness. Lakoff and Johnson note that in English "conscious is up, unconscious down."[106] We "wake up," but "fall asleep," "drop off" (into sleep), or "sink" into a coma. We have a "*sub*conscious" and can "go under" hypnosis. Lakoff and Johnson claim that the "physical basis" for this conceptual metaphor is the fact that human beings sleep lying down and stand up (or sit up) when conscious. We wake "up" because we *get* up. One problem with this physical-basis theory is that Chinese people also sleep lying down but do not use the "conscious is up, unconscious is down" metaphor in their language—at least not before it was influenced by Western language. Modern Chinese does use *xia yishi* 下意识, literally "below consciousness" for the subconscious, but this term is clearly a borrowing, established in order to translate Sigmund Freud, Carl Jung, and others. When we fall asleep in Chinese we normally *shui zhao* 睡着, where *shui* is "sleep" and *zhao* is a verbal complement indicating that the verb "takes effect" or, as we might say in

---

105. Zhang Guangda 张广达, "Shiyi shiji de yuanxing ditu" 十一世纪的圆形地图 [A round map from the eleventh century], in Cao Wanru et al., *Zhongguo gudai dituji*, pp. 19–22; see also plate 42.

106. Lakoff and Johnson, *Metaphors We Live By*, p. 15.

colloquial English, "kicks in." In *zhao* there is no sense of up or down. Spatial metaphors for going into or out of consciousness *do* exist in Chinese, but they do not have us going up or down; they have us "crossing over" an imaginary line within a horizontal plane. When *xing* 醒 'wake up' uses a spatial metaphor, it is usually *xing lai* 'wake come' or *xing guo lai* 醒过来 'wake across come'. We the wakeful are on this side of a line, and those in slumber, stupor, or coma are on the other. To faint is to *yunguoqu* 晕过去 'swoon across go'.

It would be too simple to say that English always uses concepts of up and down for entering and exiting consciousness while Chinese uses only crossing back and forth, because there are exceptions, or quasi exceptions, on both sides. For "wake up" in English we can say "come to," which is not far from the Chinese *xing lai*. And in the previous section we saw how one of the Chinese metaphors for memorize, *bei xialai*, literally means "memorize down [toward the speaker]," while not being able to recall from memory can be *shuo bu shanglai*, literally "saying [it] cannot come up." With memory, of course, we are dealing with something less radical than completely entering or exiting consciousness, but something similar is involved; we are not conscious of things in our memories until we "recall" certain items from memory's storehouse, and this process, in Chinese, is sometimes conceived as going up or down.

Despite these exceptions, it seems clear that European languages and Chinese have two different *tendencies* in conceiving the "direction" of entering and exiting consciousness and that these tendencies, in the terms of modern cognitive science, are "conceptual metaphors" that affect how people view the world. If this is so, it becomes interesting to ask whether the two conceptual tendencies might lead people in the two cultural traditions—including their philosophers—to ask somewhat different questions. Consider, for example, the famous butterfly dream from chapter 2 of the *Zhuangzi* (third–fourth century BCE). In Burton Watson's translation:

> Once Chuang Chou [i.e., Zhuangzi] dreamt he was a butterfly, a butterfly flitting and fluttering around, happy with himself and doing as he pleased. He didn't know he was Chuang Chou. Suddenly he woke up and there he was, solid and unmistakable Chuang Chou. But he

didn't know if he was Chuang Chou who had dreamt he was a butterfly, or a butterfly dreaming he was Chuang Chou.[107]

Watson translates *jue* 覺 as "woke up," which is certainly a defensible translation, yet "up" is not part of what Zhuangzi thought had happened to him.[108] In Zhuangzi's Chinese, the slide back and forth from dreaming to waking seems somehow easier than *up* and *down* suggest in modern English. This difference may arise because (as we saw in the previous section) *up* and *down* connote so much else in modern English—more or less of some thing, higher or lower status or moral standing, and so on. Zhuangzi's puzzle feels more elegantly simple—and therefore more puzzling—in Zhuangzi's ancient Chinese. A speaker (and dreamer) of modern English might also have come up with this puzzle, but perhaps not as readily. One wonders how much the wide differences between the Chinese and European philosophical traditions lie less in their different answers to questions than in the different questions that they are induced to ask and, moreover, how much the matter of "what questions are asked" is rooted in differences of language systems. I will revisit this question later when the question of nouns and "containers" arises.

The Self in Ancient Thought

The contemporary field of cognitive science has done considerable work with the notion that the "self" is often metaphorically conceived as two different things at the same time.[109] In a sentence like "I could not control myself," one self, which is the seat of consciousness, acts (or fails to act) on another; the second self is "out there" somewhere, being acted on, even though, in a larger sense, it is still the same person. "I dragged myself out of bed" is another example, as is "you're pushing yourself too hard," or "she

---

107. Burton Watson, trans., *The Complete Works of Chuang Tzu* (New York: Columbia University Press, 1968), p. 49.
108. In his translation of Zhuangzi as *Wandering on the Way* (New York: Bantam Books, 1994), Victor Mair avoids this problem by translating *jue* as "awoke" (p. 24).
109. See Lakoff and Johnson, *Philosophy in the Flesh*, ch. 13.

plopped herself down on the couch." In such cases, theorists have called the seat-of-subjectivity self a Subject and the self that is acted upon a Self. (The capital letters are conventional here.) Another version of the "two selves" metaphor occurs in examples like "I was not myself today," where one self is more exterior and ephemeral and another is deeper and more essential. In these cases, some theorists set aside the term "Subject" and refer to Self 1 and Self 2.

All such phrases are considered metaphorical because what Subject does to Self (or the relation between Self 1 and Self 2) is not literal. I do not literally drag myself out of bed and I am not literally something other than myself. What the metaphors say can often be rephrased in nonmetaphorical language. "I was not myself today" might be said nonmetaphorically as "today I did not behave as I usually do." "You're pushing yourself too hard" might be rephrased nonmetaphorically as "you are trying too hard and might suffer as a result." A sentence like "I lifted my left arm" is nonmetaphorical if you reach over with your right arm to do the lifting but metaphorical if you use the muscles of your left arm itself.[110]

Edward Slingerland, in his book *Effortless Action: Wu-wei as Conceptual Metaphor and Spiritual Ideal in Early China*,[111] uses distinctions between "Subject" and "Self," and between "Self 1" and "Self 2," to try to shed light on what he calls the "paradox of wu-wei" among pre-Qin philosophers. *Wu-wei* 無爲, literally "[taking] no [intentional] action" is an ideal human state for Laozi, Zhuangzi, Confucius, Mencius, and Xunzi. The metaphors these thinkers employed suggest a variety of methods for achieving *wuwei*, and each method, one way or another, involves a version of the paradox of "trying not to try." Some of these thinkers—Zhuangzi, Laozi, and Mencius—emphasize *not trying*, according to Slingerland. Their view, in his paraphrase, is that "we already *are* good, and we need merely to allow this virtuous potential to realize itself."[112] For this group of thinkers the difficult question becomes: if we are already there, why does anything at all have to be attempted? Why do we need philosophers to point "a way" for us? Other

---

110. See ibid., p. 271.

111. Edward Slingerland, *Effortless Action: Wu-wei as Conceptual Metaphor and Spiritual Ideal in Early China* (Oxford: Oxford University Press, 2003).

112. Ibid., p. 12.

thinkers, among whom Confucius and Xunzi are Slingerland's examples, hold that "wu-wei is a state acquired only after a long and intensive regime of training"—that is, we do have to try. For this group the puzzle becomes: how does one apply effort toward reaching a state of applying no effort? Because "wu-wei is understood as an *achieved* state," each thinker must "specify some sort of effort-ful program for attaining this state."[113]

Slingerland names these two approaches to *wuwei* "internalist" and "externalist." He finds that neither approach can solve the paradox but "merely chooses a horn of the dilemma on which to impale itself."[114] He then applies contemporary metaphor theory to the issue and asks, about the paradox, "Does metaphor theory solve anything?" He wisely demurs. It does not solve the paradox, he writes, but it does *clarify* certain issues by "demonstrating more concretely" points that before had been "merely intuitive connections."[115] For example, when we try to understand what pre-Qin thinkers meant by metaphors involving *cong* 從, *yin* 因, *yi* 依, and *shun* 順—all of which have to do with "following" nature—the distinction between Subject and Self can help, because we can see the Subject as following the Self. When I follow my nature, "the Subject," Slingerland writes, "is able to be free of exertion [i.e., *wuwei*] because the Self is allowed to do all the work"; therefore, *wuwei* can be "a state in which action is occurring even though the Subject is no longer exerting force."[116] In another kind of metaphor, which appears especially in the *Zhuangzi*, the Subject seems to "lose" or "forget" the Self. This can be a bad thing, as when a second-rate shamen quails before a true Daoist, "loses himself" (*zishi* 自失), and runs away.[117] But "losing oneself" can also be related to a state of *wuwei*, as when one "forgets [*wang* 忘] liver and spleen, loses [*yi* 遺] ears and eyes, and un-self-consciously [*mangran* 茫然] roams outside the dusty realm, wandering easily [*xiaoyao* 逍遙] in the service of *wuwei*."[118] Similarly,

---

113. Ibid., p. 38.
114. Ibid., pp. 12 and 265.
115. Ibid., p. 270.
116. Ibid., p. 28.
117. Ibid., p. 31; Watson, *Complete Works of Chuang Tzu*, p. 96.
118. This translation is from Slingerland, *Effortless Action*, p. 32, except that I have excised "his." Slingerland notes that his rendition is based on others by Burton Watson and A. C. Graham.

the distinction of a relatively superficial Self 1 and a more essential Self 2 can be useful in interpreting *ziran* 自然, or the "so-of-itself," that one finds in the *Laozi*, where *ziran* is "the way a thing is when it follows its own internal essence."[119]

These attempts to apply modern metaphor theory to the concept of *wuwei* have to do with what *wuwei* is, not how to achieve it, and therefore can be useful in interpreting the thought of both the "internalists" and the "externalists," as Slingerland refers to them. For the externalists, however, metaphor theory has the added advantage of making sense of method, that is, how to "try not to try." The separation of Subject and Self makes it easier to conceive the Subject, here and now, as "trying"—through learning, discipline, or whatever—to achieve *wuwei* for a Self, projected into the future, who then will not need, want, or use any effort to achieve it.

Can we say that any intellectual advance is involved? One might argue that clarity itself is a contribution, but is there anything else? Probably not, as far as I can tell—at least not for the serious study of Chinese thought. But on another score there is, in my view, a significant intellectual advance. This is simply the discovery that metaphor theory based primarily on modern English and other modern Western languages can make good sense when applied to pre-Qin Chinese texts. If the distinction between Subject and Self, or between ephemeral Self 1 and essential Self 2, applies in language and life as distantly separated as pre-Qin China and the contemporary United States—and this much, at least, Slingerland has shown—then there are good grounds for hypothesizing that such distinctions are fairly deep in human experience. There does appear to be a sense in which we human beings, when we look inwardly on ourselves, can view ourselves as bifurcated.

Privilege in Dyads

In many languages, one of the items in paired categories is standardly privileged over the other. The pattern is sufficiently pervasive that some theorists have hypothesized that it, too, may be "universal."

---

119. Slingerland, *Effortless Action*, p. 35.

These paired categories, sometimes called "dyads," are things like up and down, front and back, good and evil, more and less, before and after, and love and hate. There are many, many of them. In many cases, they are not much different from what grade school teachers call "opposites."[120] Linguists have noticed a pattern in the ways languages list dyads: a "plus" item often comes first and a "minus" item second.[121] Here "plus" and "minus" are conceived broadly, to encompass such distinctions as good-bad, primary-secondary, prior-subsequent, cause-effect, and others.

Studies of dyads in the 1970s were based on European-language examples, and the results were sometimes presented, with due caution, as only "our culture's view."[122] Are dyads different in different cultures? Between Chinese and English, at any rate, they are strikingly similar. In Chinese we say *hao huai* 好坏 'good and bad', not *huai hao*; and *shang xia* 上下 'up and down', not *xia shang*. These examples match English, and so do the overwhelming majority of others: *shi fei* 是非 'right and wrong', *shi fou* 是否 'is and isn't', *dui cuo* 对错 'correct and incorrect', *qian hou* 前后 'front and back', *da xiao* 大小 'big and small', *lao shao* 老少 'old and young', *gao di* 高低 'high and low', *chang duan* 长短 'long and short', *kuan zhai* 宽窄 'wide and narrow', *ai hen* 爱恨 'love and hate', and so on.[123] In English, "black and white" may seem an exception to the pattern—and so it seems in Chinese as well. The five main colors are conventionally listed in Chinese as *hong huang lan bai hei* 红黄蓝白黑 'red, yellow, blue, white, black', with *bai* coming before *hei*, but in most other expressions, such as *heibai dianshi* 黑白电视 'black-and-white television' or *diandao hei bai* 颠倒黑白 'invert black and white—turn the truth upside-down', *hei* comes first. But exceptions like "black and white" only underscore the strength of the general pattern.

---

120. Not in all cases. *Now* and *then*, and *here* and *there*, are dyads, but not exactly "opposites."

121. On this point and in much of the following discussion, I owe much to David Moser, "Covert Sexism in Mandarin Chinese," *Sino-Platonic Papers* 74 (January 1997), pp. 1–23. No one writes more clearly or incisively than Moser on the topic of structural metaphor in Chinese.

122. William E. Cooper and John Robert Ross, "World Order," in Robin E. Grossman, L. James San, and Timothy J. Vance, eds., *Functionalism* (Chicago: Chicago Linguistic Society, 1975). The phrase "our culture's view" is from Lakoff and Johnson, *Metaphors We Live By*, p. 132.

123. This list of examples is from Moser, "Covert Sexism," pp. 2–3.

In both Chinese and English, the "privilege" of the first members in dyads is reflected not only in the fact that they come first but in their being the standard term for measuring attributes of their kind. For example, if we want to know Sam's height, we say "How tall is Sam?" not "How short is Sam?" We *can*, of course, ask "How short is Sam?" but the question would suggest a special purpose. If Sam, although thirty-one years old, is not allowed on a roller coaster because of a height requirement, we might ask "How short *is* Sam?" But if we just want to ask how tall he is in the normal way, we don't use "short." Similarly, we ask "How big is Rhode Island?" (even though it is small, as states go) and can ask "How long is a microbe?" It is entirely natural to ask "How wide is the Mississippi at its narrowest?" but would seem odd to ask "How narrow is the Mississippi at its widest?" These examples show that the first member of a dyad is a "default" category. Chinese works the same as English in this regard. We ask in Chinese *Zhang San you duo gao?* 张三有多高? 'How tall is Zhang San?' (not—except in special circumstances—*Zhang San you duo ai?* 有多矮? 'How short is Zhang San?'). The principle also holds in the "choice type" questions that are so common in Chinese. "Was what she said right?" is *ta shuo de dui bu dui?* 她说得对不对? not *ta shuo de cuo bu cuo?* 她说得错不错. Similarly, *Wenti da bu da?* 问题大不大? 'Is the problem big?' (and very seldom *wenti xiao bu xiao* 问题小不小 'Is the problem small?'); *Haizhe hao bu hao chi?* 海蜇好不好吃? 'Does the jellyfish taste good?' (never *haizhe huai bu huai chi?* 海蜇坏不坏吃? 'Does the jellyfish taste *huai*—bad?').

In a very small number of cases, Chinese and English differ in their privileging. North and south is an example. In English we talk about the North and South Poles and in Chinese the *nanbeiji* 南北极 'South and North Poles'; talks between the developed and developing countries are the North-South dialogue in English, but the *nanbei duihua* 南北对话 'south-north dialogue' in Chinese.

It is also worth noting that in both Chinese and English, the conventional order of a dyad can be reversed if one has a conscious reason for reversing it. In contemporary English, when people want to compensate for the bias inherent in saying "he and she," they sometimes say "she and he." Among the talking points on "the Korea question" that Hu Jintao, the president of China, brought with him on his tour of North America in 2005 was *beinan Chaoxian zhi zheng shi xiongdi zhi zheng* 北南朝鲜之争是兄

弟之争 'the struggle between North and South Korea is a struggle between brothers'.[124] Here the reversal of the conventional *nanbei* to an unconventional *beinan* apparently was done to grant primacy to North, not South, Korea. The switch was made all the more important because of the parallel phrase *xiongdi* 'older brother and younger brother'. Unless *nanbei* were reversed, South Korea would be parallel with "older brother," which Hu apparently did not want.

The striking congruities between Chinese and English in the way dyads are conceived raises the question why this might be so. Borrowing is out of the question; the independent roots of usages in the two languages are far too obvious for that. But might there be some kind of commonality in human experience that provides an "experiential basis" for the expressions in both Chinese and English—and, perhaps, in human languages generally? Lakoff and Johnson, citing work by William Cooper and John Ross, have suggested a "me first" basis for the ordering of dyads.[125] The idea is that the first item in a dyad is somehow "closer to me"—the seat of subjectivity—than the second item. Lakoff and Johnson list "up, front, active, good, here, and now" as examples of the "me first" position that explains why we say—in these particular orders—"up and down, front and back, active and passive, good and bad, here and there, now and then." This claim raises some questions. We must assume, first of all, that "me" is conceived as *good* more than *bad*; this assumption is probably all right, in view of general human nature. We also must see "me" as closer to *now* than to *then*, and as closer to *here* than to *there*. Since "me" at other times would be *me then* (and might also be at another place, hence *me there*), we are obliged to understand "me" as meaning "my present subjectivity"—or, to use Slingerland's terms, Subject, not Self. This, too, seems fair enough. The biggest problem among the "me first" examples Lakoff and Johnson present is why *up* should be closer to "me" than *down* is. They recognize this problem but do not address it effectively.[126]

---

124. Zhang Liang, email message to author, August 29, 2005.

125. Lakoff and Johnson, *Metaphors We Live By*, p. 132.

126. They argue that "nearest is first," which would explain why *up* would be listed first once one had decided that it was nearest. But on the question whether *up* is in fact "nearest," they only state the point without arguing it. They write: "Of the two concepts *up* and *down*, *up* is oriented *nearest* to the prototypical speaker" (ibid., p. 133).

Insofar as the "me first" theory works, it works almost as well in Chinese as in English. If *front, good,* and *active* are "me first" in English and hence listed before *back, bad,* and *passive,* similarly in Chinese *qian, hao,* and *zhudong* 主动 are conventionally listed before *hou, huai,* and *beidong* 被动. *Now* and *then* are a bit problematic because *xianzai* 现在 and *nashi* 那时 are not an idiomatic pair in the way *now* and *then* are in English. A more idiomatic pair in Chinese (at least in northern Mandarin) would be *zhehuir* 这会儿 'this moment—now' and *nahuir* 那会儿 'that moment—then', and this pair does observe the "me first" pattern. A more significant divergence from the "me first" pattern in Chinese is that *zher* 这儿 or *zheli* 这里 'here' do not always refer to the position of the speaker, as *here* does in English. For example, in planning a meeting, if someone says in English "let's meet here at your place," we infer that the speaker is presently at your place. (Were he or she somewhere else, the sentence would be "let's meet *there* at your place.") This convention is mandatory in English but in Chinese is not. One occasionally hears in Chinese sentences like *zamen dou dao ni zheli lai jianmian ba* 咱们都到你这里来见面吧 (literally, "let's all meet here at your place") even if the speaker is not presently at your place.[127] In such cases, the speaker projects the center of things ("here") to the location that is associated with the listener. This pattern is not common in Chinese, where *dao ni nali qu* 到你那里去 is still much more common in such circumstances; but the fact that the usage exists at all shows Chinese to have a conceptual flexibility that English does not allow.

The "me first" explanation of the internal order in dyads is not ideal, but I do not know a better one. To say that the "plus-minus" congruities between Chinese and English in this regard are mere chance is a much weaker theory. Something is going on, and it goes on at a level that speakers of the two languages do not normally notice. David Moser has astutely

---

127. I have noted this kind of usage in my own experience on several occasions. It also appears occasionally in literature, for example when we read in Hu Fayun's 胡发云 novel *Ruyan@sars.come* 如焉 @sars.come [So it was@sars.come] (Beijing: Zhongguo guoji guangbo chubanshe, 2006), from a narrator who is not located at anyone's house, that *Damo zhiyao huicheng, jiu changchang dao Wei laoshi zher lai* 达摩只要回城, 就常常到卫老师这儿来 'whenever Damo returned to the city he made it a habit to come [here] to Teacher Wei's place' (p. 31).

observed that the evaluative connotations of "plus-minus" pairs often go unnoticed even when they relate to major and controversial social issues. Moser shows how the privileging of one or another pole can be "covert," and illustrates with the male-female dyad.[128]

In both Chinese and English, male comes first across a wide range of uses. In English we have man and woman, he and she, brothers and sisters, husband and wife, Mr. and Mrs., sons and daughters, guys and dolls, and many other examples. We also have paired names like Jack and Jill, Romeo and Juliet, Hansel and Gretel, Anthony and Cleopatra, Samson and Delilah, Roy Rogers and Dale Evans, and many others in which the male's name comes first.[129] Similarly, in Chinese we have *nannü* 男女 'male and female', *fuqi* 夫妻 or *fufu* 夫妇 'husband and wife', *fumu* 父母 'father and mother', *baba mama* 爸爸妈妈 'Dad and Mom', *xiongdi jiemei* 兄弟姐妹 'brothers and sisters' and *ernü* 儿女 or *zinü* 子女 'sons and daughters'. Slightly more abstractly, but still "male first," there are *longfeng* 龍鳳 'dragon [male] and phoenix [female]', *qiankun* 乾坤 'male and female—the cosmos', and *caizi jiaren* 才子佳人 '[implicitly male] talent and [implicitly female] beauty'. Male-first pairs of names are also common in Chinese: Liang Shanbo 梁山伯 and Zhu Yingtai 祝英台; Jia Baoyu 賈寶玉 and Lin Daiyu 林黛玉.[130] Moser notes exceptions to the pattern, such as *yin* 陰 'female element' and *yang* 陽 'male element', which are always *yinyang* in Chinese. In English, "ladies and gentlemen" appears to be an exception, although Moser notes that it is based in a kind of chivalry that makes the case problematic. "Bonnie and Clyde" is a more interesting exception because it violates not only the male-first pattern but also the rhythmic preference of TAH-ta TAH-ta over ta-ta-ta-TAH. (As we saw in chapter 1, "salt and pepper" is generally preferred to "pepper and salt.") In searching for an explanation for Bonnie and Clyde, Moser wonders if it may lie in "the sheer novelty of a female bank robber."[131] The English-language exception of Mom and Dad (or Mom and Pop) is not mirrored in Chinese,

---

128. David Moser, "Covert Sexism," pp. 1–2.
129. Ibid., p. 3.
130. Ibid., pp. 4–5.
131. Ibid., p. 3, n. 3.

where *bama* 爸妈 and *fumu* are standard. Moser notes that *mufu* "sounds utterly wrong to Chinese ears."[132]

Beyond the question of privileging within dyads is a subtler but more telling fact: categories that in theory are gender-neutral are often—in both Chinese and English—implicitly understood as male. "Male" is often a default interpretation of phrases in which gender is formally ambiguous. Moser cites stories from Chinese joke books to illustrate. One joke begins *you yige ren, laopo si le* 有一個人老婆死了 'there was a person whose wife died'. Here *ren* 人 'person' is theoretically gender-free, but the hearer understands the term as male, and this is confirmed when we hear that "the wife" died. What happens, Moser asks us to observe, if we say the same sentence but have a husband die? The sentence *you yige ren, zhangfu sile* 有一個人丈夫死了 'there was a person whose husband died' generates, according to Moser, "a slight sense of strangeness" for Chinese speakers.[133] *Ren* conjures (by the default principle) a certain expectation that the joke will be about a man; then, when we hear that "the husband" died, something doesn't fit. The listener needs to go back and recalibrate. Chinese jokes about females standardly do not begin by calling them *ren* but use a gendered term from the beginning. For example: *you yiwei xiaojie zai haitanshang shai taiyang, chuanzhe sandianshi youyongyi...* 有一位小姐在海灘上曬太陽, 穿着三點式游泳衣 'there was a young lady sunbathing at the beach, wearing a bikini...'. If we substitute *ren* in this example, Moser's insight is confirmed. The phrase generates a mild sense of contradiction. In hearing *you yige ren chuan sandianshi youyongyi* 有一個人穿三點式游泳衣 'there was a person wearing a bikini', the listener needs to understand a small but awkward gender shift halfway through.

The male gendering of "neutral" terms is further confirmed by the fact that whenever the protagonist of a joke is explicitly tagged as female (*you yiwei xiaojie...* 有一位小姐 'there was a young woman', *you yiwei lao taitai...* 有一位老太太 'there was an old lady'), it raises an expectation that her gender is going to be relevant to the story. This is not true if the protago-

---

132. Ibid., p. 4, n. 4. I have a Chinese American friend who wrote to her parents, who were natives of Taishan 台山 in Guangdong, addressing them as *mufu* 母父. But this usage may have been influenced by English.

133. Ibid., p. 7.

nist is male. Whether tagged explicitly (*you yige laotour*... 有一個老頭兒 'there was an old man') or implicitly (*you yige ren*... 有一個人 'there was a person'), there is no parallel implication that his sex is going to matter. It might or might not matter. Essentially the same is true for English-language jokes. A joke that starts "this guy goes into a bar..." can be about anything. But if a joke begins "this lady went into a bar..." the listener will wait to hear why it matters that she was female. You can test this effect by choosing any "this guy goes into a bar" joke and substituting "woman", "lady," or "gal" for "guy" but changing nothing else in the joke. Then watch your listeners' reactions. Do they wonder why you supplied "unnecessary information"? Moser cites a parallel case in which one might begin a joke by saying, "This 650-pound man walks into a bar..." and then telling a story that has nothing to do with the size of the man. Listeners would wonder why the joke-teller supplied extraneous information.[134]

Moser's choice of jokes as source materials for studying implicit attitudes is a probably a good one, because jokes are told in relaxed and relatively unguarded contexts where "default" attitudes can emerge. When telling jokes, people focus on their punch lines, not their conceptual categories. But it is important to note that this default phenomenon is not limited to jokes. It extends to many other language contexts. Liu Binyan's work of reportage *Yige ren he ta de yingzi* 一个人和他的影子 (A *ren* [man] and his shadow) tells the story of a courageous young man and would not, I think, have borne that title if the protagonist had been female.[135] When a protagonist is female, people use a gendered term to make her femaleness explicit. The Chinese language sometimes folds *nü* 女 'female' or *mu* 母 'mother' into a term that is normally used for men in order to produce a version of the term that is earmarked, as it were, "female special case." Examples are *cainü* 才女 'female talent', which is the "female exception" version of *caizi* 才子 'talented scholar', or *shengmu* 圣母 'sage mother—female sage', the female version of the (normally male) *shengren* 圣人 'sage'. More common than substitution, though, is the simple adding of *nü* as a prefix, as in *nü xuesheng* 女学生 'girl student', *nü daifu* 女大夫 'woman doctor', *nü*

---

134. Ibid., p. 6, n. 9.
135. Liu Binyan, *Liu Binyan Baogaowenxue* 劉賓雁報告文學 (Hong Kong: Mingchuang chubanshe 明窗出版社, 1987), pp. 67–136.

qiangren 女强人 'female strongman', *nü zhurengong* 女主人公 'female protagonist', *nü siji* 女司机 'female [car or truck] driver', *nü minbing* 女民兵 'female militia member', *nü yingxiong* 女英雄 'heroine', *nü yongdongyuan* 女运动员 'female athlete', and many other examples. For none of these terms is *nan* 男 'male' an appropriate prefix. The term that contains *nü* is sometimes shortened for the sake of rhythmic balance (e.g., *gongren* 工人 'worker' becomes *nügong* 女工 'female worker', *jianyu* 监狱 'prison' becomes *nüjian* 女监 'women's prison', etc.), but the use of *nü* as a tag that suggests "special case" is the same. *Niang* 娘 'woman' can be used either as a prefix (*niangzijun* 娘子军 'women's army') or a suffix (*laobanniang* 老板娘 'boss lady'); in either event the "special case" coloration of the gendered term remains the same. A male army is a *jundui* 军队 'army', not a *nanzijun* 男子军 'men's army'; and the male boss is a *laoban* 老板 'boss', not (not normally, anyway) a *laobandie* 老板爹 'boss daddy'.

The principle that the female case needs "special marking" applies even to the internal structure of characters. Moser points out that standard modern Chinese includes about 275 characters that use the *nü* 女 'female' radical, whereas a *nan* 男 'male' radical does not even exist. The generic "human being" (*ren* 人) radical apparently does all the marking that males need.[136] In the early 1930s the poet Liu Dabai 劉大白 invented a character for "him" by combining 男 and 也 to correspond to the recently invented *ta* 她 'she, her', but his effort died for want of followers.[137]

Yet we must not overstate the extent to which terms like *ren* 'human being' carry an implicit male connotation. Theoretically, the term is ungendered, and in many contexts it actually is. Moser points out that when someone is using a public telephone and we say *you yige ren zheng zai yong* 有一个人正在用 'someone is using it now' there is no presumption about the sex of the user.[138] When we talk about *ren zhi changqing* 人之常情 'common sense in human relations', it is natural to think of both sexes. If an elevator holds a maximum of twelve *ren*, no one checks sexes before deciding whether to allow a thirteenth to board. There are, moreover, a small number of ungendered terms for which "female," not "male," is the

---

136. David Moser, "Covert Sexism," pp. 12–13.
137. Ibid., p. 11.
138. Ibid., p. 5.

default interpretation. These are the names of roles in society that usually are filled by females, such as *hushi* 护士 'nurse' or *laoshi* 老师 'teacher'—provided it is a teacher at nursery or primary school. (At higher levels of education, *laoshi* takes on a male "default" interpretation.) English, too, observes these kinds of exceptions to the "male default" rule.

The close resemblance of Chinese and English in the conception and use of gendered terms seems as strong as for the other dyads we have considered above. We will look next at other examples of how far this resemblance extends.

Metaphors That Chinese and English (Pretty Much) Share

When we study conceptual metaphor across language and culture, one of the attractions is our curiosity to discover whether there are different ways to "conceive the world." A book on Chinese and English metaphor by Dilin Liu captures this aspiration in its title, *Metaphor, Culture, and Worldview*.[139] Do Chinese and English have different "worldviews"? How much? If it is true, as a variety of philosophers and cognitive scientists have claimed, that many conceptual metaphors are either determined by the common features of human experience or, perhaps, built into the structure of the human mind, then we should expect there to be considerable congruity in worldview across languages. Much as we might enjoy taking note of cultural differences, there is no getting around the fact that much of human life everywhere is obviously—boringly, one might say—similar. People have two arms, ten fingers, and a nose, walk upright, live in families, eat, sleep, feel pain when pinched, and have DNA that differs by less than 1 percent from anyone else's. Much of language, too, falls into this area where commonality is taken for granted. The basic equipment of the human mouth determines a common repertoire of oral sounds. And studies have revealed what seem to be commonalities in the brain's equipment as well. To give just one example, it seems that in all human languages, the categories that have primacy within taxonomies are those that

---

139. Dilin Liu, *Metaphor, Culture, and Worldview: The Case of American English and the Chinese Language* (Lanham, Md.: University Press of America, 2002).

are most often usable in daily life. *Chair*, for example, is more basic than *furniture* or *wooden things* on the one hand and *rocker* or *Granny's rocker* on the other.[140]

We need to recognize that when we study "culture" or "worldview" we usually have a bias toward focusing on differences. We do this because the differences are more interesting. I would not get many students in my Chinese culture courses if I spent my lectures explaining that Chinese people have two arms, ten fingers, a nose, and so on, even though these are extremely fundamental facts about Chinese life. It is more interesting to compare the culture of chopsticks with that of knife and fork, even though chewing, swallowing, sitting on a chair, digesting, defecating, and so on comprise an area of overlap that is immensely larger and more complex than the difference between chopsticks and a fork.

Yet it remains important (not merely interesting) to study cultural differences, in large part just because we human beings make such a big deal of them. (It is ironic that our zest for noticing differences is one of the many ways we are the same.) Our differences set the stage for much of what we mean by "understandings" and "misunderstandings" across cultures and also provide the basis for a wide range of activity—from university departments of national languages all the way to international rivalries and even wars. A focus on ten fingers, the nose, and DNA overlap would not lead in these directions.

In this section and the next, I want to look at a range of examples that metaphor theorists have found in English and ask how much Chinese may differ from them. I will begin with examples that seem significant for their similarity and move toward ones that seem interesting for their differences. The reader should not expect any movement toward systematic contrasting "worldviews," however. I do not find such things, and doubt that they are there to be found.

In looking for conceptual metaphors that are similar between the two languages, we need first to note the special case of borrowing. Chinese,

---

140. Objective criteria for what is meant by "primary" or "basic" here can be spelled out. See Lakoff, *Women, Fire, and Dangerous Things*, pp. 32–34; Lakoff credits Roger Brown, "How Shall a Thing Be Called?," *Psychological Review* 65, pp. 14–21, for a "classic" statement on the matter.

beginning especially in late-Qing times, has borrowed a number of conceptual metaphors from English and other European languages. Some of these metaphors have taken root in Chinese in ways that diverge from how they were used in European languages. (We saw, for example, how "yellow" evolved from "scandal-mongering" toward "pornographic" after the metaphor entered Chinese.) Other borrowings, especially more recent ones, such as *langfei shijian* 浪费时间 for "waste time," carry the obvious flavor of a loan. Sometimes the sense of "translatese" is overbearing. Ning Yu cites the example of *Zhongguo jingji zhengzai ruan zhuolu, guore de zhuangtai yijing jiangwen* 中国经济正在软着陆, 过热的状态已经降温 'China's economy is making a soft landing, and its overheated state is cooling down'.[141]

But having noted the problem of borrowings, let us now generally set these examples aside. They have limited use in revealing the conceptual habits of originally different languages. Let us turn to conceptual metaphors that are similar across languages even though they seem to spring from independent roots.

A widely noted example, for many languages, is the metaphor "affection is warmth." In English we say things like "a warm welcome" or "a lukewarm friendship," and in Chinese *relie huanying* 热烈欢迎 'warm [indeed, hot] welcome' and *reqing jiedai* 热情接待 'warm reception'. The counterpart metaphor "unaffection is coldness" has been noted as well, and in English we have "cool reception" and "sexual frigidity" just as, in Chinese, we have *lengmo* 冷漠 'cold and detached', *lengxiao* 冷笑 'cold laugh—sneer', or *lengbingbing* 冷冰冰 'frosty (in attitude)'. To brush someone off in English we can give a "cold shoulder"; in Chinese we do the same thing with the eye: *lengyan* 冷眼 'cold eye'. Lakoff and Johnson suggest that the origin of the "affection is warmth" metaphor is our experience as infants of a parent's embrace, in which warmth and affection are delivered simultaneously.[142] "Unaffection is coldness" presumably arises as a natural corollary to "affection is warmth." John Searle, on the other hand, has argued that a metaphor like "unaffection is coldness" works quite well without an experiential base and without any need for one. Searle

---

141. Ning Yu, *Contemporary Theory of Metaphor*, p. 169.
142. Lakoff and Johnson, *Philosophy in the Flesh*, p. 50.

shows in detail how the metaphorical statement "Sally is a block of ice" cannot be interpreted in terms of literal statements about Sally and ice blocks that show the two to have any common attributes.[143] Yet the metaphor is not only understandable but similar to others that have arisen in a variety of human cultures. Searle concludes that "the notion of being cold just is associated with being unemotional."[144]

If *warmth* means "affection," it is also true—in Chinese, English, and apparently many languages—that when the degree of warmth gets high, the metaphorical meaning turns from affection to anger. We get "hot under the collar" in English and *fa huo* 發火 'emit fire' in Chinese. A related metaphor sees anger as "fluid under pressure" or "fluid in a container," as when you get "steamed up," "blow your stack," or "explode" in English or, in Chinese, *sheng qi* 生气 'produce vapor—get angry', *fa piqi* 发脾气 'emit spleen gas—throw a tantrum', or become *qihuhu de* 气呼呼 'gas puff-puffy—panting with rage'. Is there a universal physical basis for these metaphors? Lakoff is impressed with experimental results from Paul Ekman and colleagues that show increased skin temperatures and heart rates when human beings become angry.[145] Lakoff hypothesizes that among "languages of the world, we will not find any that contradict the physiological results" of this study.[146]

This claim is open to doubt. Several studies, which go well beyond my brief analysis here, have shown that there is indeed considerable congruity between Chinese and English uses of "anger is heat" metaphors.[147] But

---

143. Searle, "Metaphor," p. 96.
144. Ibid., p. 98.
145. Paul Ekman, Robert W. Levenson, and Wallace V. Friesen, "Autonomic Nervous System Activity Distinguishes among Emotions," *Science* 221, no. 4616, pp. 1208–1210.
146. Lakoff, *Women, Fire, and Dangerous Things*, p. 407.
147. Ning Yu, *Contemporary Theory of Metaphor*, pp. 52–60; Zoltán Kövecses, "The Concept of Anger: Universal or Culture Specific?," *Psychopathology* 33 (2000), pp. 159–170; Brian King, "The Conceptual Structure of Emotional Experience in Chinese," Ph.D. diss., Ohio State University, 1989. Ning Yu feels that he has discovered a minor difference between Chinese and English metaphors for anger in that English uses "hot fluid in a container" (p. 51) while Chinese uses "hot gas in a container" (p. 54). But this seems simply a misunderstanding of English, where "fluid" means "liquid or gas," not just "liquid."

whether or not actual body heat is the cause of the congruity seems far less certain. The increases in blood temperature that Ekman and colleagues found during anger were only 0.08–0.10 degrees Centigrade. These are very small differences—so small that one might reasonably ask why they are not associated with "warm" affection rather than "hot" anger. "Normal" body temperatures vary in a person during a day by much larger margins. If such small differences really are the basis for "anger is heat" metaphors, it would have to be true that people notice them during anger and associate them with the anger. Do they? Are such small differences noticeable, especially when one's psyche is presumably dominated by anger? Moreover, since metaphors presumably are invented not at the very moment of anger but some time later, when one is not experiencing the anger but only recalling it, or perhaps observing it in others (in whom one would need to infer the temperature rise empathetically), we would need to postulate that the tiny temperature differences are either remembered in oneself or inferable from observation of someone else. Neither postulate seems likely.

Another problem is that Ekman and colleagues found that anger is associated not only with rises in body temperature but also with increases in the rate of heartbeat that were, proportionally speaking, much larger. During anger, heartbeat rates increased to eight more beats per minute than normal. So why, on Lakoff's hypothesis, would it not have been more likely that we generate an "anger is faster heartbeat" metaphor? Some have suggested that heartbeat increase underlies the "fluid under pressure" metaphor, and there is some prima facie plausibility to this. We do say things like "I was so angry that I almost blew an artery." But there are problems with this conjecture as well. Worry about bursting a blood vessel depends on modern understanding of the circulatory system, something that came much later than the formation of conceptual metaphor in both English and Chinese. In order to test whether an increased heartbeat could have given rise to the metaphor "anger is fluid under pressure," we would need subjectively to *feel* a sense of pressure when angry. Do we? I think so. But is it because of the increased heartbeat?

Yet another problem in identifying the origins of the "anger is fluid under pressure" metaphor is that anger is not the only feeling with which we associate an "internal pressure" metaphor. In English we say things like "bursting with pride" and in Chinese *manxin huanxi* 满心欢喜 'the heart is filled with happiness' or *annabuzhu xinzhong de xiyue* 按捺不住心中的喜悦 'cannot contain the joy in the heart'. In addition to studying subjects who were experiencing anger, Ekman and colleagues studied subjects experiencing happiness, and in the happiness cases found very slight *drops* (0.03–0.07 degrees Centigrade) in skin temperature; heartbeat rates went up, as they did during anger, but to a lesser extent. These findings raise several questions: if both happiness and anger lead to increased heartbeat, and if heartbeat indeed is a basis for the "fluid under pressure" metaphor, then would we not be better off postulating a generic "emotion is fluid under pressure" metaphor?[148] This would accord with the physiological data as well as with the metaphors that tell us that both anger and happiness can overflow, be hard to contain, and so on. It would lend support to Lakoff's "physiological universality" hypothesis, but at a higher level of generality than Lakoff proposed. It would, however, solve problems only for the "fluid under pressure" metaphor, not the "anger is heat" metaphor, for which the other problems I have pointed out would remain.

Let's move to another example. Chinese and English are very close in their use of "stinky is bad" as a conceptual metaphor. Here the underlying experiential basis is fairly obvious. The undesirability of foul odor is, like two arms and ten fingers, probably precultural. Of course, there are a few things that are stinky and yet have been attractive to human beings (cod lutefisk, jackfruit, camembert cheese), but these items are rare enough that they only underscore the validity of the basic pattern. In English, any number of things can "stink" metaphorically—a bad idea, a dull movie, a naïve plan, your school's volleyball team. Something might even "stink to high heaven." "I smell a rat" means that I have picked up an olfactory sign that something is wrong. In Chinese, *chou* 臭 is negative across a similar range of application. When someone's reputation is bad, he or she is *chou*. A stupid move in chess is a *chouqi* 臭棋 'stinking chess piece', a wild shot in basketball a *chouqiu* 臭球 'stinking ball'. When *chou* is used as an adverb it still carries a strong negative flavor, as in *choumei* 臭美 'show off disgustingly' or *chouchi chouhe* 臭吃臭喝 'eat and drink with ugly abandon'. All of

---

148. Ning Yu does speak of an "emotions are fluids in a container" metaphor (*Contemporary Theory of Metaphor*, p. 67).

these uses are in basic harmony with "stinking" behavior in English. Chinese does go a bit beyond English when *chou* metaphorically means "severely" or "intensely," as in *chouma* 臭骂 'stinky scold—deliver a tongue-lashing', but the overall connotation remains negative. *Chou doufu* 臭豆腐 'stinky [fermented] bean curd' might seem an exception to the "stinky is bad" metaphor, because people genuinely do like it. But *chou doufu* is not an exception because it is not a metaphor. It stinks literally, like lutefisk or camembert. (What separates Chinese people from Swedes or French in this regard is only truth in labeling.) The point of the term *chou doufu* is not to say metaphorically that the bean curd has a bad reputation or is showing off.

Other kinds of metaphor that Chinese and English share are metaphors for difficulties.[149] "Difficulties are burdens" is one example, as when we say in English "she's *weighed down* by responsibilities." Lakoff and Johnson suggest that the experiential basis for this metaphor is "the discomforting or disabling effect of lifting or carrying heavy objects."[150] Chinese similarly uses *fudan hen zhong* 负担很重 'burdens are heavy' both literally and metaphorically. When burdens are relieved, one can say in Chinese *ru shi zhongfu* 如释重负 'as if setting down a heavy load'. Even more common, in both languages, are metaphors in which difficulties are blockages or impediments. In English we sometimes try to "get around" regulations, "get through" a trial, or "hack our way through" a bureaucratic jungle. Sometimes we "run into a brick wall."[151] In Chinese, too, difficulties can be *zhang'ai* 障碍 'obstacles' that *zu'ai* 阻碍 'block' one's progress. The challenge is to *xiaochu* 消除 'dispel, remove' or *paichu* 排除 'shove aside, get rid of' such things. During the Cultural Revolution, Mao Zedong enjoined the Chinese people to *paichu wannan, qu zhengqu shengli* 排除万难去争取胜利 'push aside every difficulty and go pursue victory'. Specific images in Chinese often differ from those of English even while the basic conceptual metaphor remains the same. "Stumbling block" in English uses the same image as *banjiaoshi* 绊脚石 'foot-tripping stone' in Chinese; *lanluhu* 拦路虎

---

149. For a variety of examples see Lakoff and Johnson, *Philosophy in the Flesh*, pp. 188–190, and Ning Yu, *Contemporary Theory of Metaphor*, pp. 202–211.
150. Lakoff and Johnson, *Philosophy in the Flesh*, p. 50.
151. The examples are adapted from ibid., p. 189.

'road-blocking tiger' uses a different image but still illustrates the conceptual metaphor "difficulties are impediments."[152]

The English word "comprehend," which comes from Latin *com* 'jointly' plus *prehendere* 'grasp', illustrates the metaphor "understanding is grasping." This metaphor appears elsewhere in modern English in phrases like "I can't grasp transfinite numbers."[153] Chinese uses a similar metaphor when *bawo* 把握 'grasp' means "confidence" in a mental ability: *kai jiaoche wo you bawo, kai kache mei bawo* 开轿车我有把握，开卡车没把握 'I know what I'm doing driving sedans, not driving trucks'. There is a subtle difference, though. *Bawo* in Chinese is used for having confidence in how to do something, not for the more purely mental experience of "getting it" about something like transfinite numbers. For that meaning, Chinese often uses *mingbai* 明白, literally "bright white," as in *wo mingbai ni de yisi* 我明白你的意思, literally "I bright-white your meaning." This usage illustrates another systematic metaphor in which brightness, in one way or another, is "good." As an adjective, *mingbai* can mean "clear, pellucid" in a positive sense. *Ming* by itself can mean "open, honest" as opposed to *an* 暗, literally "dark" and metaphorically "hidden, covert," as in *mingren buzuo anshi* 明人不做暗事 'honest people don't do dark [untransparent] things'. *Yanming* 'eyes are bright' means sharp-eyed in *yanming shoukuai* 眼明手快 'sharp of eye and deft of hand' or *yanming xinliang* 眼明心亮 'sharp eye and bright mind—see and think clearly'. "Eyes bright" also contributes in the phrase *ercong muming* 耳聪目明 'ears sharp eyes bright', whose short version, *congming*, is the common word for "smart." *Liang* 'bright' participates in the "bright is good" metaphor independently of *ming*; when we *dakai chuanghu shuo lianghua* 打开窗户说亮话, we "open the window and say bright words"—that is, say what we really mean. After we do this, someone might say *wo xinli liang le* 我心里亮了, literally "my mind is bright now," that is, I understand. *Piaoliang* 漂亮 'spiffy-bright' is the common word for "pretty." English uses essentially the same metaphor in phrases like "a bright child" and "dark days ahead." Exceptions to the pattern tend to apply only in restricted ranges; "dark" is good in "tall, dark, and hand-

---

152. Some of the examples in this paragraph are borrowed from Ning Yu, *Contemporary Theory of Metaphor*, p. 203.

153. Lakoff and Johnson, *Philosophy in the Flesh*, pp. 54, 125.

some," but this phrase applies only in certain contexts, often to dashing young men of a certain kind.[154]

Lakoff and Johnson find "important is big" to be a conceptual metaphor of English—as when we say "tomorrow is a *big* day."[155] In Chinese, too, we say that an important official is a *daguan* 大官 'big official' and a major surgical operation is a *dashoushu* 大手术 'big operation'. Lakoff and Johnson conjecture that the connection between "big" and "important" may derive from childhood, when, in a child's view, parents are consistently both big and important. They also suggest that the connection between "big" and "important" has a parallel in the *form* of language, specifically that "more of form is more of content." For example, to say that something "is bi-i-i-i-ig," drawing out one's voice, gives the impression that it is bigger than if one just says it is big.[156] Although they do not say so, here Lakoff and Johnson are relying on another conceptual metaphor: "longer in time is more (of something)," which works in piggyback combination with "more of form is more of content." In any case, their insight, for this kind of example, does apply in Chinese as well. Something *hen da-a-a-a-a!* in Chinese is bigger than something merely *hen da* 很大 'big'.[157] *Big* and *da* might be confusing examples because the words themselves mean "big," so the idea of big is coming from both the form of the word and its referent. But the principle holds with other vocabulary as well. To emphasize that one *can* do something, in English one might say "I ca-a-a-a-n!" and in Chinese *wo h-h-u-u-u-i-i!* 我会- - -.

Lakoff and Johnson cite duplication as another case in which "more form is more content." When a noun, verb, or adjective stands for something, the same word repeated can stand for more of the same or a higher degree of it.[158] They write that the duplication principle applies, as far as they know, to "all languages of the world," but for Chinese it works only

---

154. I am grateful to Nicholas Admussen for this and other examples in this section.

155. Lakoff and Johnson, *Philosophy in the Flesh*, p. 50.

156. Lakoff and Johnson, *Metaphors We Live By*, p. 127.

157. When *hen* is not stressed, *hen da* means 'big', not 'very big'. See Ta-tuan Ch'en et al, *Chinese Primer: Notes and Exercises*, rev. ed., vol. 2 (Princeton, N.J.: Princeton University Press, 2007), p. 27, n. 7.

158. Lakoff and Johnson, *Metaphors We Live By*, p. 128.

unevenly. It often holds for nouns and auxiliary nouns, such as *renren* 人人 'person-person—everybody', *jiajiahuhu* 家家户户 'every house and home', *tiantian* 天天 'every day', and so on. When Gao Xingjian describes a potholed highway as *daochu kengkeng wawa* 到处坑坑凹凹 'pits and cavities everywhere,'[159] the idea is that there are a great many of both *keng* 'pits' and *wa* 'cavities'. But the principle does not work for other nouns, such as *baba* 爸爸 'Daddy', *meimei* 妹妹 'younger sister', *taitai* 太太 'Mrs.', *baobao* 宝宝 'baby', *xingxing* 'star' 星星, *xingxing* 猩猩 'ape', and many other examples.[160] Sometimes, especially in southwestern Mandarin (around Yunnan), noun repetition implies smallness, as in *qiuqiu* 球球 'small ball or bead'.[161] This tendency for repetition to suggest *small* or *less* contradicts the hypothesis that "repetition is more."

Lakoff and Johnson hold that "more form is more content" applies to verbs and adjectives as well, that is, that "more of the verb [or adjective] stands for more of the action [or property]."[162] But here, too, Chinese fits only unevenly. Repeated adjectives in Chinese do often intensify the degree of something, as in *chi de baobao de* 吃得饱饱的 'eaten good and full', *zhongzhong de da* 重重地打 'beat fiercely', *jiejieshishi de* 结结实实的 'strong and solid', and so on. Sometimes, though, the repetition of adjectives diminishes the strength of the adjective, or at least makes it a bit fuzzy, as in *wuzili heihei de* 屋子里黑黑的 'darkish in the room' or *yanlei wangwangr de* 眼泪汪汪儿的 'teary-eyed'.

Repeated verbs, for their part, almost never signal "more" of the verb. They are commonly "verb plus cognate object," as in *kankan* (short for *kanyikan* 看一看) 'take a look', *chichi* 吃吃 'have a bite (of something)', and so on, and, somewhat less often, are verb-plus-complement, as in *men kaikai le* 门开开了 'the door has been opened'. In both these cases, the second verb has a clear function, but it is not that of "adding more verb." There is the problem, too, that in Chinese, repetition occurs in a large variety of

---

159. Gao Xingjian, *Lingshan* 靈山 (Soul mountain) (Taipei: Lianjing chubanshe 聯經出版社, 1990), p. 1.

160. See Yuen Ren Chao, *A Grammar of Spoken Chinese* (Berkeley: University of California Press, 1968), pp. 198–210. Several of my examples here are drawn from these pages of Chao.

161. Ibid., p. 202.

162. Lakoff and Johnson, *Metaphors We Live By*, p. 128.

METAPHOR

onomatopoeic and other lively expressions that are not onomatopoeic but are close to it. Dogs say *wangwang* 汪汪 'bowwow'; something sourish is *suanbuliuliude* 酸不溜溜的 (literally 'sour-not-slippery-slippery-ish'); a chubby child is *pangdudude* 胖嘟嘟的 (literally 'fat-bunch-bunch-ish'). It is hard to pinpoint in these examples what the repetition is telling us; but it is something considerably more subtle than "more."

In a similar argument, Lakoff and Johnson hold that the metaphor "closeness is strength" can apply to form as well as to content.[163] When we say "the people closest to the prime minister" we might mean his or her loved ones, and, in political discourse, can mean the people who have the most influence on the prime minister. Chinese offers a range of similar examples: people can be *hen jin* 很近 'very close', or *guanxi hen miqie* 关系很密切 'tightly related', or, more colloquially, *tie gemenr* 铁哥们儿 'iron buddies'. That much of the "closeness is strength" metaphor seems clearly to be shared between Chinese and English.

The additional claim that "closeness is strength" applies to the form as well as to the content of language holds that a tighter grammatical structure can by itself suggest a tighter link between the items that are mentioned in a phrase. Some of Lakoff and Johnson's examples involve the way negatives are put. A sentence like "I think he won't come" is both shorter and stronger, they point out, than "I don't think he will come." Other examples involve direct and indirect objects: "I taught Harry Greek" is tighter and stronger than "I taught Greek to Harry"; the former implies more clearly than the latter that some Greek actually got into Harry. "I found the chair comfortable" is tighter and stronger than "I found that the chair was comfortable," because the former implies that the knowledge comes from direct experience: I actually sat on the chair and found it comfortable. "I found *that* the chair was comfortable" could also mean, depending on context, that I observed my grandmother and discovered it to be comfortable to her, or did a survey and found what consumers felt in general, or something like that.

Does this "grammatical closeness is strength" metaphor work for Chinese? On balance it does, although there are problems. In Chinese the most common words for "think," *kan* 看 and *xiang* 想, cannot be

---

163. Ibid., pp. 128–132.

negated,[164] so there is no handy counterpart for sentences like "I don't think he will come." We can say in Chinese *wo kan* [or *xiang*] *ta buhui lai* 我看[想]他不会来 'I think he won't come' but we do not say *wo bukan* [or *buxiang*] *ta hui lai* 'I don't think he will come'. (René Descartes would have loved Chinese. The language can make it awkward to "not think" something.) Using *juede* 觉得 'feel', however, it is possible: *wo juede ta buhui lai* 我觉得他不会来 'I think [feel] that he won't come' and *wo bujuede ta hui lai* 我不觉得他会来 'I don't think [feel] that he will come' are both all right.

If we look for a parallel in Chinese to the case of comparing "I taught Harry Greek" and "I taught Greek to Harry," we might try saying *wo jiao le Zhang San Riwen* 我教了张三日文 'I taught Zhang San Japanese' and *wo ba Riwen jiao gei le Zhang San* 我把日文教给了张三 . For these two sentences it does seem, as Lakoff and Johnson predict, that the shorter version gets more Japanese into Zhang San than the longer one. But a problem with this experiment is that in Chinese, neither of the two sentences seems very natural. They are the kind of thing one thinks of when trying to look for Western-language counterparts (which is just what we are doing here). Chinese people in normal contexts would be much more likely to say something like *wo shi Zhang San de Riwen laoshi* 我是张三的日文老师 "I was [and am] Zhang San's Japanese teacher'. In short, we will probably do better if we test the "grammatical closeness is strength" hypothesis on more native turf.

In Chinese, the example of the verbal complement might be useful. A verbal complement is a second verb that immediately follows the first and tells how the action of the first ends up. For example *ting dong* 听懂, literally "listen understand," suggests that listening (to oral instructions, a lecture, etc.) ends up in understanding (them, it). The formal relation of the two verbs is immediate juxtaposition, and the semantic connection between their senses is similarly tight. If the verbs are separated by the particle *de* 得, the connection is a bit weaker: now the idea is only that the first verb *can* result in the second. *Ting de dong* 听得懂 means something like "can understand from having listened." If *bu* 不 'no' intervenes, the connection be-

---

164. *Xiang* can be negated in its meaning of 'would like to', followed by a verb, but that is a different matter.

tween *ting* and *dong* is explicitly negated but still carries the "can" idea; *ting bu dong* is "cannot understand from having listened." It is probably significant that when even more syllables separate *ting* and *dong* in this kind of construction, the meaning is *always* negative, that is, always expresses a weak connection between *ting* and *dong*. We can say, for example, *ting bu tai dong* or *ting bu da dong* 听不太 (大) 懂, both meaning "can't understand very well from listening"; we do not say either *ting de da dong* or *ting de tai dong*, "can understand well from listening."[165] This is hardly overwhelming evidence for Lakoff and Johnson's claim that "closeness is strength" in form as well as content. But it is supportive evidence, and it is authentic.

To move to another kind of example, it might seem that the "fronts" and "backs" of things—animals, theaters, railroad trains, and many things—might be metaphors that Chinese, English, and other languages share. But it turns out that this is only partly true. In order to understand why, we need to distinguish three different criteria for determining "front and back":

1. Things whose fronts and backs are defined by the direction in which they move (e.g., animals and vehicles).
2. Things whose fronts and backs are defined by the layout and functions of their features (e.g., stores or theaters, where signs hang at the "front," one usually pays near to the "front," etc.).
3. Things (such as mountains and trees) that do not move and do not have intrinsic fronts or backs but have "fronts" and "backs" attributed to them according to the position of a speaker or writer.

In category 1, the "fronts" of animal bodies are commonly understood as the sides that face in the direction in which the animals normally move. The "fronts" of an ant, a hippopotamus, and a snake are all obvious by this criterion. Some animals, including humans, can walk backward, but we have no problem identifying such motion as exceptional. Crabs that

---

165. It is possible to say things like *ting de shifen dong* 'completely understand' 聽得十分懂 or *ting de wanquan dong* 'entirely understand' 聽得完全懂, but these are not verb-complement constructions. They are predicate constructions.

"go sideways" might be a special problem, but here category 2 can help—and it helps for many animals other than crabs—because the front is the "operational" side, the side where the eyes, mouth, and nose all do their important work. A crab eats at its "front," and appears even to be "looking" from that side; in this case we do not give serious thought to the possibility that its "front" is the edge that leads the way when it moves.

Lakoff, Johnson, and others point out that our conceptions of the "fronts" of inanimate things are sometimes done by analogy to animate ones.[166] The "front" of a bus, a train, or an airplane is the end that leads the way when the thing gets going. This rule seems to hold consistently in both Chinese and English. For things that do not move, like stores or theaters, the "front," as with animals, is the operational side, where facades, signs, box offices, and so on are located. In the case of theaters, it is interesting to note that once we enter the building and get into the big room where the show is held, front and back instantly switch. The "front row" is near the back of the building. This is because the conception "operational side" has switched. Once one is inside the theater, the stage is where the important activity is. All these points are the same in Chinese and English.

But there is a problem in holding that English and Chinese "share metaphors" of front and back. This is because what we have just considered are not metaphors but *definitions* of front and back. To observe that they are "the same" is, at bottom, tautologous. To see why this is so, try the following experiment. What if Chinese conceived the "fronts" and "backs" of things like trains and buses oppositely from English? Then *qian* would be the back and *hou* the front. But if a train came along, and a Chinese speaker pointed to the end that was in the direction of the train's motion and said *houtou* 后头 'back', an English speaker would infer—incorrectly—that *houtou* in Chinese is the same as "front" in English. Similarly, if the side of a theater building bearing the facade and harboring the box office were called the "back" in English, a Chinese speaker would have no trouble inferring that "back" is *qiantou* 前头. If we were to assign nonsense words to the box office side of the theater—say, "blint" in English and *fing* in Chinese—then "blint" would mean *fing*, and *fing* would

---

166. Lakoff and Johnson, *Philosophy in the Flesh*, p. 34.

mean "blint," and life would go on. To say that the languages "coincide" on this point would be meaningless.

However, using category 3, it is genuinely possible (and does happen) that different languages conceive front and back differently. Mountains—unless they are carved, like Rushmore—have no intrinsic fronts or backs. But a tongue twister in Chinese begins *shanqian you ge Cui Cutui, shan hou you ge Cutui Cui* . . . 山前有个崔粗腿, 山后有个粗腿崔 . . . 'in front of the mountain was a Cui Fatleg, and behind the mountain was a Fatleg Cui . . .'. Here the front and back of the mountain are defined relatively. The front is the side that the speaker and anyone standing near the speaker can see on a clear day. The back is the opposite side. If the same people climbed the mountain and went to the other side, front and back would switch. We do the same in English. Boulder, Colorado, is in front of the mountains if we are in Denver, and behind the mountains if we are in Grand Lake. But this convention is arbitrary. It could be the other way around. We could conceive the other side of the mountain, which we cannot see, as "out in front," as it were, while we are behind it. We could stand in Boulder and see Grand Lake as "in front" of the mountains. Lakoff and Johnson report that Hausa does conceive front and back in this alternate way.[167]

For a mountain itself, Lakoff and Johnson observe that English uses the metaphor "a mountain is a person." They cite the word "foothills" as evidence; in English, mountains have feet. But they classify this as an "idiosyncratic, unsystematic, and isolated" metaphor, not a "metaphor that we live by," because the "unused portions" (presumably the head, shoulders, knees, etc. of a mountain) are not standard phrases in English and would be taken as novel metaphors if a poet or other creative person were to choose to use them. Chinese also uses the metaphor "a mountain is a person" and does "live by it" a bit more than English, because in Chinese *shantou* 山头 'mountain head' and *shanyao* 山腰 'mountain waist' (i.e., halfway up) are just as acceptable as *shanjiao* 山脚 'mountain foot'.

There are myriad ways the instantiations of conceptual metaphors might differ among languages, and to try to catalogue them all would be tedious. In using the human body to describe vegetables, for example, we say *yitou dasuan* 一头大蒜 'a head of garlic' in Chinese, but a "bulb" in

---

167. Ibid., p. 34.

English; on the other hand we use "head" in English for lettuce and cabbage. The comparisons between languages that are more significant in revealing "worldviews" are those that differ in more systematic ways, and we turn to them now.

Metaphors in Chinese That Diverge from English in Significant Ways

Lakoff and Johnson make a broad claim that "the most fundamental values in a culture will be coherent with the metaphorical structure of the most fundamental concepts in the culture."[168] They are careful to point out that "be coherent with" does not mean "will always actually exist," but only that whatever values do exist will be "consistent with" the metaphorical system.[169] They suggest—but only occasionally illustrate—that different cultures observe metaphorical patterns that reflect different values.

In his book *Metaphor, Culture, and Worldview*, Dilin Liu takes up this question for the cases of modern Chinese and American English. Liu identifies a few of what he calls "dominant metaphors" in the two languages. By "dominant" he means, in part, common, but also apparently something like what Lakoff and Johnson mean by "conceptual" or "structural" metaphor in the sense of metaphor that not only reflects the ways we conceive things but actually shapes conceptions as well. Liu argues that dominant metaphors are different in modern Chinese and American English, and that we therefore can probably infer that some of the values and priorities of people who use the two languages diverge along similar lines.

For example, Liu points out that when Americans are unconvinced of an argument they might say "I don't *buy* that," whereas in Chinese, in a similar situation, one might say *wo bu chi ni nei yi tao* 我不吃你那一套 'I don't *eat* that stuff of yours'.[170] He lists many other examples where marketing metaphors are used in American English and eating metaphors in

---

168. Lakoff and Johnson, *Metaphors We Live By*, p. 22.
169. Ibid., p. 23.
170. Dilin Liu, *Metaphor, Culture, and Worldview*, p. 9. The example is Liu's, the translation mine.

Chinese. Unfortunately, he does not do actual counts of metaphor frequency in texts or oral recordings, and gives only anecdotal evidence for his claim that the thinking and values of the two cultures correspond to their metaphor preferences. Still, his broad claims do seem plausible. In addition to the marketing and eating examples, he lists sports (e.g., "the ball is in your court") and the driving of vehicles (e.g., "my wheels are spinning") as especially fertile sources of metaphor in American English and, for modern Chinese, family relations (e.g., *disidai* 'fourth generation [of leaders]') and stage performance (e.g., *chang gaodiao* 'sing high-sounding words') as especially common.

It is intuitively obvious that metaphorical uses of *chi* 'eat' in Chinese far exceed, both in frequency and in range of applicability, uses of "eat" (or "ate," "eaten," etc.) in English. Very broadly speaking, the person who metaphorically "eats" something in Chinese can either gain by the eating or suffer from it. On the gain side, there is *chi yige zir* 吃一個子儿 'eat a piece', for capturing a piece on a chessboard, or *chidiao dijun* 吃掉敌军 'eat up the enemy army' for annihilating enemy troops. To enjoy popularity is *chi xiang* 吃香 'eat fragrance', and to receive a kickback is *chi huikou* 吃回扣, literally 'eat return discount'. *Chi taiping fan* 吃太平饭 'eat great-peace food' means passing one's days in comfort. *Chi doufu* 吃豆腐 'eat bean curd' is a subtler example but also illustrates the principle that the "eater gains," because here bean curd stands for the soft white flesh that a male metaphorically nibbles when he flirts with a female. In *chi laoben* 吃老本 'eat original capital—live on past gains', the long-term consequences are a loss, but the immediate result of *chi* is still one in which the eater gains.

On the other hand—and more commonly—*chi* can suggest that the eater suffers in some way. *Chi kui* 吃亏 'eat loss' means to get the worst of something or, in a corresponding English idiom, to "come out on the short end of the stick." *Chi zui* 吃罪 'eat crime' is to take the blame for something. *Chi ku* 吃苦 'eat bitterness' means to suffer hardship, and *chi jin* 吃紧 'eat tension' to be tense or hard pressed. *Chi jing* 吃惊 'eat surprise' is to be startled or shocked; *chi bai zhang* 吃败仗 'eat defeat in battle' is to lose in battle; and *chi guansi* 吃官司 'eat a lawsuit' is to be charged in a suit. Here the "eaten" things are all abstract concepts, but concrete nouns, understood metaphorically, can also be "eaten," as in *chi heizaor*

吃黑枣儿 'eat a black date' for being hit by a bullet, or *chi cu* 吃醋 'eat vinegar' for feeling jealous. In *chibuxiao* 吃不消 'eat and cannot digest', it is not clear what is eaten or suffered except that, whatever it is, the thing is unpleasant. When a ship is loaded and, as English puts it, "draws" water to a certain depth, Chinese says *chi shui* 吃水 'eats water' to the same depth. Here the question of gain or loss seems moot, but the metaphor remains apt.

Wanting to test objectively whether Dilin Liu is right that *chi* is used metaphorically in Chinese more than "eat" is in English, I did a word search of two novels, chosen essentially at random: Lao She's novel *The Philosophy of Lao Zhang* (*Lao Zhang de zhexue* 老張的哲學) in Chinese and Mark Twain's novel *The Mysterious Stranger* in American English. In Lao She's text, *chi* accounts for one in every five hundred characters, and in Twain's text "eat" (including "ate" and "eaten") appears once in every twenty-five hundred words.[171] This difference is accountable in part to the fact that eating in a *literal* sense gets more attention in Lao She's novel than in Mark Twain's. (That fact, though, can be viewed as confirmation of Liu's claim that both references to actual eating and metaphors based on eating are especially salient in Chinese discourse.) The contrast in metaphorical uses of *chi* and "eat" was sharper: there are five instances in Lao She's novel, none in Twain's.

Another of Liu's examples of dominant metaphor in Chinese is "government is family." For this example, he is able to show how the metaphor is strong enough, or "conceptual" enough, to travel through time and over varied political terrain.[172] That the "Five Relations" of Confucianism list *jun* 君 'sovereign official' and *chen* 臣 'subordinate official' alongside family relations like *fuzi* 父子 'father and son' and *fuqi* 夫妻 'husband and wife' is already suggestive of a conceptual parallel between political hierarchy and family relations. Traditionally, *guojia* 國家, literally 'country-family', had several senses, one of which was "emperor," and in modern

---

171. I am grateful to Mao Sheng for research assistance in this effort. Mao found 177 appearances of *chi* in *The Philosophy of Lao Zhang*, which amounts to 0.19 percent of the total character count. In *The Mysterious Stranger* there were 9 instances of "eat," 7 of "ate," and 1 of "eaten," which was 0.041 percent of the total word count.

172. Dilin Liu, *Metaphor, Culture, and Worldview*, p. 8, 55–64, 131–133.

times *guojia* came to be the standard word for both "nation" and "state." In Qing times, a popular term for "county magistrate" was *fumuguan* 父母官 'parental official'. There are many ways to refer to "the people" in modern Chinese, one of which is *zhonghua ernü* 中華兒女 'sons and daughters of China'. Chinese is not unique in using family metaphors for the nation, of course; there are "founding fathers" in English, *la patrie* 'the fatherland' in French, *Mat' Rossiia* in Russian, and many other examples. But Dilin Liu may be right that the metaphor is especially salient in Chinese. Despite its traditional—or what the Communists in other contexts have called "feudal"—roots, it has extended even into the informal lingo of the Communist movement itself. When Marx and Lenin arrived in China, the Party called them *lao zuzong* 老祖宗 'old ancestors'. During the Mao era, factory workers were sometimes *gongren dage* 工人大哥 'worker elder brothers', farmers *nongmin bobo* 农民伯伯 'peasant elder uncles', and soldiers *jiefangjun shushu* 解放军叔叔 'liberation army uncles'.[173] The Soviet Union, until relations with Communist China turned sour, was a *laodage* 老大哥 'old big brother'. And the Hu Jintao cohort of top leaders was known as the "fourth generation."

Of the "dominant" metaphors that Dilin Liu finds in modern Chinese, the one that has, in my view, the deepest implications is the one he calls the "opera/acting metaphor."[174] Liu cites a number of examples to show how public presentation of behavior is important in Chinese culture and how metaphors of stage performance, many derived from Chinese opera, are used to talk and write about it. (In reference to China, by the way, "opera" should not be thought of as an elite art. Some of its modern forms are indeed elite, but most of what have for centuries been called *xi* 戏 are popular performing arts that have a wide variety of local traditions. Before the twentieth century, *xi* were the staples of popular Chinese entertainment.) Liu Dilin notes that for an official to take office is to *shang tai* 上台 'go up on stage', while to leave office is to *xia tai* 下台 'come down from the stage'. In a broader sense, any person (not necessarily an official) who takes a publicly visible stand can be said to *deng tai* 登台 'ascend the stage'. A person can get stuck on stage (i.e., publicly committed to an

173. Ibid., p. 58.
174. Ibid., pp. 103–109, 133–135.

awkward position), in which case his or her adversary, who might not want to let him or her "off the hook," as we might say in English, can *rang ta xiabuliao tai* 让他下不了台 'make it so he/she cannot get off stage'.

While a person is "on stage"—that is, visible to people who are watching—how that person performs is sometimes described using *chang* 唱 'sing'. There are a number of ways to *chang*, metaphorically speaking. To *chang honglian* 唱红脸 'sing the red face' is to play the role of the good guy. The phrase derives from the convention that a red face in opera makeup usually indicates a good person. In popular usage, it does not have to mean that one *is* a good character but only that one is presenting the good-character pose. The pose can be insincere, so that the phrase can mean, in effect, "pretend to be the good guy." Because villains in opera often have white faces, *chang bailian* 唱白脸 'sing the white face' means, correspondingly, to play the role of a bad guy. *Chang gaodiao* 唱高调 'sing a high-pitched tune' is to say fine-sounding things, often with the negative connotation of overweening self-righteousness; *didiao chuli* 低调处理 'handle things at a low pitch' is usually regarded as better. *Chang dujiao xi* 唱独角戏 'sing a solo' is to do something without partners or allies. For setting up a rival enterprise to someone else's, Chinese can say *chang duitai xi* 唱对台戏, literally 'sing opera on an opposite stage'. If you want explicitly to oppose someone, you can *chang fan diao* 唱反调 'sing a contrary tune'; if you need to go along with somebody else's pretences in order to get what you need, you might *jiaxizhenchang* 假戏真唱 'sing a phony opera as if it were real'. If you are only going through the motions of doing something you just *zou guo chang* 走过场 'walk across the scene', and if you play but a minor role, running errands and the like, you *pao longtao* 跑龙套 'run the dragon outfit'. (Imperial palace guards, when they played bit roles in operas, wore "dragon outfits.") If an enterprise collapses, one can say in Chinese *mei xi chang le* 没戏唱了 'there is no opera to sing any more'. Virtually any project at all, if it comes to naught, or was boring to begin with, can be described as *mei xi* 没戏 'no play'.

As Dilin Liu suggests, the extensive use of stage metaphors in Chinese does indeed seem to correspond to some aspects of a Chinese "worldview." Recalling the Sapir-Whorf controversies, we might want to ask whether the metaphors generate the worldview or the other way around. For a case as complex as this one, I think "both" is no doubt the right answer, and I believe we should be content to note the fact of correspondence without undertaking to unwind the directions in which causality runs. That said, there are two major features of "acting" in Chinese language and culture that seem to me worth reflecting on: the importance of *outward performance* and the *moral value* of doing the performance correctly.

The association of formal language and correct performance in China is ancient. The earliest examples of written Chinese characters, on what are called "oracle bones," often had to do with advice about action: When should the king go to war, or perform rituals? When should farmers plant? The function of language was not to say how things were but to advise on what to *do*. Speaking in general terms about pre-Qin philosophy, Roger Ames and Henry Rosemont write that "language is both performative and prescriptive; it both does something to the world and recommends how it should be."[175] They note that *dao* 道 'speak' is the same term as *dao* 道 'guiding [along the way]'.[176]

What might be called "Confucian psychology"—found in countless texts but perhaps most classically in the *Daxue* 大學 ('Great learning')—holds that classic texts contain a morality that can be internalized in a person via memorization and lead to personal cultivation, which in turn has the power to radiate outward and bring good effects, successively, to the family, to the country, even to everything under *tian* 天, the natural order of the cosmos. The same assumption of the power of morality to grow out of the study of classical language and to lead to personal cultivation and then to qualification to govern others was the main ideological undergirding for China's imperial examination system. Scholars who had mastered classical learning were supposed to be able to display not only technical ability in quoting texts or writing characters but also proper moral responses to life situations—as, for example, in producing poems to reflect the mood of poignant moments such as the seeing-off of a friend. Peasant rebels, even if barely literate themselves, still often had one or

---

175. Roger T. Ames and Henry Rosemont, Jr., *The Analects of Confucius: A Philosophical Translation* (New York: Ballantine Books, 1998), p. 31.

176. Ibid., attributing the insight to Chad Hansen, in Hansen, *A Daoist Theory of Chinese Thought* (New York: Oxford University Press, 1992), pp. 33–54.

another kind of *tianshu* 天書 'natural [righteous] document', which served as a moral warrant for their quest to change a dynasty. Even Mao Zedong, the would-be "smasher" of all "old habits, old culture, old customs, and old ideas," encouraged a system in which, during the Cultural Revolution in the late 1960s, the principles of what I am calling here "Confucian psychology" were almost exactly reproduced: young Red Guards memorized texts (containing now the words of Mao, not Confucius or other ancients), internalized the unquestionable righteousness that the texts contained, presented their resulting cultivation as qualification to set things right in the larger society, and through it all forged a connection with the highest authority under Heaven (now Mao, not an emperor).

The meanings of the correct words were paramount, of course. But the powerful sense of their rightness could be enough to imbue even their forms and vessels—written characters and oral sounds—with a special moral glow. The art of Chinese calligraphy relies only in part on what its written characters mean; the ways they are written—their "life" on paper—are important signs of the character and cultivation of the calligrapher. (This can be true even when the characters themselves are hard to identify.) At least until the mid-twentieth century, Chinese children were warned to *jingxi zizhi* 敬惜字紙 'respect paper that bears characters'. During high Maoism this "old habit," like others, persisted in altered form: it became a political crime to use a piece of newspaper bearing a Mao quote for casual purposes, such as stuffing shoes or wrapping fish.

As for sounds, the very sound of *zao zi* 早子 'sons soon' explains why dates (*zaozi* 棗子) are eaten at weddings or, as noted in Chapter 1, why a mother might pack chicken hearts (*jixin* 鸡心) in her son's school lunchbox in order to help him with his memory (*jixing* 记性). The force packed within the sounds of these two morally relevant syllables was assumed to be strong enough to span the gap from label to object, from *jixin* to chicken hearts, then to enter a boy's alimentary canal, then his bloodstream and his brain, then back across the mind-body gap from his brain to his mind, and into his behavior—where the effects would be "proper."

Some scholars have argued that in ancient Chinese texts, the criterion for deciding whether a statement is "right" is more nearly an ethical than a cognitive criterion, that is, "do these words guide action properly?" and not "are these words true?" Ames and Rosement write that "classical Chinese has no close lexical equivalent for the English "true" and "truth";[177] A. C. Graham has held that followers of Mozi (ca. 470– 391 BCE) "[do] not use a single term corresponding to English 'true' [but hold that] a name or complex of names applied to an object either fits (*dang* 當) or errs (*guo* 過),"[178] and Chad Hansen has written that "[ancient] Chinese philosophy has no concept of truth" and is built, instead, on "a pragmatic rather than a semantic interest in language"; utterances are evaluated by whether they are *ke* 可 'admissible' or 'appropriate', not whether they are true or false in the sense that attracted much attention in ancient Greece.[179]

No one argues—or could, reasonably—that in daily life over the centuries Chinese language ignores true-false distinctions any more than one might say, to go too far in the other direction, that European languages have trouble with appropriateness. Daily life in China, as anywhere, has always been full of questions and answers about truth and falsity, and it is worth noting that the kinds of Chinese literary expression that have been closest to informal daily life—songs, storytelling, popular fiction, and so on—have made much of deception, illusion, and other matters in which truth and falsity are crucial. The great novel *Dream of the Red Chamber* (or *Story of the Stone*) plays grandly with the true-false distinction, opening with a dream by a gentleman archly named Zhen Shiyin 甄士隱 (a homonym for 真事隱 'true matters concealed') and moving to the story of a Jia Baoyu 賈寶玉 (also "fake jade" 假寶玉) who lives in a very large Jia ("false") family; yet there is much to say of interest, because, after all, *jia zuo zhen shi zhen yi jia* 假作真時真亦假 'when false poses as true, true is also false',[180] and so on. Here and elsewhere in Chinese language and culture, there is no shortage of awareness of "true versus false."

177. Ames and Rosemont, *Analects of Confucius*, p. 33.
178. A. C. Graham, *Later Mohist Logic, Ethics, and Science* (Hong Kong: Chinese University Press, 1978), p. 39. Here I have converted Graham's use of Wade-Giles romanization to *hanyu pinyin*.
179. Chad Hansen, "Chinese Language, Chinese Philosophy and 'Truth,'" *Journal of Asian Studies* 44: 491–519 (1985), pp. 492, 504. I have added 'appropriate' to Hansen's 'admissible' as a gloss for *ke*.
180. The phrase appears in chapters 1 and 5. Cao Xueqin 曹雪芹, *Hongloumeng* 紅樓夢 (Hong Kong: Youlian chubanshe, 1960), pp. 5, 45.

Still, those who note a Chinese cultural tendency to assume that proper use of language is essentially ethical behavior—a performance, not a statement, of correctness—do have an important point. This assumption helps to explain why Dilin Liu can find "opera/acting metaphors" to be "dominant" in Chinese even in modern times. Notions of correct performance are embedded even in the grammar of daily-life Chinese, where they have survived through the turmoil of the modern era and its attendant language change. To "say this" in Chinese one does not *shuo zheige* 'say this' (which sounds awful), but *zeme shuo* 这么说, literally "say it this way". If a child mistakenly says two plus three is four, her mother can correct her by saying *bushi neme shuo de*—不是那么说的 "it's not said that way" or "that's not the way you say it." The child's speaking-performance did not resemble the right pattern. If the child strikes a sibling, throws food at guests, or misbehaves in any number of other ways, the mother might say *ni zheyang buxiangyang* 你这样不像样, literally "your acting this way does not resemble the [right] pattern." She might also say (and here we see how "correct language" can stand be a stand-in for "correct behavior") *ni zheyang buxianghua* 不像话 'your acting this way does not resemble [proper] words.' She might ask the child to *xuehao* 学好 'learn to be good' or *xue zuoren* 学作人 'learn to be [a proper] person'. Here *xue*, which is often translated as "study" or "learn," does not mean study or learn facts. It means "imitate." A mother's admonition to *xue baba* 学爸爸 is a call to emulate Daddy, not to research him.

For matters of *research*, in which true-or-false is the governing question, Chinese uses the word *yanjiu* 研究, but even here, more often than in modern English, there can be a subtle tendency to assume that the object of research is something worthy of emulation—a good person, good idea, or whatever. In 1980, when I was studying contemporary literature in China, I discovered some "hand-copied volumes" (*shouchaoben* 手抄本) containing detective stories, triangular love stories, martial arts stories, and so on that had been secretly copied and passed around during the Cultural Revolution for entertainment purposes. They struck me as fascinating sources on popular thought during extraordinary times, and I wrote a research paper on them.[181] Some of my Chinese friends, though,

---

181. "Hand-Copied Entertainment Fiction from the Cultural Revolution," in Perry Link, Richard Madsen, and Paul Pickowicz, eds., *Unofficial China: Popular Culture and Thought in the People's Republic* (Boulder, Colo.: Westview Press, 1989), pp. 17–36.

were perplexed. Why do you write about *that* kind of literature? What is there in it to "study" (by which they meant, implicitly, "imitate" or "learn from")? I had been aware that there were political and cultural sensitivities associated with *shouchaoben*, but the question in the minds of these friends was something a bit different: their concern was that I could get better moral sustenance by looking elsewhere.

During the same year, I did a survey of reading habits and preferences among seventy-four students at Zhongshan University in Guangzhou, and found that most of them listed *Dream of the Red Chamber* as their favorite work of fiction of all time, even though none acknowledged having read it, at least not recently, or completely.[182] Yet their answers to both questions—"What do you read?" and "What do you prefer?"—were, I feel sure, sincere. A foreign scholar was asking a formal question about the way things should be, and *"Dream of the Red Chamber"* was the right answer. Similarly, when Samuel Huntington's *Clash of Civilizations and the Remaking of World Order* appeared in 1997,[183] some Chinese intellectuals complained that Huntington should not be advocating civilizational clash. "He should write a book about harmony, not clash," a friend wrote to me in an email. She assumed that Huntington was seeking to guide behavior, not describe it.

In one interesting respect, even the grammar of modern Chinese tends to reinforce the assumption that correctness is performance. This happens with the extremely common structure that Y. R. Chao calls the "predicative complement."[184] Chinese uses this structure in many situations where speakers of European languages would use adverbs. To say, for example, "she sings (more) beautifully (than someone else)," Chinese can say *ta chang de haoting* 她唱得好听, a literal English rendition of which would be something like "her singing-manner is pleasant-sounding." In Chao's analysis, the notion of "way" or "manner" is implied between *ta chang de* 'the [noun] of her singing' and *haoting* 'is

---

182. See Perry Link, "Fiction and the Reading Public in Guangzhou and Other Chinese Cities, 1979–80," in Jeffrey C. Kinkley, ed., *After Mao: Chinese Literature and Society, 1978–1981* (Harvard University Council on East Asian Studies, 1985), pp. 256, 262–263.

183. Samuel Huntington, *The Clash of Civilizations and the Remaking of World Order* (New York: Touchstone, 1997).

184. Chao, *Grammar of Spoken Chinese*, p. 355.

pleasant-sounding'.[185] But the word-pattern itself leaves it theoretically ambiguous whether the implied noun that follows *de* is "manner" or some other noun. In *ta chang de haoting*, for example, the implied noun could just as easily be "the song" that she sings, followed by the comment that it is pleasant-sounding. Similarly *ta shuo de hen hao* 她说得很好, literally something like "her speech-performance was very good," can mean either "she said it very well" or "what she said was very good." (It can also mean both.)

Chinese speakers are accustomed to this ambiguity and very rarely feel puzzlement, in context, about what is meant. The relevant distinctions can always be made clear if necessary. Someone can ask, "Do you mean, precisely, that her meaning was good— or that she expressed it well?" and such a question is easy to understand and usually easy to answer.[186] Still, the fact that it is so very common in Chinese to speak in terms of "performing" actions that are named by verbs does make it more natural, in my view, that metaphors of stage performance are so pervasive.

In Chapter 3 we will explore ways in which "performance" of language has had special importance in political contexts. In writing about Red Guard activists during the Cultural Revolution, Anita Chan has observed that the "playing of a role in China was more than a sociological abstraction. Role-playing involved literal play-acting: a conscious assumption of the mannerisms and ways of speaking appropriate to the activist status and role."[187] More broadly—and not just for activists but for everyone in Mao's China—*zhengzhi biaoxian* 政治表现 'political performance' was something that could determine job assignments, living conditions, admissions to schools, and a variety of other crucial matters. *Biaoxian* comes literally from *biao* 'surface' plus *xian* 'appear', and this combination of notions puts the matter exactly right. A person had to present the right

---

185. Although *de* in the predicative complement is now commonly written 得, not 的, Chao explains that 的 fits better with the genesis and logic of the pattern. Ibid., pp. 356–357.

186. This can be asked, for example, as *ni shi shuo ta de neirong hao haishi ta de biaodafangfa hao ne?* 你是说她的内容好还是她的表达方法好呢? 'do you mean that her content was good or her manner of expressing it?'

187. Anita Chan, *Children of Mao: Personality Development and Political Activism in the Red Guard Generation* (Seattle: University of Washington Press, 1985), p. 214.

appearances in public even if they were different from what he or she was feeling inside. The public persona formed of one's *biaoxian* was on display in the workplace or at school. It was especially relevant during political study sessions. One had to pay attention to it, craft it, and guard it. By the 1970s, the maxim "Don't make friends within the work-unit" had arisen in Chinese cities. This was because life in the work-unit (factory, school, government office, etc.) by necessity involved the formal presentations of *zhengzhi biaoxian*, whereas friendships involved interchange that was more frank and informal. The two levels did not mix well. Informal comments made in the context of friendship, if raised to the level of political performance—whether by accident or because of betrayal by a friend— could bring serious trouble.

Conceptual Differences That Are Rooted in Metaphor

Dilin Liu's claims that metaphors of sports, marketing, and the driving of vehicles are salient in American English while metaphors of eating, family relations, and acting are more common in Chinese are claims about degree and emphasis only. Either language can use the metaphors of the other to the extent that its speakers want to. Indeed this happens in direct-translation borrowing, as when "bottleneck" in English becomes *pingjing* 瓶颈 in Chinese. But in some instances of metaphorical contrasts between languages, the differences have more to do with the structure of thought and are not so easily exchangeable. There is, in short, a useful distinction between examples that are different by *custom* and those that are different by *concept*.

A difference by *custom*, in this definition, is one in which arguably the "same" conceptual metaphor is available in each of two languages, but one language uses it more than the other. An example I have already discussed is the vertical conception of time, as in "past is up, future is down." We use this metaphor in English only rarely, whereas Chinese, as Jenn-yeu Chen has shown, uses it for about one-third of the instances in which a "time is space" metaphor is used. Other examples are metonyms for famous events, where both times and places can serve the purpose in both Chinese and English, although there is a marked tendency for Chinese to prefer times and English to prefer places. For example, in English we "remember the Alamo," but in Chinese we never forget *jiu yi ba* 九一八 'nine one eight' (i.e., September 18, 1931, when Japan invaded China's Northeast). In American English we have Watergate (and by extension other "-gates" for other scandals) and can hope that "Afghanistan is not another Vietnam." In Chinese, by contrast, we have *wusi* 五四 'five four'—the May Fourth movement, 1919, and *siwu* 四五 'four five'—the April 5, 1976, demonstration at Tiananmen to mourn Zhou Enlai's passing. The Beijing massacre of June 4, 1989, is *liusi* 六四 'six four' in Chinese and Tiananmen in English. There are exceptions, though, to this pattern of the preferences the two languages show. We have "nine eleven" and the War of 1912 in English, and in Chinese *lugouqiao* 卢沟桥 'Marco Polo bridge' can stand for the Japanese invasion of north China on July 7, 1937. Either kind of metonym works in either language; the disproportion between the two is a matter of custom.

A difference by *concept*, on the other hand, is one in which one language uses a metaphor that another just does not use. An example is the metaphor "an instrument is a companion," which in English leads to sentences like "I sliced the salami with a knife" and "she plays Ping-Pong with her left land."[188] Lakoff and Johnson claim that "with few exceptions ... in all languages of the world the word or grammatical device that indicates *accompaniment* also indicates *instrumentality*."[189] Chinese is definitely one of the "exceptions" to this generalization, and indeed would be an extreme one, because Chinese words that might be translated "accompany" (such as *gen* 跟 'follow, with'; *pei* 陪 'accompany'; *sui* 随 'follow') are *never* used metaphorically to introduce an instrument. In the Chinese mind, to say something like *daozi pei wo qie rou* 刀子陪我切肉 'the knife accompanies me in slicing meat' creates a mood reminiscent of *Alice in Wonderland*, and even in that mood the image would be hard to picture. To say "she plays Ping-Pong with her left hand" as *ta gen ta de zuoshou da pingpangqiu* 她跟她的左手打乒乓球 would ask a Chinese speaker to imagine that her left hand is at the other end of the Ping-Pong table, playing her as her opponent. To convey the notion of *instrument*, Chinese uses a nonmetaphorical

---

188. Lakoff and Johnson, *Metaphors We Live By*, pp. 134–135.
189. Ibid., p. 135.

yong 用 'use': *wo yong zuoshou da pingpangqiu* 我用左手打乒乓球 'I play Ping-Pong with [i.e., using] my left hand'. English can, of course, employ "use" in this way as well; but Chinese never uses the metaphor "an instrument is a companion."

Another family of metaphors that illustrates different conceptual approaches in Chinese and English are those that involve "looking at" or "seeing" as metaphors for "thinking" or "understanding." In some cases, these metaphors are similar. In either English or Chinese, for example, if we say someone is "covering up the facts" (*yan'gai shishi* 掩盖事实) we use a visual metaphor that suggests that our access to the facts—to knowing or thinking about them—is blocked. When we say that something is "blurry" in English or *menglong* 朦胧 'foggy' in Chinese, we are again using a metaphor of sight to describe our thinking or understanding. In some other uses, though, the *see* conceptual metaphors of Chinese and English are conceptually different.

Metaphor theorists who work from European languages have noted the metaphor "understanding is seeing." We say in English "I see what you mean," "I see they've changed their plans," or "the judge just couldn't see it my way." In these cases, "see" essentially does mean "understand." But in Chinese, neither *kan* 看 'look at' nor *kanjian* 看见 'see' works in this way: *wo kan nide yisi 我看你的意思 'I look at your meaning' and **wo kanjian nide yisi* 我看见你的意思 'I see your meaning' are both clearly wrong. The difference is systematic: *kan* and *kanjian* never work in this kind of case. But *kan* does work as a conceptual metaphor for other concepts in Chinese.

The most basic sense of *kan* 看 is deftly suggested by its Chinese character, which represents a hand over an eye, an arrangement that human beings everywhere presumably have found useful in shielding the eyes from sunlight in order to "look at" something. From the fundamental meaning of "look at," *kan* has extended meanings of watch (*kan qiusai* 看球赛 'watch a ball game'), read (*kan bao* 看报 'read a newspaper'), visit (*kan pengyou* 看朋友 'visit friends'), care for (*kan* [first tone] *haizi* 看孩子 'babysit'), "it depends" (*kan ta zenme shuo* 看他怎么说 'it depends on what he says'), and many others. The sense of *kan* that comes closest to "understand" is "think," as in *wo kan ta buhui lai* 我看他不会来 'I think he won't come'. This sense is close to the English "as I see it" or "in my view."

Kan is crucially different from "see" in the literal sense because *kan* implies only "look at," not the successful perception that is implied when we add *jian* 见 'perceive' or *dao* 到 'arrive'. (*Kanjian* and *kandao* are "see" in the literal sense.) Even the "at" in "look at" is a bit of an overinterpretation of the original sense of *kan*. One can *wangwaikan* 往外看 'peer outward' or *xiangqiankan* 向前看 'look forward' without looking at anything. *Kan* means only, as it were, "peering from [someone's] vantage point"; it does not imply seeing, let alone understanding what is seen, as the *see* metaphor does in English.

In Molière's play *Tartuffe*, Orgon tries to convince his mother that he *knows* Tartuffe has been making advances toward his wife. His mother, who venerates Tartuffe, cannot believe it, so Orgon says (act 5, scene 3): *Je l'ai vu, dis-je, vu, de mes propres yeux vu* 'I saw it, I tell you, saw, saw with my own eyes!'. Here *vu*, similarly to the translation "saw" in English, implies "know as an absolute certainty." The line is funny in part because Orgon did his witnessing while hidden beneath a table, from where he *heard* a great deal but *saw* literally nothing of what he claims by *je l'ai vu*. Molière exploits the distance between the literal and metaphorical senses of *vu* rather in the manner of a pun. In Chinese, where *kan* falls well short of meaning "know for certain" and *kanjian* is restricted to "see" in a literal sense, Orgon would seem less funny—and more just a flat-out liar—if he were to have said *wo qinyan kanjian de* 我亲眼看见的 'I saw it with my own eyes'.

But are these metaphors that "differ by concept" among languages really very significant for how speakers of the different languages think about the world? When you understand what someone else has said, in English you can say "I see what you mean," using a knowing-is-seeing metaphor, and in Chinese you might say *wo mingbai ni de yisi* 我明白你的意思 'I bright-white your meaning', using a metaphor of "knowing is bright and white." In both cases, the metaphors "differ by concept," that is, cannot be imported into the other language: *wo kanjian nide yisi* in Chinese and "I bright and white your meaning" in English are both far from acceptable. But so what, in the end? Are these not just different devices of expression, more or less like different words? The underlying ideas that get expressed are practically indistinguishable. The "conceptual difference" seems inconsequential.

In some cases, though, there do appear to be important consequences for worldviews, including the conscious worldviews that philosophers construct. To illustrate, I would like to examine a case in which the habits of metaphor in Chinese can show how concepts that are embedded in English and other European languages may not be as "given" as Western civilizations have taken them to be.

Here is the example in capsule. English and other European languages use metaphors of "containers" or "enclosures" more than Chinese does; European languages also tend, more than Chinese, to label metaphorical containers, enclosures, and other things with nouns; and Western thinkers tend, much more than do Chinese thinkers, to worry about what these "things" named by nouns "are." It is worth asking how much the philosophical puzzles—and even more, the intensity of worry about them—might be artifacts of linguistic habit.

In English we say that something is "in" a category or even "falls into" it. Guppies are "in" the tropical fish category, and swordtails "fall into" that category, too. In Chinese the simplest way to say the same thing is *kongqueyu shi redaiyu* 孔雀鱼是热带鱼, which is literally "guppy be tropical fish." In sentences like this, the single syllable *shi* does the work of the entire English phrase "falls into the category of." One reason why this works easily in Chinese is that all Chinese nouns, unless they are preceded by auxiliary nouns (also called "measure words"), are by nature abstract in the same sense that English words like "water" or "sugar" are abstract (and can be concretized only by saying things like "a *cup* of water" or "a *lump* of sugar"). To translate *kongqueyu shi redaiyu* even more literally, one might gloss it as "guppyhood fall-into-category-of tropical-fish-ness." Similarly, to say in Chinese "Zhang San is in the People's Liberation Army," one can easily dispense with *in* and just say *Zhang San shi jiefangjun* 张三是解放军, literally "Zhang San be [in the category of] People's Liberation Army." One can put in the notion of *in* if one wishes, by saying something like *Zhang San zai jiefangjun li* 张三在解放军里 'Zhang San is in the People's Liberation Army', but this is a modern usage that has been influenced by Western-language grammar. Even in this Western-influenced mode, however, Chinese does not go so far as to use "fall" as a metaphor for "belonging to" a category. To say that something belongs to a category in Chinese, one most naturally says something like *jianweiyu shuyu redaiyu zhi lei* 剑尾鱼属于热带鱼之类 'swordtails belong to the category of tropical fish'.

Other things in English that can be expressed using container or enclosure metaphors include relationships. We can say in English that we are "in" a good relationship. If in a bad one, we might find it "confining." "Falling" is sometimes involved as well; we can "fall" in love. These metaphors occur in Chinese, too, but much less often. Chinese love stories can have people sinking into enamored states, as in *xianyu chiqing* 陷于痴情 'sink into silly sentiment'; on the other hand, to fall in love with a person is often *aishang* 爱上 'love onto'. In English we can also "enter into" relationships with people as varied as coaches, lawyers, and tax advisers, whereas in Chinese we tend to *zhao* 找 'seek out' this kind of person, or *ting* 听 'listen to' them.

Using English examples, Lakoff and Johnson note that objects can *come out of* substances, as when we make statues "out of" clay. Similarly substances can be *put into* forms, as when we turn clay "into" a statue. Identifying these processes as modes of "causation," Lakoff and Johnson show how the metaphor "causation is emergence," as a metaphor we live by, can travel to other contexts: he shot the mayor "out of" desperation; he dropped "from" exhaustion, and so on.[190] But here, too, Chinese is clearly different. We don't go "into" or "out of" things for such purposes in Chinese. For making clay into a statue, in Chinese one might most naturally say *yong ni zuo suxiang* 用泥做塑像 'use clay to make statue' or *ba ni zuocheng suxiang* 把泥做成塑像, literally "take clay make to form statue"; killing mayors or falling from exhaustion would likely use a nonmetaphorical *yin* 因 or *yinwei* 因为 'because'.

There is one very common "out of" metaphor in Chinese, but it does not mean "caused by" as its English cousin does. As a complement to verbs, *chulai* 出来 'come out' can signal that the verb results in something emerging into the cognitive open, as it were, where it is more plain and perceptible than it was before. If I am wondering whether people on a bus are speaking Fuzhou or Amoy dialect, I might ask you if you can *tingchulai* 听出来 'listen come out—listen and have the answer emerge'. *Kanchulai* 'look come out' can be used when something that was originally at a dis-

---

190. Ibid., pp. 72–75.

tance, or shrouded in fog, comes visually clear; it can also be used when the visual data is right in front of you but for some reason harbors a question whose answer needs to "come out"—as, for example, when you are looking at a handsome young man but cannot tell by looking whether he is Korean or Chinese. *Xiangchulai* 'think come out' relies on no perceptual data at all; it is entirely cerebral. It is used when I am trying to figure out where I last saw someone (I cannot "think out come" where it was) or how I can reasonably explain to my mother that I skipped the geometry final (I can't "think" a good excuse "out"). In all these cases there is, implicitly, a metaphorical "place" from which the answer to a (stated or unstated) question emerges, or could emerge.

A somewhat similar conceptual metaphor in Chinese is *kai* 开, literally "open," which, when used as a verbal complement, means something like "free, away, unfettered." *Zoukai* 走开 is "walk away" (and as a command can mean "get out of the way!"), where *kai* suggests release from some tightness in the present situation. *Jiekai* 解开, literally "untie open," can be used literally for untying a knot or figuratively for solving a puzzle or getting free of a hang-up (*jiekai geda* 解开疙瘩). *Xiangkai* 想开 or *kankai* 看开 'think open' is used for release from a mental burden, as when getting over the death of a loved one.

Broadly speaking, these examples of *chulai* and *kai*, both of which suggest a notion of "release into the open," implicitly resemble some of the "container" metaphors of English. But English (like other Indo-European languages) still uses container metaphors much more than Chinese does. These container metaphors have their advantages, as we will see, but also, I will argue, might be conceptually confining in ways that Chinese avoids.

Can Conceptual Metaphors Generate Philosophical Problems?

In English, container metaphors are similar in some ways to what Lakoff and Johnson call "ontological metaphors": shorthand labels we give to phenomena whose description in literal detail would involve inordinate difficulty or tedium.[191] To spell out fully what *inflation* is would take many

---

191. Ibid., pp. 25–32.

more than three syllables; but once we "get the idea" of what it is, we settle for the one-word shorthand; then, because the abbreviation is a noun, we begin to use it in the ways we use other nouns, treating it as if it were a "thing" and sometimes even an animate thing: hence "inflation is killing us at the checkout counter," "we need to combat inflation," and so on. As noted in the Introduction, Lakoff and Johnson go so far as to say that ontological metaphors "are necessary for even attempting to deal rationally with our experiences."[192]

Here the contrast with Chinese is instructive and in some ways far-reaching. Many examples of ontological metaphors in English, including ones cited by Lakoff and Johnson, are ideas that are most naturally said in Chinese using verbs, and with no diminution at all in the "rationality of dealing with our experience." Lakoff and Johnson cite "my *fear of insects* is driving my wife crazy," where "fear," which in Chinese is almost always talked about using verbs, in English seems to be a "thing" that can do something to something else. If we try to match the English sentence closely in Chinese and say something like *wo zhi pa kunchong ba qizi bi feng le* 我之怕昆虫把妻子逼疯了 'my fear of insects drives my wife crazy', we get an awkward sentence that clearly smacks of borrowing from Western language. It would be more natural in Chinese to say *wo zeme pa kunchong qizi shoubuliao* 我这麽怕昆虫妻子受不了, literally something like "I so fear insects that wife can't take it." In the end there is no way to say that either the verb-heavy Chinese sentence or the noun-studded English one is a "more rational handling of life." One uses ontological metaphor, and the other does not; at least in this case, the use of ontological metaphor is a cultural choice, not a necessity.

Another of Lakoff and Johnson's examples is "it will take *a lot of patience* to finish this book." Here, again, experience that could well be expressed with verbs—is made into a noun, as if patience were "stuff." A Chinese speaker, encountering the same boring book, would be unlikely to think of patience as stuff. A natural, idiomatic way to respond in Chinese would be to say *zhei ben shu burenzudu* 这本书不忍卒读 'this book (one) cannot bear to finish reading', in which *ren* 'tolerate', *zu* 'finish', and *du* 'read' are all verbs. A Chinese sentence somewhat closer to the English—but still

---

192. Ibid., p. 26.

not borrowing Western grammar—would be *zhei ben shu duqilai hen feijin* 这本书读起来很费劲. It is a telling fact that this Chinese sentence is very hard to put into English *without* reverting to an ontological metaphor, even though there is no ontological metaphor in the Chinese. Of the six syllables in the predicate, *duqilai hen feijin*, only one, *jin* 'energy', is a noun. Four are verbs and one is an adverb. A superliteral translation would be "[this book] read rise come very spend energy." In more readable English, but still trying to preserve the spirit of the Chinese, one might say "it takes a lot of energy [or takes a lot out of you] to read this book." But note what happens when we do this. The metaphor of energy as "stuff"—that gets used up, or gets taken out of you—has subtly crept back in. English likes to do this.

The divergent preferences of the two languages in this regard are sufficiently strong that it can seem, at times, that some things that are sayable in English just cannot be said in Chinese. "Her feelings of frustration overcame her," for example, is hard to put into Chinese without resorting to phraseology so Westernized that it hurts the ears. But Westerners have no monopoly on the experience of frustration, of course, and it is easy to find ways to talk about frustration in Chinese—just not as a "thing" or "stuff".

English phrases that use container metaphors are especially hard to translate into Chinese. So long as container metaphors are not involved, we can say that something "disappears" in English and render it as *shizongle* 失踪了 'has lost traces' in Chinese; we can also say in English that something "is no longer there" and say *buzaile* 不在了 'no longer is [somewhere]' in Chinese. But major problems arise when the container metaphors of English come along. For essentially the same idea as "disappear," we can say in English "go out of existence"—as if one thing "exits" another. We can also say in English that a thing "comes into existence" or "is in existence." Chinese balks at all of this. Just by itself, the English noun "existence" translates into Chinese only awkwardly. A direct translation of the phrase "is in existence" as *zai cunzaili* 在存在里 sounds almost cretinous in Chinese, in part because "is" and "exist" (*zai* and *cunzai*) somehow seem redundant, but even more because, obviously, no "container" is needed here.

It is important to note that the nominalization English prefers is a matter of choice, not (as Lakoff and Johnson seem to feel) necessity. The poet Wang Wei 王維 (699–761), when he describes moonlight with the line *yuese youwuzhong* 月色有無中 'beauty of moon between there and not there', achieves a superb elegance. An English speaker viewing the same moon phenomenon that Wang Wei beheld might well have said that the moon was moving into and out of something—plain sight, the clouds, or even, poetically, "existence." There should be no doubt that a description can be effective either way, with or without container metaphors.

In saying that "either way" is viable, we must guard against supposing that one way is always the "Chinese" way and the other always the "Western" one. English can say "is no longer" as easily as it can say "out of existence," and Chinese sometimes uses ontological and container metaphors. They can be found even in the lively, natural language of comedians' dialogues. Wang Guoxiang's 1955 piece *Hu, ji, dan* 壺雞蛋 (Pot, chicken, egg) uses both a container metaphor and an ontological metaphor when it says *zhei sange "ji" litou . . .* 這三個' 急' 裏頭 'inside [i.e., among] these three "urgencies" . . .'.[193] Ning Yu cites many ontological and container metaphors in Chinese, including examples like *wo you xinxin* 我有信心 'I have confidence' (where "confidence" is an ontological metaphor) and *guoyou qiye chuyu lianghao zhuangtai* 国有企业处于良好状态 'state enterprises are [located] in good condition' (where a container metaphor is at work).[194] One could object that these examples are obviously based on borrowings from Western grammar, and that is true; but that does not mean that such examples, by now, are not authentic Chinese. By the early twenty-first century, usages such as these had become thoroughly natural, especially among younger generations of native speakers. Consider the English "inflation is killing us." Set the ontological metaphor aside and think just of the meaning. Most Chinese speakers, wanting to express such a thought, would probably say something like *dongxi gui de yaoming le* 东西贵得要命了 'things are getting unbearably [literally, "life-demandingly"] expensive'. A literal mirroring of the English—*tonghuo pengzhang zhengzai sha women* 通货膨胀正在杀我们 'inflation right now is killing us'—would seem very awkward. But something in between—a hybrid like *tonghuopengzhang yuelai yue lihai* 通货膨胀越来越厉害 'inflation is getting

---

193. In *Shuoshuochangchang* 說說唱唱 [Telling and singing], no. 3 (1955), p. 46.
194. Ning Yu, *Contemporary Theory of Metaphor*, pp. 152, 216.

more and more severe'—by the early twenty-first century, sounds quite normal.

Does English really tend to prefer nouns and Chinese tend to prefer verbs? Can we put this to an objective test? As an experiment, I chose at random a page from each of two classic works of fiction, Charles Dickens's *Oliver Twist* and Cao Xueqin's *Dream of the Red Chamber*, and counted the nouns and verbs on the pages.[195] I chose *Dream of the Red Chamber* in part because I wanted a Chinese sample that would be free from Western-language influence. Some aspects of the experiment required arbitrary judgment: for example, should a Chinese cliché like *xiaodao* 笑道 'said with a smile' count as one verb or two? Should "it" in an English phrase like "so it is" count as a noun? But such problems were relatively few, and in the end this kind of borderline question seemed insignificant because the overall result was very clear: there were 96 nouns and 38 verbs on one page of Dickens (a 2.5:1 ratio) and 130 nouns and 166 verbs on one page of Cao Xueqin (a 0.8:1 ratio). The experimental results did confirm what I thought they might.

If English grammar tends to give borders (metaphorically, the edges of containers) to "things" like existence and frustration, while Chinese is more fluid about these matters, it is worth noting that the same tendency seems to hold for the very grammatical categories of the two languages. In any language, terms can move from one part of speech to another. In English we can read a book and we can book a room; the freeway admits us at the rate of "one car per green"; and so on. But such fluidity across grammatical categories is demonstrably more common in Chinese than in English. I cited earlier the example of *ji* 急 used as a noun and translated it as "urgency." But *ji* much more commonly is a verb, as in *xian bie ji* 先別急 'first don't excite' ("don't get excited before you have to") or is an adjective (sometimes called a "stative verb"), as in *xinli hen ji* 心里很急 'in the heart excited—anxious'. I also cited *dao* 道 'speak' as a verb, but *dao* is at least as famous as a noun meaning road or way (or exalted Way). An obvious reason why Chinese is more fluid in this regard is that morphological

---

195. I used *Oliver Twist* (New York: Barnes and Noble Classics, 2003), p. 64, and *Hongloumeng* (Hong Kong: Youlian chubanshe, 1960), p. 487. The page selection was utterly at random.

change occurs much less in Chinese than in most other languages. *Fazhan* 发展 is "develop," as in *fazhan nide caineng* 发展你的才能 'develop your talents', but also "development," as in *zuijin de fazhan* 最近的发展 'recent developments', and "developed," as in *fazhan guojia* 发展国家 'developed countries' (although the latter is more common as *fada guojia* 发达国家). If we add *zhong* 中 'within' to the latter phrase, to get *fazhanzhong de guojia* 发展中的国家 'developing countries', the *zhong* might be viewed as a morphological change, but even if so, it is not as clear an example of such change as is *–ing* in the English word "developing."

Like Chinese verbs, Chinese adjectives (or stative verbs) also cross the borders of categories more easily than their English counterparts do. Chinese adjectives, when used alone, are always implicitly comparative with something else. I do not mean that they are "implicitly comparative" with a general reference group of the kind we need in order to interpret "Mary is tall" depending on whether Mary is a fourth-grader or an adult volleyball player, which, as Searle has pointed out, is a kind of implicit comparison necessary in any human language. I mean that, for example, *gao* 高 in Chinese, when used alone, does not mean "tall" but "tall*er*," and not taller than things of its kind in general but taller than some specific other thing. *Zhang San gao* 张三高 does not mean "Zhang San is tall"; it means "Zhang San is tall*er* (than someone or something else)." It is the answer to the question *Zhang San gao haishi Li Si gao?* 张三高还是李四高 'who is taller, Zhang San or Li Si?'. In order to say "Zhang San is tall" in general—parallel to the way we say "Mary is tall" in English—one needs to insert a relatively empty adverb before *gao*. *Hen* 很 'very' is the most common of these, although (in some northern dialects) *ting* 挺 'rather' and (in some southern ones) *man* 蛮 'quite' perform the function just as well: *Zhang San hen (ting, man) gao* is how one says "Zhang San is tall (compared to some appropriate reference group)." My point here is that the fundamental conception of Chinese adjectives leaves them intrinsically less static and entified than English adjectives.

A comparable "border-crossing" is visible in the conception of Chinese verbs. It is instructive to ask why the English word "try"—and comparable words in other languages—are hard to translate into Chinese. Today Chinese uses *shi* 试, but this is a modern borrowing. Was it perhaps the case that premodern Chinese people "tried" things less than other peoples?

Of course not. The difference is that the Chinese language handles the description of "trying" in a different way. The idea of "try" is built into most Chinese verbs. For example *shui* 睡 'sleep' is not, precisely, "to sleep." It is something more like "head for sleep," "set about sleeping," or "try to sleep." When a person actually falls asleep (i.e., when the attempt ends and the real experience begins), Chinese adds a complement to the verb, *shui zhao* 睡着, to signal that the *shui* effort "takes effect." Chinese uses this kind of verbal complement with great frequency, and English hardly at all. (I noted in Chapter 1 that "tickled pink" and "scared stiff" are examples in English of the kind of thing that verbal complements in Chinese do.) What English achieves by putting "try" before a verb is often the same as what Chinese achieves by using a verb and omitting any complement. When you try something in Chinese, you set about the action of the verb; if it works, you tack on a complement to indicate that it worked.[196] James Tai and Jane Chou have raised the telling example of how to say *kill* in Chinese. Chinese-English dictionaries list *sha* 殺 as 'kill', but this is not as precise as it perhaps should be. "Try to kill" might be better. In Chinese one can say *Zhang San shale Li Si liang ci dou mei ba ta sha si* 张三杀了李四两次都没把他杀死 'Zhang San tried twice to kill Li Si but didn't kill him'. In awkward English that better reflects the structure of the Chinese, one might say "Zhang San twice set about the killing of Li Si and neither time killed him into deadness." Similarly *zisha* 自杀, which dictionaries list as "commit suicide," might be more precisely listed as "attempt suicide." One can *zisha* in Chinese many times but commit suicide in English only once.

But setting aside, for now, the question of how much it might be true that Chinese verbs and adjectives "cross borders" more easily than their English counterparts do, I want to focus especially on the case of nouns, where the Western-language preference for putting things into containers has, it seems to me, some fairly profound implications.

---

196. Many complements add the additional flavor of *how* something worked. Verb-*wan* 完 says that you finished, *-hao* 好 that you finished and the result was fine, *-cheng* 成 that you formed something into something else, *-buliao* 不了 that you couldn't get to the end of the task, and there are many other examples. They all say what happened after you *tried*.

We sometimes insert nouns into English phrases for no useful purpose at all. Why, for example, do many English speakers say "on a daily basis" instead of "every day," or just "daily"? Put directly into Chinese, the "basis" idea sounds stupid. *Wo tiantian shang ke* 我天天上課 'I go to class every day' sounds fine, but *wo zai tiantian de jichushang shang ke* 我在天天的基礎上上課, literally, "I go to class on a daily basis," the *zai . . . jichushang* is superfluous and a bit ridiculous. The same kind of superfluousness can invade one-word ontological metaphors in English. For example, in the late 1990s it became fashionable in literary study in the West to speak not just of "position" but of "positionality." Both words are nouns, of course, but the *-ality* was assumed to be adding something—something new, stylish, even a bit mystical. Students from China could master the word in English, but how could they put it into Chinese? If "position" is *weizhi* 位置, then what is "positionality"? *Weizhixing* 位置性 seems inane, but to leave off *xing* 性 is to lose the *-ality*, and then position is only position.

How often, in English, do we conceive things in terms of nouns when it is not necessary to do so? For example, when electric impulses are speeding along neurons in the brain, might not a verb be best? Why does a distinguished cognitive scientist, George Lakoff, create a noun, "neural connectivity," and then conceive it as a *thing* that can act on other things, for example, "makes it natural for complex metaphorical mappings to be built"?[197] Elsewhere, in writing about conceptual categories, Lakoff explains that certain examples of a category (e.g., robins and sparrows, for the category of birds) are its "prototypes" and, through application of rules involving similarity and other criteria, can be "generators" of extension of the category to include emus, ostriches, penguins, and other birds. So far, the nouns in this explanation are probably all necessary. But then Lakoff also uses—as a writer in Chinese would not, indeed *could* not, without severe awkwardness—the abstract noun "prototypicality," which in this case allows something else, yet another abstract noun, "generativity," to occur.[198] Similarly, Amanda Scott, whose work on vertical space-for-time metaphors I have already referred to, quotes R. H. Lauer as observing not that time is

---

197. Lakoff and Johnson, *Philosophy in the Flesh*, p. 64.
198. Lakoff, *Women, Fire, and Dangerous Things*, pp. 12, 41, 44.

a fact but that "temporality is a facticity."[199] A medical researcher at the University of California at San Francisco in 2003 discussed mad cow disease in terms of its "infectivity."[200] It is easy to find similar examples, especially in the world of Western academe.

What is not so easy to say is whether this bent for nominalization does harm or good in the world of thought. Derk Bodde and others have argued that Indo-European languages, because they deal easily in abstract nouns, make abstract thinking itself more natural than it is in languages like Chinese, which see the world, as Bodde puts it, more "organically." This difference in languages helps, in Bodde's view, to explain why the scientific method originated among speakers of European languages.[201] Bodde may be right. Certainly it is a mistake to discount his view (as some have) because of its alleged disrespect for Chinese culture. What I want to do, though, is to suggest a hypothesis that leans in the opposite direction. It does not contradict Bodde's view, and both could well be true. My hypothesis, put as a question, is this: what kinds of problems might be caused by excessive nominalization in Indo-European languages? Might such problems be less troublesome when one interprets the world through verb-heavy Chinese?

Where excessive nominalization can begin to cause trouble, in my view, is the point at which a person who thinks in English begins to assume that a noun somehow says something more "real" than a verb or adjective does. "The neurons connect well" and "the neural connectivity is good" say essentially the same thing. (Good writers might prefer the former as a matter of style, but that is a separate question.) Problems enter when people begin to suppose that "neural connectivity" somehow is something special, something that *adds to* "neurons connect." Such a supposition can lead to several problems. One very simple problem is that we can be misled into thinking that a mere tautology is intellectually significant. If I

---

199. Amanda Scott, "Vertical Dimension of Time in Mandarin," p. 312; R. H. Lauer, *Temporal Man* (New York: Praeger, 1981), p. 26.

200. Joanne Silberner, "Infected Cow Born before Feed Ban Took Effect," National Public Radio, December 30, 2003.

201. Derk Bodde, *Chinese Thought, Society, and Science: The Intellectual and Social Background of Science and Technology in Pre-modern China* (Honolulu: University of Hawaii Press, 1991), ch. 7 and p. 357.

were to say, for example, "her neurons connect well because she has good neural connectivity," the emptiness of the explanation would be plain. Yet even an experienced writer like Lakoff comes close to doing this when he writes, for example, "What gives human beings the power of abstract reason? Our answer is that human beings have what we will call a *conceptualizing capacity*."[202] Lakoff goes on to explain what he means by "capacity," and his explanation, like the thing explained, is heavy with nouns. He writes that the conceptualizing capacity is an "*ability* to form symbolic *structures* . . . in our everyday *experience*."[203] My point here is not to criticize Lakoff's idea; it is to note that his thought, as he has expressed it, would be very hard to put into Chinese without completely reconceiving it (and then, if one did completely reconceive it, the question would arise as to whether or not it is the "same" thought). In Lakoff's English sentence, people reason abstractly because they "have" something (an ability, a capacity, etc.); in Chinese it is much easier to say that people reason abstractly because they "do" something. Chinese clearly prefers verbs to say this kind of thing: *fenxi* 分析 is the modern word for "analyze"; *xiang tong* 想通, literally "think through," and *xiang mingbai* 想明白, literally "think clear," are more deeply rooted vernacular expressions; *gao qingchu* 搞清楚 'get clear' is a twentieth-century colloquialism that grew out of the Communist movement. But whatever their provenance, all of them are *verbs*. Among them only *fenxi* can be used as a noun, and as such is limited to modern, Western-influenced language where it corresponds to the noun "analysis" in English. There is no way in Chinese, without seeming bizarre, to push *fenxi* further, toward a word like "analyticity."

The bent of Western languages toward nominalization might create some problems that run deeper than the relatively minor danger of redundant explanation, but these deeper problems are harder both to define and to solve. They arise mainly from an unexamined assumption that "what nouns refer to" are "things" that might or might not "exist." Most people, most of the time (here I am excluding only solipsists, certain mystics, and a few others), feel comfortable with the notion that nouns like "book," "chair," and "snowflake" refer to things that exist. A noun like

---

202. Lakoff, *Women, Fire, and Dangerous Things*, p. 280. Emphasis in original.
203. Ibid., p. 281. My emphasis.

METAPHOR 225

"unicorn" does not refer to a thing that exists, but it does refer to the kind of thing that *could* exist in the way that other referents of nouns do. Hence it is natural for speakers of Western languages, who have this kind of mental habit about nouns in their minds, to assume that nouns like "inflation" and "connectivity" also refer to things that do or might "exist." For example, when Lakoff refers to "analyticity" as a "phenomenon" that we can "make sense of,"[204] how much are we led to think in terms similar to "chair" as a "thing" that we can "put in the corner"? Because ontological metaphor works so smoothly in Western language, we normally do not ask a question like this.

Lakoff comes close to addressing this problem when he writes: "cultural categories are real and they are made real by human action. Governments are real. They exist."[205] There are two questions here. One is why we use the noun "action" to define government. Could we use the verb "acts" instead? Government collects taxes, fines you if you run a red light, runs public schools, protects you if the Canadians invade, and so on. These are things that it does. (Such a list would be indefinitely long.) We can list the actions as nouns or—as I just have—as verbs. Either works. The second important question is why, if we do decide to use nouns instead of verbs, we choose to say that abstract nouns—like "government"—are "real" and that they "exist." It is abstract to say that a government "does" things, because humans are the actual doers. Lakoff suggests as much by referring to "human" action. He probably believes that the human actions that comprise government are themselves "real," but he does not say this; his point is that human actions are what turn *governments* into real things. When this happens, governments "exist." The question that needs to be raised—and that I believe, broadly speaking, Chinese grammar prods us to raise—is to what extent English speakers are induced by the habits of their language to jump too easily from the level of "chairs exist" to the level of "governments exist," and then to conceive the two things as more similar than they are.

Does it happen, for example, that speakers of English are drawn to believe that certain things exist because nouns that claim to be their labels

204. Ibid., p. 118.
205. Ibid., p. 208.

exist? Might it be that only the labels exist? For example, Hoyt Alverson, the anthropologist I cited earlier for his argument that crosscultural similarities in the experience of time suggest a "universal template of human experience," describes the relativist position on this question, which Alverson opposes, as claiming that the "ontogeny" of time is indeterminate.[206] He explains "ontogeny" as meaning the "character" of something's "being." We have, then, the proposition that the *character* of the *being* of *time* is indeterminate. Do the nouns in this proposition refer to things that exist? In addition to time, is there a "being" of time? And if there is, is that being the kind of thing that can possess something else, as here it is supposed to possess a "character"? These problems are by no means Alverson's alone; he writes in a mode that is fairly common in English. In Chinese, though, it is almost impossibly awkward to refer to "the character of the being of time." A noun-studded literal translation like *shijian de cunzai de xingzhi* 时间的存在的性质 'nature of existence of time' is opaque in Chinese; to Chinese ears it signals that "this came out of a Western language and you might well go there to figure out what it is supposed to mean."

As noted earlier, the very word "being" (or "existence") is hard to put into Chinese. *Cunzai* is a modern term, and by the late twentieth century it had entered Chinese sufficiently to sound natural as a verb (although it remained awkward as a noun). Ancient Chinese thinkers who were concerned with being and nonbeing often used *you* 有 'there is' and *wu* 無 'there is not' to express these concerns. But *you* and *wu* are both verbs. Westerners have often translated them using nouns like "being" and "nonbeing," but within Chinese grammar they do not feel natural as nouns. This grammatical difference makes it hard, in Chinese, to pose philosophical questions about what being "is" or what "character" it might "have." From here, one can speculate on the inadequacy of the Chinese language, because certain questions cannot be raised in it. Or, to turn the matter around, one can speculate on the flaws of Western language, in which grammar permits one to raise (and waste time on) questions that are not real questions. Are English speakers better off because they can think about the "properties" of "being," or are Chinese speakers

---

206. Hoyt Alverson, *Semantics and Experience*, p. 3.

better off because they are spared this word-trap? In short, the issue of a preference for nouns in European languages and a preference for verbs in Chinese might have implications for formal philosophy in the two traditions.

Plato puzzled over "the good," "beauty," "justice," "substance," and other noun-named things some of which can be discussed just as easily as adjectives or verbs. Later Western philosophers have spent time on "mind," "autonomy," and "free will," while religious thinkers have pondered "God" and "man," "sin," and the "immortality" of the "soul." It is possible to overdraw the differences between Chinese and Western approaches in such matters, but there does seem to be a systematic difference between the two traditions, and others have noticed it. Standing back from his detailed study of pre-Qin thought, Edward Slingerland generalizes that the knowledge that ancient Chinese thinkers pursued "was not abstract knowledge *that* the good was to be defined in a certain way, but concrete knowledge concerning *how* to act in a way that was good."[207] Roger Ames and Henry Rosemont, generalizing over a broader range of Chinese thought, write that "we want to claim that English (and other Indo-European languages) is basically *substantive* and *essentialistic*, whereas classical Chinese should be seen more as an eventful language."[208] Ames and Rosemont feel that the distinction between Chinese and English holds even in modern language. They compare the sentence "The young woman who just entered the room is very bright" with a translation— *gangcai dao wuzili lai de xiaojie feichang congming* 剛才到屋子裏來的小姐非常聰明. Then they note—correctly, in my view—that somehow the young woman in the English sentence feels more "substantial" and the *xiaojie* 'young lady' in the Chinese sentence feels more "dynamic" than the counterpart in the other sentence.[209]

---

207. Slingerland, *Effortless Action*, p. 3. Emphasis in original.
208. Ames and Rosemont, *Analects of Confucius*, p. 20.
209. Ibid., pp. 22–23. I have inserted *dao* 到 into the Chinese example to make it a bit more natural. Readers who do not know Chinese and wonder why the Chinese seems more "dynamic" and the English more "substantive" might wish that I give a translation to make this clear. I apologize that I cannot improve on the translation that Ames and Rosemont provide, but I do agree with their judgment about the subtle difference in the effects the two languages create.

It would be unfair to Western philosophers to hold that their perhaps excessive focus on nouns is something that they have not noticed and that only a language like Chinese can help them to escape. Western philosophy since Plato has not lacked for critics of Plato's conception of Forms or his claiming that Forms somehow exist separately from the rest of the world.[210] Moreover, in the twentieth century, and quite without any assistance from Chinese, Ludwig Wittgenstein and others did much to show how philosophical puzzles can be born from the unexamined ways people use language. But even at the end of the twentieth century, and well after Western philosophers had had a chance to absorb Wittgenstein, the danger of creating nouns and then assuming that "things" correspond to them seems to have persisted among Western philosophers. In 1999 Colin McGinn published his little book *The Mysterious Flame: Conscious Minds in a Material World*.[211] McGinn owns a daunting intellect, and his writing is clear and incisive. In choosing his book in order to see whether the "noun trap" was still at work in Western thinking at the end of the twentieth century, I am purposefully choosing a powerful example for the test: Is even a writer as astute as McGinn vulnerable to the peril?

McGinn's book addresses the classic "mind-body problem": what is consciousness, and how does it exist in the physical world? At one point he focuses on the curious fact that our perceptions of the world are often perceptions of things in *space*, yet the perceptions themselves occupy no space. He writes:

> We need to make a distinction between the *object* of awareness and the awareness itself. When I sit in [a] ski lift and feel fear about the distance between me and the ground, the object of my fear is a spatial fact: my distance from the earth. It is not that the fear itself is a spatial thing—*it* is not a hundred feet in length![212]

---

210. Peter Abelard (1079–1142), William of Ockham (1288–1347), Thomas Hobbes (1588–1679), and Jeremy Bentham (1748–1832), among others, all polemicized in one way or another against the notion of assuming that every noun is a name for a real thing.
211. Colin McGinn, *The Mysterious Flame* (New York: Basic Books, 1999).
212. Ibid., p. 109.

Certainly the distance between a suspended chair on a ski lift and the ground below is different from a fear of falling. But why do we use nouns for both, and then believe that we are dealing with two parallel "things"? It is fairly clear that McGinn does this, that is, takes the distance and the perception of the distance as two *somethings*. He writes, "My fear has space as its object, but that which has this object—the mental state of fear itself—is not to be confused with that object."[213]

In Chinese *pa* 怕 'fear' and *haipa* 害怕 'fear' are both verbs. They can be transitive verbs, as in *pa she* 怕蛇 'fear snakes' or "stative verbs," as in *hen haipa* 很害怕 'be very much afraid'. But neither can be a noun—except in modern (and notably awkward) imitation of Western usage. *Kongju* 恐懼 'dread' works better as a noun, but it, too, is a modern term. In short, while both nouns and verbs are possible in Chinese, when I am dangerously suspended in a ski lift it is much more natural in Chinese to think "I fear" than to think "I have a fear." But right there, perhaps, is the beginning of the problem. If I think "I have a fear," then it makes sense, at least grammatically, for me to raise the question why that fear is "not a spatial thing" whereas the distance to the ground *is* a spatial thing, and this can become a puzzle. On the other hand, if I think "I fear," then no question arises of why one "thing" has spatiality and the other one does not. Again we need to ask: is it a loss or a gain that this question does not arise? Is Chinese deficient for closing off an avenue of analysis, or is English defective for allowing its grammar to entangle us in a nonquestion? The question cannot be decided on the criterion Lakoff and Johnson have suggested, that is, what we need "in order to deal rationally with our experience." *Haipa* 'fearing' in Chinese and "feeling a fear" in English are both unobjectionably rational ways to deal with the distance between a ski lift and the ground.

McGinn gives another example of how physical things occupy space and mental things do not:

> Consider the visual experience of seeing a red sphere two feet away with a six-inch diameter. The object of this experience is of course a spatial object with spatial properties, but the experience itself does

---

213. Ibid.

> not have these properties: it is not two feet away from you and six inches in diameter. . . . When we reflect on the experience itself, we can see that it lacks spatial properties altogether.[214]

The key phrase here is "the experience itself." Is there such a thing? The noun "experience" exists, but that is not the question. Does *the experience* exist? We might feel intuitively that it does. But does this intuition arise, in part, from the grammatical habit of using nouns like "experience" and assuming that they refer to things? Is there a way we can test whether our intuitions indeed are being shaped by nouns?

The English word "experience" is perhaps not the best example for doing such a test, simply because it has the same form as both noun and verb. "Feeling" might work better, because the noun ("feeling") and the verb ("feel") have different forms. In most cases, two statements of the forms "I feel X" and "I have a feeling of X" will not differ much, if at all, in meaning. But now consider this: If I say "I feel X," you cannot grammatically ask me in English "Does your feel have spatial properties?" You *could* ask, "Do you feel with (or in) length and color?" but this question, although grammatical, does not make sense. No matter how you put them, questions about the spatiality of X are hard to phrase if you use the word "feel" instead of the word "feeling." But if, on the other hand, I say "I have a feeling of X," then the same question—"Does your feeling have spatial properties?"—now does make sense. It not only makes grammatical sense, but makes enough philosophical sense to get into the writing of an excellent philosopher like Colin McGinn. So we can see here that from a starting point where there is no real difference in daily-life usage (i.e., between "I feel X" and "I have a feeling of X"), the choice of which to use can lead to (or perhaps generate?) a great philosophical puzzle if one goes in one direction and lead to no puzzlement if one goes in the other.

McGinn goes on to point out that numbers, like the experience of red spots, do not occupy space. "We cannot sensibly ask how much space the number 2 takes up relative to the number 37," he writes. "It is hardly true that the bigger the number the more space it occupies."[215] Then he writes:

214. Ibid.
215. Ibid., p. 110.

To attribute spatial properties to numbers is an instance of what philosophers call a category-mistake, trying to talk about something as if it belonged to a category it does not belong to. Only concrete things have spatial properties, not abstract things like numbers or mental things like experiences of red.[216]

In my imagination, a pre-Qin Chinese philosopher might well accept this point but then ask McGinn: Why do you experience life as "abstract things"? Is that not also a category-mistake? If I see a red spot, do I not simply see a red spot? The red spot, yes, is a thing, but "I see" is not a thing, either concrete or abstract. I see is I see. If you change it into "my sight" or "my experience of seeing," you are performing a grammatical act, but that grammatical act has no power to change the way the world is.

The Significance of Similarities and Differences among Conceptual Metaphors in Different Languages

I began my study of how conceptual metaphor compares in Chinese and English with a hope that the results might reveal alternative "worldviews" in some sort of systematic way. That hope has been largely dashed. Not only do the two languages not stand apart very clearly in their overall patterns of metaphors but—and here is a much more fundamental problem—even within just one of the languages, Chinese or English, there is a lot of metaphorical incoherence. In space-for-time metaphors, as we have seen, "before" in English can mean either past or future; and so, in Chinese, can *qian* 前. Examples such as these—and there are many—show how conceptual metaphors in a language do not have to fit together coherently. Less like auto parts that form a whole, they are more like tools in a tool bag that a person takes out, uses for a purpose, and then puts back—with no thought of how they fit together or form anything larger. When we say *houdai* 后代 'future generations', where *hou* points to the future, and also say *qiantu* 前途 'future path', where *qian* means future, it does not matter at all that *qian* and *hou* are opposites. The tools in the tool bag work, each

---

216. Ibid.

in its own way. So much for my imaginings of grand conclusions about worldviews.

But then a different sort of grand conclusion, one I did not expect, began to emerge. I noticed that the separate tool bags of Chinese and English conceptual metaphors contained some remarkably similar items. Some of these were modern borrowings, which were easy to explain and not very interesting. To recognize that *pingjing* 瓶颈 is "bottleneck" does not reveal anything very deep. More interesting were examples that are deeply and separately embedded in the two languages yet turn out to be almost uncanny in their similarity. The three different ways Chinese conceives space-for-time, analyzed earlier, are not simple patterns, either in themselves or in how they fit together. The fact that they match up so well with the ways English conceives space-for-time metaphors has been surprising to me, indeed astonishing. So have other similarities, such as the patterns of privilege within dyads.

Why do human languages as different as Chinese and English turn out to be so very similar in certain ways? As we have seen, there have been, broadly speaking, two kinds of explanation for the similarities: one is that the structure of the human brain and its perceptual apparatus determines that these things be as they are, and the other is that the commonality of human experience makes it natural for human beings everywhere to develop similar concepts . Both sorts of explanation seem clearly right in part, even though much remains to be understood about most of the details. Whatever their explanations, the commonalities have turned out to be much stronger than I anticipated, and there is something very refreshing in that fact. It seems to reinforce the valuable notion of a single human family.

In cases where conceptual metaphors differ between Chinese and English, there may be no overarching conclusions to draw yet a gardenful of interesting insights on particular questions. Cultural differences are always fun to notice, and sometimes they are enlightening. I have noted, for example, how *accompaniment is instrumentality* in many languages; in English, you can play Ping-Pong "with" your left hand, but this does not work in Chinese, where, if you say such a thing, it sounds as if your left hand has gone to the other end of the table to play against you.

There is often an even larger benefit in noticing cultural differences, however, and that is in realizing that aspects of one's culture that one has taken for granted are in fact arbitrary—because things can be conceived differently. In the modern West, *north* is so well associated with *up* (not only on maps but in words like "uptown" and even phrases like "north of thirty" to mean "over thirty years old") that it can be interesting, indeed can "turn the world upside down," to think of *south* as "up." But this is how it was in China until about a thousand years ago (and again, not only on maps but in words like *zhinan* 指南 'pointing south' to mean "compass" or to talk about a person's moral bearings). My suggestion that excessive use of ontological metaphor in Indo-European language might help to explain puzzlement over the mind-body problem in Western philosophy draws on essentially this same point. It is possible here that habits of conceptual metaphor in one's native language might prevent one from seeing that if one did not have such habits, things might look different. I doubt that insight of this variety will ever "solve" the mind-body problem. But at a minimum, it can help to explain the extraordinary amount of concern that has gone into centuries of dealing with the problem in Western languages. In Chinese the problem does not present itself in a vexing way. It is therefore not as intellectually stimulating, in Chinese, to get into the ring and wrestle with it. And that very fact may undo some of the original problem.

3
Politics

Formal political language, in many societies and in many times, has tended to diverge from ordinary talk. Vocabulary can differ, rhythms and tones of voice can diverge, and even grammar can be affected. In most cases, what creeps into political language is officiousness. A stuffy tone can claim a special authority for the speaker, who then can assume a position of elevation above an audience. This makes glibness easier to achieve and can provide a slick suit of clothes for questionable or even groundless claims. George Orwell has written that "political language . . . is designed to make lies sound truthful and murder respectable, and to give an appearance of solidity to pure wind."[1] Orwell was writing about English, but his principle applies broadly.

---

1. George Orwell, "Politics and the English Language," in *A Collection of Essays* (Garden City, N.Y.: Doubleday, 1954), p. 177.

A Bifurcation

Officialese has a long pedigree in China. In late imperial times, the lingua franca of the empire was called *guanhua* 官話 'official talk'. It was the language officials were obliged to use because they (and not many others, in those times) needed to travel among China's complex patchwork of language areas. (The term *guanhua* is reflected in the English word "Mandarin," which originally referred to these officials.) During China's late-Qing and Republican years (from about 1860 until 1949), grammatical influences from Western languages as well as a large amount of new vocabulary based on Japanese and Western terms flowed into China's official language. In most ways, though, the official language remained continuous with the earlier *guanhua*.

The cataclysmic events of the late Mao era, from the late 1950s to the early 1970s, then brought a significant change. The bifurcation between official language and ordinary language in China grew much sharper and more pervasive than it had ever been before. In the Anti-Rightist Movement of 1957, people were forced to explain in public how they had come to be, officially speaking, "anti-Party" and "antisocialist"—even though these words did not correspond at all to their inner feelings. During the Great Leap Forward, people had to speak of "great bountiful harvests" at the same time that the largest famine in world history was unfolding. Not only was the gap between official language and daily-life reality suddenly much larger than before; it was now no longer just the officials but nearly everyone in society who had to learn to negotiate the official language. Moreover, the penalties for missteps were more severe than they had even been.

China's eminent journalist Liu Binyan has written of his personal discovery of this language bifurcation. Liu was labeled a "Rightist" in 1957 and sent to work among dirt-poor farmers during 1958–60. There, in a gully in the mountains,

> a struggle began to rage deep inside me: how could two diametrically opposed "truths" coexist in the world? The longings of the peasants were one truth, and the policies of the higher-ups and the

propaganda in the newspapers were quite another. Which should I follow?[2]

After some soul-searching, Liu opted for the "bottom up" truths that he saw in the daily lives of farmers. But at the same time (and here he was like most people in Chinese society) he learned to handle both versions of the Chinese language. A person had little choice. If you wanted to get certain things done—buy a bicycle, get a marriage license, or take a family photo, for example—simply saying so would not get you very far; you had to manipulate the official language rather as one manipulates the pieces in a chess game, referring to such things as "revolutionary needs," "class stands," or your desire that "policy be correctly implemented," being careful to put things in such a way that small matters like your bicycle, your marriage license, or your photograph seemed almost incidental. If you suffered political attack, the need for skill in language manipulation became even more critical; your words offered in defense had to fit with the words in the attack or they would not count; wrong political terminology could confirm that your politics were wrong, and that could confirm the original charges.

Even when the official language was not needed for such vital purposes, it was a good idea to stay in touch with it. It was, after all, "another kind of truth." It could tell a person about policy, and policy was important to know about regardless of what one thought of it. When policy during the Great Leap Forward called for planting rice stalks much closer together than ever before, it suddenly became crucial for farmers to know the policy even if they also knew that the stalks would die if planted in such a way. One's livelihood, even one's life, could depend on knowing what the policies were. In addition to learning about policy, sophisticated readers could find ways to mine official language for ordinary-life truths that were buried inside it. Wu Zuxiang, an author of splendid short stories in the 1930s and later a professor of Chinese literature at Peking University, put it this way:

---

2. "Listen Carefully to the Voice of the People," in Liu Binyan, *Two Kinds of Truth: Stories and Reportage from China*, ed. Perry Link (Bloomington: Indiana University Press, 2006), p. 31.

> There is truth in Chinese newspapers, but you have to know how to find it. This often means reading upside down. If they say great strides have been made against corruption in Henan, you know that corruption is especially bad in Henan. If they say dozens of police were hurt in a clash with students, you know hundreds of students were injured if not killed.[3]

Wu was speaking in 1980, four years after the death of Mao Zedong and at a time when Chinese society was emerging from the extreme repression of the late Mao years. By 1980 ordinary talk about nonpolitical things had returned to the public sphere in China in ways that had not been possible under Mao. But the juxtaposition of the two kinds of language in public life only accentuated the sense of artificiality of the official language. It became more and more apparent that in using it people were only shuffling words that had been drained of the ideals and principles they had originally represented.

The bifurcation was sufficiently well established by 1980 that people living their daily lives tended not to notice it. It was just the way things were in the Chinese language. But to an outsider like me, who first lived in China during 1979–80 (I had been to China before, but only for short trips), the distinction of levels was both startling and fascinating. In newspapers, on the radio, in classrooms, at formal meetings, or in official welcomes to foreign guests, there was one kind of language. Buying fish in the market, asking your sister-in-law to pass the soy sauce, or shouting at a child to get out of the rain, there was a very different kind of language. By "language" I do not mean just tone, or what linguists call "register." I mean also vocabulary, pronunciation, and grammar. To be sure, it was all "Chinese," but the two kinds of Chinese presented a sharp and pervasive distinction. Even later, in the 1990s and the early twenty-first century, as linguistic influences surged into China from the outside world through travel, television, and the Internet, the official language has remained largely intact. It has kept its distinctive diction, grammar, and

---

3. Interview, July 18, 1980, Beijing.

aura, and has continued to occupy a special plane within Chinese language use.[4]

One way to test for the large but often unnoticed gap between the official and unofficial languages in China is to observe how mixing of the two levels produces incongruity that people find laughable. Judith Shapiro and Liang Heng, observing Chinese student life in 1983, note that "a form of black humor was common among young Chinese . . . the repetition of any of the [official] slogans in ordinary conversation was almost certain to bring a laugh."[5] I observed this phenomenon myself around the same time at a dinner party in Shanghai. Someone put a delectable morsel on the plate of a friend, and the friend responded, as is normal, *bie keqi, ziji lai* 别客气,自己来 'don't be polite, help yourself'. The morsel deliverer then responded—*not* normally—by saying *buyaojin, wo wei renmin fuwu* 不要紧,我为人民服务 'that's all right, I'm serving the people'. The phrase precipitated sharp laughter from everyone within earshot. The Maoist slogan "Serve the People" belonged to such a different level of language that it was highly incongruous, and therefore funny, to insert it into such a relaxed and informal context. (The laughter probably also derived, at least in part, from the sense of relief that comes when the tension involved in use of the official language is made to dissolve in mirth.) Near the end of Jiang Zemin's rule in China in 2002, there were popular jokes about "three [people] wearing wristwatches" (*sange dai biao* 三个戴表) because the phrase was a pun on Jiang's pretentious phrase for the new roles of the Communist Party as "The Three Represents" (*sange daibiao* 三个代表).[6]

---

4. The last time I visited China, in the summer of 1996, I was detained at the Beijing airport (no reason was given) and held overnight in a nearby hotel by four Chinese policemen before being sent back to the U.S. The police used official language to tell me the rules of my stay: I could not exit the room, I could not make a phone call, I could not leave their company, etc. That done, the four of them, who were young and curious, reverted to a very different level of language to ask: "How much did your watch cost?" "How did you learn Chinese?" etc. For details see my essay "Beijing yiyou" 北京一遊, in *Banyang Suibi* 半洋隨筆 [Notes of a semiforeigner] (Taipei: Sanmin chubanshe, 1999), pp. 93–98.

5. Judith Shapiro and Liang Heng, *Cold Winds, Warm Winds: Intellectual Life in China Today* (Middletown, Conn.: Wesleyan University Press, 1986), p. 41.

6. The three things that the Communist Party should represent, according to Jiang Zemin at the Sixteenth Party Congress in November 2002, are (1) the requirements of

Even officials sometimes played with this kind of pun, and records of such play sometimes found their ways into internal Party documents. At a 1979 Party meeting to discuss how to repress a cartoon strip that, in the view of certain high officials, showed the violence of the Cultural Revolution in excessively stark terms, officials who opposed the repression satirized it by punning on politically charged terms. What the people on the repressing side stood for, they quipped, was not *lishi weiwuzhuyi* 历史唯物主义 'historical materialism' but *lishi weiwu zhuyi* 历史为无主义 'history-is-nothing-ism'. And it was the same people, they said, who had turned a *wenhua dageming* 文化大革命 'Cultural Revolution' into a *wuhua dageming* 武化大革命 'militarized revolution'.[7]

Puns by nature trade on the incongruity of two levels of language, but in this kind of politically loaded pun the contrast is sharper, and the resultant laughter often stronger, than what puns normally provide. When I did research at Zhongshan University during the 1979–80 academic year, students of English sometimes sought me out for language practice. On one occasion a group wanted to learn the game of charades. After I explained the game's principles, some of the students went into an adjacent room to plot what they were going to act out, and they suddenly burst into irrepressible laughter. Someone had suggested that they do "class struggle," which, as a euphemism for attack on people during the Cultural Revolution, was still a phrase that inspired fear. In this case the release of tension was far more than what a mere pun could have achieved.

I was visiting the university to study "scar" literature, which consisted primarily of short stories that lifted the curtain on the fear, violence, and other trauma of the late-Mao years. Scar literature was parallel in many ways to the "thaw" literature that helped Russians begin to look at the pain and repression of the Stalin years after Stalin died in 1953. One reason why Chinese readers loved scar stories was that they could help to release tensions and animosities that had long been repressed; at the same time,

---

the development of China's advanced productive forces, (2) the orientation of the development of China's advanced culture, and (3) the fundamental interests of the overwhelming majority of the people in China.

7. *Guanyu lianhuanhua "feng" de zuotanhui fayan jilu* 关于连环画"枫"的座谈会发言纪录 (Transcript of the conference on the comic strip "Maple"), comp. Editorial Offices of *Lianhuanhua* 连环画 [Comic strips], August 11, 1979, pp. 17, 18.

and in part because of precisely that incendiary potential, the stories were sometimes "politically sensitive." Officials at several levels worried about whether they personally might be recognizable in the ostensibly fictional portrayals of villains, while the rulers at the very top monitored the question of whether the overall outcry might rock their whole system and threaten their monopoly on power. These two sides of the response to scar literature—popular enthusiasm and official apprehension—were expressed, respectively, in both of the two levels of language, official and nonofficial, that we have been considering here. In classrooms in which I was an auditor, professors of Chinese literature used the official language to lecture to students on the Party-approved history of modern Chinese literature; but during the breaks between classes (which, because of the infectious interest in scar literature, grew longer than they were scheduled to be), the same professors and students spoke in lively ordinary language about the latest scar stories.[8] During the day, government bureaucrats pronounced warnings, in austere official language, about how some scar stories were going too far, but in the evenings, after hours, those same officials sometimes went home to discuss the same stories with their children, in informal language and in much more positive terms. Hu Yaobang, minister of propaganda of the Communist Party of China at the time, delivered a major speech on scar literature in February 1980, in which he acknowledged this problem of public versus private commentary on politically sensitive works. "What you might say casually at home," Hu told an assembly of officials, "doesn't matter very much. But to speak in public is to do official thoughtwork, and this produces social effects . . . that can be good or bad."[9] Hu was accepting the political bifurcation of the Chinese language and simply trying to ensure that the two kinds of language operated in their proper spheres.

8. Personal observation of classes on modern Chinese literature taught by Professors Wang Jinmin 王晋民 and Huang Weizong 黄伟宗, Zhongshan University, spring 1980.

9. Hu Yaobang 胡耀邦, *Zai juben chuangzuo zuotanhuishang de jianghua* 在剧本工作会议上的讲话 (Talk at the conference on playwriting), February 12–13, 1980. Published in 1980 as a pamphlet with no date or place listed. Once available on the Internet at http://news.xinhuanet.com/ziliao/2005-02/04/content_2548212.htm, but not available as of June 29, 2012.

In certain ways the official language in contemporary China has always had more power than the ordinary language. It conveys the ideas of "leaders," and these ideas, one way or another, do have important effects on ordinary life. It hardly follows, however, that the official language is itself more infused with life; indeed the opposite is almost always the case. The official language normally is colorless and boring. People tolerate it, and sometimes study it, because of its possible impacts—but not, usually, because of any intrinsic attraction to it as language. Mark Salzman, who taught English for two years in China after he graduated from Yale in 1982, wrote this after observing some official meetings at his school:

> The Chinese have, by necessity, increased their endurance manyfold by making listening optional. During meetings they talk with one another, doze, get up and stretch or walk around, and in general do not pretend to pay attention. This does not seem to offend the speaker, who, in general, does not pretend to be interested in what he or she is saying.[10]

If the speaker is as bored as the listeners, why, one might ask, do such meetings happen at all? In broad terms, the answer to this question is that their purpose is largely ritual; the point is to mark the fact that everyone present subscribes to the content of the speech. At meetings where decisions are actually made or argued about—and these would be meetings that a young foreigner like Salzman certainly would not have been allowed to observe—the atmosphere is more lively and, significantly, the language itself is often much more informal. At a confidential Party meeting on literature and art in Guangxi in the winter of 1980, for example, some delegates were arguing against the continued influences of Maoism on literary policy by saying that Mao could not even control his wife, Jiang Qing (leader of the discredited "Gang of Four"). People present at the meeting report that this thought spread among the conference delegates in the earthy phrase *lian laopo dou mei fa guan, zenme neng guan wenyi ne?* 连老婆都没法管，怎么能管文艺呢？ '[Mao] had no way to handle even his old woman, how could he handle literature and art?'. In response, Hu

---

10. Mark Salzman, *Iron and Silk* (New York: Vintage Books, 1986), p. 162.

Yaobang, the Party's top propaganda official, reportedly warned "we have to get away from this tendency" of saying Mao "could not even corral his own wife."[11] Around the same time Hu Qiaomu, who for years had been a secretary to Mao, was deputed to deliver good news to a young playwright named Zhao Zixiong 赵梓雄. The message was that Zhao's play *The Future Beckons* (*Weilai zai zhaohuan* 未来在召唤), which had drawn heavy criticism from Party authorities, would not likely land the youngster in prison. The published criticism of Zhao's work had all been in formal language. But Hu Qiaomu's reprieve, which was delivered privately, used lively informal language. These words were, as reported by witnesses, *xi ge zao, shui ge jiao, zhe shi bu hao xi* 洗个澡, 睡个觉, 这是部好戏 'have a bath, take a nap, this is a good play'.[12] More recent examples of informal language at very high levels in Chinese politics are not hard to find. In the 1990s Deng Xiaoping was widely quoted as saying that the Communist Party's Politburo "should have only one mother-in-law" (i.e., one boss, himself); otherwise, it would be a "many-headed horsecart" and get nothing done.[13]

In considering the differences between official and unofficial language, therefore, it is important *not* to think of them as two different kinds of language that two different groups of people speak. They are, rather, two ways of speaking, and people of many kinds draw on them as needed. To be sure, officials use the official language more than ordinary people do, but that is only a matter of degree. The two kinds of language can even be interlarded within the same conversation. In a formal interview a person might break from official language to say something informal, as if parenthetically. Sometimes the volume of a person's voice will drop in such

---

11. The reports of what was said at the meeting came from Chen Huangmei 陈荒煤, the deputy director of the Institute for Literary Research of the Chinese Academy of Social Sciences, and Li Yingmin 李英敏, the acting chief of the literature and art bureau of the Propaganda Department of the Communist Party of China. They were relayed to me by Wang Jinmin 王晋民, professor of Chinese at Zhongshan University.

12. The sources here are the same as those in note 11.

13. See Bao Pu, Renee Chiang, and Adi Ignatius, eds., *Prisoner of the State: The Secret Journal of Zhao Ziyang* (New York: Simon and Schuster, 2009), p. 209; and Yan Jiaqi 严家其, "'Santou mache' de lishi kaocha" "三头马车" 的历史考察 (A historical examination of 'the three-headed horsecart'), appendix to Gao Gao 高皋, *Santou mache shidai* 三头马车时代 (The era of the three-headed horsecart) (New York: Mirror Books, 2009).

cases. A softer tone can seem to say "here's a little unvarnished item for you." Credibility can go up as volume goes down.

In the next section I will explain some of the formal and conceptual features that set China's official language apart from the language of daily life.

Characteristics of the Official Language

Every living language changes, and so does what I am here calling China's "official language." Today's modern bureaucratese has roots in China's late-Qing years and took further shape during the republican era. My focus below is on Communist-era official language, but even that has been through changes. In 1951 the distinguished Chinese linguists Lü Shuxiang and Zhu Dexi lent their scholarship to a government-sponsored effort to standardize the national language and "purify" it, that is, rid it of several things, including Western syntax, classical influences, and borrowings from dialects.[14] None of this was easy to do, or could be achieved to perfection, but after a government campaign to get the messages out in print and over the radio, considerable standardization did result, at least in the official language. Some Chinese writers have argued that Lü and Zhu laid the foundation for what became known (and sometimes deplored) as the "Maoist literary style" (*mao wenti* 毛文体) that dominated in the 1960s and 1970s. A number of scholars, including T. A. Hsia, H. C. Chuang, Lowell Dittmer, Chen Ruoxi, Xing Lu, and Ji Fengyuan, have written incisively on what might be called "the language of high Maoism" and on its influences on how people conceptualize things.[15] My own focus

---

14. Lü Shuxiang and Zhu Dexi, *Yufa xiuci jianghua* 语法修辞讲话 (Lectures on grammar and rhetoric) (Shanghai: Kaiming shudian, 1951).

15. T. A. Hsia, *Metaphor, Myth, Ritual, and the People's Commune* (Berkeley: Center for Chinese Studies, University of California, 1961), *A Terminological Study of the Hsia-Fang Movement* (Berkeley: Center for Chinese Studies, University of California, 1963), and *The Commune in Retreat as Evidenced in Terminology and Semantics* (Berkeley: Center for Chinese Studies, University of California, 1964); H. C. Chuang, *The Great Proletarian Cultural Revolution: A Terminological Study* (Berkeley: Center for Chinese Studies, University of California, 1967), and *The Little Red Book and Current Chinese Language* (Berkeley: Center for Chinese Studies, University of California,

in what follows will be primarily on the official language of China's late-Mao and post-Mao years, from the 1960s through the early twenty-first century. No cut of the temporal spectrum can be clean, however. Much of what I address below are habits inherited from earlier times.

Another line that cannot be drawn clearly is any between post-Mao official Chinese language and the official languages of societies and governments elsewhere in the world. There are differences, yes, but also many common features. I have already noted the relevance of Orwell's famous essay "Politics and the English Language," and there is plenty to study in the spin-meistering of American politics. Comparisons between Chinese officialese and the official languages of other authoritarian governments, especially Marxist-Leninist authoritarian governments, will be even more obvious, and admirers of Czeslaw Milosz, Miklos Haraszti, and Vaclav Havel are sure to find many resonances in what I address below.[16] Comparisons can be useful, and I will make some, but I do ask readers to bear in mind that my focus below is on post-Mao China. When I assert something about the political language of post-Mao China, I do not mean to imply that the same is either true or not true anywhere else. Where I want to make those further claims, I will make them.

Let us now turn to five features of post-Mao official Chinese, which I will call, for convenience, lexicon and metaphor, grammar and rhythm, moral weight, goal orientation, and "fit" as a kind of truth.

1. Lexicon and metaphor. In Chapter 2 we saw how English, like other Indo-European languages, tends to invent nouns to handle abstract concepts.

1968); Lowell Dittmer, "Thought Reform and Cultural Revolution: An Analysis of the Symbolism of Chinese Polemics," *American Political Science Review* 71 (1977), 67–85, and with Chen Ruoxi, *Ethics and Rhetoric of the Chinese Cultural Revolution* (Berkeley: Center for Chinese Studies, University of California, 1981); Ji Fengyuan, *Linguistic Engineering: Language and Politics in Mao's China* (Honolulu: University of Hawaii Press, 2004); Xing Lu, *Rhetoric of the Cultural Revolution: The Impact on Chinese Thought, Culture, and Communication* (Columbia: University of South Carolina Press, 2004).

16. Czeslaw Milosz, *The Captive Mind*, trans. Jane Zielonko (New York: Knopf, 1953); Miklos Haraszti, *The Velvet Prison: Artists under State Socialism*, trans. Katalin and Stephen Landesman (New York: Basic Books, 1987); Vaclav Havel, *Living in Truth* (London: Faber and Faber, 1989).

When neurons connect we have neural "connectivity"; and so on. Lakoff and Johnson called such uses ontological metaphors,[17] and we saw how they are much less common in Chinese—at least in Chinese before the end of the nineteenth century, when neologisms derived from Western languages began to enter the Chinese language in large numbers. Nouns like *zhengzhi* 政治 'politics', *jingji* 經濟 'economics', and *shehui* 社會 came in, and such terms were called *mingci* 名辭 'terminology', which itself was another example of the new noun-borrowing. Nearly all of the new terms had been invented in Meiji Japan, where Japanese modernizers had used Chinese characters to invent counterparts to Western abstract nouns. For Chinese, to borrow the terms felt like only half-borrowing, since they were already expressed in Chinese characters. Later, Chinese began making adaptations of their own, and eventually there were nouns like *ziyouhua* 'liberalization' 自由化, *zhutixing* 'subjectivity' 主體性, and many others. Many items of ordinary vocabulary in Chinese (*da* 打 'beat', *gou* 狗 'dog', *xi* 洗 'wash', *tou* 頭 'head'—the examples are legion) are monosyllables. Most of the new Western-derived terms, though, were polysyllabic. In 1959 a survey found that 98 percent of "new verbs" and 95 percent of "new nouns" were polysyllables.[18]

This influx of polysyllabic, Western-derived abstractions into the Chinese language played a major role in the formation of modern official Chinese. Premodern official Chinese could also be pretentious—turgid, sometimes excessively ornate, and sometimes opaque. But the distinctive flavor of modern official Chinese—simultaneously austere and vacuous, intimidating yet elusive, in short stuffy and puffy at the same time—owes its foundations to European habits of abstract conception that were brought into Chinese in the late nineteenth century. Orwell recognized essentially the same problem when, in 1946, he deplored the "pretentious diction" of European (especially Marxist) political language:

---

17. George Lakoff and Mark Johnson, *Metaphors We Live By* (Chicago: University of Chicago Press, 1980), pp. 25–32.

18. See San Duanmu, "Stress and the Development of Disyllabic Words in Chinese," *Diachronica* 16 (1999), p. 31. For "old" (i.e., traditional) vocabulary, 27 percent of verbs and 83 percent of nouns (which included nouns with vestigial suffixes like *zhuozi* 桌子 'table' and *yizi* 椅子 'chair') were polysyllables.

Words like *phenomenon, element, individual* (as a noun), *objective, categorical, effective, virtual, basic, primary, promote, constitute, exhibit, exploit, utilize, eliminate, liquidate*, are used to dress up a simple statement and give an air of scientific impartiality to biased judgments.[19]

Orwell's worry about "an air of scientific impartiality," which he finds "pretentious," has to do with the texture of language—the use, for example, of multisyllabic words of Latin or Greek origin when plainer Anglo-Saxon words would be clearer and livelier. But it also has to do importantly with abstraction—speaking of *phenomena* instead of *sunsets*, of *insects* instead of *ladybugs*, and so on.

The Chinese political commentator Cao Changqing has found the same tendency toward abstraction in contemporary official Chinese and calls it *shuiguo yuyan* 水果语言 'fruit language'.[20] When we hear the word "banana" or "apple," Cao notes, we can picture an image in our minds. When we hear "fruit" we don't know what to picture. To a Party official charged with delivering policy, the ambiguity of fruit language is precisely its virtue. If an official says "fruits are good," and it turns out that a higher-up decides that bananas are bad, the official can say "I meant apples." Fruit language preserves an official's options and might even save his or her career. For example, in the days before the Beijing Massacre in June 1989, two groups of leaders, headed by Li Peng and Zhao Ziyang, respectively, differed over the fateful question of whether to order a military crackdown. Luo Gan, a high official who had recently been minister of labor, approached both the Zhao and Li camps with a bit of fruit language: "I am certain justice will prevail," Luo said.[21] That made it possible for Luo, once the massacre was over and officially "correct," to claim that he had been siding with Li Peng. But had matters gone the other way, he could have been on the other side.

Liu Binyan has pointed out other examples in which phrases are abstract enough that they can accommodate different or even opposite interpretations. In Liu's examples the beneficiary is not an individual person, as in

---

19. Orwell, "Politics and the English Language," p. 167.
20. Cao Changqing 曹長青, "Yuyan baoli: Jiquan tongzhi de weishe liliang" 語言暴力: 極權統治的威懾力量 [Linguistic violence: The power of intimidation in authoritarian rule], *Zhongguo zhi chun* 中國之春 [China spring], January 1992, p. 49.
21. Reported to me orally by Zhang Zuhua, June 18, 2008, in Princeton, New Jersey.

the Luo Gan example, but a political group—usually part or all of the Communist Party. In such cases the point of abstract language is to preserve a veneer of unity over controversies that remain unresolved beneath the surface. Liu's examples are from 1991,[22] when Party policy was *jianchi sixiang yuanze, jixu gaige kaifang* 坚持四项原则, 继续改革开放 'persist with the Four Basic Principles and continue with reform and opening'. The two parallel phrases, which represented countervailing impulses despite their syllabic balance, presented an overall meaning that allowed radical ambiguity. People on one side could say it meant *weile jianchi sixiang jiben yuanze, women yiding yao gaige kaifang* 为了坚持四项基本原则, 我们一定要改革开放 'in order to continue with the Four Basic Principles, reform and opening absolutely have to be pursued', while people on the other side could say *gaige kaifang jue buneng weifan sixiang jiben yuanze* 改革开放决不能违反四项基本原则 'reform and opening must never be allowed to violate the Four Basic Principles'. Another of Liu's examples is the policy watchword *gaohuo guoying dazhongxing qiye shi yige zhengzhi wenti* 搞活国营大中型企业是一个政治问题 'to bring large and medium-sized state enterprises to life is a political question'. People with different interests used this phrase under fundamentally different assumptions about what the key "question of politics" was. Liu writes:

> One group said that it meant "if you don't solve this problem, the economy will go nowhere, and if that happens the people will oppose you and your socialism will be smashed, as it was in Eastern Europe and the Soviet Union." The other group said it meant "it's fine to enliven state enterprises, but current political arrangements must not be changed, which means the 'political core functions' of Party secretaries must stay in place and not be taken over by factory managers."[23]

The ambiguity of this kind of carefully crafted, overarching phrase had, in Liu's view, a number of advantages for officials. For high officials, the phrases had the advantage of allowing one to stand above two contradictory

---

22. Liu Binyan 劉賓雁, "Yi jiu jiu yi: Zhongguo yin zhuan duo yun" 一九九一: 中國陰轉多雲 [1991: The skies in China beginning to clear], *Mingbao yuekan* [Ming Pao monthly], no. 12, 1991, p. 79.
23. Ibid.

positions and appear to represent a sort of transcendent unity that subsumed both. To others, who were lower in the power structure, the ambiguity allowed room to squeeze their own viewpoints into phrases that had already been anointed from above as "correct." But the purest examples of the advantages of abstraction, for officials, are the ways the two- or three-syllable terms that Cao Changqing calls "fruit terms" can generate an air of authority even while their meanings remain vague.

Abstract nouns that carry an "air of scientific impartiality," as Orwell put it, are easy to spot in Communist political jargon: *xingshi* 形势 'situation', *jumian* 局面 'condition', *qingkuang* 情况 'circumstances', *cuoshi* 措施 'measures', *dongxiang* 动向 'trends', and many others. Although most such terms are nouns, other parts of speech are affected as well—both in the abstraction and the accompanying air of authority. Verbs like *jiayi* 加以 'add' and *jinxing* 进行 'carry out' can be prefixed to other two-syllable verbs (and in the process turning those verbs into nouns) to yield examples like *jiayi kaolü* 加以考虑 'add consideration', *jiayi fenxi* 加以分析 'add analysis', and *jiayi taolun* 加以讨论 'add discussion'; or *jinxing fangwen* 进行访问 'carry out visitation', *jinxing caice* 进行猜测 'carry out estimation', or *jinxing gaige* 进行改革 'carry out reform'.[24] *Jiayi* and *jinxing* almost never contribute any useful meaning: *jinxing taolun*, *jiayi taolun*, and just plain *taolun* almost always amount to the same thing, except for the airs. *Tiyan* 体验, literally "personally experience," is similar. Normally one "lives" (*shenghuo* 生活), but to *tiyan shenghuo* 'personally experience living' is more formal and political; it pretends to an experience that is somehow more scientific, more correct.

Adverbs like *xiangdang* 相当 'fairly, considerably' and adjectival modifiers like *yiding de* 一定的 'definite' are similarly useful in political language because, like the nouns and verbs just mentioned, they claim authority but lack any content that can be pinned down. If an official wants to give public credit to someone but has little idea what, if anything, the person has actually accomplished, he can say that comrade so-and-so's work is *xiangdang hao* 相当好 'considerably good' or that he *zuo chu le yiding de gong-*

---

24. See James H-Y. Tai, *Syntactic and Stylistic Changes in Modern Standard Chinese in the People's Republic of China since 1949* (Washington, D.C.: United States Information Agency, 1977), p. 7.

xian 做出了一定的贡献 'has made a definite contribution'. Some political modifiers originate in standard meanings but then take on a spiffy veneer when they turn political. Eventually, the spiff can overshadow the original meaning. For example, *guangda de* 广大的 'broad' is used in Communist jargon only to modify politically correct groups: *guangda de qunzhong* 广大的群众 'broad masses', *guangda de ganbu* 广大的干部 'broad (masses of) cadres', and so on.[25] The actual size of a *guangda* group is not as important as its political pedigree. An assembly of imperialist running dogs, no matter how large, could never be *guangda de zougou* 广大的走狗 'broad running dogs'. In short, much of the original meaning of *guangda* leaks away, leaving it, like the verb *jiayi* or the noun *xingshi*, primarily a vehicle for airs.

Pretentious nouns, verbs, and other parts of speech can combine to produce sentences that seem all the more irrefutable just because everything fits together on the same plane. The resulting verbiage, as Orwell has put it, can make even "lies sound truthful and murder respectable." During the Cultural Revolution, people were terrorized, torn from their families, even killed—events that a plain-speaking person might call *jiapo renwang* 家破人亡 'literally, family-broken-person-perished' or *hunfei posan* 魂飞魄散 'literally, soul-flies-ghost-disperses'. But official language, in describing the same events, could seal off all the pain, pull people to a distance from it, and apply layers of varnish with phrases like *caiqu cuoshi jinxing zhengdun* 采取措施进行整顿 'adopt measures to carry out rectification'. Cao Changqing calls the result *qiti yuyan* 气体语言 'gaseous language', which he characterizes as language that "says everything and yet says nothing."[26]

At the same time that some words, elevated to an abstract level, lost their concrete meanings and began to drift within the official fog, others came to moor on meanings that were indeed useful but sometimes different from what they had originally been. *Guangda* 'broad', cited above, is one kind of illustration; it came to mean something like "politically amicable" as much as it meant "broad." A more complete shift of meaning is visible in a word like *fandong* 反动 'reactionary'. The literal sense of this

---

25. Ibid., p. 100.
26. Cao Changqing, "Yuyan baoli," p. 49.

term is "oppose movement." During the 1930s and 1940s the Communists were on the move, and it made sense for them to refer to their opponents, the Kuomintang and others, as "opposing movement." But after the installation of a nationwide bureaucracy in the 1950s, the matter of who was moving and who was blocking movement underwent fundamental change. By the end of the 1970s, one of the favorite targets of popular "scar literature" was the unmoving and unmovable Communist bureaucrat: whatever you said, the bureaucrat had a way of smiling and spinning jargon—but doing nothing (and then sometimes, behind your back, arranging to punish you for having spoken up). Yet while the social role of Communists had largely turned around, the word *fandong* 'reactionary' persisted as a standard term of abuse. *Fandong* still meant "opposing the Communists," but that now meant, ironically, that people who wanted their society to move could be officially labeled as "opposing movement."

In a similar way, the political terms *zuo* 左 'left' and *you* 右 'right' drifted away from their original meanings during the Mao years and began to take on new and sometimes paradoxical senses. In the 1940s, when the Communist movement stood in opposition to an authoritarian Kuomintang regime and was publicly associated with the interests of society's downtrodden, its designation as "left" made sense. But in the 1950s, especially with the Anti-Rightist Movement of 1957, a difficult ambiguity arose. The critics of the Party who were labeled "rightist" in 1957 stood for things like free speech, a free press, fairness, the interests of the downtrodden, and other notions that fifteen years earlier had been called "left." Meanwhile, the label "left," in the 1950s and 1960s, continued to refer to orthodox followers of the Party line. By the late 1970s, after Mao died, this doctrinaire group had become known as *baoshou* 保守 'conservative'. Their critics also called them *jizuopai* 极左派 'ultraleftists'—and so it happened that "ultraleft" and "conservative" became synonyms. In the late 1980s, when the *xinzuopai* 新左派 'new left' appeared, its members had to face the awkward question of what the "new left" had to do with the "old left." The new left's inspiration arose in part out of academic liberalism in the West, and the word "liberal," in this Western sense, might have been a good label for them. But, unfortunately, the term "liberal," which in literal translation would be *ziyoupai* 自由派, was out of the question, because *ziyoupai* was already in use in China to refer to critics of the regime whom the old left was still calling "rightist." It will likely take some time—and probably will not be possible before the end of Communist rule in China—to completely untangle this semantic knot.

The official language includes a number of characteristic metaphors. Some are "dead metaphors" so well established that people no longer think of them as metaphorical. Some fit together in patterns and constitute "conceptual metaphors" in the sense that I discussed in the previous chapter. The "stage metaphors" we considered are an example. An official who takes a post may be said to *dengtai* 登台 'ascend the stage' and later, leaving power, *xiatai* 下台 'come off stage'; political support from behind the scenes is *houtai* 后台 'backstage' support; an opponent can *chang fandiao* 唱反调; and so on. Stage metaphors are deeply rooted in the Chinese language and were in wide use well before the Communist period. They appear not only in language from official sources, but, at least as often, in the informal talk of daily life. When protesting students in the spring of 1989 called for the ouster of Premier Li Peng, they chanted *Li Peng xia tai* 李鹏下台 'Get off stage, Li Peng!'

But if stage metaphors are deeply rooted, certain other metaphors in the official language of contemporary China appear to have grown directly out of the Communist movement. Many scholars have observed, for example, the prominence of military metaphors in recent decades, and it is generally agreed that these arose from guerilla war terminology, which had infused the Communist movement during the 1940s and was transferred to the project of building a new society in the 1950s. When "struggle" was no longer literally warfare but the "struggle to build socialism," a whole constellation of new metaphors was born. T. A. Hsia has traced how production became *zhandou* 战斗 'fighting a battle' and a production worker a *zhanshi* 战士 'fighter'; a workplace became a *zhanxian* 战线 'battle line' and a person's place within it a *gangwei* 岗位 'sentry post'.[27] Did this happen only because Mao and his comrades could not imagine a different vocabulary? Probably not, in the view of many scholars. It is more likely that the militarization of language was part of a deliberate strategy. Ji Fengyuan, who has made this argument, plausibly advances two rationales for it as "to teach [people] to subordinate themselves utterly to the leaders" and "to transfer the urgency . . . of wartime struggles" to present

---

27. Hsia, *Metaphor*, quoted in Ji Fengyuan, *Linguistic Engineering*, pp. 87–88.

concerns.[28] Since Mao's passing, the frequency of war metaphors in official publications has declined, but they remain latent in the official repertoire and resurface from time to time, especially when China's rulers see a need to stimulate nationalist sentiment. When Tibetans rioted in March 2008, for example, an editorial in the Communist Party's *Tibet Daily* announced a *ni-si-wo-huo de diwo douzheng* 你死我活的敌我斗争 'fight to the death between enemies', in which the goal was to "resolutely counterattack, thoroughly vanquish the reckless effrontery of the enemy forces, and seize total victory in this battle."[29] That the opponent in this battle was the Dalai Lama was not a reason to alter the metaphors; the reason for using them was to stimulate and channel the allegiances of Chinese readers.

From the arena of pure politics, military metaphors have spread into official language in most other spheres, including science, social trends, and literature and art. In all cases, the prominence of military metaphors seems to be greater when political sensitivities are higher. During the Mao years and for several years thereafter, poems and short stories could become tools of battle. A story might be well written, or especially illuminating—or praiseworthy in other ways—but as soon as it broached political comment, it could become a "weapon" in a "struggle" on a literary "front." When post-Mao scar stories began to appear in 1977 and 1978, one critic praised them for *fahui le duanpian xiaoshuo zhenchabing de zhandou zuoyong* 发挥了短篇小说侦察兵的战斗作用 'utilizing the battle function of short stories as advance scouts'.[30] At a conference on the politics of

---

28. Ji Fengyuan, *Linguistic Engineering*, p. 89. There are obvious parallels to totalitarian language elsewhere. Henry Friedlander shows how Nazism "took technological terms and applied them to human beings"; "The Manipulation of Language," in Henry Friedlander and Sybil Milton, eds., *The Holocaust: Ideology, Bureaucracy, and Genocide* (Millwood, N.J.: Kraus International, 1980), p. 108 and elsewhere.

29. In Chinese: Jianjue huiji, chedi ba didui shili de xiaozhang qiyan da xiaqu, duoqu zhei chang douzheng de quanmian shengli 坚决回击, 彻底把敌对势力的嚣张气焰打下去, 夺取这场斗争的全面胜利, in "Zhenfeng xiangdui jianjue huiji, quebao Xizang zizhiqu shehui wending" 针锋相对坚决回击确保西藏自治区社会稳定 [Focus squarely and counterattack resolutely to ensure social stability in the Tibet Autonomous Region], editorial, *Xizang ribao* [Tibet daily], March 17, 2008.

30. Liu Xicheng 刘锡诚, "Tan dangqian duanpian xiaoshuo chuangzuozhong de jige wenti" 谈当前短篇小说创作中的几个问题 [On a few questions in the creation of contemporary short stories], *Guangming Daily*, March 30, 1979.

comedians' dialogues (*xiangsheng* 相声) in 1980, an official sought to defend the sarcasm of certain comic lines by saying they *xiang bishou yiyang cixiang diren* 像匕首一样刺向敌人 'are like daggers pointed at the enemy'.[31]

In later times, after China's economy began to flourish, military metaphors carried over into the commercial realm. In this context, they largely shed their political connotations but still carried a special zing. For example, in 2007 a television commercial for a brand of cell phones touted the devices as *shoujizhong de zhandouji* 手机中的战斗机 'the fighter planes of cell phones'.[32] Here a *qiyan* rhythm (see Chapter 1) garnishes the military metaphor with added stylishness. Such pizzazz apparently diverted attention from the question of whether one would really want a fighter plane in one's pocket.

Many writers have noted how military metaphors in the official language of mainland China eventually seeped into daily-life usage as well. That such usage stems specifically from the Communist experience seems to be attested by the fact that Chinese speakers from Taiwan, Hong Kong, and elsewhere can find it strange. To refer to the "education battle front" sounds odd in Taiwan or in New York's Chinatown, but *jiaoyu zhanxian* 教育战线 raises no eyebrows inside China. On a Beijing bus in 1994, I heard a little boy tell his mother he had to pee. His mother explained to him that Uncle Busdriver could not just stop in the middle of traffic for him. He would have to hold on. *Ni jianchi yi xia!* 你坚持一下 'persevere a bit!' she ordered him, using a phrase that I doubt would have occurred to a mother in Taiwan, who more likely would have said something like *ni ren yi ren ba* 你忍一忍吧? 'can you hold on a bit?'. We need not assume that the Beijing mother's feelings toward her son were really more militaristic than those of the imaginary Taiwan mother with whom I am comparing her. But her idiom, and its roots, are different. In 2007 a law student from Wuhan published an article in *Southern Weekend* decrying the prevalence of "violent slogans" in Chinese society. Her concern was less with metaphorical violence in official language than with how it had rubbed off and

---

31. Xiangsheng chuangzuo zuotanhui bangongshi 相声创作座谈会办公室, ed., "Xiangsheng chuangzuo zuotanhui jianbao" 相声创作座谈会简报 [Bulletin on the conference on creating comedians' dialogues] (n.p., 1980), day 1, p. 4.

32. I am grateful to Mao Sheng for the example.

been absorbed into common use by ordinary people. Why, for example, would a sign against garbage dumping go so far as to read "the dumping of garbage is strictly prohibited, on pain of death to your entire family!" (*yanjin dao laji, fouze quanjia si guangguang!* 严禁倒垃圾否则全家死光光!)?[33] Cao Changqing has argued that the pervasiveness of violent language in contemporary Chinese establishes an underlying "atmosphere of fear" that brings "psychological pressure" to people and eventually becomes accepted as a normal part of daily life.[34]

Another kind of metaphor that became prevalent in official Communist language, especially in the realm of literature and art, was medical. This family of metaphors originated in the Yan'an years, lasted through the Mao years, and remained common through most of the Deng era. In a 1957 speech Mao referred to certain works of fiction as *ducao* 毒草 'poisonous weeds',[35] and the term spread quickly during the Anti-Rightist Movement that unfolded later that year. The opposite of poisonous weeds were "correct" literary works. *Zhengque* 正确 'correct' was a technical term in all ideological matters, and correct literary works, in the medical metaphor, were *jiankang* 健康 'healthful', where "health" could refer to the well-being either of an individual reader or the overall society that readers inhabited. "Incorrect" works—everything from dissidence to "hooligan" culture to pornography—were *bujiankang* 不健康 'unhealthful'. In the late 1970s, after Mao's death, *shanghen* 伤痕 'scar' joined this family of metaphors. The term was borrowed from the title of Lu Xinhua's story "Shanghen," but was also understood as referring broadly to literary works that looked back at the Cultural Revolution and served a healing function for readers and society. Writers who probed deeply were said to "dissect" (*jiepou* 解剖) society, using their pens as scalpels. Terms like "poisonous weeds" had two lives: they rang of Gang-of-Four extremism, which was now officially under attack, yet persisted in both formal and informal language. In 1980, in a major policy speech, Hu Yaobang

---

33. Li Fenglin 李凤林, "'Baoli biaoyu' keyi xiu yi" "暴力标语"可以休矣 [Let us be done with "violent slogans"], *Nanfang zhoumo* [Southern weekend], June 21, 2007.

34. Cao Changqing, "Yuyan baoli," p. 48.

35. Mao Zedong, "Speech at the Communist Party's National Conference on Propaganda Work," in *Selected Readings from the Works of Mao Tsetung* (Beijing: Foreign Languages Press, 1971), p. 496.

said: "comrades in literature and art are sensitive, so I don't use the words 'poisonous weeds' very much. But poisonous weeds do, in fact, objectively exist."[36] A year later, in another major speech, Hu again insisted that literature and art contained "unhealthful [*bujiankang*] and negative things that hurt [*you hai yu* 有害于] the people."[37]

It is worth standing back for a moment to ask why the abstractions, decentered meanings, and special metaphors of official language arise in the first place. Why do states and their leaders prefer such things to plain, concrete language? Reminding the reader that officialese is a widespread phenomenon, and that by commenting on Communist Chinese society I do not mean to suggest that the same conditions cannot be found elsewhere, I would like to probe the reasons, which appear to be several.

One of the most basic reasons seems to be that the associations of "abstract" with "high" and of "high" with "good" are deeply embedded in the conceptual metaphors of Chinese, English, and many other human languages. As we have seen in Chapter 2, both Chinese and English use the metaphor "up is good": *gaoshang* 高尚 'high' character is good character, a "high-minded" person does not take the "low road," and so on. Both languages also use the metaphor "abstract is up": a more general level of analysis is a "higher" level, a position of broader authority within a bureaucracy is a "higher" position, and so on. Both of these metaphors are human conventions, not natural facts, but they are sufficiently well established in our minds to condition the way we think. And political authorities naturally like the combination because it reflects well on their own "high" position. The implicit claim of superiority in abstract language can transfer to the speaker, supplying him or her with pomp.

A second advantage of abstract language is its utility in supplying syllables when one actually has little notion of what one is talking about, that is, where the abstract level is in fact the only level that can be made to be coherent. This advantage explains why words like "concrete," "individual," and "praxis" are so useful in political language. They indirectly acknowledge

---

36. Hu Yaobang, *Zai juben chuangzuo zuotanhuishang de jianghua*.

37. Hu Yaobang 胡耀邦, "Zai Lu Xun dansheng yibai zhounian jinian dahuishang de jianghua 在鲁迅诞生一百周年纪念大会上的讲话 [Talk at the memorial assembly for the hundredth anniversary of Lu Xun's birth], *Guangming Daily*, September 26, 1981.

the need to speak of nuts and bolts even though the speaker or writer cannot provide them. They are a way to be concrete in an abstract way. Doris Lessing has observed that phrases like "concrete steps," "contradictions," and "interpenetration of opposites," are useful in political language because they "fill up as much space as possible without actually saying anything" while exuding an air of authority.[38] They can cover up ignorance—or fuzzy understanding at best—with something that sounds like wisdom.

A third benefit of abstract language can be to associate the speaker with political trends and styles. Cao Changqing writes that "people use their familiarity with the official language—in speaking, writing articles, 'revealing their thoughts' at meetings, and preparing reports—to demonstrate how they 'stick tightly' to the line of the times and show 'political depth.'"[39] A general benefit of stylishness in any context is to provide the security that comes from group participation; if I am stylish in the right way, I am exempt from criticism by others who follow the same style. In the authoritarian line-following that Cao Changqing analyzes, an important additional security comes from hiding beneath what people above me are saying. If my expression is "on message," then I cannot be criticized unless people "higher" than I am are also criticized. In order to be "correct," I do not need to know anything about nuts or bolts. I need only to manipulate verbiage correctly.[40]

Ignorance or vague ideas may be the most common weaknesses that official language covers over, but there are others, and some are more insidious. When Orwell speaks of making "murder respectable," he has noticed the utility of official language as euphemism. In such cases, the user of abstract language might be quite clear on the nuts and bolts that lie below and turn to abstract language precisely in order to cover them up. For example, twentieth-century authoritarian regimes of several kinds have used "cleansing" or "purification" as metaphors for systematic killing. Hitler's *Säuberrungsaktion* 'cleansing action', Mao Zedong's *qingli jieji*

---

38. Doris Lessing, "Questions You Should Never Ask a Writer," op-ed, *New York Times,* October 13, 2007, p. A15.

39. Cao Changqing, "Yuyan baoli," p. 49.

40. As an academic, I feel a bit guilty in making the points about official language in the preceding three paragraphs, since all three—and others—apply to pomp and abstraction in academic jargon as well.

duiwu 清理阶级队伍 'cleansing the class ranks', Pol Pot's "purification" of Cambodian society, Slobodan Milosevic's "ethnic cleansing" of Kosovo, and others all draw from essentially the same ghastly metaphor. These phrases now burn in our consciousness; they stand out, and we notice them. But euphemism of a more pedestrian sort often goes unnoticed, even though it surrounds us every day. To pick a representative example at random, when unnamed Chinese people were accused of plotting to protest at the Asian Games in Beijing in 1990, the Chinese government's Ministry of Public Security noted that police were going to deal with them as "international terrorists." Would they be arrested? Jailed? Tortured? Killed? The announcement said this: *Zhongguo yi caiqu cuoshi jinxing daji* 中国已采取措施进行打击 'China has already adopted measures to carry out attacks [on them]'.[41] Just what measures, doing exactly what, were not things the Ministry wished to reveal.

This example illustrates another way official language uses euphemism. The authorities, not wanting to acknowledge that their police, or secret police, or military police have done something, say that "China" did it. In the decades of Communist Party rule in China, it has become standard in the official language to use the word "China" to refer to the views or actions of the state, or of the Party, or even just an elite level within the Party. Examples that refer to the views of "China" on climate change, or anticorruption measures, or the Dalai Lama—views that statistically represent only a part, sometimes not a very large part, of the Chinese populace—are easy to find. Young people are trained to equate *ai guo* 爱国 'love of country—patriotism' with *ai dang* 爱党 'love of Party'. A word like *zuzhi* 组织 'organization', originally abstract and colorless, took on a connotation of fear and gravity during China's Mao years because of what it meant at the concrete level; the "organization department" in a "work-unit" controlled not just your career but your entire fate in life. In Hitler's Germany the *Organization* and in Pol Pot's Cambodia the Angkar, "Organization," used the abstraction in similar ways.[42]

---

41. Quoted in "Shi ri yao wen" 十日要闻 (Main news of the last ten days), in *Xinwen ziyou daobao* 新闻自由导报 [News freedom herald, April 30, 1990, p. 1.

42. Henry Friedlander, "Manipulation of Language," p. 106; and Someth May, *Cambodian Witness: the Autobiography of Someth May*, ed. James Fenton (London: Faber, 1986), p. 149.

Below the elite who ran the "organization" in China were the *renmin* 人民 'people', but this, too, was an abstract term whose practical uses served the interests of the elite. In his incisive article "'Non-people' in the People's Republic of China," Michael Schoenhals has shown how only *some* of the people are *renmin* 人民 'people'. Schoenhals quotes Central Committee member Bo Yibo in 1981: "'People' includes workers, peasants, the urban poor, intellectuals, etc., but certainly not landlords and comprador bourgeois elements."[43] And even among the workers, peasants, and other favored categories, only those who are docile qualify as "people." A worker who seriously misbehaves can become a "bad element," which is a separate category from "people." "No wonder," Schoenhals concludes, "the Party loves the People. Here is a semantic entity that by definition is incapable of rebelling."[44] In Party parlance, the word *qunzhong* 群众 'masses' is similar, but has been used a bit differently from *renmin*. *Qunzhong* shares with *renmin* the connotation of "from below": opinions from below, reactions from below, and so on. But there are a few additional levels of meaning in a phrase like *qunzhong yijian* 群众意见 'mass opinion'. Formally, it is supposed to mean the opinions of the majority in society. But these opinions are hard to know, and are often unknown to the very people who use the term. Within bureaucracies, *qunzhong yijian* means, practically speaking, "opinion that the next lowest level in the bureaucracy claims to be the views of everybody below them." Bureaucrats at a given level are supposed to "reflect mass opinion" to the level above them; practically speaking, however, *qunzhong yijian* can be the opinion of the bureaucrats themselves. Since the people above them have little access to the actual views of the people below them, bureaucrats in the middle can, and do, present their own views as *qunzhong yijian*.

Terms that refer to democratic ideals are often welcomed in China's official language, because they sound good, even if they in fact are used in ways that indirectly support authoritarianism. For example, a policy toward the press that is *kuansong* 宽松 'relaxed' is referred to as "democratic"

---

43. Michael Schoenhals, "'Non-people' in the People's Republic of China: A Chronicle of Terminological Ambiguity," *Indiana Working Papers on Language and Politics in Modern China*, no. 4 (July 1994), p. 3.

44. Ibid., p. 16.

even though the fact of relaxation simultaneously implies the existence of a control mechanism that could easily tighten any time authorities wished it to. State control, be it tight or relaxed, is something different from democracy, but the label is used anyway. The dissident astrophysicist Fang Lizhi, writing in 1987, objected to official language that described "people's representatives" (ostensibly a democratic term) who came to "inspect" (*guancha* 观察) the university where he was vice president. People's representatives, he argued, are supposed to be listening to our opinions and passing them upward, not coming to inspect us. "We are accustomed to this term [*guancha*]," Fang wrote, but in terms of democratic theory "it is entirely incorrect."[45]

Fang was unusually astute; most users of the official language do not notice such implications. But in other ways—in ways the official language itself encourages—ordinary people could become attuned to fine distinctions of political usage. Victims of the 1957 Anti-Rightist Movement, for example, were said to "wear rightist caps" (*dai youpai maozi* 戴右派帽子). To get the label removed was to get the cap off your head, but there were two ways to do this, *zhai maozi* 摘帽子 'remove cap' and *pingfan* 平反 'overturn [label]', and the difference between them was tremendous. *Zhai maozi* 'remove cap', which happened to some rightists in the 1960s, meant that you were no longer a rightist but a "former rightist." Still a stigma followed you, rather the way the label "former sex offender" does in U.S. society. The implication that you had once been evil was indelible. *Pingfan*, which happened to many people in the late 1970s, implied that your original capping was a mistake. You never should have been capped in the first place. Your reprieve now, at least in theory, was complete. Similarly fine-tuned distinctions could apply to a person's *lishi* 历史 'history'. If you made political mistakes in the past, but then looked at them squarely, confessed, showed contrition, and so on, your personal file might record the notation *lishi qingchu* 历史清楚 'history is clear'. That was good, but not as good as a file that said *lishi qingbai* 历史清白 'history is pure', which meant that

---

45. He Lilang 何澧朗, "Fan zi neibu pipan cailiao: Fang Lizhi Liu Binyan yanlun" 反资内部批判材料: 方励之刘宾雁言论 [Classified antibourgeois criticism material: The words of Fang Lizhi and Liu Binyan], *Jiushiniandai* 九十年代 [*Nineties*], no. 6 (1987), p. 39.

there never had even been a problem that had to be cleared up. If a politically sensitive appointment were at stake at the organization department in one's work unit, the difference between a *lishi* that was *qingbai* and one that was *qingchu* would be crucial. People knew this, and so it became important never to "make a mistake," even of the correctable kind, and never even to be accused of making a mistake. This is one reason why bureaucratic inertia became so heavy within China's socialist system.

While officials used the official language in these ways, ordinary people sometimes borrowed its devices to use it "from the other end," as it were. A worker, instead of saying *wo shi gongren* 我是工人 'I am a worker' could choose to say, in more abstract political language, *wo shi gongren jieji* 我是工人阶级 'I am [of] the working class' and by doing so lay claim to a status that could make a difference in a plea for some kind of access or privilege.[46] We will look further at such matters in the section "The Popular Response to the Language Game."

2. *Grammar and rhythm.* Premodern official Chinese used rhythms, employed clichés, and sometimes obeyed set forms, but these patterns were importantly different from the grammar rules, borrowed largely from Western language, that contemporary official Chinese observes. Premodern Chinese could omit subjects and elide meanings in a variety of flexible ways, and punctuation, if any, was used more to mark rhythms or emphases than to clarify conceptual relations. By contrast, in the official language of contemporary China, sentence structure obeys an organization that Western-style grammar imposes, and punctuation is used to keep that kind of structure clear.

The officially published works of Mao Zedong are a good example. Mao's sentences are long and sometimes convoluted, but are impeccably grammatical and carefully punctuated. We know from several sources that Mao's oral language was not like this. It was colloquial, earthy, and certainly not "Western" in the manner of his officially published works. There is irony, of course, in the Party's decision to bring Western grammar into Mao's thought. The assumption of those who engineered this conversion—mainly Hu Qiaomu and others at Yan'an—seems to have been

---

46. I am indebted for the example to Chen Ping, letter to author, May 16, 1992.

that Western grammar makes something seem more clear, more scientific-sounding, more authoritative, or in any case, better. Yet it was also the grammar of people who were considered, at another level, imperialists and the enemy. How Hu Qiaomu and others handled this irony, or whether they even noticed it, is not well understood.

The effects of Western grammar are especially noticeable in the ways in which terms in the official Chinese language change parts of speech to match Western-language usages. Nouns can become adjectives, for example. In the early twentieth century, the word *yingxiong* 英雄 'hero' was a noun whose corresponding adjective was *yingyong* 英勇 'heroic': Qiu Jin was a *nüyingxiong* 女英雄 'heroine', but one spoke of a *yingyong de Qiu Jin* 英勇的秋瑾 'heroic Qiu Jin'. But at some point during the Cultural Revolution years, *yingxiong* slipped, in Maoist language, to become an adjective, and then there could be *yingxiong de renwu* 英雄的人物 'heroic characters'. Lexical slips of this kind, from nouns to adjectives, sometimes became not only standard but especially "correct," so that they were used even in the presentation of Chinese language to foreigners. A standard textbook of Chinese for foreigners, published in 1971, was called *Jichu Hanyu* 基础汉语 (literally, "foundation" Chinese).[47]

In the mid-1970s, James H-Y. Tai did a systematic survey of this kind of category-shift in the grammar of China's official language during the Communist era.[48] In addition to nouns becoming adjectives, Tai found verbs becoming nouns. *Tigao* 提高 'raise', which in modern Chinese before the Communist era was a verb, could now be a noun in a sentence like *sheyuanmen shenghuo you le hen da de tigao* 社员们生活有了很大的提高 'the lives of commune members had [i.e., saw] major raises'. The commune members could also make *hen da de jinbu* 很大的进步 'big progress', where *jinbu*, originally a verb, is used as a noun, and their example could *dedao quanguo de puji* 得到全国的普及 'gain nationwide dissemination', where *puji* 'spread', another verb, again is used as a noun.[49] Western languages commonly use the same kind of category switch, of course. In English,

47. *Jichu Hanyu* 基础汉语, formal English title *Elementary Chinese* (Beijing: Shangwu yinshuguan).
48. Tai, *Syntactic and Stylistic Changes*.
49. Ibid., pp. 46–47.

"progress" can be a noun or verb with only an accent change to mark the difference. But in English is it generally not the case that the category switch corresponds to a borderline between officialese and ordinary language.[50]

Tai also notes how adjectives (also called "stative verbs") imitate Western-style adverbs in Communist-era officialese. *Genghao* 更好 'better' plays this role in a phrase like *genghao de wei renmin fuwu* 更好地为人民服务 'serve the people better', in which the particle *di* 地 is inserted to convert *genghao* from adjective to adverb. The same is true of *genggao* 更高 'higher' in a sentence like *women yao genggao de juqi geming de qizhi* 我们要更高地举起革命的旗帜 'we must raise the revolutionary banner even higher'.[51] Tai is right that these usages are distinctive to the official language. No teacher in the daily life of a third-grade classroom would tell a child *ni dei genggao de ju ni de shou* 你得更高地举你的手 'you must in-a-higher-manner raise your hand'.

Even more commonly, and again with a strong flavor of officialese, adjectives can turn into transitive verbs. *Huopo* 活泼 'lively' becomes a transitive verb in a statement like *zhei jian shiqing huopo le ta de gongzuo ganjin* 这件事情活泼了他的工作干劲 'this matter enlivened his working spirit'. The same is true of *fengfu* 丰富 'lively' in *tamen fengfu le xiangcun wenhua huodong de neirong* 他们丰富了乡村文化活动的内容 'they enriched the content of rural cultural activities'.[52]

Nouns can turn into transitive verbs in the official language. In stressing the need for "stability" in Tibet in the spring of 2008, the *Tibet Daily* used *guanxi* 关系 'relation' as a verb to warn that *xizang wending guanxi quanguo wending* 西藏稳定关系全国稳定 'Tibetan stability relates to stability in the whole country'.[53]

James Tai makes the astute observation that Communist official language tends to use the "aspect marker" *le* 了 more than it is used in ordinary

---

50. Generally but not always. For a time in the 1990s it was stylish in American officialese, for example, to use *interface*, originally a noun, as a verb: "we interfaced for twenty minutes," etc. Such usage, as in the Chinese cases, serves as a marker that "this is official language"; ordinary people in daily life speak more plainly.

51. Tai, *Syntactic and Stylistic Changes*, pp. 39, 41.

52. Ibid., pp. 43, 45.

53. "Zhenfeng xiangdui jianjue huiji, quebao Xizang zizhiqu shehui wending."

language. One of Tai's examples is *ta shoudao le shisheng he pinxiazhongnong de zanyang* 他受到了师生和贫下中农的赞扬 'he received praise from the teachers and students and the poor and lower-middle peasants'.[54] Tai does not offer an explanation of this use of *le*, but—since so many other features of official-language grammar are borrowed from Western grammar—it may be that this usage is born of an impulse to reflect Western-style past tense. Chinese does not use tense, and therefore has no tense markers. But if one were looking for a way to reflect a past tense, this minor abuse of *le* would be one way to do it. Whether or not this speculation of mine is correct, there is no doubt that this sort of use of *le* was common in official language by the late 1980s. News reports of meetings where officials gave speeches commonly used phrases like XXX *shizhang jiang le hua* 市长讲了话, YYY *fushizhang ye jiang le hua* 副市长也讲了话, ZZZ *tongzhi ye jiang le hua* 同志也讲了话 'Mayor XXX spoke, Deputy Mayor YYY also spoke, and so did Comrade ZZZ'. *Le* in such phrases, like other usages derived from Western-style grammar, carries a subtle assertion of pomp.

Tai goes on to observe that in tandem with the rise of *le* in the official language, the corresponding aspect marker *zhe* 着 'in the process of' also became more common. Tai lists examples such as *tamen zhijian youzhe feichang miqie de guanxi* 他们之间有着非常密切的关系, literally something like "between them there exists an extremely close relationship."[55] Again Tai is right to point out the subtle abnormality of official language. In ordinary Chinese the same thought would probably just be *tamen de guanxi feichang miqie* 他们的关系非常密切 'their relationship is extremely close', or something like that.

In general, the more intensely the official language focused on telling people what to do, the more structurally rigid it became. To illustrate, let us revisit the example from the Introduction, of the Cultural Revolution phrase *weida de guangrong de zhengque de Zhongguo gongchandang* 伟大的光荣的正确的中国共产党 'the great, glorious, correct Communist Party of China'. During the tense times when that slogan was used, you could, if you chose, refer to the Party without using any adjectives at all; but if you did choose to use adjectives in public contexts, then "great," "glorious,"

---

54. Tai, *Syntactic and Stylistic Changes*, p. 76. I have changed the translation slightly.
55. Ibid., p. 76.

and "correct" were the three that you used—and if you used all three, they had to be in that order. If you were to mix the order, and refer, for example, to the "glorious, great, correct" Party, the "correct, glorious, great" Party, or the "great, correct, glorious" Party, you would sound less than great, not very glorious, or—most dangerously—not correct. If your wrong word order were perceived as intentional, your phrase could even smack of subversion and mean very serious trouble for you. The "correctness" of a set phrase inhered very much in its form, not just its content. The more politically charged the phrase was, the more form mattered.

As we saw in Chapter 1, form in official language was sometimes reinforced by rhythms, which could make phrases easier to memorize and enhance the sense that they are inevitably "right." This sense of rightness could survive even when concrete content was hardly clear. It is hard to say, for example, exactly what a person was supposed to do when following the rhythmical Cultural Revolution slogan *linghun shenchu gan geming* 灵魂深处干革命 'make revolution in the depths of your soul.' Make revolution deep inside myself? What exactly am I supposed to do? Rebel? Against what? Obey? Obey what? But whatever the phrase was supposed to mean, one point was clear: it was *correct*. And here is one reason why this sort of rigid and rhythmical language has been useful to authoritarians. It says, in essence, "stop thinking and just accept official correctness." Young Red Guards during the Cultural Revolution could head off to "struggle," sometimes even to their deaths, under the spell of rhythmic and spellbinding—but essentially contentless—phrases such as *xia ding juexin, bupa xisheng, paichu wannan, qu zhengqu shengli!* 下定决心, 不怕牺牲, 排除万难, 去争取胜利 'firm your resolve, fear no sacrifice, cast aside every obstacle, go forth and seize victory!' Or even more bluntly: *yi bupa ku, er bupa si* 一不怕苦, 二不怕死 'first, don't fear hardship; second, don't fear death'.

This last example exhibits not only rhythm but *repetition*, which, in combination with rhythm, can enhance the implicit sense that "this is right, there is no need to think about it." Other examples from the Mao era, also cited in Chapter 1, are *daming, dafang, dazibao* 大鸣大放大字报 'big outcry, big release, big-character posters', in which the repetition of *da . . . da . . . da . . .* hammers away as if to proclaim that there is no way that the thrust of this phrase can or should be stopped; and *loushang louxia, diandeng dianhua* 楼上楼下电灯电话 'electric lights and telephones upstairs and down', where the parallel repetition of *lou* and *dian* also somehow creates a sense that only a fool would gainsay the rightness of what is said. Although less common in the Deng, Jiang, and Hu years than it was under Mao, hammer-like repetition has continued to be used in political rhetoric, especially when the topic is high priority. In March 2008, in response to the Tibetan uprising in Lhasa, a political editorial in the *Tibet Daily* arrayed a set of seven consecutive four-character phrases: *tigao jingti, caliang yanjing, mingbian shifei, qizhi xianming, tuanjie yizhi, tongzhou gongji, tongchou dikai* ... 提高警惕, 擦亮眼睛, 明辨是非, 旗帜鲜明, 团结一致, 同舟共济, 同仇敌忾 ... 'raise vigilance, keep the eyes open, distinguish clearly between right and wrong, take a clear-cut stand, come together in unity, help one another, hate the enemy together ...' This barrage was followed by three six-character phrases and then three longer phrases each of which began with *baowei* ... 保卫 ... 'safeguard ...'[56] The extremely important political topic apparently called for unusual attention to linguistic craft.

Repetition in official rhetoric strengthens the demand on the listener to accept the correctness of a phrase. It adds to what rhythm alone achieves in this regard. But why should this be? Why should the repetition of words or phrases lend them more authority? John Frankenstein has offered the interesting hypothesis that repetitive rhythmic phrases tend to "infantilize" the listener. The phrase (cited in the Introduction) *gaogao xingxing chucheng zou* 高高兴兴出城走 'happy-happy out-of-city go—have a happy trip leaving the city' has, Frankenstein points out, a childlike flavor. *Daming, dafang, dazibao* 大鸣大放大字报 'big outcry, big release, big-character posters' carries it, too, although to a lesser degree. Children's language, especially in Chinese, uses a lot of repetition: *mama* 妈妈 'Mama', *baba* 爸爸 'Papa', *baobao* 宝宝 'precious (little one)', *guaiguai* 乖乖 'well-behaved (little one)', and so on. Might it be that such language draws the minds of listeners partway back to childhood, to a time when they were more accepting of paternalistic authority?[57] Is this part of why an authoritarian government finds such language useful?

---

56. "Zhenfeng xiangdui jianjue huiji, quebao Xizang zizhiqu shehui wending."
57. John Frankenstein, email message to author, September 15, 2002.

As a broad generalization, Chinese-language political slogans from outside the People's Republic are less childlike than Beijing's slogans. Political slogans in Taiwan tend to draw more on classical Chinese. For example in 1996, when the Taiwan leader Li Denghui wanted to advise entrepreneurs from Taiwan on how to invest on the mainland, he announced a slogan of *jieji yong ren* 戒急用忍 'be not hasty, use patience'. Mainland slogans also sometimes use classical language, but it is worth noting that when they do, they are slogans directed at other members of the ruling elite, not at the (infantilized) "masses." When Deng Xiaoping wanted to set a strategy in foreign policy during China's economic rise in the 1990s, he advanced the classical-language phrase *tao guang yang hui* 韬光养晦 'hide capacity and await the time'. This was a phrase that others in leadership positions needed to hear; it did not need mass consumption.

The use of numbers in Communist-era slogans has achieved effects that are similar to those of repetition. Many scholars have noted this practice, and examples are legion. In 1928 Mao Zedong laid out *san da jilü ba xiang zhuyi* 三大纪律八项注意 'three great disciplines and eight points for attention' for the People's Liberation Army. In the early 1950s, urban China was consumed by the *san fan* 三反 'three antis' and *wu fan* 五反 'five antis' movements. In the Cultural Revolution, the population was divided into the *hong wu lei* 红五类 'five red categories' and *hei wu lei* 黑五类 'five black categories'. Oracular wisdom descended from Mao as *yi fen wei er* 一分为二 'one divides into two'. Stalin's (and Mao's, after his death) errors and credits were summed up as *sanqikai* 三七开 '30 percent versus 70 percent'. Deng Xiaoping's new direction from the late 1970s was called *sige xiandaihua* 四个现代化 'the Four Modernizations', but Deng insisted as well on the *sige jiben jianchi* 四个基本坚持 'Four Basic Principles'. A politeness campaign called *wu jiang si mei* 五讲四美 'five pay-attentions and four beautifuls' arose from the Deng era as well. Jiang Zemin, in his time, added *san ge daibiao* 三个代表 'three represents', and later Hu Jintao sponsored *ba rong ba chi* 八荣八耻 'eight honors and eight shames'. These are only a few of many examples. What do the numbers contribute? What explains their perennial attraction for the people who devise the slogans? It is a special characteristic of Communist Chinese language. Other authoritarian systems have used numbers, too, and so does Chinese culture in other spheres. But not as much.

Might the use of numbers, like the use of repetition, be a way of infantilizing the people to whom slogans are addressed? At a minimum, the numbers seem to be saying, "here is a list of the things to focus on, and we are numbering them to help you be sure none are overlooked." Cao Changqing has noted two other functions of numbers in slogans. One is that, as with other lexical items in the official language, they are a bit "gaseous" in the sense that they draw attention away from content and toward the form of phrases—and form alone, as we have seen, can deliver a sense of correctness. The other contribution of numbers is what Cao calls *gaikuoli* 概括力 'completeness of coverage'.[58] If I tell you, in official cadence, that there are "eight honors and eight shames," the implication is that these sixteen points pretty well sum up *everything*. There is nothing else you really need to know, or to ask. If you have grasped the "five pay-attentions and four beautifuls," then you are ready to be a fully polite person; there is no need to go (or think) further.

3. Moral weight. Official language in contemporary China regularly assumes a strong position of moral rectitude. Certain words, grammatical patterns, and rhythms carry a strong connotation that "this is right." It is another feature that tends to stifle independent thought, because who will argue with something that is automatically right? The automaticity of the implication depends on the official context. Words and phrases that have ordinary meanings in ordinary contexts take on a connotation of moral rightness when used officially. We saw this briefly in the example of *guangda qunzhong* 广大群众 'broad masses', where *guangda* clearly takes on the connotation of "good." We saw it also, in the Introduction, with the example of *zui* 最 'most', which consistently had positive connotations during the late Mao years in phrases like *zui zui zui weida de Mao zhuxi* 最最最伟大的毛主席 'the most, most, most great Chairman Mao'. Phrases with negative connotations, also with early roots in the Communist movement, include *yixiaocuo* 一小撮 'a small bunch',[59] and 极少数 'tiny minority'.

---

58. Cao Changqing, "Yuyan baoli," p. 49.

59. The phrase was used in a xiangsheng "comedian's dialogue" piece, *Zhi laohu* 纸老虎 [Paper tiger], published in 1950. See Xi Xiangyuan 席香远 and Sun Yukui 孙玉奎, eds., *Zhi laohu* (Beijing: Sanlian shudian, 1950), p. 26.

Even rhythms can carry connotations of right and wrong. In Chapter 1 we saw how *wuyan* and *qiyan* rhythms, in many kinds of official, commercial, and daily-life contexts, can carry subtle suggestions that the ideas they help to communicate are somehow more natural, authoritative, or exalted than the same ideas would be if expressed without the rhythms. In political language, especially in high-pressure political contexts, this kind of effect is strong and easy to observe. Consider again this example, cited in the preceding section: *xia ding juexin, bupa xisheng, paichu wannan, qu zhengqu shengli!* 下定决心, 不怕牺牲, 排除万难, 去争取胜利! 'firm your resolve, fear no sacrifice, cast aside every obstacle, go forth and seize victory!' The phrase has a strong and clear rhythm: TAH, TAH, ta-TAH! . . . TAH, TAH, ta-TAH! . . . TAH, TAH, ta-TAH! . . . ta-TAH-ta-TAH! TAH! The words themselves, of course, also have strong positive meanings. Can we separate these positive meanings from the contribution of the rhythm? Does the rhythm, by itself, have a positive connotation? I believe that it does, and that we can easily see this by doing another experiment with word substitution. What happens if we insert words that have negative connotations while keeping the same rhythm? What if someone said: *paihuai, panghuang! bimian xisheng! jiawei taopao! chiuh jieshou shibai!* 徘徊彷徨! 避免牺牲! 夹尾逃跑! 去接受失败! 'dither and vacillate, avoid sacrifice, tuck tail and run, go and accept defeat!' The expression sounds funny—not just odd, but literally funny, and the reason it generates humor is that the austere, positive implications of the rhythm are incongruous with the negative content of the words.

There is a well-rooted custom in Chinese culture of choosing names for children that express parental hopes. Names have often mentioned moral virtues such as honesty, sincerity, and learning, or, especially for boys, strength or bravery, and for girls, purity and refinement. At the height of Maoism, some of these traditional notions were jettisoned as "feudal" and politics often entered the process of coosing names. Children born in the late 1960s and early 1970s received names like Xiangdong 向东 'toward the East' or 'toward [Mao Ze]dong', Xuegong 学工 'learn from workers', and even Miezi 灭资 'annihilate capitalism'.[60] There are anecdotal accounts of experiments with keeping to the left on roadways (since left is inherently

---

60. For more examples see Ji Fengyuan, *Linguistic Engineering*, pp. 153–154.

better than right), and having a red light (red is good) mean go, not stop. The color red was powerful enough that it could turn the word *hong* 红 'red' into a transitive verb, as when socialist flowers *hong bian renjian* 红遍人间 'redden the entire world'.[61] Red served as the opposite, morally speaking, for both black and white. A *baizhuan* 白专 '[politically] white expert' was evil compared to a red expert, but so were any of the *hei wu lei* 黑五类 'five [politically] black categories' of landlord, counterrevolutionary, rich peasant, rightist, or bad element.[62]

On the whole, animals have not fared too well within the moral landscape of the official language of Communist China. Some examples of negative connotations—of dogs, for example—were inherited from pre-Communist times. But the general trend during the Mao years turned more sharply against animals. Donkeys, crabs, lizards, flies and insects, tigers and leopards, and other species of real animals joined with cow ghosts and snake spirits, devils, demons, ghosts, monsters, vampires, and other imaginary beasts in a menagerie whose abiding unity, despite its superficial diversity, was that all were used metaphorically to denigrate one or another kind of human being. With or without modifiers, animal terms were meant and understood as negative.

Terms that have turned intrinsically positive in the official language include *kexue* 科学 'science, scientific', whose uses Michael Schoenhals has analyzed.[63] During the Mao years *kexue* sometimes meant little more or less than "good" or "politically correct." A sentence like *ni zheige kanfa bu kexue* 你这个看法不科学 'this view of yours is unscientific' did not have to refer to a point of science or to any claim that the scientific method had not been properly applied. It could just be a general way of saying "I don't like your view." The term *wenhua dageming* 文化大革命 'Great Cultural

---

61. Hsin-cheng Chuang, *The Great Proletarian Cultural Revolution: A Terminological Study* (Berkeley: Center for Chinese Studies, 1967), p. 8, cited in Ji Fengyuan, *Linguistic Engineering*, p. 190.

62. See also Elizabeth J. Perry and Li Xun, "Revolutionary Rudeness: The Language of Red Guards and Rebel Workers in China's Cultural Revolution," Indiana East Asian Working Paper Series on Language and Politics in Modern China, no. 2 (July 1993), pp. 9–10.

63. Michael Schoenhals, *Doing Things with Words in Chinese Politics: Five Studies* (Berkeley: Center for Chinese Studies, 1992), p. 9.

Revolution' is another illuminating example because it had strong positive connotations during the last years of Mao; but then, after Mao, the Deng Xiaoping regime sought to purge the phrase of its positive connotations even while continuing to use it. An order went out to China's media that, beginning in August 1980, the term should bear quotation marks: not Cultural Revolution but "Cultural Revolution." Here was a way the positive connotations that one leadership group added to a term could be peeled off by another group.

4. Goal orientation. The official language of Communist China has a tendency to stress goals, often in absence of comment on how to achieve the goals. The tendency is visible at several linguistic levels: from the structure of general policies down to the level of slogans and even to single words. It is also evident in many spheres of life, ranging from military orders to literary policy.

For example, at the level of general policies, after the Third Plenum of the Eleventh Congress of the Communist Party of China in 1978, China's writers were exhorted to *jiefang sixiang* 解放思想 'liberate [their] thought'. They should not *xin you yuji* 心有余悸 'harbor residual fears' because of what happened to them and others during the Cultural Revolution. At the same time, though, they were cautioned to observe *sige jiben jianchi* 四个基本坚持 'Four Basic Principles': the leadership of the Communist Party, Marxism-Leninism-Mao-Zedong-thought, the dictatorship of the proletariat, and the socialist system. These contradictory guidelines created a problem for the writing process. How, in actually writing a story or poem, could one follow both sets of instructions? It seemed that one was being told to go and stop at the same time.[64] The official language had set forth goals, but the problem of how to reach the goals was left to individual writers. Similarly, but in a very different context, on June 3, 1989, soldiers of the Chinese army in Beijing were ordered to clear Tiananmen Square of protesting students "resolutely," with "absolutely no delays . . . by 6 a.m. [on June 4]"; at the same time, there was to be "no bloodshed

---

64. This was, in fact, a standard tool in the project of inducing self-censorship in writers, and we will consider it further in the section below "How the Game Is Played."

within Tiananmen Square—period."[65] Soldiers were given rifles and machine guns. How, exactly, were the twin goals of finishing on time and ensuring no bloodshed to be achieved? This was left to the ones receiving the orders. The official message was just "Get it done."

At the word level, the project of stating a goal without specifying a means is well reflected by the widespread use in mainland China of the "dummy" verb *gao* 搞, a word that in isolation is almost impossible to translate because it usually means literally nothing except "do," "pursue," or "bring about" the noun that follows it. All of the freight of a *gao* phrase is carried by the verb's direct object. *Gao* has been especially useful in official language because its dummy-verb nature is perfect for officials who want to say "get [something] done" without committing themselves about just what to do. An order to *gao shengchan* 搞生产 'do production' tells a worker simply to produce more output—one way or another. Slogans like *gao shehuizhuyi* 搞社会主义 'pursue socialism' and *quanxin quanyi gao sihua* 全心全意搞四化 'pursue the Four Modernizations with all your heart and mind' all lay emphasis on the desired results, even though, in these two examples, the results themselves are expressed only vaguely. Eventually, *gao* spread from the official language into many other spheres of life. By the end of the Mao years, what a janitor did was *gao weisheng* 搞卫生 'do sanitation', a physicist would *gao wuli* 搞物理 'do physics', a young person *gao duixiang* 搞对象 'pursue a [romantic] partner', an artist *gao meishu* 搞美术 'do art', and so on.

Gao is also used in Taiwan and overseas Chinese communities, but not nearly as much as on the mainland. The usage has roots in regional dialects (notably of Hunan, the native province of a number of Communist leaders) and was sometimes used as a euphemism in sexually suggestive phrases such as *gao nüren* 搞女人 'mess with women' and *luangao nannü guanxi* 乱搞男女关系 'be promiscuous in sexual relations'. But by the middle of the twentieth century, *gao* had become a mainstream term within the Communist movement and was neutral in connotation and flexible in usage. In

---

65. Zhang Liang, *The Tiananmen Papers: The Chinese Leadership's Decision to Use Force against Their Own People*, ed. Andrew J. Nathan and Perry Link (New York: Public Affairs, 2001), p. 370.

1951 Lao She, the master of Beijing brogue who had returned to China from the United States in order to support the new Communist society, used *gao* in phrases like *sixiang ruoshi mei gao tong*... 思想若是没搞通... 'if you don't get your thinking clear...'.[66] In the summer of 1980, during a coordinated government effort to get writers to "liberate thought," meetings and headlines commonly used the phrase *ba wenyi gao huo* 把文艺搞活 'bring literature and art to life'. In an internal speech on literature and art policy, Hu Yaobang used *gao* more often than any verbs other than *shi* 是 'is' and *you* 有 'have'. Urging that there be national guidelines on what topics to write about, Hu said (I will leave the elusive *gao* untranslated here):

> First, we must help writers to *gao* planned design. Cultural departments, the National Artists Association and the Writers Associations at all levels should do what they can to *gao* a few conferences in this regard. Of course, for an artist to *gao* creativity is different from *gao*-ing manufacturing... so we must not oblige literary artists to *gao* collective design in a mechanical way.[67]

The snippet shows how pervasive *gao* had become in official language, especially in contexts where officials were speaking casually. The convenience of *gao* as a dummy verb for telling people to just "get it done" continued for many more years. In the early 1990s, when Chinese students overseas were denouncing the June Fourth massacre, personnel in Chinese consulates received instructions to find ways to discredit those who spoke out most vociferously. Exactly how to discredit them—by rumors of corruption, sexual misconduct, or whatever—did not matter, as long as the discrediting worked. The instruction was simply to *gao chou* 搞臭 'cause [them] to stink'.

The overwhelming importance of the goal in this kind of usage tends to leave moot the questions not only of means but also of the actor. "Get it done" can leave ambiguous the question *who* should get it done. This as-

---

66. Lao She, "Wenyi zuojia ye yao zengchan jieyue" 文艺作家也要增产节约 [Writers must be productive and frugal, too], in *Shuoshuo changchang* 说说唱唱 [Speaking and singing] 4, no. 6 (1951), p. 9.

67. Hu Yaobang, *Zai juben chuangzuo zuotanhuishang de jianghua*.

pect of "goal orientation" is visible in the fact that nearly all Chinese political slogans grammatically are free-floating predicates. They are clauses that could take subjects but do not: *dadao sirenbang* 打倒四人帮 'down with the Gang of Four', *quanxin quanyi gao sihua* 全心全意搞四化 'pursue the Four Modernizations with all your heart and mind', and *buyao xin you yuji, xiangqian kan* 不要心有余悸, 向前看 'do not harbor residual fears, look to the future' are all examples. Slogans in English, in contrast, do sometimes name the subjects, for example, "Hell, no! We won't go!" during American protests of the Vietnam War. But even when English-language examples do not state a subject, they differ in one crucial way from most slogans in Chinese. Compare, for example, "down with the Gang of Four" to *dadao sirenbang*. The English phrase has no subject and grammatically cannot accommodate one. You cannot say "I down with the Gang of Four" or "You down with the Gang of Four." But the Chinese phrase, the free-floating predicate, can do this. You can say *wo dadao sirenbang* 'I knock down the Gang of Four', *ni dadao sirenbang* 'You knock down the Gang of Four', or *zanmen dajia yikuair dadao sirenbang* 咱们大家一块儿打倒四人帮 'all of us together knock down the Gang of Four'. With no subject stated, Chinese slogans are not exactly imperative and not exactly descriptive, either. They mean something like "would that it be that [predicate]."

Yet Chinese slogans as free-floating predicates that *can* take subjects, if one wants, have the flexibility (as English-language slogans usually do not) to turn themselves into imperatives by implying subjects. The phrase *tiba nianqing ganbu* 提拔年轻干部 'promote young cadres', which has been used several times since the Mao era, is an example, as is *jianjue fandui tiaoji shangfang* 坚决反对跳级上访 'resolutely oppose the jumping of levels in petitioning', which was used in the Hu Jintao era to try to prevent people who were petitioning the government from approaching higher levels without going first through lower levels. Such slogans are grammatically the same as *dadao sirenbang*, yet in their political contexts their imperative mood emerges more clearly. They carry less a sense of "would that it be that . . ." and more a sense of "you should . . ."

Why, in this kind of case where the subject is fairly clear, does the official language still prefer subjectless slogans? Why not just name the subject and say "*You* must promote young cadres," "*You* must prevent level-jumping," and so on? Hu Ping has observed that the reason for omission of the subject can be a sense of embarrassment at the fact that one is giving orders. Officials in authoritarian governments—perhaps in China's more than others—tend to feel better when they pretend they are not being authoritarian. They seem to like to say "Let's have X done, but let's not say that *I* am telling *you* to do it." The point is especially clear in cases where the message itself is potentially embarrassing. When Deng Xiaoping said in 1985 *yibufen ren xian fuqilai* 一部分人先富起来 'a part of the people [may] get rich first',[68] Chinese people watched as, unsurprisingly, well-connected Party members became that special "part" who got rich first. *Yibufen ren xian fuqilai* became a pleasant-sounding catchphrase, but it was also an order to lower-level officials to allow disparate enrichment to take place. When the latter point needed to be made unmistakably clear (even at the cost of some embarrassment), the word *rang* 让 'let' was appended: *(rang) yibufen ren xian fuqilai* '(let) a part of the people get rich first'.

5. *"Fit" as a kind of truth.* In his incisive book *Doing Things with Words in Chinese Politics*, Michael Schoenhals points out the special power and importance of *tifa* 提法 'ways of putting things' in the official Chinese language of the Communist era. He quotes an authoritative 1978 statement in the *People's Daily* that *tifa* "are very serious matters that must be resolved scientifically.... Where the *tifa* is off by one millimeter, the theory will be wrong by a thousand kilometers."[69] Among the illustrations Schoenhals offers is one from a 1965 speech by the vice president of the Central Party School to a group of students. It is all right, the official said, to refer to China's current society as a *you jieji de shehui* 有阶级的社会 'a society that has classes' but not a *jieji shehui* 阶级社会 'class society'. Schoenhals comments that "here the distinction between socialism on the one hand and capitalism, feudalism, and slave society on the other rested on the presence or absence of a *de*."[70] Even when the issues at stake were less weighty, an assumption prevailed that key political phrases had to be *just*

---

68. "Deng Xiaoping: rang yibufenren fuqilai" 邓小平: 让一部分人先富起来 [Let part of the people get rich first], http://news.xinhuanet.com/newscenter/2005-01/16/content_2467918.htm, accessed June 29, 2012.

69. Schoenhals, *Doing Things with Words in Chinese Politics*, p. 7. I have altered the translation slightly.

70. Ibid.

so—and that it was, somehow, a serious error if they were not. During the brief interregnum of Hua Guofeng after the death of Mao Zedong, it was "correct" to refer to *weida de Mao zhuxi* 伟大的毛主席 'the great Chairman Mao', *jing'ai de Zhou zongli* 敬爱的周总理 'the beloved Premier Zhou', and *yingming de Hua zhuxi* 英明的华主席 'the wise Chairman Hua'. The three rulers had to be mentioned in that order if all three were mentioned; moreover, the three adjectives that had been selected to match "scientifically" the nature of the men they referred to could not be switched around without incurring the definite sense that the speaker had made a mistake. *Tifa* became an extension of grammar.

Schoenhals calls the rigidity of *tifa* a "form of power." This simple claim has greater profundity than may appear on the surface. In an obvious sense, it means that holders of power can insist that people say certain things in certain ways and expect that, over time, thought and behavior will follow. *Aiguo, aidang, airenmin* 爱国爱党爱人民 'love the country, love the Party, love the people' has lilt, repetition, fixity, and a sense of rightness that sinks in after a while. The power of *tifa* can sometimes be used to turn things entirely upside-down. During the spring of 1989, the demonstrations at Tiananmen were called a *xuechao* 学潮 'student protest' or a *minzhu yundong* 民主运动 'democracy movement' up until the moment when they were suppressed. Then, almost overnight, government media began to call the same events a *fan'geming baoluan* 反革命暴乱 'counterrevolutionary riot'. It was a formulation most people would not have dreamed of using only a week earlier, but now it had become a correct *tifa*, and people had to begin using it, in public contexts, on pain of punishment for being "incorrect." The phrase remained in place and entered textbooks and the media, and twenty years later many people in a younger generation of Chinese knew no better than to accept *fan'geming baoluan* as what had happened.

But *tifa* are "forms of power" not just because brutish power can stand behind them and force their acceptance. They have an intrinsic power, too, when they cut off alternative ways of thinking and limit the conceptual horizons of the people who adopt them. This phenomenon is observable in many kinds of ritualized language, be it in politics, religion, song, or elsewhere. Maurice Bloch, after studying rituals of the Merina people of Madagascar, gained insights that, without much alteration, can apply to the use of *tifa* in Communist China:

> In a highly formalised or ritualised political situation there seems no way whereby authority can be challenged except by a total refusal to use the accepted form which is compulsory for this type of occasion, i.e., a total refusal of all political conventions.[71]

Since very few people can find the will for "total refusal," formalized authority comes to be accepted. Its "ceremonial trappings," Bloch writes, "seem to *catch* the actors so that they are unable to resist the demands made upon them."[72] If authoritarian language provided for a *range* of alternatives for how to express something, then that language still might not be so constricting (from the point of view of users) or such a lever of power (from the point of view of authority). But Bloch's key point is precisely that a range of alternatives is denied. He calls the language of political or religious ritual an "impoverished" language in the sense that "many of the options at all levels of language are abandoned so that choice of form, of style, of words and of syntax is less than in ordinary language" and concludes that "as soon as you have accepted a form of speaking in an appropriate way you have begun to give up at a bewilderingly rapid rate the very potential for communication."[73]

The tradition of giving fixed names to things in Chinese political language has a long pedigree. Many have noted how Confucius, in the *Analects*, offered instruction on governance to a newly ascended ruler by saying *zheng zhe zheng ye* 政者正也 'to govern is to rectify [names]'.[74] And Xunzi (in Burton Watson's translation) held that:

> When the ruler's accomplishments are long lasting and his undertakings are brought to completion, this is the height of a good government. All of this is the result of being careful to see that men stick to the names which have been agreed upon.[75]

---

71. Maurice Bloch, "Symbols, Song, Dance and Features of Articulation *or* Is Religion an Extreme Form of Traditional Authority?," *Archives Européennes de Sociologie* 15, no. 1 (1974), p. 59.

72. Ibid., pp. 59–60.

73. Ibid., pp. 60 and 61.

74. *Lunyu* 論語 [The analects], Yan Yuan 12 顏淵第十二.

75. *Xunzi: Basic Writings*, trans. Burton Watson (New York: Columbia University Press, 2003), p. 145.

On the basis of bits of text such as these, as well as official histories in intervening years, scholars have observed that the role of the official naming of things in Chinese tradition has been prescriptive as much as descriptive; it is *right* that things be put a certain way, and be referred to in the same way. I noted in Chapter 2 that, within some of the strains of ancient Chinese thought, the modern notion of "true" is not as useful a way to measure the worth of utterances as are notions of *dang* 當 'fitting' or *ke* 可 'admissible' or 'appropriate'.[76]

The power-engineering of the official language of contemporary China has even stronger roots in modern authoritarianism, especially Soviet Leninism. There are, however, some important differences between ancient and modern notions of politically correct "fit." Perhaps most fundamental among these is how the two kinds of language relate to truth or falsity of fact. In ancient China, when a statement was *dang* 'fitting', its truth could be part of what made it fitting. Xunzi says, for example, *fei wo er dang zhe wu shi ye* 非我而當者吾師也 'the person who criticizes me appropriately is my teacher'.[77] Here we assume that what "my teacher" says in criticizing me is factually true, but that truth alone is only part of what makes the criticism "fitting." It is fitting because it is factually true *and* designed to help me. In short, factual truth cooperates in the project of making a statement *dang*. In modern authoritarianism, by contrast, the project of establishing certain *tifa* as "fitting" is often done *in rivalry with* factual truth, or even in outright opposition to it.

For example, imagine yourself as a Chinese citizen during the Hua Guofeng interregnum in the late 1970s. If you were to say, in an official context, *weida de Hua zhuxi* 伟大的华主席 'the great Chairman Hua', your statement could be criticized as incorrect, and the grounds for calling it incorrect would not be truth or falsity in a factual sense. Hua Guofeng might or might not have been "great," however one chose to define that word, but that would not be the point, and you would not be criticized in those terms. You would be criticized with a sentence like *zhe wenti bushi neme tifa* 这问题不是那么提法 'that is not the way this matter is put', and the reason would be that you had produced an

---

76. See section "How Do Metaphors Work in Ordinary Language?," in Chapter 2.
77. Xunzi: Xiushen 荀子: 修身 (Xunzi: Cultivating oneself); see Watson, *Xunzi: Basic Writings*, p. 24.

inappropriate match of adjective with leader's name. Yet your "incorrectness" would be just as clear as if truth versus falsity had been the criterion. "The notion of true or false," as Bloch observes, generalizing over a number of cases, "has been eliminated by the way the proposition has been put."[78]

In short, "fit" and "truth" have become parallel entities in China's modern authoritarian language. Both are standards for measuring the affirmability of statements, and both are positive. Each is opposite, but in a different way, to *cuowu* 错误 'mistaken'. This bifurcation of fit and truth distinguishes modern official Chinese from its ancient counterpart, in which standards like *dang* or *ke* could stand as the lone measure of a statement's affirmability. The fact that the modern official language has two standards, not one, has produced a range of problems for ordinary language users. I have noted Liu Binyan's perplexity in 1958 over how to handle "two kinds of truth."[79] (Liu, who knew Russian, was fond of the "old joke" in Moscow that the only thing worse than living without truth was living with two of them.)[80] The resulting "language game" that citizens of the People's Republic of China became obliged to engage with will occupy most of the remainder of this chapter.

The Language Game

During China's Mao years, and especially after 1957, Chinese people became more and more accustomed to constructing their public assertions by asking not just "do they reflect reality?" but also "do they fit politically?" As the bifurcation of language spread more and more widely through society, a second order of reality—an image of "the official version of things"—seemed to take on a life of its own whenever topics with political implications were being discussed. This second order of reality was not idle puffery. It could have real consequences in the world, and in

---

78. Bloch, "Symbols," p. 66.

79. Liu Binyan, "Listen Carefully to the Voice of the People," p. 31.

80. A version of the joke, attributed to Alexander Fadeyev during the post-Stalin thaw in the Soviet Union, is cited in Harold Swayze, *Political Control of Literature in the USSR, 1946–1959* (Cambridge, Mass.: Harvard University Press, 1962), p. 253.

that sense was itself very real. You had to deal with it in order to get certain things done, and people became accustomed to this fact. The British scholar William Jenner, who lived in Beijing during the late Mao years, wrote in 1978 that "in daily life our Chinese friends can cope perfectly well with the distinction between what actually happens and the required formulations that keep things functioning."[81] Even if you opted to avoid the official language (which could mean having to settle for *not* getting certain things done), you still could be forced to use it when others used it against you. Some people got very good at manipulating the official language, and benefited; others were less talented and could suffer.

Ji Fengyuan, writing about the Mao years, when political combat sometimes got heavy, has written that "revolutionary language became little more than a weapon in a low-grade civil war."[82] Words and phrases were tools—verbal chisels, clubs, and levers, as it were. Ji writes of high Maoism, when this kind of language use reached an extreme. For other, less extreme times, a better metaphor for official language use is a game, especially an intellectual game like chess. The metaphor is apt for several reasons: in both cases there are rules, tactics, and goals; in both cases skills can be honed and a person usually gets better with experience. On one point the analogy does not work well: games are normally entered into freely, but China's language game, especially during the years of high Maoism, was not optional. You had to play. If you withdrew into silence, the silence itself was viewed as a political position—indeed, almost always, an "incorrect" one. One had to "perform" a correct "appearance." A few years after Mao's death, a young farmer told Andrew Nathan in interview: "I don't know what socialism is anymore; I only know how to talk about it."[83] Since those years the language game has receded somewhat from daily life, but it has never entirely disappeared and has remained important, especially on politically sensitive topics, well into the twenty-first century.

---

81. W. J. F. Jenner, "Is a Modern Chinese Literature Possible?," in Wolfgang Kubin and Rudolph G. Wagner, eds., *Essays in Modern Chinese Literature and Literary Criticism: Papers of the Berlin Conference 1978* (Bochum: Brockmeyer, 1982), p. 213.

82. Ji Fengyuan, *Linguistic Engineering*, p. 293.

83. Andrew J. Nathan, *Chinese Democracy* (New York: Knopf, 1985), pp. 175, 235.

Mark Salzman records an illuminating story from the mid-1980s about what happened when he, a foreign teacher on a Chinese campus, killed a rat as part of a general rat extermination campaign. People who brought in dead rats were given rewards, and Salzman lined up for his. There was a problem, though, because officially foreigners were not supposed to know that there were rats in China. That information was "internal." The fact that a foreigner had killed a rat was true in the real world but could not be true in the parallel world of the language game. Campus officials, facing a dilemma, decided to deny Salzman his reward. So long as there was no reward, they could avoid acknowledging that a foreigner knew about rats. Salzman later asked one of his students if all of this was not a bit silly. "Oh, of course it is very silly," he records the student as answering. "But the comrades in the office, like anyone else, would rather do something silly than something stupid."[84] To violate the language game in the name of common sense would be obtuse.

In this story, campus officials were playing the language game defensively. In cases where a person decides to be proactive in the game, the reason is usually some kind of expediency: Will my move get something done? Will it serve my interests (or those of my family, or my group)? I mentioned in the Introduction the example of my friend in Guangzhou who wanted a bigger apartment for his family and went to his Party leader in 1979 with the question "Do you think we can concretize Party Central's policy on intellectuals?" His goal was a bigger apartment, and his language-move was crafted with that goal in mind. It was a clear case of the language game having consequences in the real world.

In other cases, causality between the real world and the language game flows in the opposite direction. People sometimes make real-world changes in order to shift the terms of play in the language game. For example, during the prodemocracy demonstrations at Tiananmen in the spring of 1989, Fang Lizhi, the famous astrophysicist who two years earlier had been a hero to prodemocracy students in Hefei, Anhui Province, and who in 1989 was living on the outskirts of Beijing, deliberately stayed away from the prodemocracy demonstrations in the city's center. Why? Lack of interest? No. Lack of sympathy? No. Only because he did not want the

---

84. Salzman, *Iron and Silk*, p. 201.

government to be able to *say* (even though it would have been false, and even though government leaders would likely have known it to be false) that he was an instigator of the demonstrations. Fang had recently been expelled from the Communist Party under the label "bourgeois liberal." That label was a poor fit with reality but had been effective in the regime's language game. Fang knew that any association he might have with the 1989 demonstrators could allow the regime to transfer the label from him to the demonstrators. In short, he foresaw a possible language move on the government's side and altered his real-world behavior in order to obviate it. So he stayed away from Tiananmen Square.

There is one respect in which utterances in the official language game are more reliable than ordinary assertions about truth and falsity. In ordinary language, a statement might or might not be true, and if a speaker means deliberately to deceive a listener, the statement is called a lie. But in the language game, where the standard is not "Is it true or not?" but "Does it serve the speaker's interests or not?" the counterpart of a "lie" is not possible. The person who hears a statement can be 100 percent sure that "this speaker believes that this statement serves his or her interests." It might not be easy to figure out exactly what the specific interest is, but one can be sure that the speaker is aiming at it. It also can happen that a speaker miscalculates in the choice of which words will actually serve his or her interests. But that, too, does not change the principle that the speaker *believes* that the words will be expedient. To experienced players of the language game, this "impossibility of a lie" is a useful fact. One can use it to analyze what a speaker is doing with words.

Let us look at some more examples. When Tibetans protested in the streets of Lhasa and elsewhere in March 2008, and when Uighurs did likewise in Urumchi and elsewhere in July 2009, why did the players of the language game within China's media bureaucracies say that the demonstrations had been "planned and instigated abroad"? Because they believed this to be true? Did they really believe that the Dalai Lama and Rebiya Kadeer were pulling strings from distant places? This seems highly unlikely. They were adequately informed on what was happening in these places and would not have subscribed to such a far-fetched theory in the ordinary-talk world of "is it true or not?" It is quite possible that they did not even give much thought to questions of true versus false.

Their duty in their work was not to act as observers of events but to pursue results within the flow of those events. Their goals included discrediting the protesters by making them seem to be puppets; intimidating the Dalai Lama and Rebiya Kadeer into not speaking out from overseas (by saying, in essence, "by speaking out you only confirm what we are saying about you"); stimulating Chinese nationalism and presenting the Communist Party of China as its champion; and distracting the attention of people inside China from problems of corruption, inequality, pollution, and so on where the Party's image was under strain. To choose as *tifa* that Kadeer was the "mastermind" of the Uighur protests or that the Dalai Lama is "a jackal clad in Buddhist monk's robes" disregards plausibility,[85] but plausibility was not the standard the fashioners of such phrases were using. The standard was "what will work?" and by that standard the *tifa* seemed right.

The distinction between truth and utility as standards for evaluating statements in the language game struck me most clearly in 2001, in a conversation that I had with the distinguished Chinese writer Su Xiaokang not long after the publication of *The Tiananmen Papers*, which I had helped to edit.[86] In February 2001, the Chinese compiler of those papers, who used the pseudonym Zhang Liang, was able, through friends who were highly placed in the Chinese government, to get access to the record of a meeting of the Politburo of the Communist Party of China that was held on February 8, 2001.[87] At that meeting Jiang Zemin, China's president at the time, addressed the matter of the publication of *The Tiananmen Papers* and said, according to the terse notes on the meeting that reached me, that this leak of state secrets was the largest in the history of the Party and showed that people of ill will, who wish to overthrow the Communist Party and the socialist system, were hiding in high places inside the Party. The record also shows Jiang saying that the leaking of the papers was a naked sale of state secrets to Americans and that whoever did it has lost qualification to be Chinese. Farther down the list—at point 5—the summary reads: "Andrew Nathan and the other two so-called American editors

---

85. China Central Television, July 7, 2009; Edward Wong, "Dalai Lama's Defeat to Be a Holiday in Tibet," *New York Times*, January 19, 2009.

86. See note 65.

87. Zhang Liang email to Andrew Nathan, February 28, 2001.

[i.e., Perry Link and Orville Schell] are by no means pure and independent scholars; they wear the overcoats of scholars in order to use scholarly status while they work for the CIA."

This statement interested me and raised a question. I have never worked for the CIA, or any branch of the U.S. government, but here was the top leader of the world's largest government saying that I did. I wondered what, in Jiang's own mind, he might have been thinking he was doing with his words. It seemed a rare chance to try to figure out how official language is used at the highest levels of the Communist Party of China.

If Jiang's words had been broadcast to all of the Chinese people, then I could have understood them as an attempt to manipulate public opinion. But that was not the case. Jiang was addressing a small group of his fellow rulers at the top, in a context where, I imagined, there should have been no barrier—at least for a question such as this one—to presenting the truth as well as one could. So I began to wonder: Did Jiang himself believe what he had said? If so, how had he formed his opinion? By listening to intelligence briefings? Could it be that intelligence reports to the leader of the largest nation on earth are as inaccurate as this? That seemed frightening. But had Jiang perhaps *not* believed what he had said to the Politburo? Would he use manipulative language on this question in addressing even his highest-level colleagues? That, too, seemed a bit frightening. I decided to poll a number of my Chinese friends, including writers and former officials who had had extensive experience with China's official language. "When Jiang Zemin told the Politburo that I work for the CIA," I asked, "how do you think it felt to him in his own mind? Did he think he was telling the truth? Or doing something else?"

The poll results split almost evenly. Some said Jiang likely felt that he was telling the truth. The CIA does have a record of undercover activity around the world, and the general lore that surrounds the CIA in the subculture of Chinese Communism exaggerates this record in flamboyant ways. The Chinese intelligence services might or might not have had good information on specific people like Nathan, Link, or Schell, but the people in those services also have incentives, especially in sensitive cases, to tell top leaders what they want to hear. Jiang could well have heard a briefing that said Nathan, Link, and Schell were only wearing the outer clothing of scholars.

On the other side, just as many in my poll felt that Jiang likely had not believed the things he was saying. On politically dangerous questions it was important for leaders, even among their top-level colleagues (who, after all, are also their potential rivals for power) to adopt politically unassailable positions. The pose of blaming the CIA was one that, whatever else happened, no one could characterize as "soft." *Ning zuo er bu you* 宁左而不右 'better [to err to] the left than the right' was a reliable maxim for hazardous times, and its value outweighed less important questions about the accuracy of this or that detail.

In all, though, Su Xiaokang gave me the answer that taught me the most. He began by chiding me for a wrongheaded question. Jiang Zemin, in that situation, doesn't even ask the question you are asking, Su said. It doesn't occur to him. He doesn't care whether the words are "true or not"; he only wants them to *work*. Is he telling the truth to his colleagues, or deceiving them? Neither, said Su. In Jiang's own view, he is merely supplying to his colleagues the words that he thinks will be useful in getting done what needs to be done. Does he expect his words to be believed? That's the wrong question, said Su. He expects his words to be *put to use*.[88]

If Su is right, then the record of this Politburo meeting might be viewed an example of how *tifa* originate. Starting from a high level (although not necessarily as high as the Politburo), *tifa* spread downward and outward to the rest of government and society, where they turn into standard tools in the playing of the official language game. They might seem rigid or awkward at first, but with repeated use and the passage of time, people learn to accept them as normal and to use them in a variety of situations. In 1980 a literary scholar at Zhongshan University in Guangzhou told me about his complaints about the slogan *xingwu miezi* 兴无灭资 'promote the proletarian and annihilate the bourgeois' that Hua Guofeng had unveiled in 1976 when he was Party chairman. The scholar said he had no problem with the theory of *xingwu miezi*. The Marxist ideal was all right with him. The problem was that this four-character phrase became a nasty little club in the hands of the local stewards of political

---

88. Based on a conversation with Su Xiaokang, spring 2001, Princeton Junction, N.J. I have omitted quotation marks because this is a summary, not a transcript, of what Su said.

correctness—Party secretaries, chiefs of Organization Departments, and the like. These people did not understand much Marxism themselves, and were not inclined to go read about it either. But they needed tools in order to do what they saw as their job, which was to *guan ren* 管人 'manage people'. If a student wore bell-bottom trousers, or hair that was too long, or if a professor taught from an unapproved book, it would be too much to go read Marx in order to know what to do, but with a convenient little phrase like *xingwu miezi* an official could get moving.

With the decline of the work-unit system in recent decades, the use of official phrases to control people's daily lives has also receded considerably. But it has not disappeared. Special phrases in the official language live on within bureaucratic subcultures; careers have been built around terminology and the ideas that they enshrine, and people who live within the subcultures cling to the vocabulary of language games in part because their livelihoods are invested in doing so. In analyzing the repression in Tibet in March 2008, Phuntsog Wanggyal, a Tibetan who had spent years as a high Party official in Tibet, observed that the doctrine of *fan fenlie* 反分裂 'anti-splittism' had deep roots in the bureaucracies that were charged with Tibetan affairs. The very term had taken on a sort of transcendent status. Careers had been invested in the idea, and no one would think of questioning it. The Dalai Lama could explicitly say that he did not favor *fenlie* 'splitting', but still the banner of *fan fenlie* had to be held high. Too many people were already known for it, good at it, and paid to do it. Other *tifa* this group depended on to justify its work included *daoluan fenzi* 捣乱分子 'trouble-making elements' and *didui waiguo shili* 敌对外国势力 'hostile foreign forces'. Such phrases were useful as explanations for anything that might go wrong; they were also enduring justifications for the vigilance that "anti-splittist" officials were providing to the motherland.[89]

Harsh terminology such as this does not dominate in the official language, even on a "sensitive" topic like Tibet, but it is always available in abeyance, ready to emerge as needed. A good example of "as needed" use of formulaic language is the written confession. A ubiquitous device in the Chinese police system, the confession is a way to establish guilt and justify

---

89. Interview with Wang Lixiong, March 2008; see also Wang Lixiong, "The Cry of Tibet," *Wall Street Journal* op-ed, March 28, 2008.

punishment; but it is also a tool in the language game. It is a way of drawing a person into the language-world and thus (if it works) into the thought-world of the political authority. I recall my own single experience of writing a confession for the Chinese police. This happened after I failed, in the fall of 1988, to register the Beijing Office of the Committee on Scholarly Communication with China (CSCC) as a "business" within the prescribed thirty-day period for doing so. The CSCC was not, in fact, a business, which was the root of my original misunderstanding with the police; learning to call it a business was part of my initiation into this particular corner of the language game. After several hours of negotiation the officers and I settled on a confession document, which I signed, admitting that I had failed to register within thirty days. But I remember being surprised at how much back-and-forth the police seemed to want during the negotiation. At several points one of them would say something like "you broke rule X because you did not do Y by day Z!"—and then look at me, eyebrows raised, as if to ask, "What do you have to say? Do you want to rebut anything? Explain anything?" I reflected that an American policeman, in a similar situation, would just write out a ticket, hand it to me, and be off. But for the Chinese police, to get me involved in the language game, and to see me perform properly within it, seemed to be an important goal in itself. They seemed to assume that if the accused uses language in the right way, step 1 has been achieved in bringing his or her thought into line.[90]

It is not only an accused, or ordinary people in general, who can make "mistakes," of course. Officials can, too, and the penalties for misspeaking can be costly to a bureaucratic career. For this reason the language game has developed a range of vocabulary whose functions are to buffer officials from mistakes. These vocabulary items are not official terms, not formally approved *tifa*. They are natural outgrowths of the language game, invented by its users, that eventually become widespread and standard. In the 1980s, for example, a bureaucrat who heard a request for something—and who

---

90. I have written up this episode in "Jingguan qiyu: Liang ci sange yiwai" 警官奇遇: 兩次三個意外 [Strange encounters with police: Three surprises, twice], in *Banyang Suibi* 半洋隨筆 [Notes of a semiforeigner] (Taipei: Sanmin chubanshe, 1999) pp. 68–72.

did not want to make a mistake—would often say, instead of "yes," *wenti buda* 问题不大 'there's no big problem'. Instead of "no," he or she might say *youxie kunnan* 有些困难 'there are some difficulties', and instead of "maybe," might use *yanjiu yanjiu* 研究研究 'we'll study it' or *kaolü kaolü* 考虑考虑 'we'll think it over'. The hallmark of such terms is their vagueness; they combine easy fluency with the impossibility of being pinned down. Essentially defensive, they are born of the dilemma of how to satisfy (or mollify, or perhaps just cause to go away) the person making the request, and, at the same time, avoid committing to a position that might later prove to have been "incorrect."

One of my own personal experiences with this kind of vocabulary came in 1979 when I was living at Zhongshan University in Guangzhou. I wanted to go into the city to buy socks. The Foreign Affairs Section at the university was in the habit of providing a car whenever I went off campus, but I felt that a car was a bit excessive for a mere sock-buying expedition, so suggested that I ride my bicycle instead. The official at the Foreign Affairs Section was affable and said *wenti buda*. This told me that, from her point of view, there was "no big problem." But what did that mean? Did she approve or not? I later asked some Chinese friends, and they said that I should take it as a yes. But it was a yes that, from the point of view of the Foreign Affairs official, also said "I am not officially on record as saying yes." If something had happened to me on that bicycle trip, the official could have been in trouble if she had given explicit approval. Later, when I heard officials answer requests with *youxie kunnan*, I came to understand that this really meant no, but they preferred the vaguer phrase because it allowed them to avoid the embarrassment of saying no bluntly. Then I came to understand that the "maybe" responses—*yanjiu yanjiu* or *kaolü kaolü*—were generally used to buy time in which the official could hope that the request would simply go away or, if it did not, could ask for guidance from above. Sensitive questions could get passed successively to higher levels, and clogging near the top could mean that some questions never actually reached any desk for decision. Comedians and cartoonists satirized this pattern at considerable length in the 1980s, often playing on the near-pun between *yanjiu* 研究 'study' and *yanjiu* 烟酒 'cigarettes and liquor', items that were useful as small bribes to get things moving.

Vagueness has several uses in the official language. We have seen how abstract vocabulary can create a special sense of authority. In this section, we have seen how vagueness can be useful in avoiding bureaucratic responsibility. And we will see below how vagueness is useful in inducing self-censorship by obliging people to guess what a vaguely stated prohibition might mean. Note in passing, though, that while vagueness in the official language has all of these uses, the preference of ordinary people in daily-life language is often in the other direction, toward the concrete. Popular sayings sometimes borrow the form of official phrases and fill them with very practical, concrete content. For example the phrase *hai lu kong* 海陆空 'sea, land, air', which is an abbreviation for "navy, army, and air force" in the official language, during the Cultural Revolution was a popular nickname for homemade sandals cut from the rubber of worn-out tires. Why were they called "sea, land, and air"? Apparently because they could withstand any conditions, including water, dust, and sun. In any case, later, when policies of "reform and opening" in the late 1970s suddenly made it all right to admit to material desires and overseas connections, the same phrase, *hai lu kong*, became a popular catchphrase for what a young woman could ask as a condition of marriage: *hai* meant *haiwai guanxi* 海外关系 'overseas connections'; *lu* was a two-speaker or four-speaker *luyinji* 录(陆)音机 '(stereo) recorder', and *kong* was *kongtiao* 空调 'air conditioning'. Other popular phrases imitated the practice in official language of numbering things (three antis, Four Modernizations, etc.). As an alternative to demanding *hai lu kong*, prospective brides in the late 1970s could ask for the *sanzhuan yixiang* 三转一响 'three turns and one sound', meaning a watch, a bicycle, and a sewing machine (three things that turn) plus a (sound-making) recorder.

Part of the popular enjoyment of such phrases is that they evoke the abstraction and pomp of official phrases but bring them down to earth by inserting concrete and practical content. In 1987, Deng Xiaoping sought a linguistic watchword that would promote reform and opening, and continued economic growth, but also maintain Leninist political control. These were conflicting goals, and the task of unifying them in a single phrase was not easy. Eventually, Deng announced a formula of *yige zhongxin, liangge jiben dian* 一个中心, 两个基本点 'one central concern and two basic points'. The "central concern" was economic development. The two basic points were (1) the Four Basic Principles (the socialist system, dictatorship of the proletariat, Party rule, and Marxism-Leninism-Mao-Zedong-thought), and (2) the policy of "reform and opening." From the Party's point of view, this may have been an excellent phrase. But it was far too abstract for ordinary people, who satirized it by making it concrete in irreverent ways. A website for students returning from overseas said a person's "central concern should be health" (*yi jiankang wei zhongxin* 以健康为中心) and two basic points should be to be *xiaosa yidian* 潇洒一点 'on the cool and easy side' and *hutu yidian* 糊涂一点 'a bit muddle-headed'.[91] A joke on the oral grapevine was even less respectful; it said the "one central concern plus two points for attention" was only "a bikini policy." Jiang Zemin's formula of "the three represents" (*sange daibiao* 三个代表) was satirized, as we have seen, as "three [people] wearing wristwatches" (*sange daibiao* 三个戴表), and later Hu Jintao's "harmony" (*hexie* 和谐) was turned into a "river crab" (*hexie* 河蟹).

If part of the popular response to China's official language has been to stand apart from it and even to satirize it, another side of the response—as we have seen in several examples—has been to accommodate it, manipulate it, and "play the game." This raises an important question we considered in Chapter 2 in connection with the "Whorf hypothesis": how much do habits of language use induce habits of thought? The question has worried a wide variety of contemporary Chinese thinkers and observers of China.

For me the question first arose during a visit to China in May 1973. In those days foreigners were so rare on the streets of Chinese cities that my group and I nearly always attracted a long train of curious onlookers, especially children, who followed us in polite silence whenever we walked on the sidewalks. At one point, on a street in Xi'an, I turned around to see if I could talk to some of the children in the crowd. A group of about eight or ten, who appeared to be perhaps ten to twelve years old, formed a sort of semicircle and showed rapt attention. I asked if they had seen foreigners before, and they shook their heads. I asked what they wanted to be when they grew up. Nobody answered. One boy let me catch his eye, so I asked him directly, "What would you like to be when you grow up?" He

---

91. www.haiguinet.com/forum/viewtopic.php?t=1010621, accessed June 29, 2012.

took a step forward, stood erect, and said, with verve, *wo yao dao zui jianku de difang wei renmin fuwu!* 我要到最艰苦的地方为人民服务! 'I want to go to the most stressful place to serve the people!' I said "Great!" and turned to another child. "What about you? What would you like to be when you grow up?" The child answered, in the same tone of voice, *wo yao dao zui jianku de difang wei renmin fuwu!* I asked two or three more, and each said *wo yao dao zui jianku de difang wei renmin fuwu!* The first child had clearly set an example—in what, with a foreigner watching, must have felt to them like a performance situation. The fact that each child pronounced the sentence in exactly the same way, without the variation of a single syllable, suggested that the phrase itself had likely been taught somewhere, perhaps in school or at a Young Pioneers meeting.

It left me wondering about what was going on in their minds. How much did the linguistic formula that they had repeated correspond to their inner thoughts? Had they used it to cover up various other ideas about, perhaps, being a Party secretary, a teacher, doctor, or fireman? Or had the "right answer" of *dao zui jianku de difang wei renmin fuwu!* temporarily—or maybe not so temporarily?—obliterated such other thoughts? The question, which of course applies to adults as well as to children (if not necessarily to the same degree), is how the playing of the language game comes to affect the ways a person thinks. Ritualized language, according to Maurice Bloch, by its very nature "both excludes explanation and hides this exclusion."[92] When Bloch notes that "you cannot argue with a song,"[93] he means that songs and other ritualized language not only tell you what to think, but, even more importantly, cut off your ability to look squarely at things that you otherwise should want to look at. In cases where ritualized language is backed by a strong political authority, any inclination even to try to argue, or to look elsewhere, is powerfully discouraged.

In looking at situations of repression in the modern world, many writers have noted that when a dominant ideological language takes hold, it tends to pervade a culture as a whole, including its victims. Henry Friedlander, surveying the language of the Nazi Holocaust, finds that "not only the perpetrators, but also the victims spoke the language of Nazi totali-

---

92. Bloch, "Symbols," p. 67.
93. Ibid., p. 71.

tarianism," including euphemisms for transporting, sorting, and killing of victims. "Nazi language was a prison language," and "both jailers and convicts spoke it."[94] Bloke Modisane, recalling his youth in South Africa, records instances of slipping into apartheid language—sometimes without meaning to, and at other times quite deliberately, as he wished to manipulate it to his advantage.[95] Someth May shows similar examples of adaption to, and manipulation of, the official language during Pol Pot's devastation of Cambodia.[96] Anna Wierzbicka finds an "unofficial, underground language of antipropaganda" in Soviet-dominated Poland.[97] Sarah Cook finds ordinary people playing a "language game" in Syria in the early twenty-first century.[98] Other examples are not hard to find.

Still we can ask: how much do patterns of *thinking* change because of language-game use? How much are people's worldviews affected? We know at least that the whole system of "thought reform" in China has always *assumed* that there are effects. Many veterans of the system, too, have noticed them. The philosopher Liu Xiaogan has this to say:

> The hot iron of "struggle worship" has left its mark upon the language habits, patterns of thinking, and ways of behavior of the Chinese people. In the lexicon of mainland Chinese, "struggle," "revolution," "rebellion," "resolute," and "thoroughgoing" are unequivocally positive in their connotations; they symbolize nobility and glory. On the other hand words like "retreat," "negotiate," "compromise," "tolerance," "gradualism," and "improve," have at times all been broadly rejected as terms with negative connotations, terms that symbolize shame and dishonor.[99]

---

94. Friedlander, "Manipulation of Language," p. 111 and p. 113, n. 28.

95. Bloke Modisane, *Blame Me on History* (London: Thames and Hudson, 1963), pp. 41, 59.

96. Someth May, *Cambodian Witness: The Autobiography of Someth May*, ed. James Fenton (London: Faber, 1986), pp. 146–151 and 175.

97. Anna Wierzbicka, "Antitotalitarian Language in Poland: Some Mechanisms of Linguistic Self-Defense," *Language in Society*, no. 19 (1990), pp. 1–59.

98. Sarah Cook, "The Language Game: Words of Power and the Power of Words in Syria and China." unpublished manuscript, 2010.

99. Liu Xiaogan 刘笑敢, "Mao Zedong yu douzheng chongbai lungang" 毛泽东与斗争崇拜论纲 [Mao Zedong and the worship of struggle: An outline], unpublished paper, 1996, p. 20.

The official language game of the Mao era, in Liu's view, forged the linguistic tools—the words, phrases, syntactic patterns—in which everyone in the culture talked and thought.

In Hu Fayun's novel *So It Was@Sars.come*, an elderly writer who was persecuted cruelly during the Mao era worries about how Chinese memory and cultural expression—including even his own, despite his conscious wishes—have been colored by Maoist politics. He tells friends how he recently found himself humming a tune and then felt shock to realize that the lyrics were "lifting my head, I gaze at the Big Dipper; in my heart, I long for Mao Zedong."[100] He then reflects:

> Even our own most personal emotional memories are soaked in an all-encompassing, all-pervading ideological culture. . . . Within a few decades, they took from us our ability to express suffering and sorrow. They took our ability to express love. What they gave us instead were fraudulent stand-ins. . . . Even today we *do not have* an authentic, untainted cultural vehicle with which to record our lives. . . . Other countries have it. Even the poorest and most backward countries have it. But the country with the largest population and the longest history on earth does not have it—you have to admit there is something horrifying about this. The long-term effect on our nation's psyche is still something that no one can measure.[101]

Other writers have observed how hard it can be to get "outside" the mindset of a political language game even when one wants to. Ji Fengyuan notes that Jung Chang, the well-known author of *Wild Swans: Three Daughters of China* and *Mao: The Unknown Story*,[102] viscerally detested Mao Zedong's Cultural Revolution as early as 1966 but could not conceive the notion of

---

100. Hu Fayun 胡发云, *Ruyan@sars.come* 如焉 *@sars.come* [So it was@sars.come], ch. 25. This passage was censored from the version of the novel published in Beijing, but has been restored in the translation by A. C. Clark, *Such Is This World@sars.come* (Dobbs Ferry, N.Y.: Ragged Banner, 2011), pp. 131–132.

101. Hu Fayun 胡发云, *Ruyan@sars.come* 如焉 *@sars.come* [So it was@sars.come] (Beijing: Zhongguo guoji guangbo chubanshe, 2006), pp. 75–76.

102. Jung Chang, *Wild Swans: Three Daughters of China* (London: Flamingo, 1992); and *Mao: The Unknown Story* (New York: Knopf, 2005).

blaming Mao himself until, in 1974, she happened across a piece of writing that came from outside the Maoist modes of expression.[103] Similarly, the literary critic Li Tuo, in analyzing the life-course of the famous modern writer Ding Ling, who absorbed the outlook of Maoist language at midcareer and apparently could not extricate herself from it even as she suffered two decades of banishment by the regime that it supported, comments in summary that "once a person enters within a certain discourse, to exit it becomes extremely difficult."[104]

A number of Chinese writers since the 1980s have recognized this problem and have sought, as it were, to "climb out" of official language and its worldview. This is not easy, because the act of climbing out of a language still requires a language, and one must use the language one has. The effort can become something like trying to climb out of one's skin. In the 1980s, for example, Li Tuo tried to abandon *zui* 最 'most' in his personal language use just because the term had been so abused during the Mao years (in phrases like *zui zui zui zhengque* 最最最正确 'most, most, most correct' . . . ; as mentioned ealier). But it was not easy to keep his promise to himself. Li found himself saying, inadvertently, things like *wo zui buxihuan zhei zhong yuyan* 我最不喜欢这种语言 'I can't stand this kind of language'.

One method for trying to exit official language has been to dive into another. Li Tuo has held that the true breakthrough in language—and therefore thought—in Chinese literature of the immediate post-Mao years was "misty poetry" (*menglong shi* 朦胧诗) more than the more numerous and widely read works of "scar" literature. Others have pointed out that one reason why Zhong Acheng's story "The Chess Master" seemed so fresh and new when it appeared in 1984 was that its language was fundamentally different from Maoist style.[105] It avoided not only Maoist political usage but much of the Western-influenced vocabulary and grammar that had come into Chinese since late-Qing times. In its phrase

---

103. Ji Fengyuan, *Linguistic Engineering*, p. 290.

104. Li Tuo 李陀, "Ding Ling bujiandan: Maotizhixia zhishifenzi zai huayu shengchanzhong de fuza jiaose" 丁玲不简单: 毛体制下知识分子在话语生产中的复杂角色 [Ding Ling is remarkable: The complex role of intellectuals in the production of discourse under the Maoist system], *Jintian* (Today), no. 3 (1993), p. 236.

105. Zhong Acheng 锺阿城, "Qiwang" 棋王 [The chess master], *Shanghai wenxue* [Shanghai literature], July 1984, pp. 15–35.

structure it resembled the simulated oral storytelling style of Ming-Qing fiction, a style that may have come easily to Zhong because "The Chess Master" and others of his stories had, in fact, originated in his oral storytelling to friends. Other critics have observed that one attraction of modernist language to Chinese writers in the 1980s (Mo Yan, Can Xue, Ma Yuan, Ge Fei, and others) has been, in part, its utility in breaking free from political and social conventions of standard written Chinese.[106] Ha Jin chooses to write in English, not his native Chinese, for similar reasons.

During the protest demonstrations of the spring of 1989, the issue of whether and how to climb out of official language generated controversy. Intellectuals who drafted the May 16 Declaration, a sharply worded critique of how the government was handling the protests, differed over what kind of language the declaration should use. Should the statement include words like *tongzhi* 同志 'comrade', *shehuizhuyi zuguo* 社会主义祖国 'socialist motherland', *jiefanghou* 解放后 'after Liberation', and *sanzhong quanhui* 三中全会 'third Party plenum'? To some degree these were questions about how much to identify the authors of the declaration with the Party-state. But they were also, more deeply, questions about whether use of official terminology draws one into a certain mind-set.

That such drawing-in can happen is clear from some of the language of overseas dissident groups in the years following the June Fourth massacre. Now driven into exile, where they were more free to state things as they wished, some of their phrases continued to resemble officialese: *wei Zhongguo minzhu er nuli fendou* 为中国民主而努力奋斗 'strive hard for Chinese democracy' *xianshen yu weida shiming* 献身于伟大使命 'devote oneself to the great mission', and so on. As I noted in the Introduction, in the summer of 1989 when refugees met to form a "Chinese Democratic Front," one faction argued that the use of preexisting officialese for the slogans they were writing would make them more effective, while the opposing faction felt that any use of such language whatsoever was too compromising.

In sum, the question of how much a political language game shapes a person's thought appears to have no easy answer. There can be little doubt

---

106. For example, Yang Xiaobin 杨小滨, "Fan yuyan: Xianfeng wenxue de xingshi wenti" 反语言: 先锋文学的形式问题 [Anti-language: The question of form in avant-garde literature], *Wenlunbao* [Hebei], July 25, 1988.

that it does contribute to the closing of minds, at least sometimes and to some extent. But it is also true that people resist language games, consciously and perhaps unconsciously as well. Moreover, because the games themselves can change, people sometimes just outlast them, or at least parts of them. Perhaps easier to analyze and to illustrate are questions about the ways people who have been involved with the contemporary Chinese language game have tried to cope with it or to exploit it to their own advantage. I turn next to those questions. I divide them into the two broad categories of how the game is played by (1) the rulers, who on the whole have been the originators of the game, and (2) the ruled, who have needed to adapt and respond to the game in various ways. In making this division I do not mean to suggest that every tactic within the game neatly falls on one or the other side of the divide. The push and pull of the interaction is more complex than that; my division is only a matter of organizational convenience.

How the Game Is Played: From the Side of the Rulers

When we turn to analyze the ways people in the Chinese government play the language game, there is a certain danger of focusing on parts and not seeing the whole. The regime's tactics have comprised a wide variety and have operated at several levels: in the connotations of words, in pressuring individual people, in political meetings within work-units, in society-wide campaigns, and so on. Each topic deserves attention, but to look at them one by one runs the risk of overlooking perhaps the most important point of all, which is to see how pervasive the whole enterprise is. Its parts work in concert, and the whole is stronger than the sum of the parts. It is not easy to encompass the whole picture at once, but Cao Changqing, in the opening paragraph of his essay "Linguistic Violence: The Power of Intimidation in Authoritarian Rule," has done as well as anyone:

> The most distinctive feature in the ideological project of the Communist Party of China is its language. The Party mobilizes not only its propaganda organs but all state organs to spread and implement its language system, the purpose of which is to influence, mold and

manipulate the language and thought processes of ordinary people in order to control how they think about certain questions and what they say about them. In this cause the Party has mustered the print and electronic media, book publishing, "political study" meetings, meetings that are supposed to be non-political, "confidential chats" with leaders, written "reflections on experience" and "reports on personal thinking," speeches at big assemblies and discussions within small groups, and other devices whose number and variety are constantly renewed with changing times, all with the goal of forcing people into a language system where they learn how to speak in conformity with the requirements of the Party: what to say, what not to say, how to put things, and what vocabulary to use.[107]

The breadth of scope of the regime's linguistic engineering is matched by the persistence with which its key tenets are pressed. When a political point matters, its assertion in the official language is unremitting. Zhou Liming, who was a vice consul in charge of propaganda at the Chinese Consulate in San Francisco until he defected after June 4, 1989, spoke as an insider as he explained, in a speech in 1991, how sheer repetition was a deliberate part of government strategy. As part of his explanation for how people could come to accept the whitewash of a massacre, Zhou cited Joseph Goebbels's famous line "If you tell a lie big enough and keep repeating it, people will eventually come to believe it."[108]

In a study of the Anti-Rightist Movement of 1957, Michael Schoenhals compiled a list of terms that were used to drive home, through repetition, the labels that indicated the ways "rightists" were evil. These included "rightist hard-core element," "old-line rightist," "rightist pathbreaker," "vicious rightist 'counselor,'" "rightist careerist," "utterly evil rightist element," "rightist wolf in sheep's clothing," "sinister and ruthless rightist element," and others. Schoenhals found these phrases in official newspapers that were published between July 27 and September 4, 1957. From the same sources, he compiled another list, this one of phrases that described

---

107. Cao Changqing, "Yuyan baoli," p. 46.
108. "Communist Propaganda: The Art of Deceiving People," *China Forum Newsletter* 1, no. 1 (January 1991), p. 4.

rightists with the word *fan* 反 'anti-'. The word had appeared in abundance, apparently in order to make it clear that rightists, whatever their descriptions, were united in their opposition to the Party, the people, and Communism. Schoenhals lists these terms: "utterly arrogant and utterly reactionary and utterly despicable anti-Party element," "anti-Communist and anti-People conspiratorial activist," "anti-Party buffoon-gang accomplice," "anti-Party careerist, traitor, and spy turned anti-Communist vanguard," "anti-Communist specialist," "anti-Party 'eulogist,'" "anti-Communist 'valiant general,'" "anti-Communist black gang strategist," "old-line anti-Communist," "anti-Party clique 'military counselor,'" "anti-Communist 'rocket gun,'" and "rightist element oozing anti-Communist toxin from the depth of the soul."[109] Later in the Mao years this sort of compulsive political language reached even into dictionaries. Ji Fengyuan has compared dictionaries published at different times in contemporary China and finds that the end of the Mao era was a high point in the politicization of dictionary examples. A 1976 English-Chinese dictionary illustrates the verb "live," for example, with the sentence "without the Party and Chairman Mao I could not have lived to see today's happiness"; "attribute" is illustrated by the sentence "we attribute all our successes to the wise leadership of the Communist Party of China"; and "wherever" gets the example "we will go wherever the Party directs us."[110]

The true power of this kind of repetitive, insistent, and pervasive political terminology shows itself not in things like dictionary examples, where an editor has a right, after all, to pick examples arbitrarily. Strong-arm language is most impressive when it contradicts a person's own perceptions and own memory—and wins anyway. For example, Beijing citizens appearing on state-run television in the days following June 4, 1989, used "counterrevolutionary riot" to describe events that until two days earlier everyone had been calling a "democracy movement" or "student protests"—events that were likely to have been extremely vivid in their own memories. We can only imagine the anxiety and inner turmoil that

---

109. Michael Schoenhals, "'Non-people' in the People's Republic of China: A Chronicle of Terminological Ambiguity," *Indiana Working Papers on Language and Politics in Modern China*, no. 4 (July 1994), p. 13.

110. Ji Fengyuan, *Linguistic Engineering*, pp. 233–234.

must have accompanied the mismatch between memory and politically correct usage. Orwell dramatizes this problem in his famous episode in *1984* in which Winston Smith, attached to a torture machine, is asked how many fingers are the four that are held before his face. Four? "And if the party says that it is not four but five—then how many?"[111] After stumbling, Winston finally gets the right answer: "Five! Five! Five!" A similar dramatization lives in the lore of Chinese tradition in the episode, recorded by Sima Qian in *The Records of History* (*Shiji* 史記), in which a powerful imperial official tested the loyalty of courtiers by presenting a deer to the second emperor of Qin and asking that the assembled courtiers acknowledge it to be a horse. When the exercise was over, the official found ways to put to death all who had called a deer a deer.[112]

In the official language of contemporary China, this sort of "strong-arm lie" technique draws some of its power from the mutual reinforcement of interlocking parts. Medium-sized lies fit together in ways that allow a big lie to take shape. Not only, for example, did unarmed protesters in 1989 suddenly turn into "rioters" and "hooligans." They were also—despite their large numbers—a "tiny minority." Worried for the future of their own country, they took actions that were "instigated by foreigners." Daring to tell the truth, they were "spreading rumors." And so on. These various linguistic tags were not matters of accident. For a long time, ever since the 1950s, it had been part of the job of the Communist Party's Department of Propaganda to keep media workers aware of exactly which terms to use in characterizing politically sensitive people and events. Labels change, and are updated, as the political needs of the Party—as viewed by its top leaders—go through stages. Michael Schoenhals has edited a collection of instructions that were sent to news editors in the year 1979 through a publication called *Xuanchuan dongtai* 宣传动态 (Propaganda trends). Topics such as the following are addressed, with reasons for the specific word choices noted: "Henceforth, no longer refer to *Dalai's Renegade Clique*," "Do Not Accuse the Vietnamese of *Lack of Gratitude*,"

---

111. George Orwell, *1984*, pt. 3, ch. 2.
112. Sima Qian 司馬遷, *Shiji* 史記 [Records of history] Qinshihuang benji 秦始皇本紀. The passage is translated by Yang Hsien-yi and Gladys Yang in Szuma Chien, *Selections from Records of the Historian* (Peking: Foreign Languages Press, 1979), pp. 192–196.

"Phase Out *Educated Youth*," "Use *Appeasement* with Care," "We suggest *Achieve Wealth Through Diligence*," and "Criteria for Writing about the Seamy Side of Socialism."[113]

Such guidelines are ephemeral. They enter and exit political grace according to the regime's needs of the day. But certain others are perennial. They sink in, begin to seem normal, and eventually become so well established that people overlook the fact that originally they were rooted in political design. An example is the word *renmin* 人民 'people', which is nearly ubiquitous in the names of government-related things. The names of the currency, the post office, the media, many buildings, and nearly every government office at every level include the word *renmin*. The original purpose of using the term was to claim that these Party-controlled institutions "belong to the people"; after decades of use, however, the word *renmin* became so routine as to have, in practice, no content at all. By the early twenty-first century, only a bookish person might notice any irony when the People's Armed Police suppress a protest by the people.

The term *lingdao* 领导 'leader(ship)' may be an even better example. In their original meanings, the two components of this phrase, *ling* and *dao*, are both verbs that describe the leading of a person who *follows willingly*, even gratefully. A paradigmatic example of *ling* is what an usher does in a church or a theater; *dao*, originally, is something like what a tour guide does. Do these activities resemble what a *lingdao* does within China's political system? Hardly. Overwhelmingly, people in China follow their *lingdao* because they have to, not because they choose to. Words like "authority," "ruler," or "boss" would be more literally descriptive of what a *lingdao* does, but if one puts such words directly into Chinese—using terms like *quanwei* 权威, *dangju* 当局, or *laoban* 老板—the rhetorical flavor changes immediately. The *lingdao* themselves view such terms as "hostile to the socialist system." They prefer the euphemism, which saves their face, because face is one root of their power. A term like *lingdao* has the added advantage that it makes any objector seem, at least at the rhetorical level, to be wayward or ungrateful.

---

113. Michael Schoenhals, ed. and trans., *Selections from* Propaganda Trends, *an Organ of the CCP Central Propaganda Department* (Armonk, N.Y.: M. E. Sharpe, 1992).

Do words like *renmin* or *lingdao* actually affect the ways people think and behave, or have they become—like the "dead metaphors" we considered in Chapter 2—so ordinary that they are simply standard tags? In many cases, no doubt, they are standard tags. The *People's Daily* is just the name of a newspaper. Still, their persistence in fossil form does ground concepts in a certain way, subtly softening the image of authoritarian rule. The fresh, unfossilized political usages of the kind that appear in *Xuanchuan dongtai* no doubt have more immediate effects. The Soviet theoretician L. O. Resnikov, in summarizing the views of Lenin and Stalin on this general question, wrote that "language [is] a powerful tool which can be used to affect thoughts, feelings, and especially behaviour" and that this is something that "Marxism teaches us."[114] This Soviet approach to language as a tool in thought-engineering arrived in China primarily in the 1950s, when it merged with assumptions that were deep in Chinese tradition about speech as moral performance. The result, for China's rulers, was an enduring confidence that government-prescribed words could indeed produce "correct" behavior in citizens.

In her book *Linguistic Engineering*, Ji Fengyuan shows—at least for the extreme case of the late Mao years in China—that this confidence was justified. Government-sponsored terminology, applied with both force and subtlety, did have substantial effects. Ji draws on theoretical literature as well as China studies to sort out some of the psychological mechanisms that went into the "engineering" of thought. She offers a useful summary,[115] which includes the following. *Mere exposure* to terms makes a significant difference; in addition, a *validity effect* takes hold when a person is aware of being part of a large group (i.e., when everyone accepts something, then I tend to as well). Group pressure is brought more intensely into focus in *political study* sessions where "correct" oral performance is required. Personal *models* are important in showing people how to speak and behave correctly, and *self-perception theory* can explain how going through the outward motions of believing something can lead a person into actually believing it. *Higher-order conditioning* can explain how the well-known connotations of

---

114. Cited in J. W. Young, *Totalitarian Language: Orwell's Newspeak and Its Nazi and Communist Antecedents* (Charlottesville: University Press of Virginia, 1991), p. 211.

115. Ji Fengyuan, *Linguistic Engineering*, pp. 27–37.

certain words (like the negative connotations of a word like "poverty" or "disease") can spread, through repeated association, to political terms (like "capitalism").

"Higher-order conditioning" has a good example in the 1983 campaign against "spiritual pollution." The targets of this campaign were foreign influences—everything from AIDS to rock music to ideas about human rights. People naturally had differing opinions about whether some of these things are good or bad, but the blanket label *wuran* 污染 'pollution' was hard to argue against. Negative connotations "leaked" from the label to all of the items that it covered, and anyone defending "pollution" in any form started from a position of obvious weakness. In a parallel manner, positive connotations could also leak from one item to another. For example, *aiguo* 爱国 'patriotism' has been overwhelmingly positive in Chinese since late-Qing times, but in the Communist era it has routinely been paired with *aidang* 爱党 'love the Party' to form *aidang aiguo* and has even gone on to form the mellifluous *qiyan* phrase *aidang aiguo airenmin* 爱党爱国爱人民 'love the Party, love the country, love the people'. The phrase rolls off the tongue and gives the air, by its rhythm and its repetition, of being inexorably right. It is hard for any person using it to stop and say, "Wait! Why is a political party heading up this phrase?" The phrase arrives as a whole package.

It can be a problem, for the Party's language engineers, that politically correct phrases sometimes gain momentum on their own. The Propaganda Department sometimes acknowledges this problem when it issues orders—such as those published in *Propaganda Trends*—to *stop* using certain phrases. When phrases sound good, and feel good, and users get used to thinking in the terms that they set, it is not always easy to apply the brakes. In the late 1970s, for example, the term *fanshi pai* 凡是派 'whateverists'— which was used to refer to doctrinaire Maoists because they insisted on "whatever" Mao said—turned out to be so appealing to people who were fed up with Maoists that it continued in popular use even after officials, embarrassed at the term's spurt in popularity, had called for its end.

The problem of the momentum of phrases also appears when top-level policy takes a sharp turn and language use cannot turn as quickly. During the Cultural Revolution, for example, it was common to say that the people needed to "struggle" against "anti-Party" people like "revisionists" and "capitalist-roaders" who were "opposed to socialism," aimed to "usurp power," and so on. Then, in October 1976, the political landscape changed abruptly when leaders of the Cultural Revolution, now relabeled the "Gang of Four," were arrested. Writers and editors across China were called on to denounce the Gang of Four, but what language were they to use? Ji Fengyuan quotes from an English-language textbook that apparently was hastily pulled together in Henan Province in 1977. Two young people are in dialogue:

A: The Gang of Four Anti-Party clique wanted to usurp Party and state power and restore capitalism. We Red Guards, never allow them!

B. That's right. The struggle against the Gang of Four is a life-and-death struggle between the proletariat and the bourgeoisie, between socialism and capitalism, and between Marxism and revisionism.[116]

It would be harsh to conclude that the English teachers who constructed this dialogue, who after all may have been terrified at the time, could not think except in jargon. They may have been well aware that to say that the former leaders of the Cultural Revolution are now, suddenly, representatives of the bourgeoisie does not make any sense; they may have opted (and who could blame them?) to play their language game in a way that seemed to maximize their possibilities for safety. Still, the poverty of their options in vocabulary was a problem. They apparently felt that their only reliable store of negatively charged terms lay inside the same old bag that they had long been using—and now were using anachronistically.

In a broader sense, the entire corpus of post-Mao "scar" literature has sometimes been criticized for aiming to expose the excesses of the Mao years but doing so in language and literary forms that in many ways inherited Maoist style.[117] There is considerable merit in this criticism. Fiction written in the immediate post-Mao years tends, just as during the Mao years, to be set in a good-and-evil world in which heroes and villains vie over political right and wrong. The continuity is worth pondering,

---

116. Ibid., p. 307.

117. Li Tuo, for example, makes this criticism, in "Xiandai hanyu yu dangdai wenxue" 現代漢語與當代文學 [Modern Chinese and contemporary literature], *Xindi wenxue* [New land literature], no. 6, p. 40.

because more than just style and form are at stake; patterns of thinking—conceptual categories and worldview—also seem to carry over, despite claims that a watershed has passed. This kind of subtle but powerful continuity is part of what Li Tuo has uncovered in his careful study of Ding Ling.

As an aside on the topic of the "momentum" of political phrases in Chinese, it can be amusing to note how some sayings in Chinese Communist history have taken on an iconic status, not only in China but around the world, even though their origins are not what most people suppose. For example, the phrase *mozhe shitou guo he* 摸着石头过河 'cross the river by feeling the rocks' is routinely attributed to Deng Xiaoping, who felt that China needed a gradual and practical approach to the uncharted task of economic reform. Deng did hold these views, and did use that phrase, but the political use of the phrase originated with Deng's rival Chen Yun, first in 1950 and again in a major speech in 1980.[118] Deng is also famous for the phrase *buguan bai mao hei mao, zhuo dao laoshu jiushi hao mao* 不管白猫黑猫，捉到老鼠就是好猫 'it matters not whether a cat is white or black; if it catches mice it is a good cat'. The phrase is a famous emblem of Deng's pragmatism: don't be bothered with ideological labels; if something works, then let it work. It is far from clear, however, that that white cat was not in fact brown. A Sichuan aphorism (Deng was from Sichuan) says *huang mao, hei mao, zhiyao zhuazhu laoshu jiushi hao mao* 黄猫黑猫只要抓住老鼠就是好猫 'brown cat, black cat, if it catches mice it's a good cat'. We also hear via Zhuo Lin, Deng Xiaoping's wife, that Deng was fond of Pu Songling's collection of stories *Liaozhai zhiyi* 聊斋志异 (Strange tales of Liaozhai) and liked to bring it with him while traveling; the section of the novel called *quguai* 驱怪 (Expelling demons) contains the sentence 黄狸黑狸，得鼠者雄 *huang li hei li, deshuzhe xiong* 'brown cat, black cat, the rat-catcher is the more powerful'.[119] Another example is the phrase *zhifu guangrong* 致富光荣, rendered in English as "to get rich is glorious," which is widely accepted as a hallmark of the Deng era. Scholars have not been

---

118. Chen Yun, "Zhongyang gongzuo huiyishang de jianghua 中央工作会议上的讲话 [Speech at the Central Work Committee], December 16, 1980.

119. Ma Ruifang 马瑞芳, *Yangzhou xinwenwang* 扬州新闻网 [Yangzhou news net], March 14, 2008; www.28gl.com/html/86/t-30786.html, accessed June 30, 2012.

able to establish whether Deng invented this phrase, or indeed whether he even said it.

Iconic phrases from Mao Zedong have also grown reputations that exceed their origins. Mao is widely believed, for example, to have proclaimed at Tiananmen on October 1, 1949: *Zhongguo renmin zhan qilai le* 中国人民站起来了 'the Chinese people have stood up'. In fact, Mao opened his famous speech that day with the words *Zhonghua renmin gongheguo zhongyang renmin zhengfu jintian chengli le* 中华人民共和国中央人民政府今天成立了! 'the central people's government of the People's Republic of China today is established!' The phrase about the people standing up is authentic but was delivered ten days earlier, on September 21, at a meeting of the Chinese People's Political Consultative Conference. Mao is also well known outside China for having said, apparently in 1968, "women hold up half the sky," but this phrase in English translation (and translations into other languages) oddly omits a key word. In Chinese, what Mao is quoted as having said is *funü neng ding banbiantian* 妇女能顶半边天 'women *can* hold up half the sky', not that they do in fact hold it up. It does not take a feminist to recognize that Chinese peasant women, in their many kinds of hard work, had already been holding up half or more of the sky for several centuries before Mao made his comment. In asserting only that an equal contribution from women is possible, not actual, Mao was hardly the feminist that many in the West took him to be.

Many of the ways the regime "plays the language game" have to do with force. I have referred to the "forceful lie," "psychological conditioning," and political terms that have "momentum." All these might be called, broadly speaking, the "push" side of the regime's language engineering, but there is another side, a "pull" side, that is at least as important. Here the effort is to induce willing compliance from people, to cast the world in such a way that it seems only right that the regime should be in charge, only right that people should want to obey, and wrong, indeed peculiar, to consider going astray.

The fundamental principle of the "pull" side of language engineering is to place the Party, especially the highest levels of the Party, at the moral center of the world, so that anyone who opposes it is automatically on the defensive. One way this is done is through implications about the sizes of groups. The official language makes it clear that a majority—the mainstream of "the people"—is always on the side of the Party. The Party's opponents are therefore always a minority, and often a "tiny" one. Sometimes—especially in times of emergency—this centrality of the Party is stated baldly. After the 1989 Beijing massacre, for example, when the moral image of the Party was at a nadir, the *People's Daily* flatly announced a "socialist education" campaign in which "patriotism means love of the socialist People's Republic of China. To carry out socialist education is to carry out love of the Party."[120] In more normal times this kind of overt statement about the lovability of the political center is avoided, though, because there is a certain loss of face in having to make the claim in such a straightforward way. It is preferable to *imply* the moral centrality of the Party.

Such implication is achieved in several ways. One, as noted, has been the use of the word *renmin* 'people' in the names of innumerable institutions and offices involving Party rule. The usages become so ordinary, so accepted, that it seems axiomatic that the Party and the people are at one. Any opponent of the Party-plus-people is *automatically* (1) a minority, (2) removed from the center, and (3) morally inferior. These three notions (minority status, displacement from the center, and moral inferiority), although analytically separable, are assumed in the terms of the official language to imply one another. A rival group to the mainstream one in the top leadership, for example, can be called a *jituan* 集团 'clique'. In the official language a *jituan* might be powerful, and thus dangerous, but it is always decentered and can never be truly popular. Chiang Kai-shek, even as president of China, headed a *jituan*. Liu Shaoqi and Lin Biao, in their times, had *jituan*. Mao Zedong's wife, Jiang Qing, was at the political and moral center until Mao died, when suddenly she, too, headed a *jituan*.

People who are as fully decentered and wrong as a *jituan*, but not as high-ranking or powerful, tend to be only *fenzi* 分子 'elements'—a term the Chinese Communists borrowed from Soviet-era Russian. There have been *dizhufenzi* 地主分子 'landlord elements', *youpaifenzi* 右派分子 'rightist elements', *zichanjiejifenzi* 资产阶级分子 'bourgeois elements', *bufafenzi* 不法分子 'illegal elements', and many other kinds. A blanket category called simply *huaifenzi* 坏分子 'bad elements' has included everything

---

120. *Renmin ribao* 人民日报 [People's daily], June 2, 1991, p. 1.

from criminals to drug addicts to dissidents to gays. After the 1989 massacre, there were *liusifenzi* 六四分子 'June Fourth elements'. A small number of *fenzi* words do not carry heavy negative coloration. *Zhishifenzi* 知识分子 'intelligentsia', which is a loan word from the Soviet Union, is probably the most obvious example.

We have noted how the terms *yixiaocuo* 一小撮 'a small bunch' and *jishaoshu* 极少数 'tiny minority' have been used since the early years of the People's Republic to label groups that rulers wish to denigrate. These terms have continued in use into the twenty-first century to refer to Tibetans, Uighurs, Falun Gong adherents, democracy advocates, and others. In a *Tibet Daily* editorial on the disturbances in Lhasa in March 2008, *jishaoshu* and *fenzi* were combined in the double-barreled negative label *jishaoshu bufafenzi* 极少数不法分子 'tiny minority of illegal elements'.[121] Examples such as this show the implicit connection in the official language between the ideas of *tiny, evil,* and *potent.* The smallness of the opposition reinforces the implication that it is evil, and if something is both tiny and evil it must be fairly potent and therefore is dangerous. Note that these ideas in their origins—outside the language game—do not have these connotations. Normally, if things are as disparate as the word *fenzi* suggests, as well as extremely few in number, they would be something like needles in haystacks, or marbles in the ocean. There would be no reason to get very upset about them. But in official rhetoric, a "tiny minority" can be enough to warrant a call for hundreds of millions of people to *tigao jingti* 提高警惕 'raise vigilance' and *jianjue fandui* 坚决反对 'resolutely oppose' the small group. Because of the connection between *tiny, evil,* and *potent,* phrases such as *yixiaocuo* and *jishaoshu* have the paradoxical effect of belittling and magnifying their object at the same time. But the paradox does not matter in the playing of the language game. Indeed it helps, because the point of terms like *yixiaocuo* and *jishaoshu* is not, after all, to seriously estimate the size of an opposition but to establish that it is evil and dangerous. The implicit contradiction of "little group" and "big problem" helps to do this because it shows how strong the evil little group can be.

Phrases like "small bunch" and "tiny minority" have the added advantage of leaving plenty of room for the average citizen, at the receiving end

---

121. "Zhenfeng xiangdui jianjue huiji, quebao Xizang zizhiqu shehui wending."

of the rhetoric, to choose to join the majority. If troublemakers are a small minority, then the choice for you, the average citizen, is easy: come to the center and join the mainstream. If you do, the safety of knowing that the authorities approve is reinforced by safety of numbers. A person who joins the mainstream does not have to defend the choice.

Official language can create the illusion of a mainstream where originally none existed. On any given subject, before the official language game begins to address it, people might have a natural variety of views, and many might have no view at all. Is long hair attractive? Is Falun Gong good for one's health? Is the Dalai Lama a sincere man? Without official intervention, it is unlikely that Chinese people would have much consensus on such questions. But once it becomes an official view that long hair suggests spiritual pollution (as happened in 1983), that Falun Gong is an evil cult (after 1999), or that the Dalai Lama is a splittist (several times, but especially in 2008), then people everywhere in China have an incentive to join in these views, and a "mainstream opinion" is manufactured. This sort of opinion is artificial in its origins, but eventually it can turn into a very real thing—if not "opinion" in the original sense, then at least recognition of what the officially "correct" view is. In extreme cases, a manufactured view can represent opinion that differs radically from what original opinion was. In the late Mao years, for example, farmers in many parts of China wanted to dismantle "people's communes" and return to family farming. But as long as Mao was alive, the official view, accepted as mainstream, was that people loved the people's communes. In a society that lacked press freedom, and where "incorrect" expression of any kind was suppressed in public, it could happen that a large majority of people might in fact have a consensus but have no way of knowing that this was so. If numbers alone were what mattered, then, on the question of whether to dismantle the communes, Mao and his lieutenants, the creators of the "mainstream view," in fact were the small minority.

The claim of moral correctness at high levels in the Party-state is further enhanced in the official language by abstract vocabulary of the kind I have analyzed above under "lexicon." Party Central does not think things over, it "applies consideration" (*jiayi kaolü* 加以考虑); unlike ordinary people, who simply do things, Party Central "adopts measures" (*caiqu cuoshi* 采取措施). On matters of *yuanze* 原则 'principle', the Party cannot but *jianchi*

坚持 'be resolute', and so on. Such vocabulary, consistently applied, generates a lofty, august atmosphere. It is the verbal counterpart of the physical arrangements in the great meeting halls where major Party meetings take place: huge glossy red banners bearing gold-colored Chinese characters, long tables covered in red cloth, bearing neatly arrayed white teacups, one before each chair, spaced as if by a machine. All of this, the verbal and the nonverbal together, is *paichang* 排场 'ceremonial extravagance'. *Paichang* has deep roots in Chinese culture and has taken on an especially exaggerated form in Communist China, due in part to borrowings from Soviet culture. *Paichang* is not just for show; it contributes importantly to face, prestige, and political power. To be able to present a decorous display of language is an important way of claiming political power and attracting respect for it.

The assumption is well established in Chinese culture that correct language use, when properly internalized in a person, leads to personal "cultivation," which gives rise to appropriate moral behavior, which in turn provides legitimate authority to rule. Such things as a person's calligraphy, or the ability to write a good poem, have been seen as outward signs of moral character. These assumptions, despite Maoist campaigns to "destroy the four olds," have survived well into the Communist period and thrived even within Maoist culture itself.

Mao supplied his own calligraphy to many institutions, where it stood as signs both of his political patronage and of the receiving institution's fealty to him. Recipients included the *People's Daily*, the *Guangming Daily*, and many provincial newspapers, as well as universities, publishing houses, railway stations, and—as Richard Kraus points out in his fascinating book about calligraphy and politics in the People's Republic *Brushes with Power*—even such obscure places as the mosquito nets at Fujian Teachers College.[122] In 1978 students at Zhongshan University wanted to start a student-run literary magazine but were having trouble getting political permission from campus authorities to do so. When the central literary commissar Zhou Yang came to Guangzhou for a visit, the students went

---

122. Richard Curt Kraus, *Brushes with Power: Modern Politics and the Chinese Art of Calligraphy* (Berkeley: University of California Press, 1981), p. ix.

to see him and asked if he would be so kind as to donate his calligraphy for the front cover of their inaugural issue. Zhou did, and with that imprimatur the students were able to launch their magazine. Around the same time, Marshal Ye Jianying donated his calligraphy for the front gate of Zhongshan University, an act that symbolized his broad endorsement of the university as well as its loyalty to him.

The political symbolism of poetry has been important as well. As noted in Chapter 1, Mao Zedong coveted his image as poet, and Zhou Enlai's admirers used countless poems to praise Zhou. In 1978 Chen Yi, a former mayor of Shanghai and foreign minister of the People's Republic, published a collection of his poems in two thick volumes.[123] (A significant difference between Chinese political culture and that of the modern West emerges if one imagines, just as a thought experiment, what the reaction might be if a leading Western politician were to announce publication of a collection of poems.) Since the 1980s, the publication of poetry and donation of calligraphy by high-ranking Communists has declined, but the underlying assumption that formal political language carries an air of exaltation and is related to the personal power of leaders has remained very much in force. Such language is still common at formal meetings and in the media, where it continues, in its presentation and delivery, to underscore the connection between proper language, morality, and political legitimacy.

One consequence of this persisting tradition is that whenever a problem arises—whenever something appears that might detract from the *paichang* that supports power—it is difficult to face the matter squarely. To face it squarely, or to name it plainly, can entail a loss of face, might damage the aura of exaltation, and such damage, in the terms of the political culture, might be detrimental to power. Problems are therefore dealt with indirectly—by looking askance, using euphemisms, or the like.

For example, after Wei Jingsheng wrote his famous poster in 1978 calling for democracy as a "fifth modernization," he was arrested and sent to prison not for the challenge that he had issued, direct address of which

---

123. Chen Yi 陈毅, *Chen Yi shici xuanzhu* 陈毅诗词选注 [Annotated collection of the poetry of Chen Yi] (Beijing: Beijing chubanshe, 1978).

would have embarrassed China's rulers, but for "passing military secrets to a foreigner." Many others who have challenged the ruling authority by raising questions about corruption, fraud, environmental damage, and other such topics have been punished on charges that are beside the point, and often false, but convenient to the rulers from a cosmetic point of view. To argue over the real issues would detract from the aura that supports power.

One of the most common of these charges-of-convenience has been "revealing state secrets" (applied with no sense of the irony of the resulting association of things like corruption and fraud with state secrets). It is one of the most feared charges, because it can carry heavy penalties. Other such charges have been rumor mongering, various kinds of sexual misbehavior, and corruption. (He Qinglian has documented cases in which journalists who expose corruption are charged with corruption.)[124] The blind lawyer and dissident Chen Guangcheng, who defended women who were resisting forced abortion, was imprisoned in 2006 after charges of assembling a crowd to disrupt traffic.[125] The conflation of sexual misbehavior and political misbehavior, in which the former is stated when the latter is meant, has been recurrent. In the 1983 campaign to "oppose spiritual pollution," long hair, premarital sex, drug use, and political dissidence all counted as spiritual pollution. Since then, intermittent campaigns to *yan da* 严打 'strike hard' have aimed at "hooligan crime"—robbery, rape, kidnapping, and so on—but have prominently included, especially in the early 2000s, *sao huang* 扫黄 'sweeping up the yellow [i.e., pornography]'. This expression has been used as a broad label for various things that authorities identify as obscene, including dissident politics. It, too, is *huang*, and can be swept away during a *yan da* campaign. In May 2009 the Ministry of Industry and Information Technology announced that every personal computer sold in China beginning July 1 of that year would need to include "Green Dam Youth Escort" software designed to avoid "the poi-

---

124. See He's accounts of the cases of Gao Qinrong and Zhang Chongbo, quoted in Perry Link, review of He Qinglian, *Zhongguo zhengfu ruhe kongzhi meiti* 中国政府如何控制媒体 [How the Chinese government controls the media], *New York Review of Books* 52, no. 3 (February 24, 2005), p. 37.

125. Philip P. Pan, "Chinese to Prosecute Peasant Who Resisted One-Child Policy," *Washington Post*, July 8, 2006, p. A12.

soning of our youth's minds by harmful information on the Internet."[126] The order characterized "harmful information" as *disu zhi feng* 低俗之风 'vulgarity', but Chinese Internet users were quick to complain that disapproved political opinion was covered as well.

The foregoing examples of euphemism might seem clumsy and simpleminded, but their functions in repressive politics are far-reaching and worth analyzing in more detail. In some cases, the point of a euphemism is to disguise the identity of the person who causes others to suffer. This can be as simple as the naming of a scapegoat. For example, when horrific accounts of the Great Leap famine were reported to Mao and other top Party leaders in the summer of 1960, and when it could not have been more obvious that Mao and others at the top were responsible, Mao said: "many landlords, rich peasants, counterrevolutionaries and bad elements have seized political power and committed evil acts."[127] Other techniques of disguise are more subtle. We have seen above, for example, how Chinese political slogans often omit subjects. In the *yan da* 'strike hard' campaigns of the 1990s, exactly *who* was instructing the police to be severe? It was convenient that the grammar of Chinese slogans allows this item to remain unspecified. No one had to be named as possible perpetrator. (A similar effect in political English is achieved by use of the passive voice: "It has been decided that . . .") Even when a doer is named, the connection to past wrongdoing can remain fuzzy. In 1980, for example, China's official media began to list Kang Sheng, the much-feared head of the secret police under Mao, as one more post-Mao villain, alongside Lin Biao and the Gang of Four. But the references to Kang, even in blaming him, skirted the delicate question of his role of running the secret police. Instead, the standard reference to him was *lilun quanwei* 理论权威 'authority on theory'.

Political euphemisms, in China and elsewhere, are used not just to mask perpetrators but, even more commonly, to obfuscate what they have done. Orwell shows how this can be done through abstraction, or what he calls "sheer cloudy vagueness":

126. Human Rights in China, "Chinese Government Orders Computer Manufacturers to Pre-install Filtering Software," www.hrichina.org/content/301, June 8, 2009, accessed June 30, 2012.

127. Yang Jisheng, *Tombstone: The Great Chinese Famine, 1958–1962*, translated by Stacy Mosher and Guo Jian (New York: Farrar, Straus and Giroux, 2012), p. 61.

> Defenceless villages are bombarded from the air, the inhabitants driven out into the countryside, the cattle machine-gunned, the huts set on fire with incendiary bullets: this is called *pacification*. Millions of peasants are robbed of their farms and sent trudging along the roads with no more than they can carry: this is called *transfer of population* or *rectification of frontiers*. People are imprisoned for years without trial, or shot in the back of the neck or sent to die of scurvy in Arctic lumber camps: this is called *elimination of unreliable elements*. Such phraseology is needed if one wants to name things without calling up mental pictures of them.[128]

Nazi language avoided "calling up mental pictures" by using euphemistic words like *Aktion* 'action'. There were *Grossaktion* 'big actions', *Kleinaktion* 'small actions', *Einzelaktion* 'individual actions', *Studentenaktion* 'student actions', *Allgemeine Befriedungsaktion* 'general pacification actions', and others, and they referred to things like roundups, incarcerations, deportations, and murder.[129] A similar euphemism in Mao's China was *jieji douzheng* 阶级斗争 'class struggle', which became a dreaded phrase, especially at the height of the Cultural Revolution. The word *douzheng* originally means "struggle," so it might not seem entirely a euphemism. But we should view it that way, because the intensity and variety of the cruelty involved went well beyond ordinary "struggle." It included ransacking homes, burning books, public humiliation, beatings, torture, eye-gougings, killings, demands that families pay for the bullets that killed their loved ones, and even—as Zheng Yi has carefully documented—such extreme atrocities as the ritual eating of bits of flesh of murdered "class enemies."[130]

The term *jieji douzheng* dwindled quickly from view during the post-Mao years, but other well-known euphemisms lived on. *Laodong jiaoyang* 劳动教养 'education through labor', which lasted well into the twenty-first century, was even more feared than *laodong gaizao* 劳动改造 'reform through labor'. Both were euphemisms for labor camps, but "education

---

128. Orwell, "Politics and the English Language, p. 173.
129. Friedlander, "Manipulation of Language," pp. 110, 113.
130. Zheng Yi 鄭義, *Hongse jinianbei* 紅色紀念碑 [Red memorial] (Taipei: Huashi wenhua gongsi, 1993), pp. 2–51.

through labor" was actually worse than "reform through labor" because it was an administrative measure, not a criminal punishment—which meant that it had no fixed terms of service. One received (was grateful for?) "re-education" as long as authorities said one needed it. In 2009, when Chinese government censors closed certain websites for the sake, they said, of President Hu Jintao's ideal of "harmony" (*hexie* 和谐), Chinese netizens turned the euphemism on its head by inventing the use of *hexie* as a transitive verb. To write that a website *bei hexie* 被和谐 'has been harmonized' came to mean that authorities had closed it down.

Political euphemisms not only turn unpleasant things into abstractions—or, as Orwell says, make them "cloudy"—but also prettify them. "Education" sounds better than "forced labor," and "harmony" of course sounds better than "coercion." I have noted how metaphors of "cleaning" or "purifying" were attractive to several twentieth-century authoritarian regimes as they carried out unspeakable acts of cruelty. It is worth probing the reasons why the perpetrators of violence or repression like to prettify. What exactly does this achieve? Superficial pleasantness is one reason, of course, but there are others.

One is that even if a person believes that a certain violent act is right, the same person is often aware that other people, observing, may not agree. In these cases, prettification serves the purpose of deflecting criticism others might bring, even if the doer, left to his or her own conscience, might not think that euphemism is necessary. A chilling example of this sort of mind-set is that of Nazi Special Services militiamen who, as Simon Wiesenthal has reported, felt no need for euphemism because no evidence of their killing would survive to be observed: "we will destroy the evidence together with you," they said to prisoners. "And even if some proof should remain and some of you survive, people will say that the events you describe are too monstrous to be believed."[131]

In other cases, third-party observers are not relevant. The need for prettification can arise wholly inside perpetrators of outrageous acts when their consciences or moral upbringing conflicts with something else—an order from above, pressure from peers, or aroused passions within

---

131. Simon Wiesenthal, *The Murderers Are Among Us*, quoted in Primo Levi, *The Drowned and the Saved* (New York: Vintage, 1989), pp. 11–12.

themselves—and they are led to do things that their better selves would rather not have done. In such cases, euphemism helps the perpetrator *whether or not* other people are looking. Primo Levi offers a number of examples of this kind of inner conflict in people whom he observed running Nazi death camps. "The person who has inflicted the wound," Levi writes, "pushes the memory deep down, to be rid of it, to alleviate the feeling of guilt."[132] In the organization of the camps themselves, Levi shows, a number of arrangements made it possible that people would not have to look squarely at what was happening: the Special Services (SS) personnel, who ran the crematoria, "were kept rigorously apart from the other prisoners and the outside world"; the SS itself was staffed at the bottom levels by Jews who themselves would soon be killed—an arrangement that allowed the transfer of guilt for the act of killing away from those who ordered it and onto people who were victims in any case, and who, in addition, would soon be dead and therefore incapable of making a report.[133]

Another reason for degrading human beings before killing them, in Levi's analysis, was that it could subtly allow people on the killing side to feel that they were killing things that were less than fully human. If the inmates of death camps are called "vermin," then killing them is killing vermin and not, after all, murder. Should this be called "euphemism"? It might seem an odd term, since euphemism is supposed to make something sound good and calling people vermin does the opposite. But the essence of euphemism is still at work here, because the function of the word "vermin" is still to deflect a square look at what is happening. It makes it possible for the perpetrator of a vile act to view the act as less vile. Azumo Shiro, a Japanese soldier during World War II, noticed a similar utility of animal metaphors in recalling the mind-set he and his fellow soldiers had during the Nanjing Massacre in China in 1937. They had gotten used to referring to the Chinese as pigs, bugs, and other animals. Azumo remembers an instance when they raped a Chinese woman and then shot her in the back as she ran away. They killed her because Japanese army regulations forbade rape (even though, on another level, the practice was tolerated and even encouraged). The soldiers wanted to erase any evidence of the rape. "Per-

---

132. Levi, *Drowned and the Saved*, p. 24.
133. Ibid., pp. 51–52.

haps when we were raping her, we looked at her as a woman," Azumo wrote, "but when we killed her, we just thought of her as something like a pig."[134]

That facile conversion within the mind—from human being to pig, in order to cushion a perpetrator's conscience—has a grisly parallel in Zheng Yi's account of the politically induced cannibalism that happened in Wuxuan County in Guangxi during the summer of 1968. There was no official policy to promote cannibalism at the time, but, in the feverish competition to demonstrate "final victory" over "class enemies," activists sometimes disemboweled their victims, removed their hearts and livers, and challenged villagers to participate in eating bits of the internal organs. Zheng Yi shows how the ghastly political rituals that resulted led to psychological conflicts for villagers who wanted to—or at least felt pressure to—participate in the political campaign but at the same time could not face the prospect of eating human flesh. Leaders in one village, according to Zheng, found a middle way through this dilemma. They ordered that human flesh and pork be cut into equal-sized pieces and boiled together in a large pot in the village square. They suspended the pot above eye level while villagers passed by to receive one piece of meat each. All villagers could then say "I have shown a firm class standpoint" but could also say, perhaps only to themselves, "It is possible I have not eaten human flesh."[135] The village leaders had figured out a way to use ambiguity in order to avoid looking squarely at something awful. Their technique resembles that of firing squads in twentieth-century America that loaded all rifles but one or two with blank cartridges, so that no man on the squad would have to carry the burden of knowing for sure that he had killed someone. This sort of avoidance reflex apparently is a deeply rooted human response.

In yet another version of the avoidance response, the doer of an unpleasant deed can pretend "I am doing not exactly *this*, but something else." In China the device has many examples in the area of the political criticism of literature. In 1979, for example, three young playwrights wrote the play *What If I Really Were?* It features a young man who pretends to be the

---

134. Quoted in Iris Chang, *The Rape of Nanking: The Forgotten Holocaust of World War II* (New York: Penguin, 1997), pp. 49–50. See also p. 218.

135. Zheng Yi, *Hongse jinianbei*, pp. 90–91.

son of a high official in order to get a ticket to a theater show.[136] His ruse succeeds, but then, to his dismay, he finds he cannot extricate himself from it. Others—most of them ambitious officials—take him at his word, shower him with food, gifts, and invitations, introduce him to potential girlfriends, and follow up their favors with requests for reciprocity. In its context, the play was a bold exposé of official corruption. It was an immediate hit in China, and its written text circulated widely underground even after its stage performance was banned. Then, in 1980, in a number of Propaganda Department meetings that were followed by austere articles in the press, the play was denounced.[137] It was criticized for having encouraged young people to sympathize with a deceitful impersonator, a "swindler." To audiences who had loved the play, the criticism was odd. The whole point of the play had been not to encourage deceit, hypocrisy, bribery, sycophancy, or string-pulling but to satirize and denounce those very things. Audiences had perceived these vices not in the ne'er-do-well young impersonator but in the menagerie of officialdom that surrounded him, and that reminded them of officials they had encountered in their own experience. Yet, viewed against its own goals, the focus of the official criticism on the swindler was brilliant. It drew attention away from the sore point—the play's devastating comment on officialdom—and toward an issue where officialdom had not only face but the upper hand. Sympathize with a trickster? Socialist China may have its problems, but we need socialist solutions, not bourgeois-individualist ones, said the Party-run media. This was the lesson readers of the criticism were to take home— even though in the play itself there was no suggestion that the protagonist's little trick was any kind of solution, either for society or for himself. At the play's end (and the end of a literary work, in traditional Chinese storytelling as well as in socialist realism, is where the "lesson" appears), the young man is crushed.

136. Sha Yexin 沙叶新, Yao Mingde 姚明德, and Li Shoucheng 李守成, "Jiaru wo shi zhen de?" 假如我是真的? [What if I really were?], *Qishiniandai* [Seventies] (Hong Kong), no. 1 (1980), 76–96.

137. Hu Yaobang led the criticism in *Zai juben chuangzuo zuotanhuishang de jianghua*. The leading written criticism was by Chen Yong 陈涌, "Cong liangge juben kan wenyi de zhenshixing he qingxiangxing" 从两个剧本看文艺的真实性和倾向性 [The realism and the tendencies of literature and art as seen in two plays], *Renmin ribao* 人民日报 [People's daily], March 19, 1980, p. 5.

The official criticism of *What If I Really Were?* implicitly warned Chinese audiences that if you sympathize with a trickster then *you*, not just the trickster, are a problem. You should reflect on your own thinking and make appropriate changes before you get into more trouble. This general way of inducing self-censorship has been fundamental in the Chinese Communist movement ever since its years in Yan'an in the 1940s. Compared to their Soviet predecessors, the Chinese Communists have used censoring mechanisms that rely less on physical and bureaucratic controls (where a censor blots out or changes what a writer writes) and more on psychological engineering (where an authority induces a writer to conform to what the authority clearly wants). The self-censorship system is grounded in the principle of fear. At times, especially during the Maoist campaigns of the 1940s–1960s, this was an intense and immediate fear: a person could be taunted, ostracized, raided at home, and in other ways "struggled." More normally, though, and especially in the decades since Mao's death, the fear that anchors self-censorship has not been a clear and present sense of panic. It is more like a dull, well-entrenched leeriness that people who deal with the censorship system have gotten used to and have accepted as a normal part of their environment. In daily life it is so routine as to go largely unnoticed, but its controlling power is impressive nonetheless. It operates almost in the manner of a traffic light: people control themselves because of it, and a person who chooses to disobey seems not so much courageous as stupid.

While fear anchors this system, linguistic vagueness plays a major role. Abstract words name things one is supposed to avoid, even though they are hard to define: rightism, revisionism, ultraleftism, spiritual pollution, bourgeois liberalization, splittism, anti-China tendencies, and many others. The *evaluative* components of the meanings of such terms could not be more clear: no one should dream of being a splittist, a purveyor of pollution, or the like. But the *denotative* meanings of such terms are always vague. What exactly is "rightism"? Telling unapproved truths in print, as exemplified by Liu Binyan and other famous "rightists"? Owning a degree from the University of Chicago or having family members who live in Indonesia, as other cases show? What about "spiritual pollution"? Exactly what is it? Listening to Hong Kong music? Wearing long hair? (How long? Am I safe at eight centimeters? Twelve?) It has always been impossible to know such things, and it has always been a part of the deliberate design of the control system that people must make their own guesses at the answers. As soon as I am made to guess, the system has successfully turned me into my own censor: if I'm not sure about the rule on long hair, maybe I should be conservative and keep mine at six centimeters.

In addition to vagueness about the exact borderlines of what constitutes an error, vagueness over the punishments that are applied if one commits the error also creates anxiety, and this, too, strengthens self-censorship. If I am judged to be guilty of spiritual pollution, will I be criticized at school? Punished by a bad job assignment when I graduate? Or worse, perhaps, be expelled? These questions were impossible to answer during the Anti-Spiritual Pollution Campaign in 1983. It is also well known that punishments are applied irregularly. People from well-connected families can get away with more, on a wide range of issues, than ordinary people can. So where—each person must ask—does my case fall?

It is worth trying to list the several ways linguistic vagueness serves official purposes. Here are some:

1. *Vague warnings frighten more people than precise warnings do.* If I don't know what "spiritual pollution" or "bourgeois liberalization" is, then it could be virtually anything; therefore, it could be what *I* am doing; therefore, I pull back. (Result: many people begin to censor themselves, often unnecessarily.) If I could know exactly what the rules were, then I could tailor my speech and behavior precisely to avoid mistakes, which would then leave me relatively free and relaxed to speak and behave in all other areas. (Result: many fewer people would pull back.) Clarity serves the purpose of the censoring state only when it wants to silence a specific person or action; when it wants to intimidate a large group, vagueness works much better.

2. *A vague threat pressures an individual to curtail a wider range of activity than a precise prohibition does.* If I don't know exactly what it is that the authorities are prohibiting, then I have to guess for myself. If I am living in fear of being punished for my possible mistake, then my imagination of what topics could be risky might run far and wide, perhaps well beyond anything that the authorities originally had in mind, or even knew about. (They might not know, for example, that I listen to Australian radio—and they might not even care; but I know, and fear that they might care, so I cut back on my listening.)

3. *Vague charges allow for arbitrary targeting.* It is probably a rule of human nature that people who exercise arbitrary power like to disguise the

real reasons for their actions, because this allows people to look respectable even while doing whatever they want. In a culture like China's, where the leader's "face" represents his morality, which in turn affects his political legitimacy, the desirability of appearing to be moral is especially strong. The need for such pretense only increases as a particular leader's moral behavior worsens. In this context, the availability of vague and even self-contradictory guidelines can be very useful. When a guideline says "long hair is spiritual pollution" at the same time that some people do have long hair and are not bothered, it is the authority alone, in the privacy of his or her own mind, who can decide whether or not to punish a given person for violating the rule. The same space for arbitrary power is opened when a rule says "internal-circulation materials must not be made public" at the same time that many such materials are openly available in bookstores. The authority can punish a given person *for whatever reason the authority wishes* and still be able to point to an official rule as justification for the punishment. China's constitution itself illustrates this useful flexibility. It provides that citizens have freedom of speech, of assembly, and of the press. But its preamble also sets down the inviolability of Communist Party rule, Marxism-Leninism-Mao-Zedong-thought, the dictatorship of the proletariat, and the socialist system. The huge space between these two contradictory poles (both of which, by the way, are poor descriptions of the actual patterns of life in China) gives leaders immense room to be arbitrary while still claiming to be legal.

 4. *Vague accusations are useful in eliciting information from detainees.* When a person is arrested or detained in a political case, police normally do not explain to the accused what the accusations are. Formal charges are vague or sometimes entirely absent. "You yourself know the reason," the accused is often told. It is then up to you, the accused, to "earn lenience" by "showing sincerity"—which means opening up and telling everything that you know. The police often begin by saying they already possess an exhaustive amount of information on your activities and that the purpose of the interrogation is not to get information but to measure your sincerity by observing your confession. But this can well be a lie. Usually the point is precisely to extract new information, which can then be used against either you or someone else. Clarity about the original accusation would obviously render this tactic useless.

5. Unclear or contradictory instructions can be used in order to shift responsibility for mistakes away from leaders and onto the people who are receiving the instructions. We have seen above two examples of this tactic: telling writers in the late 1970s to "liberate their thought" but also to adhere to "Marxism-Leninism-Mao-Zedong-thought," and telling soldiers at Tiananmen in June 1989 to clear the square by 6 a.m. "absolutely" but to do it without bloodshed. In such cases, the authority figure can "have it both ways": if something goes wrong in either this direction or that, the giver of the order can always avoid responsibility by pointing to the side of the instructions that said the mistake should not have happened. The blame falls to the person who was trying to carry out the contradictory orders. The efforts of such a person to avoid both a Scylla and a Charibdys naturally intensify self-monitoring and self-censorship.

6. Occasionally, in high-profile political cases, the purpose of vagueness is to veil the identities of the people who are being attacked. In 1967, for example, the official Chinese press began to use the phrase "the top person in authority taking the capitalist road" to refer to Mao's chief rival, Liu Shaoqi. In this case, the point was not really to withhold information (it was no secret who the "top person in authority" was) but to provide a layer of face-saving indirection: to be naming him without naming him. Similarly in 1974, in a campaign to "Criticize Lin Biao and Confucius," Mao and the people close to him were using Confucius as a stand-in for Zhou Enlai, who was their political target at that time. In the Confucius case, most ordinary people did not know that Zhou was the behind-the-scenes target, and hence were left with the very considerable puzzle of why two people as different as Lin Biao and Confucius were being lumped together. But the elite knew what was going on, and that, for the purposes of Mao and his associates, was enough. To them it probably seemed just an incidental bonus that people at all levels, regardless of what they knew, began self-censorship of anything that might seem bad about Confucius.

In sum, there are many ways language itself has been a tool of the Chinese Communist Party's efforts to maintain its control of Chinese society. The use of both forceful, domineering language and vague, abstract, or indirect language may seem in some ways an opposition, but there is unity between these practices in their pursuit of the common goal of shaping the ways people think, speak, and behave. Still, we must not claim too much for language alone. Although it plays an important role—and a role whose power often goes unnoticed—it is only part of a wider array of techniques the Party uses to maintain its power. Those other techniques include, for example, financial incentives (You want your business to thrive? It might be best to cooperate) and appeals to patriotism (You want to be proud of your country? Then be proud of "your" Party). During the Mao era, when the commune and work-unit systems were dominant (the work-unit system remained important through the 1980s as well), many kinds of daily-life questions—housing, education, medical care, permission to travel, marry, even buy a bicycle or sewing machine—all depended on one's political credentials in the eyes of Party officials. By the early twenty-first century these controls had largely disappeared, and nothing so comprehensive has replaced them. But Party leaders have shown flexibility in finding alternate means of applying pressure. One of these, for example, is the use of China's borders to exact compliance from citizens who dare to criticize the government. The technique is used regardless of the direction in which people want to cross the border. You want a passport in order to travel abroad? Be obedient, or you won't get it. You are an exile who wants to come back to China for your mother's funeral? Sign the "confession" we have prepared for you, or better yet give us information on overseas dissidents, and we will let you back in. And in the end, behind all of the myriad ways "soft" techniques are used to shape people's incentives, there stands the police—uniformed police, plainclothes police, cyber police, quasi-military People's Armed Police, and others, including simply thugs for hire. This book is about language and cannot address the full range of the Party's tools and techniques of social control. That would need another book, or several. My focus will now turn to some of the ways citizens in the People's Republic, including ordinary people as well as protesters, have responded to the official language game.

How the Game Is Played: From the Side of the Ruled

On the whole, Chinese people have used adaptation more than resistance in response to their government's political use of language. They have found ways to adjust to the language game, defend themselves within it, and use it to advance their own interests. For people who stand on the weaker side in a governing relationship, such an approach is only prudent.

The Chinese Communist Party's special use of language for political purposes originated during the 1930s and 1940s, before Communist accession to power in China as a whole in 1949. During the early 1950s, many in the Chinese population were still largely unaware of the language game. To most, slogans like "serve the people," "oppose corruption," and "join cooperatives" had straightforward meanings that implied idealistic purposes. There seemed no reason to feel distance from such terms or to second-guess what they might mean. As we have seen earlier, it was only in the late 1950s, with the Anti-Rightist Movement and the Great Leap Forward, that the bifurcation between official language and ordinary language became pervasive and began to impinge on daily life in ways that obliged almost everyone to adjust to "two kinds of truth." Now people had to learn how, when speaking officialese, to set aside ordinary norms of truth and falsity and make words "fit" prescriptions of what was "correct."

People began to use ordinary language to talk about how to handle the official language: "You can just say X" or "If they say Y, you can say Z," and so on. In this way of speaking, X, Y, and Z, however high-sounding, become mere tools. Victor Erlich noticed essentially the same mechanical use of language in the Soviet Union, where it emerged a few decades before it came to China. Erlich writes that "what had been a rhetoric of crude yet genuine ideological commitment becomes a threadbare rationale for crass personal materialism."[138] Statements can be true or not, far-fetched or not—that sort of thing does not matter—so long as a job gets done or a goal gets reached. A detailed example might best show how this works. In 1988 my work with the Committee on Scholarly Communication with China involved arranging for a group of American scholars to do fieldwork in Zouping County, Shandong Province, where a group of local county officials was in charge of hosting them. This work allowed

---

138. Victor Erlich, "Post-Stalin Trends in Russian Literature," *Slavic Review* 23, no. 3 (September 1964), p. 407. Erlich is commenting on "the Drozdovs," a phrase made famous by the character Drozdov in Vladimir Dudintsev's novel *Not by Bread Alone*.

me some close-up views of how these officials handled their government's language game, and I later wrote this about it:[139]

> As part of their compensation [for hosting the Americans], the officials wanted my assistance in purchasing an American Jeep. In order to get a loan from Chinese banking authorities, they needed a formal statement from my office that the Jeep would be for use by the American scholars in the rural county. When I pointed out that this was not strictly true, they explained that the statement was only a "formality," and made it clear that it would be quite unfriendly of me not to write the statement. So I did. Then a few weeks later, with their loan secured, the same county officials came back asking for another formal statement, this one certifying that the Jeep *would not* be used by Americans. If the Jeep were for Americans, they explained, regulations required that it be bought in foreign exchange currency rather than Chinese currency. I decided to call the Bank of China to point out the directly contradictory regulations and to ask for guidance. This decision perplexed the rural officials. "Why do *that?*" they asked indignantly. "Just write another statement. It doesn't matter." To them, contradictory statements were a mere nuisance that should not impede the task of acquiring a Jeep.
>
> Eventually the officials did get their Jeep. Before I got around either to calling the Bank of China or to writing a statement, they made a separate appeal to my Chinese office assistant, who, acting on the principle that I was a generally well-intentioned person who of course would want to help, wrote a statement for me and affixed the official CSCC chop to it.

If this incident illustrates how people use ordinary language to talk *about* the official language—how to manipulate it to get things done—the reverse could also happen. People could use official talk to focus on things that had been said informally. This happened often during the Mao era

---

139. Perry Link, *Evening Chats in Beijing: Probing China's Predicament* (New York: Norton, 1992), p. 187. Certain other examples below are also drawn from *Evening Chats in Beijing*, pp. 181–190.

(and sometimes during the immediate post-Mao years as well) and could be frightening. If person A at a formal political meeting reported that person B had, in an unguarded moment, made politically incorrect statement X, then statement X, originally not intended as an item in the language game, entered the game willy-nilly. At the height of the Maoist frenzy in the late 1960s, even something as informal as talking about one's cat (*māo* 猫, a near homonym for Máo 毛) could, if overheard by a dim-witted or mean-spirited neighbor, be brought to a political meeting, where it could cause one great harm.[140] By the end of the Mao era, an aphorism had arisen in the unofficial culture: "Choose your personal friends outside of your work-unit." If you made friends and spoke informally with people at work, you would always have to guard your words, even in informal contexts. That was no way to relax. Even if you trusted your friends to keep confidences, you would also have to trust that your friendship would never, for any reason, lapse—because people have memories and could report you later. That was no foundation for friendship.

On the other hand, the work-unit *was* the right place to learn how to manipulate required terms and phrases. During political study sessions, this kind of language use was, in any case, required, and to get good at it was seen as a worthwhile skill. A person who was quick to sense a political drift and to articulate it with a bit of eloquence could be said to *zhudong fucong* 主动服从 'take an initiative in obeying'. In ordinary language such a phrase might seem contradictory, because *zhudong* suggests an actor with a mind of his or her own, while *fucong* suggests the opposite. But in a Mao-era political meeting, *zhudong fucong* was a virtue. (Whether or not people viewed it as a virtue *outside* the political meeting is another, more complex question.) A similar example is *jiji kaolong* 积极靠拢 'actively fall in [with the Party line]'. In ordinary language, *jiji* suggests an activist and *kaolong* a follower. *Jiji kaolong* thus produces the odd notion of "lead in following," but in a formal political study session it was unquestionably a smart thing to do.

The value of being "active" or "taking an initiative" in such contexts deserves some analysis. At bottom, *following* is the main point in a politi-

---

140. Cao Guanlong 曹冠龙, "Mao" 猫, in "San'ge jiaoshou" 三个教授, *Anhui wenxue* [Anhui literature] 1 (1980), pp. 17–31. Translated by John Berninghausen as "Cats," in Perry Link, ed., *Roses and Thorns: The Second Blooming of the Hundred Flowers in Chinese Fiction, 1979–80* (Berkeley: University of California Press, 1984), pp. 123–130.

cal study session; why stress "initiative"? Such words show, first of all, energy, enthusiasm, and an example for others to imitate (i.e., follow). More subtly, but at least as important, they underscore the fiction that the activist is acting *independently*, guided by his or her own enthusiasm. In a system that claims to be a "democratic" dictatorship within a "people's" government, it is important to preserve the fiction that the people are indeed the ones who come up with ideas such as "oppose revisionism," "oppose bourgeois liberalization," and "root out rightist tendencies to reverse verdicts." In Mao-era political meetings, it was common to refer to *wo geren de kanfa* 我个人的看法 'my personal opinion' even though the phrase was seldom used actually to lift the curtain on a person's private thoughts. It had two other uses: (1) to provide a buffer in case the opinion was criticized (one could always say that my *geren de kanfa* was mistaken and now I see that the Party's view is correct), and (2) to maintain the democratic fiction that all of us, in this Party-run political meeting, are expressing our individual views. The general practice of using words to claim conformity to democracy has extended well beyond the Mao period. Official language in the early twenty-first century continues in several ways to rely on the pretense of pursuing alignment with majority opinion.

The foregoing are several examples of how people adapt to the official language game. Some of the commonest ways they avoid or resist it depend on the language "bifurcation" that I have noted in several contexts earlier. To the extent that officialese and ordinary talk are different and operate in separate spheres, each can maintain its own outlook, at least to some extent. Alexander Yashin describes Russian farmers in the Soviet era who were very good at manipulating official language during Party meetings but then, in informal contexts—as if shedding a layer of clothing—spoke in a very different mode and were full of lively complaints about the officiousness of higher-ups.[141] Similar behavior has been noted by many Chinese writers, among them Gu Hua, who describes rural officials in Hunan during the Cultural Revolution this way:

> For years they had trained themselves to be two-faced, trained themselves in double-talk.... By day, they attended classes to "struggle

---

141. "Levers," in Hugh McLean and Walter Vickery, eds., *The Year of Protest, 1956: An Anthology of Soviet Literary Materials* (Westport, Conn.: Greenwood, 1956), pp. 193–210.

against the self and combat revisionism," then they smuggled home plexiglass and imported stainless steel to make a table-lamp or four-poster double bed. During meetings they contrasted past bitterness with present joys; but once home they griped because the commune's co-op had no kerosene, or even candles. They passed the day drinking tea, smoking, reading the newspaper [all clichés for "official" behavior], and stressing the long-term importance of suppressing revisionism; the evenings, however, were spent jockeying for promotion or finding jobs for their relatives or places in the army or in college for their children.[142]

Even when speaking in a wholly informal context, like that of these commune members during their evenings, the sliding back and forth from unofficial to official language could be useful when special circumstances arose. The official language was generally more formal and imposing, and could be useful if someone felt a need to make a claim of authority or to issue a threat. A vivid example in my own memory is from 1980 in Guangzhou, when I saw a young woman from a politically well-connected family enter an argument over whether *liangbei* 两倍 'twofold' in Chinese means "double" in English or properly should be viewed as "triple" because *yibei* 一倍 'onefold' can also mean "double." The debate grew fierce, and then it grew personal. The well-connected young woman suddenly decided to call her opponent a *baizhuan* 白专 '[politically] white expert'. A few years earlier, during the Cultural Revolution, this had been a fearful label. It had serious implications. In 1980 it seemed a bit out of place, but still, because of psychological associations that remained alive in the minds of everyone present, and because of the political pedigree of the speaker, it delivered a chill to the room. It had no intellectual connection to the question of "double" versus "triple." It was simply a linguistic club that the young woman had decided to borrow for use in combat.

The most common way of avoiding the official language game is to take refuge in informal contexts where ordinary language is the norm. But

---

142. Gu Hua, "Futuling," trans. Gladys Yang, in *Pagoda Ridge and Other Stories* (Beijing: Panda Books, 1985), pp. 131–132.

people also achieve avoidance or resistance in many other more specific ways. A review of some of them follows. I have chosen the examples in part for their intrinsic interest and in part for what they reveal about the nature of the language game.

One common tactic of resistance has been to play dumb. Who made a certain anti-Party remark? One can say "I don't know." And where did you hear it? "Forgot." Who else is in your group? "What group?" And so on. This tactic arose during the Mao era, and by the 1980s seems to have taken on some fairly standard forms. One ready answer to the question "Where did you hear it?" came to be "in the public toilet"—because no person could be expected to identify a fellow toilet-user any more specifically than that. In 1988 in Beijing I heard the following joke, which seems to be an embroidery on the standard "heard it in the toilet" line. It is a dialogue between an interrogator (I) and a citizen (C):

I: What did the person look like?

C: Don't know.

I: How can you not know? What clothes was he wearing?

C: No clothes.

I: Hunh?

C: We were in a public bath.

I: I see. Well then, how tall was he?

C: Don't know . . . we were sitting down in the water.

I: What did his face look like?

C: Hard to say. There was steam rising from the water.

The need to use such ploys has declined since the Mao era but has by no means disappeared. Students used essentially the same tactic during the crackdown after the Beijing Massacre in 1989, and signatories of Charter 08, the citizens' manifesto for human rights and constitutional democracy that appeared at the end of 2008, used it throughout 2009 to respond to interrogation about their movement. In the early twenty-first century, the Internet replaced the public bath or toilet as the safest place to say, untraceably, that one had heard something.

Although the "playing dumb" tactic takes the official language at its face value and answers it at the same level, other methods make use of the distance between official and unofficial language. We have seen Wu Zuxiang's description of how intellectuals had learned, by the end of the Mao era, to read the newspaper "upside down". They understood that the report of a heroic rescue of a few people in an earthquake, a fire, or a mine collapse should be read as a report that a much larger number of people had likely perished. From an official positive X, one could reliably infer an unofficial negative Y. The inference could work the other way around, too: a negative X could be grounds to infer a positive Y. For example, when Mao and his associates criticized Deng Xiaoping in 1976, they distributed samples of Deng's speeches in which he called for more intellectual freedom, more emphasis on economic growth, and less class struggle. People were supposed to read these speeches and denounce Deng. And Deng was indeed denounced—widely, loudly, and insincerely. Witnesses to the events have attested that at least some of the denunciation was mere play-acting, and that, in their own minds, some of the denouncers identified with the very views they were denouncing.[143] The campaign to denounce Deng in fact was spreading his views. Essentially the same thing happened to the dissident astrophysicist Fang Lizhi after 1987, when he was expelled from the Party as a "bourgeois liberal." His speeches advocating democracy and human rights were sent to universities as *fanmian jiaocai* 反面教材 'reverse teaching materials'—meaning materials to instruct students in what not to think. Two years later, Fang concluded that this teaching-materials campaign had spread his ideas to many more students than he could ever have reached by himself. The attempt to use his speeches "in reverse" had itself worked in reverse.

The double entendre that the official language makes possible and the satire to which it opens the door have been exploited primarily by China's intellectuals. But others in society—farmers, workers, and others—have also made use of double meanings. In the 1950s, for example, the Party needed to recruit large numbers of soldiers. As an antidote to traditional prejudices against soldiers, slogan-makers in the Party revised the traditional Chinese aphorism *haotie bu da ding, hao nan bu dang bing* 好铁不打

---

143. Jung Chang, *Wild Swans: Three Daughters of China* (London: Flamingo, 1992), pp. 654–656; Ji Fengyuan, *Linguistic Engineering*, p. 302.

钉, 好男不当兵 'good iron doesn't go to make nails, good men don't go to be soldiers' as *hao nan cai dang bing* 好男才当兵 'only good men go to be soldiers'. Rural families across China were willing to accept this new politically correct formulation, but many gave it an inversion of meaning. For them, "good men" did not mean only "men who will make good soldiers" (be obedient, willing to die, etc.). It could also mean men who found a way to get out of the villages and into the cities. City life had long been viewed as more attractive than rural life, but permits to live in cities were not easy to get. Now, under the new slogan, joining the army was a way a "good man" could get to a city, and maybe even establish a beachhead there for the rest of the family.

In some cases, double meanings are used not just to play the system for personal advantage but to engage in verbal combat with officialdom. In 1980, for example, Party officials held a meeting with practitioners of *xiangsheng* comedians' dialogues as a way to warn them to be less sharp in their comment on corruption, special privilege, and other politically sensitive problems. Some of the performers (and these people were, after all, masters at wordplay) fought back with double entendre. Jiang Kun, a rising *xiangsheng* star at the time, announced that the interests of the Party and of *xiangsheng* were *yizhi* 一致 'at one'. The phrase was officialese and could not be gainsaid. He went on to say that *xiangsheng* "speaks what is in the minds of the masses."[144] This, too, was politically correct verbiage and impossible to oppose. But it harbored the second-level meaning that "the masses" were angry at corruption, special privilege, and all those other topics whose repression was precisely the reason officials had convened the meeting in the first place. Officials then felt they had to answer Jiang, but they could not contradict him without contradicting their own language.

Another example of combative use of double entendre (to choose but one among a plethora) came in the late 1970s in Guangzhou with a play on the word *tiaozheng* 调整 'adjust'. Skilled people in urban work-units—universities, hospitals, museums, libraries, and so on—had had no salary raises, and had often suffered reductions, during the final decade or more of the Mao years, and now the government was promising to *tiaozheng gongzi* 调整工资 'adjust salaries'. A member of the Guangdong Political

---

144. Xiangsheng chuangzuo zuotanhui bangongshi, "Xiangsheng chuangzuo zuotanhui jianbao" p. 1.

Consultative Conference punned on the official phrase to complain that so far the raises had been tiny. We only got *weitiao* 微调 'fine-tuning', she said. Another wag invented a pun that spread widely in the Guangzhou area. The government gave us *kongtiao* 空调 'air conditioning'. The same two Chinese characters, pronounced the same way, can mean "empty adjustment," that is, raises of zero.

But double entendre is only a part of what language bifurcation makes possible. The gap between what the Party says it is doing and what it actually does is a pervasive fact, with examples that are grounded in fundamental institutions. The Chinese constitution guarantees freedom of assembly, yet people can be put in prison for joining unapproved groups. Political cases are handled in "trials," but only after authorities have decided what the outcomes will be. An official can accuse a writer of "bourgeois individualism," when the writer's actual offense was to expose corruption. The large space between pretense and practice that examples like this establish leaves much room for people to use the language game as a tool for resistance.

In early 1989, for example, shortly after his speeches on democracy spread as "negative teaching materials" in reverse, Fang Lizhi applied for permission to travel from Beijing to Taiwan. The Chinese government had recently announced, as a part of a delicate game of words and face with the Taiwan authorities, that it would now allow Chinese intellectuals to visit Taiwan. Mainland authorities, of course, were not thinking of people like Fang when they announced this policy, and Fang knew this, and knew that an application from him would certainly be rejected, but decided to play a round of the language game anyway. His goal was not to get to Taiwan but to expose pretense. And why do that? Because pretenses such as these were struts that supported the regime's face and claims to legitimacy. Fang's gesture was small, but its purpose was not.

Later in the spring of 1989, student protesters at Tiananmen made more explicit use of the gap between pretense and actuality in officialese. They were protesting corruption, special privilege, and authoritarian rule, all of which were "sensitive" topics whose mention could be risky. Repeatedly, they used official language as cover. They held up a banner that read "Citizens of the People's Republic of China have freedom of speech, publication, assembly, formation of groups, demonstration, and protest (Article

35 [of China's constitution])." They also drew words—carefully selected for relevance—from China's national anthem: "Arise, ye people who would not be slaves.... The most perilous hour for the Chinese nation has arrived," and so on. The Communist anthem "The Internationale," translated from the French, provided an even larger trove of stirring, double-edged words:

> Arise, wretched of the earth, convicts of hunger ...
> let us wipe the slate clean ...
> the world is about to change ...
> we are nothing, let us be all, this is the final struggle ...
> there are no supreme saviours ...
> let us save ourselves ... so that the spirit be pulled from its
>   prison ...
> hideous in their self-glorification, kings of the mine and rail—
>   have they ever done anything other than steal work?

Understood one way, such words were unspeakably seditious. But how could the authorities order people to stop singing a classic Marxist anthem? (What they could do—and did—was to play the language gambit in reverse by claiming that the students felt a basic loyalty to the socialist motherland because they were, after all, singing a Marxist classic.) At Beijing University, students invented perhaps the most sarcastic double entendre in all of the song lyrics that emerged that spring. They revived the tune—widely popular in the 1950s—"Without the Communist Party There Would Be No New China" but now sang it, poker-faced, without comment on whether "New China" was a good or bad thing.

After the June Fourth massacre, when officials across China held meetings to promote the correctness of the "necessary military action," people found ways to turn even applause into sarcasm. After a political speech to students at Peking University, an official was greeted with silence. Then a *pop!* as one pair of hands came together, alone. Then a pause and another random *pop!* here, and another there, and then a faster but irregular pattern of isolated popping. What could the authorities do? Find the people who had clapped and charge them with clapping? Ban applause after political speeches? At a required political meeting at a major publishing house in Guangzhou, people were asked to discuss Deng Xiaoping's report on why the June Fourth crackdown was correct. Inwardly, this group of well-informed intellectuals felt rage at the massacre. But what could they say? After an awkward silence, someone thought of calling out *hao!* 好 'good!' and then repeated the word several times, ending with an extended *h-h-h-h-a-a-a-o-o-o-o-o-o!* It was biting irony, of unmistakable intent.

In the early twenty-first century, people working in China's *weiquan* 维权 'support rights' movement have continued the tradition of exploiting pretense in language. A small but influential group of "rights lawyers" use a strategy of following the rules in the Chinese legal code and showing how officials themselves violate these rules. It is well known on all sides that political cases are decided by Party leaders, not by legal rules, yet the pretense that the law is supreme remains vital to the Party's claims to legitimacy. What rights lawyers say, in essence, is "all right, if you pretend that you follow the rules, then so will we, and we will hold you to them." The strategy can yield two kinds of benefit. Occasionally, it can actually do some good for individual defendants. But, more important, it challenges the entire system by exposing its hypocrisy—and does so in a way that is theoretically unassailable because it depends only on the following of rules. (One reason why the regime so often avails itself of spurious charges—corruption, traffic obstruction, etc.—is that the actual offenses of rights lawyers and other activists are that they follow rules, but the written law does not include the "crime" of rule-following.) Vaclav Havel has put the matter very well in writing about Czechoslovakia in the 1970s, and it is perhaps relevant to quote Havel because Chinese rights lawyers in the 2000s have taken direct inspiration from him:

> A persistent and never-ending appeal to the laws—not just to the laws concerning human rights but to all laws—does not mean at all that those who do so have succumbed to the illusion that in our system the law is anything other than what it is. They are well aware of the role it plays. But precisely because they know how desperately the system depends on it—on the "noble" version of the law, that is—they also know how enormously significant such appeals are. Because the system cannot do without the law, because it is hopelessly tied down by the necessity of pretending the laws are observed, it is compelled to react in some way to such appeals. Demanding that the laws

be upheld is thus an act of living within the truth that threatens the whole mendacious structure at its point of maximum mendacity.[145]

In June 2009 the poet and literary critic Liu Xiaobo, who a year and a half later was awarded the Nobel Peace Prize, was arrested and charged with "inciting subversion of state power" because of his support for Charter 08. In defending him, the famous rights lawyer Mo Shaoping made exemplary use of the strategy Havel describes. Liu had originally been detained on December 8, 2008, on the authority of a document on which the space for the item "suspected of the crime of . . ." was left blank. To leave this blank was illegal, Mo pointed out. Then Liu was held for six months under "residential surveillance." This, too, Mo showed, was illegal because Liu was not kept at his own residence and was denied access to his family and his lawyers. When the maximum period allowed by Chinese law for "residential surveillance" had expired, Liu continued to be held without charge. This, too, was illegal, Mo showed. When formal charges were announced two weeks later, the police told Mo that he could not defend Liu because he, Mo, had also signed Charter 08. This also was outside the law.[146] Did Mo believe that his pointing out of these various legal infractions would lead to redress within the system? Probably not. Was his inveterate appeal to law a mode of support for the regime? Hardly. (One could view it this way only if the regime itself were fully and sincerely supporting the law.) In defending Liu Xiaobo, Mo was playing a language game whose proximate goal was to help Liu if possible but whose larger, long-term enterprise was to push China further toward rule of law by exposing the hypocrisy in the way things currently were.

Mo and other rights lawyers use their real names, but most resisters and language-game players do not. Most are ordinary citizens—purveyors of *shunkouliu*, oral jokes, graffiti, text messages, tweets, blogs, and so on— who hide behind anonymity for the sake of freedom and safety. In the first decade of the twenty-first century the Chinese government passed

---

145. Vaclav Havel, "The Power of the Powerless," in *Living in Truth* (London: Faber and Faber, 1989) p. 98.

146. A 2009 open letter by Mo Shaoping in defense of Liu Xiaobo appears in Perry Link, *Liu Xiaobo's Empty Chair: Chronicling the Reform Movement Beijing Fears Most* (New York: New York Review E-books, 2011), pp. 52–56. See also letters from Zhang Zuhua and signers of Charter 08, *New York Review of Books* 51, no. 13 (August 13, 2009), p. 76.

laws banning the use of pseudonyms on the Internet, and, although the government can track down almost anyone if it really wants to, with hundreds of millions of people using the Internet, it is not hard for most netizens to speak anonymously. Messages often list no author or only a pseudonym. Like jokes in the West, material often passes from person to person often without either the passer or receiver knowing who the original author was. But while authorship and readership remain fluid and largely obscure, the principle of exploiting the gap between official pomp and actual life remains constant. For example, in a dormitory restroom at Capital Normal University in early 2009, a sign that hung above the men's urinal read:

Shengming shaobuliao wenming yongyu 生命少不了文明用语
Renqun shaobuliao huansheng xiaoyu 人群少不了欢声笑语

Speech in life should be polite
People should laugh in delight.

Beneath the sign an anonymous graffiti artist had added:

Guanfang shaobuliao wuliao biaoyu 官方少不了无聊标语

Official slogans are always trite.[147]

It is important to note here that the *content* of the official sign is not the main object of satire. Apparently some official, somewhere, had had the idea—not a bad idea—of making use of the few seconds during which a person urinates to remind people to be happy and polite. Who could argue with that? It was not the sign's idea but its source and its style—officialdom, using its official voice, rendered pompous by the adoption of rhythm and parallelism—that apparently inspired the sarcasm of the graffiti artist.

When economic recession threatened the world in early 2009 and it looked as if only China's labor-intensive growth engine could save international capitalism, an anonymous wordmeister in China reached back to

---

147. I am grateful to David Moser for the example. Email message to author, February 17, 2009.

Mao-era officialese to create a *shunkouliu* that, for its wizardly cleverness, spread widely:

1949 *nian: zhiyou shehuizhuyi cai neng jiu Zhongguo*	1949 年: 只有社会主义才能救中国
1979 *nian: zhiyou zibenzhuyi cai neng jiu Zhongguo*	1979 年: 只有资本主义才能救中国
1989 *nian: zhiyou Zhongguo cai neng jiu shehuizhuyi*	1989 年: 只有中国才能救社会主义
2009 *nian: zhiyou Zhongguo cai neng jiu zibenzhuyi*	2009 年: 只有中国才能救资本主义

1949: Only socialism can save China.	(Mao's assertion)
1979: Only capitalism can save China.	(as Deng turned a corner from Mao)
1989: Only China can save socialism.	(as socialism collapsed across eastern Europe)
2009: Only China can save capitalism.	(as Western capitalism fails)

Almost continuously since the early 1950s, official discourse has claimed that the Party has been campaigning against corruption, combating bureaucratism, rooting out waste, and so on. Such claims are satirized in the following *shunkouliu* about SARS, the infectious and sometimes fatal flu-like disease that spread through China in 2003 precipitating extraordinary health measures and forcing bureaucrats, on this issue, into unaccustomed transparency. The piece is called "What the Party Can't Cure, SARS Can":[148]

dachidahe dang zhibuliao, feidian zhi le;	大吃大喝党治不了, 非典治了;
gongkuan lüyou dang zhibuliao, feidian zhi le;	公款旅游党治不了, 非典治了;

---

148. Cited in Hong Zhang, "Making Light of the Dark Side: SARS Jokes and Humor in China" in Arthur Kleinman and James Watson, eds., *SARS in China: Prelude to Pandemic?* (Stanford: Stanford University Press, 2005), p. 152. Zhang gives an excellent translation, but here I have used my own.

wenshanhuihai dang zhibuliao, 文山会海党治不了, 非典治了;
feidian zhi le;
qishangmanxia dang zhibuliao, 欺上瞒下党治不了, 非典治了;
feidian zhi le;
maiyin piaochang dang zhibuliao, 卖淫嫖娼党治不了, 非典治了。
feidian zhi le;

The Party couldn't stop rampant banqueting, but SARS did;
The Party couldn't stop junkets on the pubic till, but SARS did;
The Party couldn't stop interminable meetings, but SARS did;
The Party couldn't stop cover-ups, but SARS did;
The Party couldn't stop traffic in sex, but SARS did.

A piece from early 2008 satirizes the habit in official language of packaging political catchphrases in numbers (the Gang of Four, the Four Modernizations, the Four Basic Principles, etc.). It is called "The Four Clears and the Four Unclears":

Wei shenme kai hui buqingchu, kai hui zuo nar qingchu;
Shei song li bu qingchu, shei mei song li qingchu;
Shei gan de hao buqingchu, gai tiba shei qingchu
He shei shui bu qingchu, shui jiao gan shenme qingchu.

为什么开会不清楚, 开会坐哪清楚;
谁送礼不清楚, 谁没送礼清楚;
谁干得好不清楚, 该提拔谁清楚;
和谁睡不清楚, 睡觉干什么清楚。

Why hold a meeting?—Unclear
But who sits in what spot?—Clear
Who brought what gifts?—Unclear
But who brought *no* gift?—Clear
Whose work has been good?—Unclear
But who should be promoted?—Clear
Who sleeps with whom?—Unclear
What happens in bed?—Clear

Other anonymous authors have not been this coy about "what happens in bed." The piece "New Year's Wishes for 2007" lists ten sexually laden wishes for men and ten more for women in the new year. Each wish plays on the name of a top leader. For men, it is wished that *jiahuo xiang Li chun yiyang chang* 家伙象李春一样长 'the thing is as long as [propaganda chief] Li Changchun', that it *jueqi xiang Wu guo yiyang bang* 崛起象吴国一样棒 'rises as magnificently as [National People's Congress chair] Wu Bangguo', plus eight more. For women, the wishes are that *jiahuo xiang Hu tao yiyang jin* 家伙象胡涛一样紧 'the thing is as tight as [President] Hu Jintao', that *pigu xiang Wu guan yiyang zheng* 屁股象吴官一样正 'buttocks are as proper as [chief of discipline inspection] Wu Guanzheng', and eight more. I include this example not to be salacious but, in part, to illustrate the extremes to which people can go when protected by anonymity.

During times of extreme political pressure, such as the late Mao years, even authorial anonymity might not be enough to protect one from a misstep in the language game. Merely *repeating* incorrect words, regardless of who had originated them, could be a political crime. Zhang Xianliang, in his fictionalized memoirs of labor camp experience in the late 1950s, tells of meeting a man named Ma Weixiao and talking with him, while the two are alone in a field, about the causes of the terrible famine they were experiencing. Ma ventures the view that Mao Zedong planned the famine intentionally. The government "has plenty of grain," Ma says. "Yes, they have it, but they aren't bringing it out to feed the people. They want the people hungry." Zhang Xianliang's protagonist asks how that could possibly be. What would be the point in starving the people? "It's the best way there is of reforming people," Ma answers. Ma follows with a lengthy explanation of why persuasion and education cannot get done what Mao wants to get done. Freezing and fire will not work, either. Only hunger works, because everyone has to eat.[149] Hearing these words, Zhang knows that he cannot repeat them. Normally, in the Mao era, a person could earn political credit by reporting the counterrevolutionary words of another. But not in this case, because "what Ma had said was enough to get both listener and speaker executed." Zhang knew this, and Ma knew it,

---

149. Zhang Xianliang, *Fannao jiushi zhihui* 烦恼就是智慧, translated by Martha Avery as *Grass Soup* (Boston: Godine, 1993), pp. 177–179.

too. He knew that, ironically, "the more counterrevolutionary one's words were, the safer one would be."[150]

Informal codes have sometimes been useful in avoiding the danger of saying things explicitly. In the summer of 1988, the widely watched television series *Heshang* (River elegy) fed a national debate over whether China and its Communist Party were still mired in a mentality that was left over from the imperial era. It was very much a political debate but was called—for the sake of indirection—a *wenhua re* 文化热 'cultural fever'. It included the problem of how the Communist Party operates but did this under the rubric of discussing "feudalism," not Leninism. Mao Zedong and Deng Xiaoping were not mentioned by name, but emperors and "despotism" were analyzed. All these were, in a sense, codes. A few months later, when students demonstrated at Tiananmen, many used the two-fingered "V for victory" sign, and then, after the June Fourth massacre, when it suddenly became too dangerous to flash that V sign, the sign persisted in code as people asked *yao mai huichong yao ma?* 要买蛔虫药吗? 'do you want to buy roundworm medicine?' The understood answer was *liang pian!* 两片! 'two tablets', using the fingers to illustrate the number of tablets wanted: a V sign. The gesture became an improvised *xiehouyu* 歇后语 'implied-end phrase'[151] that allowed the V-sign to be conjured without actually being flashed.

Coded terms expanded greatly in the early 2000s, with the rise of the Internet and the need to evade government filters. Internet police began using software to intercept words such as *minzhu* 民主 'democracy', *renquan* 人权 'human rights', and *liusi* 六四 'June Fourth', and Chinese netizens in response began inventing coded substitutes. For a time, June Fourth, for example, became 陆肆—the traditional way accountants wrote *liu* and *si* in tamper-proof style. The term lingba xianzhang 零八宪章, "Charter 08," was blocked shortly after it appeared on the Internet, so users began referring to it in several other ways, one of which was the near-homonym

---

150. Ibid., pp. 180, 181.

151. *Xiehouyu* resemble riddles in English except that they are terser than riddles, and what is guessed is a word, not a thing. They always rely on puns or other double meaning. "A hen on an empty nest," for example, implies *bujian dan* 不见蛋 'no egg in sight', a pun on *bujiandan* 不简单 'not simple—complicated' or 'not easy—impressive'. The indirection of *xiehouyu* allows a speaker to say something that otherwise would be embarrassing or dangerous.

linba xianzhang 淋巴县长 'lymph county-magistrate'. Coded substitutes such as these are easy for the police to discover and to block. But it is just as easy for netizens to reinvent new codes and stay one jump ahead.

Some codes in popular usage are brought about less by political repression from the government than by broader social attitudes. In the early 2000s, for example, people in gay and lesbian subcultures in China began referring to one another as *tongzhi* 同志 'comrade'.[152] Here the oppressing force was not (or not only) the Party-state, hence it becomes an interesting fact that the code word chosen by the oppressed side was a classic political term. It did not have to be; the subculture could have chosen a word like "gay" or "queer". Apparently, an assumption had taken root that the terms to which coded language refer are most naturally Communist officialese, whose vocabulary was already well suited for irony.

Group loyalties based on any number of factors—hometowns, lineages, classes in school, and so on—have given rise to senses of "we" versus "they" in Chinese society, both in the Communist era and well before. The Mao years, though, brought an important new sense of *tamen* 他们 'they' into the Chinese language. The term became a nickname for the ruling authority. When used without an antecedent, *tamen* was understood to mean the Communist Party, the *lingdao* 'leadership', the people who control our lives. It implied a distance. One was circumspect in dealing with *tamen*, who could be arbitrary. (Party jargon may have exacerbated this sense, without meaning to, by its frequent reference to itself as *wo dang* 我党 'me [our] Party'.)

During political campaigns, especially in the Mao years, activists who were not originally part of the ruling authority, not part of *tamen*, sometimes chose to speak as if they were. This was usually done in pursuit of political advantage, but the tactic could backfire as well, because it could undermine one's position among one's peers. Ji Fengyuan, a veteran of Maoist campaigns, explains the difference between the normal, defensive use of the official language and this sort of political opportunism:

> People were forced to protect themselves and seek advancement by verbal displays of revolutionary conformity. Words were cheap and

---

152. Ji Fengyuan writes that the usage spread to mainland China from Hong Kong. *Linguistic Engineering*, p. 317.

everyone knew it. So while everyone understood, and respected, a decent compliance with the norms of linguistic virtue, those who excelled often became not admired models but objects of skepticism.[153]

Skepticism of this kind could turn into alienation from the redder-than-red. Liu Binyan, in his classic reportage "People or Monsters?" writes:

> Language is a strange thing. When Commissar Yang pointed to Wang Shouxin as having a "completely red family," he had meant to praise her. Yet, in the mouths of the common people, the same phrase—"completely red family"—was said as a curse.[154]

During the Mao years, farmers in agricultural brigades and communes sometimes referred to Party secretaries as *tuhuangdi* 土皇帝 'local emperors'.[155] Political operators who were good at manipulating personal relations got the nickname *wanneng jiao* 万能胶 'all-purpose glue'.[156] There are many other such epithets, and they exhibit great variety, but they have in common a sense of distance, alienation, a divide between us and them.

The same kind of division has appeared in the popular language of other Leninist states. In Poland in the 1980s, for example, Anna Wierzbicka finds a "polarization between 'them' (the people in power) and 'us' (the bulk of the nation)" and that "the language of official propaganda gives rise to its opposite: the unofficial, underground language of antipropaganda."[157] Vaclav Havel's brilliant exposé of the language of pretense in "The Power of the Powerless" is based on Czechoslovakia in the 1970s.[158] Miklos Haraszti *(The Velvet Prison)* for Hungary and Vladimir

---

153. Ibid., p. 299.
154. Liu Binyan, "Renyao zhi jian" 人妖之间, trans. James Feinerman, in Liu Binyan, *Two Kinds of Truth: Stories and Reportage from China*, ed. Perry Link (Bloomington: Indiana University Press, 2006), p. 60.
155. Kate Zhou, *How the Farmers Changed China: Power of the People* (Boulder, Colo.: Westview Press, 1996), p. 29.
156. Xiangsheng chuangzuo zuotanhui bangongshi, "Xiangsheng chuangzuo zuotanhui jianbao," day 5, p. 2.
157. Wierzbicka, "Antitotalitarian Language in Poland," pp. 1, 2.
158. Havel, *Living in Truth*, p. 45 and elsewhere.

Voinovich (*The Fur Hat*) for the Soviet Union highlight the difference between writing honestly and writing for and with "them."[159]

A noteworthy feature of all these cases is that the context of repression gives to ordinary language the potential to be extraordinary. Without repression, a plain statement might be just plain, but under repression, it can seem uplifting, inspiring, or even profound. Victor Erlich, writing of Soviet literature in the 1950s, has observed that "when bureaucratic euphemisms displace the unbearable actuality and explain it away, the simple act of calling a spade a spade, of naming the unspeakable, becomes an epiphany. When fraudulent official semantics distorts the normal relations between the sign and referent, responsible and accurate use of language is a blow for personal dignity."[160] The additional power that writing gets when done in defiance of repression has enhanced Chinese dissident voices since the 1950s. The enthusiastic response to Liu Binyan's work in both the 1950s and the 1980s is largely attributable to Liu's willingness to write down truths about corruption and abuse of power in plain, clear language, forming a sharp contrast with the surrounding official language. In the late 1980s, a group of students in Beijing experimented with the power of calling a spade a spade at the level of single words. Is *minhang* 民航 'the people's airline' really the people's airline? No, they reasoned, so let's call it *guanhang* 官航 'the officials' airline'. As an experiment, they tried out terms such as *guanhang* on others in society. They found that people at first were startled, but then, after reflecting for a moment, "got it." We should observe that there would have been no joke to "get" if the distance between *guan* and *min* had not already been broadly assumed and accepted. We now turn to some reflections on how significant that kind of broad acceptance might be.

Effects of the Language Game in the Mao and the Post-Mao Eras Compared

In 2009, at the sixtieth anniversary of the founding of the People's Republic of China, many analysts drew a distinction between the regime's "first

---

159. Miklos Haraszti, *The Velvet Prison: Artists under State Socialism*, trans. Katalin and Stephen Landesman (New York: Basic Books, 1987); Vladimir Voinovich, *The Fur Hat*, trans. Susan Brownsberger (San Diego: Harcourt Brace Jovanovich, 1989).

160. Erlich, "Post-Stalin Trends," *Slavic Review* 23, no. 3 (September 1964), p. 418.

thirty" (1949–79) and "second thirty" (1979–2009) years. And indeed, there has been a considerable difference. From the first to the second of these two periods, political control of daily life declined considerably, the country opened much more to the world, and the economy began to operate in very different ways. Party policies have changed, too, sometimes so radically as to become the very opposite of what they were before: capitalism was excoriated, then embraced; Confucius was denounced as a root of "feudalism," then exalted as a symbol of Chinese pride; memory of Japanese war atrocities was at first discouraged, then purposefully stimulated.

On the other hand, some key elements in the Communist Party's political tradition have remained the same: one-party rule, a Leninist governing structure, domination of political power at the top by the same group of families, and the mobilization of the tools of governance (including the police, media, education, and penal systems) to support the preservation of the political and economic interests of the elite.

Along this spectrum of change and continuity, official language and the playing of the language game are intermediate examples. Some of the basic structures are the same, but there has been considerable evolution, too. To trace every facet of change would be to write an encyclopedia, which is beyond our scope here. But we can at least take stock of how the language game in the two periods has seemed to relate, in general, to the ways people think and behave. Two Western writers, Jean-François Billeter and David Moser, have written brief but astute analyses of the social-psychological consequences of official language use in the Mao era and the post-Mao era, respectively. They are worth our consideration.

Billeter grounds his analysis in the Mao regime's claim that its rule is based on virtue. This claim has strong antecedents in Confucian culture, even if the contents of Confucian and Maoist "virtue" have been fundamentally different. Any regime that bases its legitimacy on a virtue-claim, Billeter argues, is "naturally unstable given the fact that, unlike qualifications of birth, virtue is not objectively measurable or certifiable. In this kind of regime, everyone had better be virtuous, or at least seem virtuous." Next, Billeter argues, the need for everyone to present appearances of virtue (and to play the language game, as I have been considering it here) naturally makes "all virtue come to appear suspicious." People dress up self-interest as virtue, or—even when they do not do this—are *suspected* by others of doing it. What Billeter calls a "pathology of virtue" becomes pervasive:

> Suspicion, hypocrisy, and opportunism settle in. Everyone is in danger of being justifiably or unjustifiably accused of hypocrisy or opportunism. A defense is sought in refusing to take risks or in refusing to expose oneself to any criticism whatsoever, in other words, in conformism. This is all the more true since the surest way of displaying revolutionary virtue is to denounce the lack of revolutionary virtue in others.[161]

Another question that is beyond the scope of this book but is well worth asking is what have the long-term psychological consequences been, for the generation whose formative years were the Mao era, of growing up with feigned virtue and suspicions of feigned virtue so natural a part of life. We have seen, above, many examples of how the language game during the Mao era was shaped by the need to negotiate a world in which the pretenses and suspicions Billeter identifies were dominant. When the question "Can I have a bigger apartment?" is expressed as "Do you think we can concretize Party Central's policy on intellectuals?" Billeter's point is illustrated. When an answer of no is expressed as "the policy may have difficulties," it is illustrated again. If the whole matter is dismissed because you are a "white expert," we have yet another example.[162] Billeter writes that the "pathology of virtue" can be "catastrophic" for society.

Moser, who worked for many years in Beijing for CCTV, finds a different sort of "pathology" in the public's accommodation of official language. Looking primarily at the years since 2000, he refers to "schizophrenia," a word that he means not in the clinical sense but in the popular sense of "split perception."[163] He finds that the official language game operates within certain spheres of life—the politically important spheres—but also

---

161. Jean-François Billeter, "The System of 'Class Status,'" in Stuart R. Schram, ed., *The Scope of State Power in China* (Hong Kong: Chinese University Press, 1985), pp. 147–148.

162. See the examples in the Introduction at note 17 and in this chapter in the paragraphs following notes 90 and 142.

163. David Moser, "Media 'Schizophrenia' in China," www.danwei.org/media_and_advertising/media_schizophrenia_in_china_b.php, accessed June 30, 2012.

floats, like a block of styrofoam, in an ocean of other kinds of language use with which it is fundamentally incompatible.

The situation came about, in Moser's analysis, largely because the Communist Party could not control the world revolution in digital technology. During the 1980s, when the Party was combating such things as "bourgeois liberalization" and "spiritual pollution," Party leaders could rely on their ability to seal out unwanted influences. They could never do this absolutely, but they could always make it work pretty well. Newspapers, radio, and television could be censored, foreign broadcasts could be jammed, the importation of foreign films could be monitored and rationed, and there was no Internet to speak of. Then, Moser writes,

> this all changed in the mid-90s, when digital technology hit China like an atomic bomb. Virtually overnight, waves of pirated CDs, software, computer games, and VCDs became available through underground bootleg channels. The effect was not merely the opening of a spigot; China was suddenly inundated by a tsunami of foreign "memes" and intellectual products. Outdoor stalls in the open-air markets began to offer counterfeit versions of Windows 95, Jane Fonda workout videos, music CDs from Mozart to Megadeath, and movies from *Bambi* to *Basic Instinct*. . . . TV junk food like *Get Smart* and *Charlie's Angels* suddenly appeared on Chinese screens, sandwiched between Peking opera and news footage of Li Peng.

What could the Party do? The tsunami could not be turned back. It was too big and, moreover, liquid in the sense that it seemed flexible at a molecular level. During the Mao era, and even in the 1980s, people watched films and plays in large groups, and much newspaper reading was done in open offices or at billboards in public parks. Such activity could be controlled through censorship and mutual surveillance that induced self-censorship. But now people could stay at home, make their individual choices of what to listen to and look at, and, if they liked, keep their activity pretty much private. So long as there was strong demand and money to be made, illicit traffic in digital content was nearly impossible to stop. Moser provides a photo taken in Kunming of a bootleg DVD shop right next door to a police station. In short, Moser writes, "the propaganda machine's worst nightmare had come true."

On the other hand, the Party could not just walk away from its claim that official language embodies an immutable political correctness or the myth that such language represents the unitary voice of "the Chinese people." To retreat on these fronts would be to risk the Party's grip on power. So the official language continued to march along, lonely in its own sphere and immaculate in its internal consistency even while it became impossible, indeed unthinkable, that it be integrated into the multiplicity that surrounded it. The result, Moser finds, is that Chinese media content has split clearly between "the news" (i.e, the official news in the state media, plus a few other topics that need the imprimatur of being officially correct) and "everything else."[164]

The incommensurability of the two realms has caused practical problems for media workers. Leakage from unofficial language into official spheres has been hard to avoid and has caused what Moser refers to as problems of "schizophrenia." He relates a story about Qin Minxin, a deputy director of the international department of CCTV's Entertainment Program Center. Qin was considering whether to air the American sitcom *Friends* on CCTV. For years, *Friends* had been infectiously popular among young Chinese, who passed it around on bootleg DVDs. Should CCTV now air it? Qin was not sure:

> I had thought the play focused on friendship, but after a careful preview I found each episode had something to do with sex . . . the attitudes of the six close-knit young friends in the play cannot be generally accepted by Chinese audiences yet.

Could he cut the parts that refer to sex? That would not work, Qin thought, because

> most youth on the Chinese mainland have watched the show and feel passionate about it. If we make too much trimming, I'm afraid they will not agree. But it is also impossible that we accept it uncritically . . . much content of *Friends*, although considered healthy in the United States, is unacceptable to the Chinese.

---

164. Moser notes in passing how an opposite trend emerged in the U.S. media over the same years; in the U.S., entertainment and news reporting has merged, and the distinction has become blurred.

Moser then analyzes the several ways Qin has to struggle as he tries to bring together the pretend world of CCTV language and the actual world that surrounds it. Chinese audiences "cannot accept" the sexual implications of *Friends*, but CCTV must not censor this content because it attracts audiences. Contradictory? Yes—but also no, because "cannot accept," in the official language, is pretend language for "should not, in our opinion, accept." In the pretend world, "the people" do not do anything they should not do. It therefore also becomes meaningful for CCTV officials to ponder whether to "expose" people to *Friends* despite the fact that they are already well exposed to it. (Indeed, the fact that viewers find the show attractive is the very reason why CCTV is considering its "introduction.") By the end of Moser's analysis, one almost sympathizes with Qin. He needed to juggle two worlds, a real one and a pretend one.

The ersatz flavor of the pretend world can be sensed even when explicit comparison to the real world is absent. It is enough for the real world to exist only vaguely in the background. One of Moser's examples of the self-revelation of pretense is the annual CCTV Chinese New Year variety show:

> The lavish costumes, the unrelenting upbeat tone, all the glitz and flashy production values seem designed to distract from the empty core of the affair, an over-compensation for the impossibility of offering anything that reflects real life.

Moser calls the presentation of real life an "impossibility," not just an omission, because of the closed nature, and ultimately the fragility, of the official language system. If a performer were to step out of line and crack a joke about current affairs, or satirize a leader, or present a "national minority" person who was not wearing colorful native garb and a toothy smile, the aberration would not stand on its own. It would threaten the entire world of pretense. The failure of protocol at point A would expose its artifice at all other points. Moser writes: "Since performers do not—and cannot in principle—relate to the audience in an honest fashion . . . no wonder the shots of the audience so often reveal a sea of stony-faced spectators applauding robotically on cue."

Does the pretend world of official language in the post-Mao era pose a danger to the whole of society in the way that language based in a "pathology of virtue," in Billeter's analysis, did during the Mao era? Probably not, at least not to the same extent. Official language in post-Mao times can no longer dominate as it did under Mao. Significant dangers do remain, however. I see primarily two, one potential and one actual.

The potential danger is an intensification in the use of the official language to stimulate and exploit nationalism. After the June Fourth massacre of 1989, when the image of China's rulers was at a low point, Jiang Zemin (backed by Deng Xiaoping) made the strategic decision to use nationalism to try to recoup the Party's image. A number of measures—including the Beijing Olympics, the Shanghai World's Fair, the denunciation of "splittism" in Tibet, Xinjiang, and Taiwan, the injection of chauvinist sentiment into news reports of conflicts with Japan, the United States, and other countries—have met with considerable success in this regard. A stress on nationalism serves the interest of the ruling authority in two important ways: first, it distracts attention from problems that citizens otherwise complain about—corruption, special privilege, pollution, rights violations, a growing wealth gap, and so on—and second, it helps to change the image of Party leaders. Instead of being the targets of popular resentment because of all the problems, these leaders can present themselves as standard-bearers and heroes of the Chinese nation. The danger, as of the second decade of the twenty-first century, is that nationalism could be magnified even much more. It could draw deeper on Chinese national pride and on the sense of aggrievement about the history of the previous two centuries. The nation's textbooks already stress this aggrievement, and the potential to magnify it further, and to marshal energies behind the idea that China should be "number one," is very considerable. I am not ready to predict that an outsized chauvinism will appear in China. But one is possible, and it would be bad news for both China and the rest of the world if it should come.

In my view, the greatest *actual* social-psychological cost of the official language game has been something rather different: it is the general acceptance by the Chinese citizenry that the demands of the official language game are "normal" and should be accepted as a part of daily life. The game's demands prohibit certain topics from public discussion: the disasters of the Mao era, the 1989 June Fourth massacre, misbehavior among top leaders or their family members, the Falun Gong movement, political questions relating to Taiwan, Tibet, and Xinjiang, the prospect of an end to one-party rule, and a number of others. All these are important topics on which a healthy society would conduct open debate. But many Chinese citizens have grown so accustomed to avoiding these topics that their absence from the public sphere seems unremarkable. People go through daily life—making money, enjoying fashions, playing sports, traveling, finding romantic partners, and doing other things that people could not easily do during the Mao era—while simply avoiding the areas in the world of ideas that could cause "trouble." This is, in a sense, a rational way to behave. Why should a person spoil a good thing? Dissidents report that their colleagues, neighbors, and even families sometimes find it odd, and even a bit stupid, that they venture into politically forbidden zones and do things that, although idealistically aimed to help the whole of society, in fact are likely to hurt themselves. Most of the public wants to be "smarter" than that. It is smarter to stay out of trouble and take what you can get. My main worry about this pattern is not just that it isolates the "dissidents"—the people who are courageous enough to speak about ideals. My worry is that, for the public at large, a myopic outlook on the world comes to seem ordinary and normal.

In his essay on "schizophrenia," David Moser relates an incident in which he was invited to be a guest on a CCTV talk show on the topic of the Internet. Before the taping the host sought to put him at ease. "Just relax and say anything you want," the host counseled, "and it should be okay." Moser reports feeling surprise at the man's apparent nonchalance. "*Anything* that comes to mind?" Moser asked. "Does that include how the government blocks sensitive sites and news sources? Can we freely discuss Internet pornography? Or how chat rooms are monitored and censored?" The host backed off. "Yes, well, *almost* anything," he said, as if reminded of another way to look at the world. The value of this anecdote is not just to give yet another example of the well-known fact that China's Internet is censored. The more significant point is that a CCTV host can become so accustomed to self-censorship, so relaxed with it, that even a word like "anything" can be severely stunted in his usage without his seeming to have noticed. He accepts the rules of a language game so completely that, unless reminded, he does not realize he is doing so.

Epilogue

To view the matter superficially, I chose the three themes in this book—rhythm, metaphor, and politics—simply because they are facets of the modern Chinese language that I have found interesting over the years. I had taken a lot of notes on them.

But this explanation harbors a deeper question: why did *these* particular aspects of the language, and not others, draw my attention? Why was I not taking notes on the *bai hua* vernacular movement, on debates over romanization, or on conventions of punctuation or paragraphing? The topics one might choose to study are almost endless. Why these three? Do they share anything in common?

They do, I believe. Two commonalities in particular stand out.

One is that all three are features of language whose use normally *goes unnoticed*. A few people—professional linguists and others—are consciously aware of them, but people in daily life seldom are. Most speakers of Chinese just "absorb" them—and use them correctly in both speech and writing—but are unaware of doing so. This inadvertency contrasts sharply with the very conscious manner in which other aspects of language are learned. Chinese children are highly aware of what they are doing when they labor to master character writing or punctuation rules; their parents and teachers, too, pay plenty of attention when checking their work for errors. Advanced students of Chinese literature, in their conscious work, study such topics as genre, form, narrative point of view, intertextual influences, and the ideology and historical contexts of literary works. Only a few scholars, working in linguistics or cognitive science, turn conscious attention to how prosody or conceptual metaphor work in daily-life language.

For example, the overwhelming majority of speakers of Chinese are unaware—and do not need to be aware—of how a 2–2–3 (*qiyan* 七言) rhythm can serve to formalize or exalt a piece of ordinary language; or how the structural metaphor *guo* 过 'cross over' works in expressions about entering or leaving consciousness (*yunguoqu* 晕过去 'faint and go-over', *xingguolai* 醒过来 'awaken and come-over', etc.); or how, in political language, a phrase like *jishaoshu* 极少数 'tiny minority' adds a nonlexical derogation that causes the phrase to mean something like "tiny (troublemaking) minority." Still—and this is the interesting part—*speakers of Chinese completely master these conventions and rely on them in daily life.* In order for daily-life communication to work, rules that people do not know about are just as important as those of which they are consciously aware.

The other commonality among the three topics of rhythm, metaphor, and politics is that despite the inadvertency of their use, each of these elements *affects meaning*, that is, makes a difference in what is communicated. This is not something that can be said of all linguistic inadvertencies. For example, English speakers who insert "filler" phrases like "you know" and "I mean" in their sentences and Chinese speakers who use similar fillers such as *zheige, zheige, zheige* 这个, 这个, 这个 . . . (this, this, this . . .) or *neige, neige, neige* 那个, 那个, 那个 . . . (that, that, that . . .) are normally adding nothing to the meanings of the overall sentences they are uttering. At most, such words are but floor-holders, whose "meaning" might be said to be "I would like to keep on talking even though I have not yet figured out what it is that I want to say next." (The English word "like" in a sentence such as "He asked me to dance and I'm—like—*what?*" also appears empty but probably is not entirely so. It does have a sliver of meaning, as attested by the fact that, at least sometimes, it cannot easily be omitted; but that sliver of meaning is extremely hard to articulate.)

By contrast, the "meanings" of rhythm, metaphor, and political connotation that I have examined in this book are usually more substantial than this, and often can be at least partly articulated. The exaltation *qiyan* provides, the spatial conception of consciousness *yunguoqu* implies, and the denigration *jishaoshu* connotes are all fairly clear. Moreover, we can count them as "meaning" (and not just ad hoc flavors) because they remain reliably the same among the very large community of speakers of Chinese who pass them back and forth. In using the *qiyan* pattern to make a phrase, one can assume that one's listeners will correctly apprehend the exaltation; the negative connotation of *jishaoshu*, when used in political contexts, is equally standard. This sort of "meaning," to be sure, is vaguer than that of a word like *zhuantou* 砖头 'brick'. But even its quality of vagueness is something that travels effectively from speaker to speaker.

The combination of these two commonalities—inadvertency and meaningfulness—is especially interesting because of the paradox it seems to imply. We normally think of meaning as something that we *mean*, and what we normally understand by "mean" is that we are aware of what we are doing. If I step on your toe accidentally, I can apologize that I did not *mean* to. In this book, though, we have studied aspects of meaning that we do not notice. *Meaning that we do not notice?* The phrase almost seems self-contradictory. But there can be no denying the phenomenon. It is there. This book offers a range of examples of it, and my examples are only a smattering of what is there to be found.

How should we describe this kind of "unnoticed meaning"? Metaphors of plumbing, or of anatomy, come to mind. We are dealing with the undergirding of language, with functions that are vital even if they are not obvious on the surface. Our awareness of these quiescent workings of words is usually about as good as our awareness of our pancreas. Our life depends on our pancreas, though we seldom think about it and (except for a few of us) do not understand it or even try to. An analogy to bicycle-riding seems useful as well. Most people who ride bicycles do not understand why it is possible to ride a bicycle.

For such things—pancreases, bicycles, or the undergirdings of a language—it is appropriate to ask the question, "Why study them?" Understanding for its own sake is, of course, always a defensible answer to this question. But are there more practical benefits? In the case of the pancreas, avoidance of severe pain or death from pancreatitis is an obvious practical payoff. What about the undergirdings of language use? Are there any practical payoffs?

I believe that there are, and that some of the examples in this book can show this to be so. For one, there is value in becoming consciously aware of the ways "meanings" can be delivered inadvertently—bypassing, as it were, the critical judgment that one normally would want to apply. For example, when a message expressed in *qiyan* rhythm strikes us as being authoritative, it can be useful to realize that the sense of authority comes in part from the rhythm alone, not necessarily from any special stature of the issuer of the words or from any special wisdom of the words themselves. This does not mean that we should turn rebellious when we see a street sign in *qiyan* that says *yi kan, er man, san tongguo* 一看, 二慢, 三通過 'first look, then go slowly, then cross' or when a political leader commands *linghun shenchu gan geming!* 灵魂深处干革命 'make revolution in the depths of the soul!' We can still choose whether to respect authority or not. The value of becoming aware of the rhythm is that we can also be aware of the claim to authority the rhythm places on us. We can remind ourselves that rhythms per se have no grounds to make such claims, and that we can set them aside if we like. This leaves us more free to think for ourselves.

Parallelism, alliteration, song, and other embellishments of words can have similar effects. Chiasmus, as we have seen, is an especially clear example of this kind of imposition on our intellect. Chiasmus seems to claim special access to wisdom, and it is important that we be able to set this claim aside if we like. When a politician says that Enron executives were "either criminally stupid or stupidly criminal," the art of his phrase, and the power it generates, almost seem to say to us, "This is so obviously right that you needn't think about it anymore." The politician may, of course, have an excellent point about Enron. But we are better off if we probe further and find exactly what that point is than if we allow ourselves to be transfixed by chiasmus and cut off our thinking.

Many of the examples I considered in Chapter 3 illustrate benefits that can be had simply by understanding what political language is and how it differs from daily-life language. The person who is officially labeled part of a "tiny minority" (*jishaoshu*) is obviously better off if he or she can understand that the phrase is not a description of the actual size of the community that shares his or her opinion but a pejorative term that a Party-state uses in order to serve a purpose. In the late 1950s, learning to play the official language game began to be a required part of Chinese daily life, and in ensuing decades people grew skilled at using the official language not only to defend themselves but to pursue interests of their own. This kind of conscious use of official language brought the political underpinnings of language to the surface more clearly than the others—those relating to rhythm and metaphor—that this book has addressed. As of the early twenty-first century, Chinese speakers remain much less aware of the rhythmic and metaphorical undergirdings of their language than they are of the political ones. This imbalance is understandable, of course. It has sometimes been vitally important to understand what a phrase like *jishaoshu* is doing, whereas understanding the hidden connotations of a conceptual metaphor like *yunguoqu*, or of a *qiyan* rhythm, has been much less important.

In cases where political language combines with either a rhythm or a conceptual metaphor, it can be enlightening to observe how the undergirdings sometimes clash. Metaphors and rhythms—because people have examined them less than political language—are sometimes employed even when they contradict conscious political messages. In metaphor use, for example, the conscious ideology of the Communist movement says workers are the "leading class" and officials "serve the people." But conceptual metaphors—in both official and unofficial language—have consistently used *shang* 上 'up' for people who have more power and *xia* 下 'below' for people who have less. When workers make a report to their leaders, the report inevitably "goes up" (*shangqu* 上去), even though in the political ideology, the workers are already at the top and the officials theoretically should be serving them from "below." In the case of rhythm, we saw in Chapter 1 several examples of how Maoist culture used *wuyan* and *qiyan* rhythms to exalt politically correct things, including Mao himself, even while the same Maoist culture, at the conscious level, was denouncing things like ancient rhythms under the rubric of "the four olds" (customs, culture, habits, ideas). There is value in noticing these inconsistencies, and the value is not merely in noticing that the human mind can handle conceptual inconsistencies and still get along in daily life. The additional value, indeed the greater one, is in perceiving the double standards they reveal. With rare exceptions, it has never *really* been true that leaders in the Communist system have conceived of themselves as servants of the working class, and understanding the inadvertencies of their daily-life metaphors can help to make this point explicit. Similarly, Maoist culture never *really* succeeded in rooting out "the four olds"—even from itself, as its frequent use of *wuyan* and *qiyan* rhythms makes clear.

In a broader sense, study of the inadvertencies of language considered in this book can help us to understand how the human mind works. For the cognitive scientists whose work I drew on in Chapter 2, this line of inquiry has been the main goal. With rare exceptions, though, the subfield of cognitive science that works on conceptual metaphor has not done too well at testing its hypotheses against non-European languages, and there is something to be gained by trying to do so. By comparing Chinese and English uses of fundamental conceptual metaphors such as "space for time"—as Ning Yu does, for example—one can shed at least some light on the elusive question of to what extent conceptual metaphor varies with culture and to what extent it springs from structures that are likely universal in the human brain. To what extent the timeless "mind-body" problem might be related to habits of metaphor use is but one example of the possible benefits of studying conceptual metaphor comparatively.

At a more mundane level, awareness of how conceptual metaphors can differ from one culture to another can help us avoid cultural misunderstanding. In Chapter 2, I related an anecdote about how two eminent scholars, one Chinese and one American, became very unhappy with each other over a misunderstanding about what "yellow" meant. Their exchange would have been entirely different—very friendly—if they had understood the same connotations for the term; but they did not, and the result was powerful anger. Such a pure example of metaphorical misunderstanding is rare, but it illustrates a more general danger that affects many other and more complicated cases. The metaphorical connotations of "dog," for example, are generally more negative in Chinese than in English, so that a Chinese phrase like *zougou* 走狗 'running dog' loses some of its sting when translated literally into English; on the other hand, the English word "watchdog" can take on an unintended negative connotation if translated too literally into Chinese. In any case, everyone is better off to be aware of such things than not to be. It can be useful, as Dilin Liu has shown, to reflect on the prominence of metaphor families in particular cultures. American English makes much use of sports metaphors and car-driving metaphors; Chinese has special predilections for metaphors of eating and of stage performance, as well as—in the Mao and the post-Mao eras—military metaphors. It is hard to be precise about how significant these tendencies are, but it would likely be a mistake to say that they have no significance at all.

More generally—although this, too, would be hard to show concretely—I suspect that any person who notices the undergirdings of his or her daily-life language, whether comparatively or not, is likely to reap benefits just from thinking, and therefore speaking and writing, more clearly and consistently. There are so many examples of this that one can cite them almost at random. For conceptual metaphors, it is useful to understand why the phrase *houdai de qiantu* 后代的前途 'the future of future generations' is not contradictory despite its surface appearance of being so. To be clear about the two space-for-time metaphors that it combines is to be able to use *qian* and *hou* metaphorically, in any number of contexts, with more precision and confidence. Finally, to understand linguistic undergirdings can simply be enjoyable, even if no practical advantages are at stake. By "enjoyable" I mean here something a bit more than the phrase "understanding for its own sake" that I used above. Understanding for its own sake can be fun, but need not be. I find it particularly fun to notice that a 3–3–7 rhythm appears in a Chinese nursery rhyme (*ni pai yi, wo pai yi, yige xiaohair kai feiji* 'you pat one, I pat one; one little child flies the plane') and also appears in an English rhyme ("this old man, he plays one, he plays knick-knack on my thumb"), and to wonder why, and to discover a complex history that begins at least fifteen hundred years ago and originates (separately?) at two ends of the Silk Road as well as in Europe. Similarly, I think, it is fun to note that the Maoist slogan *gongye xue Daqing* 工业学大庆 'industry should learn from [the] Daqing [oilfields]' employs an ancient Chinese rhythm. What would Stalin say? (What, indeed, would Mao have said, had he noticed?)

There is also something fun—but even more than fun, something deeply satisfying—to see how many up-and-down metaphors, space-for-time metaphors, color metaphors, and other fundaments of the conceptual apparatuses of Chinese and English are the same, even though speakers of the two languages often like to think that they and their cultures are "very different" from the other. The commonality of the human experience seems underscored by such discoveries.

Acknowledgments

My interests in the topics of this book have grown on their own, without a clear plan and in unforeseen ways, beginning primarily in the early 1990s and thanks to conversations with a wide variety of people. I hesitate to begin listing their names because I know that any list will be incomplete. I cringe to think of readers who might scan the following list for their own names, not find them, and then judge me, rightly, to be either forgetful or insufficiently ungrateful. Still, to say nothing at all would be even worse, so I will try.

I owe everything to Rulan Pian, who started me in Chinese at Harvard in 1963–64, and to her genius-father, Yuen Ren Chao, whose books and articles have not only taught me much but have set standards for me and others to emulate. My mentor and dear friend Ta-tuan Ch'en at Princeton taught me an immense amount over decades of working together. Chapter 1 on rhythm owes much to Feng Shengli. Sam Glucksberg provided crucial help in the field of conceptual metaphor for Chapter 2. David Moser has given many examples and astute advice on all three chapters. Others who have provided materials, offered insights, or reviewed drafts include Nicholas Admussen, An Kun, Robert Bagley, Anthony Barbieri-Low, Chen Ping, Joanne Chiang, Chih-ping Chou, Duanmu San, John Frankenstein, Harry Frankfurt, Meow Hui Goh, Adele Goldberg, Hu Ping, Monica Link, Liu Binyan, Victor Mair, Mao Ruxing, Mao Sheng, Daniel Osherson, Andrew Plaks, James Pusey, James Richardson, Patricia Russel, Michael Schoenhals, Su Wei, Su Xiaokang, Tong Yi, Wang Haicheng, Wang Lixiong, Wang Wei, Xiao Qiang, Ye Minlei, Yu Maochun, Yu Ying-shih, and Bell Yung. None of these, of course, bears responsibility for my mistakes.

I am grateful for the support of the Chiang Ching-kuo Foundation for research support during 1994–95, when research for this book first began in a serious way; to Chinese University Press for its permission to use, in Chapter 1, portions of my essay "The Secret History of Classical Rhythms in Modern Chinese," from *The Scholar's Mind: Essays in Honor of F. W. Mote*, ed. Perry Link (Hong Kong: Chinese University Press, 2009); and to Tong Yi, Daniel Link, and Samuel Link for their graceful indulgence of my use of time.

Index

Abstract nouns, 222–223, 244–245, 248, 255–256
Acting metaphor. *See* Stage performance metaphors
Adjectives: in conceptual metaphors, 220; nouns as, 261; in official language, 262; repetition of, 192–193
Adverbs in official language, 248
Advertisements: military metaphors in, 253; parallelism used in, 105; rhythmic patterns in, 34–35
"Affection is warmth" metaphor, 185
Al-Kāshgarī, Mahmūd, 169
Alverson, Hoyt, 115, 226
Ambiguity: in official language, 247–248, 255–256, 287–288, 318–320; and self-censorship, 317; and stage performance metaphors, 208
Ames, Roger, 203, 205, 227
Analects (Confucius), 276
Anatomy metaphors, 351
"Anger is heat" metaphors, 186–187
Animals, 269, 314
Anonymity of Internet, 334
Anti-Rightist Movement (1957), 33, 235, 250, 254, 259, 296–297, 322
Anti-Spiritual Pollution Campaign (1983), 318
Apartheid, 291
Aspect markers, 262–264
Austin, J. L., 83

Authoritarian regimes: metaphors used by, 256–257; numbers used by, 266–267; and official language, 258, 277
Authority: and abstract language, 256; and ambiguity, 288; and fourth tone, 94–95; and *qiyan* patterns, 352

Baigujing xianxingji (Ma Ji), 32
Bartholomew, Terese, 100
Basic Color Terms (Berlin & Kay), 148
Beijing Massacre (1989): metonyms for, 210; and military metaphors, 19; and political language game, 16, 246, 270–271, 275, 294, 297–298, 320, 327; and stage performance metaphors, 251
Being, 226–227
Berlin, Brent, 148–149
Billeter, Jean-François, 342–343
Black, 149, 154
Bloch, Maurice, 90, 275–276, 278, 290
Bo Yibo, 258
Bodde, Derk, 223
Book of Odes, 90
Boroditsky, Lera, 130, 131, 132, 133, 146
Borrowing of metaphors, 184–187, 232
Brightness metaphors, 190
Brushes with Power (Kraus), 308

Calligraphy, 204
Camel Xiangzi (Lao She), 24
Can Xue, 294

Cao Changqing, 246, 248, 249, 254, 256, 267, 295–296
Cao Xueqin, 219
Cao Yu, 84
The Captive Mind (Milocz), 13
"Causation is emergence" metaphor, 214
Censoring mechanisms, 317
Central Chinese Television (CCTV), 34–35, 345–346
Ceremonial trappings, 276
Chan, Anita, 208
Chang, Jung, 292
Chao, Y. R., 2, 22–23, 41, 72, 83, 102, 207
Charges-of-convenience, 310
Charter 08, 327, 333, 338
Chaucer, Geoffrey, 75
Chen Dengke, 101
Chen Duxiu, 43
Chen Guangcheng, 310
Chen, Matthew, 62
Chen, Jenn-yeu, 131, 137, 144, 209
Chen Yi, 309
Chen Yun, 303
Cheng Dachang, 167
"The Chess Master" (Zhong Acheng), 293–294
Chiang Kai-shek, 305
Chiasmus, 106–109
Children's names, 100–101, 268
Chomsky, Noam, 11, 115, 129, 133, 134
Chou, Jane, 221
Chuang, H. C., 243
Clapper-tales, 30
Clash of Civilizations and the Remaking of World Order (Huntington), 207
"Closeness is strength" metaphor, 193–195
Coded language, 338
Cognitive science: on color metaphors, 150; and metaphors, 116, 117–118, 354; on time metaphors, 145
Color metaphors, 147–155, 355
Committee on Scholarly Communication with China (CSCC), 2, 286, 322
Community memory, 84
Completeness, 93
Conceptualizing capacity, 224
Conceptual metaphors, 116. *See also* Metaphors
Confucius, 172, 173, 200, 276, 320, 342
Consciousness metaphors, 9, 122–123, 169–171
Conservative, 250

Consonants, 96–101
Container metaphors, 213–214, 215, 216–218, 221–222
The Contemporary Theory of Metaphor: A Perspective from Chinese (Ning Yu), 138
"Control is up" metaphor, 159–160
Cook, Sarah, 291
Cooper, William, 177
Cooperative principle, 119
Covert sexism, 180–183
Credibility, 243
Cultural memory, 84
Cultural Revolution. *See* Great Proletarian Cultural Revolution
Cultural T-shirts, 27

Daily-life language: and language game, 278–341; metaphors in, 115–128; *qiyan* patterns in, 25–26; rhythm patterns in, 24–37; *wuyan* patterns in, 25–26
Dalai Lama, 252, 257, 281–282, 285, 307
Darkness metaphors, 190
Dead metaphors, 121, 251, 300
Deception, 91
Defining concept, 119
Deng Xiaoping: Mao's criticisms of, 328; metaphors used by, 8; and official language, 242, 270, 274, 288–289, 303; repetition used by, 266
Descartes, René, 11
Determinacy, 161
Dickens, Charles, 219
Difficulty metaphors, 189–190
Ding Ling, 293, 303
Dingell, John, 108
Direction. *See* North and south metaphors
Dittmer, Lowell, 243
Doing Things with Words in Chinese Politics (Schoenhals), 274
Dominant external rhythms, 54–59
Dominant metaphors, 198–209
Double meaning, 100, 328–329, 330
Down. *See* Up and down metaphors
Dream of the Red Chamber (Cao Xueqin), 205, 207, 219
Driving of vehicles metaphors, 199, 209, 354
Drumsinging, 30
Du Fu, 12, 81
Duanmu San, 37, 51, 52, 53–54, 68, 73, 88
Dummy verbs, 17–18, 271
Dyads, privilege in, 174–183

"The East Is Red" (song), 12
Eating metaphors, 198–200, 209, 354
Effortless Action: Wu-wei as Conceptual Metaphor and Spiritual Ideal in Early China (Slingerland), 172
"Eight Honors and Eight Shames," 34, 266
Ekman, Paul, 186, 187, 188
English language: color metaphors in, 147–155; consciousness metaphors in, 169–171; container metaphors in, 216–218; dominant metaphors in, 198–209; dyad privilege in, 174–183; left-to-right orientation of, 144; length and volume as spatial metaphors in, 132; lexicon of, 244–245; meanings of rhythmic patterns in, 86; pitch differences in, 101; recessive rhythms in, 56; stress patterns of syllables in, 21–22; time metaphors in, 115, 133, 136–147; up and down metaphors in, 145, 155–162, 255
Erlich, Victor, 322, 341
Euphemisms, 311–314
Existence, 226–227
External rhythms, 54–59

False verb-object compounds, 72
Falun Gong, 306, 307
Family relations. *See* "Government is family" metaphor
Fan fenlie doctrine, 285
Fang Lizhi, 259, 280–281, 328, 330
Fear: and ambiguity in official language, 318; and ontological metaphors, 216; and self-censorship, 317; and violent language, 254
Feng Menglong, 63
Feng Shengli, 51, 53, 58–59, 60–61, 67
Fiction: official language in, 302–303; *wuyan* and *qiyan* patterns in, 25–26
Filler verbs, 17–18, 271
First tone, 101
"Fit": as kind of truth, 274–278; and meanings of rhythms, 90; and parallelism, 103
"Five black categories," 66, 266
"Five pay-attentions and four beautifuls," 112
"Five Relations," 200
Five-syllable strings, 62–63, 64–66. *See also Wuyan* patterns
Flexibility, up and down metaphors to convey, 161

Focal colors, 12, 149–150
Fodor, Jerry, 129
Formality: of official language, 234, 242–243; and stage performance metaphors, 203; up and down metaphors to convey, 161
Foul odor metaphors, 188–189
"Four Basic Principles," 247, 266, 270
"The Four Clears and the Four Unclears" (anonymous), 336
"Four Modernizations," 266
Four-syllable patterns: in daily-life language, 27; in Great Leap Forward period, 44–45; in recessive rhythms, 61; speaker's awareness of, 111; in *xiangsheng*, 31
Fourth tone, 94–96, 101–102
Frankenstein, John, 265
Freud, Sigmund, 123, 169
Friedlander, Henry, 290
Friends (television sitcom), 345–346
Front and back metaphors, 195–197
Fruit language, 246, 248
The Fur Hat (Voinovich), 341
The Future Beckons (Zhao Zixiong), 242

Gang of Four, 302, 311
Gao, 17–18, 271–273
Gao Xingjian, 192
Gao Yubao, 71
Gay subculture, 339
Ge Fei, 294
Gendered terms, 180–183
Gender-neutral dyads, 179–180
Glucksberg, Sam, 123
Goal orientation of official language, 270–274
Goebbels, Joseph, 296
"Government is family" metaphor, 200–201, 209
Graham, A. C., 205
Grammar: and meaning, 54–55; moral weight of, 267; of official language, 234, 235, 237, 260–267; recessive rhythms altering, 73–74; rhythmic patterns determined by, 37; and three-syllable phrases, 51
Gravity, 130, 146
Great Leap Forward: euphemisms used in, 311; four-syllable phrasing used in, 44–45; and official language, 235, 236, 322; parallelism used in, 103; pattern 3-3-7 used in, 80; rhythmic phrasing used in, 45, 93

Great Proletarian Cultural Revolution: aspect marker use in, 263–264; chiasmus used in, 106; difficulty metaphors used in, 189; grammar use in, 261; and official language, 249, 269–270; pattern 3-3-7 used in, 80; rhythmic phrasing used in, 16, 33, 45, 66; and stage performance metaphors, 204
Greek language: length and volume as spatial metaphors in, 132; time metaphors in, 133
Green, 152
"Green Dam Youth Escort" software, 310–311
Grice, Paul, 119
Gu Hua, 325
Guo Moruo, 26
Guo Qiru, 31

Ha Jin, 294
Happiness, 157–158, 188
Haraszti, Miklos, 13, 244, 340
Havel, Vaclav, 244, 332–333, 340
He Chi, 33
He Qinglian, 310
Heat. See "Anger is heat" metaphors
Heng, Liang, 238
Heshang (television series), 152, 338
Hidden meanings, 100
Higher-order conditioning, 300–301
Historical materialism, 239
Hitler, Adolf, 256, 257
Homonyms, 100
Horizontal movement metaphors, 125, 130, 138, 143, 144, 147, 170
Hou Baolin, 31, 100
Hsia, T. A., 243, 251
Hsu, Mei-ling, 164
Hu Fayun, 292
Hu Jintao, 34, 176–177, 201, 289, 313
Hu Ping, 273–274
Hu Qiaomu, 242, 260
Hu Shi, 43, 106
Hu Yaobang, 240, 241–242, 254–255, 272
Hu, ji, dan (Wang Guoxiang), 218
Hua Guofeng, 275, 277, 284
Huntington, Samuel, 207

Implied conditionals, 70
"Important is big" metaphor, 191
Indonesian language: length and volume as spatial metaphors in, 132; time metaphors in, 133

Infantilization, 265
Informality: codes for, 338; and official language, 323–324; of ordinary language, 242–243; up and down metaphors to convey, 161. *See also* Daily-life language
"Instrument is companion" metaphor, 210–211
Internal pressure metaphors, 187–188
Internet, 310–311, 334, 338–339
Irony, 120–121
Item lists, 66–67

Jenner, William, 279
Ji Fengyuan: on military metaphors, 251; on mindset of political language game, 292; on official language, 243, 279, 297, 302; on psychological effect of political language, 300, 339–340
Jia Baoyu, 179, 205
Jiang Kun, 329
Jiang Qing, 241, 305
Jiang Zemin, 238, 266, 282–283, 284, 289
Jichu Hanyu (textbook), 261
Jituan, 305–306
Johnson, Mark: on "affection is warmth" metaphor, 185; on "causation is emergence" metaphor, 214; on "closeness is strength metaphor," 193, 195; on conceptual metaphors, 116–117, 119–122; on consciousness metaphors, 169; on cultural values in metaphors, 198; on difficulty metaphors, 189; on front and back metaphors, 196; on "important is big" metaphor, 191; on intonation, 102; on metaphors and thought, 8–11, 128–130, 133–134; on "mountain as person" metaphor, 197; on ontological metaphors, 15, 215–216, 245; on privilege in dyads, 177; on repetition in metaphors, 192–193; on time metaphors, 145; on up and down metaphors, 157–158, 159
Jung, Carl, 169
Jusczyk, Peter W., 77–78

Kang Sheng, 311
Kant, Immanuel, 11, 115, 134
Kay, Paul, 148–149, 150–151
Kennedy, John F., 106
Keysar, Boaz, 124
Köhler, Wolfgang, 97
"Kong Yiji" (Lu Xun), 4, 56

Kövecses, Zoltán, 158
Kraus, Richard, 308

Lakoff, George: on "affection is warmth" metaphor, 185, 186; on "causation is emergence" metaphor, 214; on "closeness is strength" metaphor, 193, 195; on color metaphors, 150–151; on conceptualizing capacity, 224; on conceptual metaphors, 116–117, 119–122; on consciousness metaphors, 169; on cultural values in metaphors, 198; on difficulty metaphors, 189; on front and back metaphors, 196; on "important is big" metaphor, 191; on intonation, 102; on metaphors and thought, 8–11, 128–130, 133–134; on "mountain as person" metaphor, 197; on nominalization, 225; on ontological metaphors, 15, 215–216, 245; physiological universality hypothesis of, 188; on privilege in dyads, 177; on repetition in metaphors, 192–193; on time metaphors, 145; on up and down metaphors, 157–158, 159
Language game in politics, 278–341; Mao vs. post-Mao era effects of, 341–348; ruled side of game, 321–341; rulers' side of game, 295–321
Lao She, 24, 200, 272
Laozi, 172
Lauer, R. H., 222–223
Left-to-right orientation, 143–144, 250–251
Length as spatial metaphor, 132
Lesbian subculture, 339
Lessing, Doris, 256
Levi, Primo, 314
Lexicon of official language, 244–260
Li Bai, 12, 81
Li Denghui, 266
Li Peng, 16, 88, 246, 251
Li Shangyin, 168
Li Tuo, 13, 19, 293, 303
Liang Shanbo, 179
Liberal, 250
Limericks, 55–56, 74, 87
Lin Biao, 69, 305, 311, 320
Lin Daiyu, 179
Linguistic Engineering (Ji Fengyuan), 300
"Linguistic Violence: The Power of Intimidation in Authoritarian Rule" (Cao Changqing), 295–296

Liu Binyan, 181, 235–236, 246–247, 278, 317, 340, 341
Liu, Dilin, 183, 198, 200, 201, 206, 209, 354
Liu Shaoqi, 305, 320
Liu Xiaobo, 333
Liu Xiaogan, 291
Logos, left-to-right orientation of, 143–144
Lu Bingfu, 37
Lü Shuxiang, 243
Lu Xinhua, 254
Lu Xun, 4, 15, 56
Luo Gan, 246

Ma Ji, 32
Ma Weixiao, 337
Ma Yuan, 294
"The Magical Number Seven, Plus or Minus Two" (Miller), 77
Male-female dyad, 179–180
Mao: The Unknown Story (Jung Chang), 292
Mao Zedong: awareness of rhythmic patterns, 41–42, 57; calligraphy of, 308; and chiasmus, 106; criticisms of Deng Xiaoping, 328; difficulty metaphors used by, 189; and "five black categories," 66; and *gao*, 18; and "government as family" metaphor, 201; grammar use by, 260; and language game in politics, 341–348; and literary style, 302–303; metaphors used by, 256–257; and official language, 14, 15, 235, 241–242, 243, 292, 304, 307; and parallelism, 104–105; poetry of, 309; repetition used by, 265, 266; rhythmic phrasing of, 4–5, 33, 47–48, 92, 353–354; and self-censorship, 317; and stage performance metaphors, 204, 208; up and down metaphors used by, 155
Maps, 163–166
Marketing metaphors, 198–199, 209
May Fourth movement (1919), 210
May 16 Declaration (1989), 294
McEwan, Ian, 56
McGinn, Colin, 228–229, 230–231
McGlone, Matthew, 123
Meanings: and chiasmus, 106–109; and consonants, 96–101; contributory features, 94–109; double meaning, 100; and grammar, 54–55; of metaphors, 350; negative, 54; and parallelism, 103–106; and pitch, 101–103; of rhythm, 5–6, 82–94, 350; speakers' awareness of, 109–112; and three-syllable phrases, 51; of tones, 94–96; and vowels, 96–101

Meaning-transfers, 100
Medical metaphors, 254
"Me first" theory, 177–178
Memory, rhythm as aid for, 84, 92–93
Mencius, 172
Metaphor, Culture, and Worldview (Dilin Liu), 183, 198
Metaphors, 113–233; "affection is warmth," 185; of color, 147–155; conceptual differences rooted in, 209–215; of consciousness, 169–171; in daily-life language, 115–128; dead metaphors, 121, 251, 300; divergences between Chinese and English languages, 198–209; dominant, 198–209; meanings of, 350; mixed, 124, 136–137; north and south, 162–169; in official language, 244–260; philosophical problems generated by conceptual metaphors, 215–231; and privilege in dyads, 174–183; psychology of, 125; and self in ancient thought, 171–174; shared by Chinese and English languages, 183–198; significance of conceptual metaphors in different languages, 231–233; speakers' awareness of, 349–350, 353; and thought, 128–136; of time, 136–147; up and down, 155–162
Metaphors We Live By (Lakoff & Johnson), 8–9, 102, 116, 128, 135
Metaphor theory, 117–118
Metonyms, 209–210
Military maps, 165
Military metaphors, 19, 251–252, 253, 354
Miller, George, 77
Milosevic, Slobodan, 257
Milosz, Czeslaw, 13, 244
Mind-body problem, 150–151, 228–229, 233, 354
Misty poetry, 293
Mixed metaphors, 124, 136–137
Mo Shaoping, 333
Mo Yan, 294
Modisane, Bloke, 291
Molière, 212
Moral weight: and language use, 206, 304–308; of official language, 267–270; and stage performance metaphors, 203; of up and down metaphors, 155–156
Morphemes, 37–39
Morrison, Toni, 107
Moser, David, 158, 178–179, 181, 182, 342, 343–347, 348

Mountain as person metaphor, 197
Mozi, 205
Music, 55, 75, 89
"My Humble Opinion on the Reform of Literature" (Hu Shi), 43
The Mysterious Flame: Conscious Minds in a Material World (McGinn), 228
The Mysterious Stranger (Twain), 200

Nanjing Massacre (1937), 314–315
Nathan, Andrew, 279, 282–283
National Football League logos, 143–144
Nationalism, 347
Nazis, 256, 257, 290–291, 312, 314
Negative meanings, 54, 193, 267
"The Neural Lyre" (Turner), 77
Neutral tone, 49, 60
"New Year's Wishes for 2007" (anonymous), 337
Niehaihua (novel), 108
1984 (Orwell), 298
Ning Yu, 125, 138, 139, 141–142, 143, 145, 158, 185, 218, 354
Nominalization, 223–224
Nonhead stress rule, 52, 53, 68–69
North and south metaphors, 162–169
Noun repetition, 192–193
Nouns: abstract, 222–223, 244–245, 248; as adjectives, 261; and container metaphors, 213–214; cultural preference for, 219, 222
Numbers: and metaphors, 230–231; official language use of, 266–267, 336; patterns to memorize, 84, 92

Odor metaphors, 188–189
Official language, 243–278; "fit" as kind of truth in, 274–278; goal orientation of, 17, 270–274; grammar in, 266–267; lexicon of, 244–260; metaphor in, 244–260; moral weight of, 267–270; rhythm in, 260–267. *See also* Politics
Oliver Twist (Dickens), 219
"On Establishing a New Literature" (Hu Shi), 106
"On Literary Revolution" (Chen Duxiu), 43
Onomatopoeia, 96, 98, 193
"On the 'Natural Foot' in Chinese" (Feng Shengli), 58
Ontological metaphors, 9–10, 15, 215–216, 218, 245
Opera/acting metaphor. *See* Stage performance metaphors

INDEX

Orwell, George, 15, 234, 244, 245–246, 248–249, 256, 298, 313
Ouyang Xiu, 62

Paired categories, 174–183
Parallelism: in daily-life language, 3, 4; and meanings, 103–106; in official language, 34–35, 352; in popular sayings, 29; and rhythm, 103–106; speaker's awareness of, 43, 110
Pathology of virtue, 343
Peck, Graham, 113–114, 137, 141
Pekinese Rhymes (Vitale), 80
Peking University, 42
Peng Ruigao, 34
"People or Monsters?" (Liu Binyan), 340
People's Daily: parallelism used by, 105; rhythmic patterns used in, 45–47, 48–49; on *tifa*, 274
Philosophical problems generated by conceptual metaphors, 10–11, 172, 215–231, 233
The Philosophy of Lao Zhang (Lao She), 200
Phuntsog Wanggyal, 285
Physiological universality hypothesis, 188
Pianwen, 63
Pinker, Steven, 128–129, 133, 134
Pitch and meanings, 101–103
Plato, 227, 228
Playing dumb, 327–328
Plumbing metaphors, 351
Plus-minus pairs, 179. *See also* Dyads, privilege in
Poetry: dominant vs. recessive rhythms in, 57; meanings of rhythm in, 91; misty poetry, 293; pattern 3-3-7 used in, 81; political symbolism of, 309; *qiyan* patterns in, 25; rhythmic patterns in, 41–42, 55, 77, 85; *wuyan* patterns in, 25
Pol Pot, 257, 291
Politics, 234–348; bifurcation of official and unofficial language use, 13–14, 235–243; characteristics of official language, 243–278; and language game, 278–341; Mao vs. post-Mao era effects of language game, 341–348; of nationalism, 347
"Politics and the English Language" (Orwell), 15, 244
Positionality, 222
Power: of official language, 241; *tifa* as form of, 275; up and down metaphors to convey, 156–157

"The Power of the Powerless" (Havel), 340
Predicative complement, 207
Privilege in dyads, 174–183
Propaganda: and official language, 298, 301, 316; rhythms in, 32
Prosody, 21. *See also* Rhythms
Psychology of metaphor, 125
Pu Songling, 303
Puns, 100, 239, 330

Qiao Shi, 88
Qin Minxin, 345–346
Qiyan patterns: in advertising, 253; in daily-life language, 25–26; defined, 2–3; and item lists, 67; and meaning, 89; meaning in, 352; moral weight of, 268; pattern 3-3-7 combined with, 78–79; in recessive patterns, 73; in recessive rhythms, 56; as rhythmic preference, 61–62, 75
Quyi, 30–31

Rebiya Kadeer, 281–282
Recessive external rhythms, 54–59, 61; of favor, 60–67; structural effects of, 68–74
The Records of History (Sima Qian), 298
Red, 11, 149, 153, 269
Redundant syllables, 69
Repetition: in metaphors, 191–192; of nouns, 192–193; in official language, 264–265, 296; of verbs, 192–193
Resnikov, L. O., 300
Responsibility-shifting, 320
Rhythms, 21–112; and chiasmus, 106–109; in Chinese vs. other languages, 37–40; and consonants, 96–101; dominant external, 54–59; external, 54–59; fads in, 44–49; meanings of, 5–6, 82–94, 350; as memory aid, 84, 92–93; moral weight of, 267, 268; in official language, 16, 234, 260–267; and parallelism, 103–106; and pitch, 101–103; prevalence of patterns in daily-life Chinese, 24–37; recessive, 54–74; roots of, 49–54; speakers' awareness of, 40–44, 109–112, 349–350, 353; and tones, 94–96; universality of preferred rhythms, 74–82; and vowels, 96–101
Ritualized language, 290
Role-playing, 208. *See also* Stage performance metaphors
Romantic relationship metaphors, 122
Roosevelt, Franklin, 92

Rosemont, Henry, 203, 205, 227
Ross, John, 177
Ruoxi, Chen, 243

Sadness, 157–158
Salzman, Mark, 241, 280
Sapir-Whorf hypothesis, 128, 202
SARS, 335
Scar literature, 239–240, 250, 252–253, 293, 302–303
Schell, Orville, 283
Schoenhals, Michael, 13, 258, 269, 274–275, 296–297, 298
Scientific method, 223
Scott, Amanda, 137, 146, 222–223
Searle, John, 117, 185–186, 220
Seat-of-subjectivity self, 172
Second tone, 101
Self, 126, 171–174
Self-censorship, 317, 318, 344–347, 348
Self-cultivation, 126
Self-perception theory, 300
Semantic inversion, 3, 106
Semantics and Experience (Alverson), 115
Seven-syllable strings, 62–63, 64–66. *See also* Qiyan patterns
Shakespeare, William, 75, 86, 119
Shandong "fast tales," 75
Shanghai Municipal Propaganda Bureau, 34
"Shanghen" (Lu Xinhua), 254
Shapiro, Judith, 238
Shiro, Azumo, 314
Shunkouliu, 30, 84, 335
Sima Qian, 298
Six-syllable strings, 63, 64
Slingerland, Edward, 90, 126–127, 172–174, 177, 227
Smith, Craig, 34
So it was@sars.come (Hu Fayun), 292
South. *See* North and south metaphors
Spanish language: spatial metaphors in, 132; time metaphors in, 133
Spatial metaphors, 131–133, 134
Speakers' awareness: of four-syllable phrases, 111; of meanings, 109–112; of metaphors, 353; of parallelism, 43, 110; of rhythm, 40–44, 109–112, 349–350, 353
Sports metaphors, 199, 209, 354
Stage performance metaphors, 199, 201–206, 209, 251, 354
Stative verbs. *See* Adjectives
"Stinky is bad" metaphor, 188–189
Storytelling, 30

Stress patterns, 21–23. *See also* Rhythms
Strong-arm lie technique, 298
Structural metaphors, 116. *See also* Metaphors
Struggle metaphors, 251–252, 291
Su Xiaokang, 152, 154, 282, 284
Subconscious, 123, 169. *See also* Consciousness metaphors
Sunrise (Cao Yu), 84
Suppression of Counterrevolutionaries campaign, 45
Syllabic balance, 49, 71, 87
Syllabic elongation, 103
Syllabic stress patterns, 21–22
"Symbols, Song, Dance, and Features of Articulation" (Bloch), 90

Tai, James, 221, 261, 262–263
Tamaki, Ogawa, 82
Tartuffe (Molière), 212
Thaw literature, 239
Thought and metaphors, 128–136
"Three loves," 112
"Three Represents," 238–239, 266, 289
Three-syllable strings, 50
3-3-7 pattern, 28–29, 78–82
The Tiananmen Papers (Zhang Liang), 282–283
Tibetan protests (2008), 252, 265, 281–282, 285, 306
Tibet Daily on protests, 252, 262, 306
Tifa, 274–278
Time lines, 131, 136–137, 143, 147
Time metaphors, 9, 114–115, 136–147, 209–210, 232, 355
"Tiny minority" phrasing, 16, 306–307, 352
Tones: and irony, 121; meanings of, 94–96; of official language, 234
Topographic maps, 165
Transitive verbs, 161, 262
Truth: fit as kind of, 274–278; and official language, 281; and stage performance metaphors, 205, 206–207
Truth and Reconciliation Commission (TRC, South Africa), 156–157
Turner, Frederick, 77, 89–90, 91
Tutu, Desmond, 156–157
Twain, Mark, 200
Two Kinds of Time (Peck), 113
Two-syllable adjectives, 54
Two-syllable strings, 60

Uighur protests (2009), 281–282, 306
Unconsciousness metaphors, 122–123

"Understanding is seeing" metaphor, 211–212
Unofficial language. *See* Daily-life language
Up and down metaphors, 155–162; conceptual clashes for, 125; cultural preference for, 355; in official language, 255; for time, 130, 137, 144, 147
Updike, John, 56

Vacuous syllables, 69
Validity effect, 300
The Velvet Prison (Haraszti), 340
Verb-object constructions, 51
Verbs: cultural preference for, 219; dummy verb, 17–18, 271; false verb-object compounds, 72; in official language, 248; repetition of, 192–193; transitive, 161, 262
Vertical movement metaphors. *See* Up and down metaphors
Violent language, 253–254
Virtue, 155–156, 342–343
Visual metaphors, 211–212
Vitale, Guido, 80
Vocabulary of official language, 234, 237
Voinovich, Vladimir, 340–341
Volume as spatial metaphor, 132
Vowels, 96–101

Wakeman, Frederic, 154
Wang Anyi, 4
Wang, David, 108
Wang Guoxiang, 218
Wang Huo, 26
Wang Luxiang, 152
Wang Shuo, 70
Wang Wei, 218
War metaphors, 19, 251–252, 253, 354
Warmth. *See* "Affection is warmth" metaphor
Watson, Burton, 170–171
Wei, James, 100
Wei Jingsheng, 309–310
What If I Really Were? (play), 315–317
"What the Party Can't Cure, SARS Can" (anonymous), 335–336
White, 149, 153
Whorf, Benjamin, 128, 130, 133, 135

Wierzbicka, Anna, 291, 340
Wiesenthal, Simon, 313
Wilde, Oscar, 91
Wild Swans: Three Daughters of China (Jung Chang), 292
Wittgenstein, Ludwig, 83, 228
Worldview and metaphor, 183–198, 202, 213
Wu Zuxiang, 236–237, 328
Wuwei, 172–174
Wuyan patterns: in daily-life language, 25–26; and item lists, 67; and meaning, 89; moral weight of, 268; in recessive patterns, 73; as rhythmic preference, 61–62

Xiangsheng, 30–31, 32, 253, 329
Xing Lu, 243
Xu Zhenya, 4
Xu Zhimo, 74
Xunzi, 172, 173, 276, 277

Yan Dongsheng, 154
Yashin, Alexander, 325
Ye Jianying, 309
Yellow, 11, 154
Yellow journalism, 154
Yu Gong shanchuan dili tu (Cheng Dachang), 167
Yulihun (Xu Zhenya), 4

Zhang Heng, 168
Zhang Liang, 282
Zhang Xianliang, 337
Zhao Zixiong, 242
Zhao Ziyang, 246
Zhen Shiyin, 205
Zheng Yi, 315
Zhong Acheng, 293–294
Zhonghua Book Company, 168
Zhongshan University, 14, 207, 239, 287, 308–309
Zhou Enlai, 25, 73, 309, 320
Zhou Liming, 296
Zhou Yang, 308–309
Zhu Dexi, 243
Zhu Yingtai, 179
Zhuangzi, 9, 170–171, 172
Zhuo Lin, 303